CURRICULUM THEORY AND METHODS

Perspectives on Learning and Teaching

Wendy Frood Auger
Nipissing University

Sharon J. Rich
University of New Brunswick—Fredericton

With the Collaboration of
Helen Langford
Nipissing University

BICENTENNIAL
1807
WILEY
2007
BICENTENNIAL

John Wiley & Sons Canada, Ltd.

Library and Archives Canada Cataloguing in Publication

Auger, Wendy E., 1940-
      Curriculum theory and methods : perspectives on teaching and learning / Wendy Frood Auger & Sharon Rich.

Includes bibliographical references and index.
ISBN-13: 978-0-470-83774-0
ISBN-10: 0-470-83774-8
      1. Teaching--Textbooks.   2. Learning—Textbooks.   3. Educational psychology—Textbooks.   I. Rich, Sharon   II. Title.
LB1051.A7465 2006   370.15   C2006-904190-3

Production Credits

Acquisitions Editor: Michael Valerio
Editorial Manager: Karen Staudinger
Publishing Services Director: Karen Bryan
Marketing Manager: Joan Lewis-Milne
Developmental Editor: Daleara Hirjikaka
Cover Design: Swap Advertising + Design
Cover Image: David Roth (Getty Images)
Interior design: Adrian So
Anniversary Logo Design: Richard Pacifico
Printing and Binding: Tri-Graphic Printing Limited

Printed and bound in Canada
1 2 3 4 5 (Tri) 10 09 08 07 06

John Wiley & Sons Canada, Ltd.
6045 Freemont Blvd.
Mississauga, Ontario L5R 4J3
Visit our website at: www.wiley.ca

DEDICATION

This book is dedicated with love to our children Elizabeth, David, Tasha, Galan, and Courtney, who remind us always why good teachers are important, to Michael whose patience is legendary, and with great appreciation to our mentors, Dr. Elizabeth Thorn, Faculty of Education at Nipissing University and Alice Yardley, Principal Lecturer at Nottingham College of Education—half a world apart but together in a common message.

ABOUT THE AUTHORS

Wendy Frood Auger

Throughout her career, Wendy Frood Auger has taught in the primary, junior, and intermediate divisions, as well as at the university level. In addition, she has taught in Canada, England, and France. She holds Bachelor of Arts and Master of Education degrees from the University of Toronto as well as a Bachelor of Education degree from York University. She worked as a Primary/Junior Consultant, a Mathematics Consultant (Junior Kindergarten to Grade 8), and an Area Support Teacher with responsibilities in Special Education and Enrichment (Junior Kindergarten to Grade 8) for the former Scarborough Board of Education. She was an Associate Professor at York University and an Assistant Professor at Nipissing University, teaching in-service and pre-service courses in Curriculum Methods. Her in-service teaching has involved teaching and coordinating Primary/Junior courses at the Basic, Part I, Part II, and Specialist levels both in Ontario and in England for Nipissing University and York University respectively. Currently, she works for Nipissing University on a contractual basis.

She is the author of numerous curriculum resource units for teachers (Scarborough Board of Education), co-author of a textbook series in mathematics (*Holt Math System* for Harcourt Publishing), and most recently, the author of a series of 13 literacy/mathematics books for young children (Math Readers for Rubicon Publishing and Thomson Nelson). She has also co-authored the Primary Additional Basic Qualification course for Nipissing University. Wendy has contributed regularly to educational journals and presented workshops throughout Ontario as a speaker for the former Federation of Women Teachers of Ontario. She has also conducted workshops in the United States, England, France, and Ireland.

Sharon J. Rich

Currently, Dean of Education at the University of New Brunswick, Sharon Rich is no stranger to the Canadian education scene. She has taught primary, junior, and intermediate levels as well as pre-service and graduate education programs in Ontario and New Brunswick. She holds a Bachelor of Arts degree from the University of Western Ontario, a Masters degree from the University of Alberta and a Doctorate from the University of Toronto. Her work at the University of Western Ontario (UWO), where she was an Associate professor, included developing the online program in Continuing Teacher Education. Her research at UWO was informed by her work in language and literacy education and stimulated her on-going interest in the development of professional learning communities.

Sharon's research into learning communities has resulted in several papers in educational journals including the *Language Arts, The Brock Journal of Education* and *Education Canada* as well as several co-authored book chapters. She has also been involved in developing text books in language arts and literacy learning for classroom use including *the Irwin Writing Project* and *Ginn Journeys Language Arts*. A noted speaker, Sharon has presented nationally in most provinces and internationally in Australia, the United States and Malawi.

PREFACE

As instructors teaching Curriculum Methods courses for many years, we have been continually reminded of not only the importance of the theoretical component of curriculum delivery, but the need to foster an awareness in our students of *how* theoretical concepts inform effective classroom practice. The primary goal of this text then is modelled on the notion of helping the teacher candidate and in-service professional create PRAXIS—the making of connections between theory and practice. Teaching curriculum should not be considered merely a technical endeavour. Our goal in writing this text has been to help build a heightened awareness of how theoretical concepts and practical ideas work together. We have aimed to provide enough background information on aspects such as learning and child development so that a common base of understanding is created in the reader. This in turn will help create an appreciation of the connections between developmental and curriculum theory, and how student learning can be accomplished.

ORGANIZATION AND FEATURES OF THE TEXT

Every effort has been made to ensure that *Curriculum Theory & Methods* is a reader-friendly and informative text. The text is divided into thirteen chapters to make it useful for a one semester course. The content itself is divided into four thematic sections. Part I: Learning & Teaching provides important theoretical knowledge of development and learning. Part II: Creating the Road Map for Teaching and Learning adds specific information relating to the teacher's role in the learning process across the various subject areas. Part III: Enhancing Children's Thinking deals with strategies for enhancing and extending children's learning. Part IV: Looking at the Big Picture provides background and strategies to encourage ongoing professional growth.

The text makes extensive use of pedagogical elements to help make it practical and informative. The pedagogical elements are strongly focused on helping the reader make the connections between theory and practice, and to emphasize the practical value of theory in the classroom. The key pedagogical elements are:

CHAPTER OPENERS

Each chapter begins with Study Objectives and an Introduction to help set the context of the chapter and to help reader comprehension.

GLOSSARY

In order to highlight important terms, a running **Glossary** has been incorporated into the margins of each chapter. Glossary terms appear in blue and are defined in the margin. This allows the reader quick access to definitions as they are encountered in the text.

INFORMATION BOXES

To assist the reader in searching for more information on important topics covered in the text, **More Information** boxes have been placed in the margins of each chapter. In addition to providing immediate assistance for the interested reader, these boxes also highlight key concepts.

PERSONAL STORIES

To emphasize the importance of connecting theory to practice, **Personal Stories** boxes have been integrated throughout the text. These engaging first-person accounts and cases are designed to show how theory is implemented in the classroom to aid in the student's understanding.

REFLECTIVE PRACTICE

These boxes highlight insights, realizations, and the importance of critical reflection in order to provide a context for professional growth. **Reflective Practice** activities encourage professional development and show how theoretical concepts can continually be applied throughout a teacher's career, and help put into practice the ideas and concepts contained within the text.

SUMMARY AND CHAPTER ACTIVITIES

Chapter summaries at the end of each chapter go over the chapter content, reemphasize key concepts, and help make connections to the subject areas covered. Each chapter then ends with an activity specially designed to encourage critical reflection and practical strategies to implement theoretical concepts.

ACKNOWLEDGEMENTS

Our gratitude goes to the reviewers for their insightful comments and guidance throughout this project. Even before work on the text began, colleagues willingly provided feedback on the proposal. We would like to thank the following reviewers who read through the initial book proposal; their thoughtful comments helped us in the writing of this text:

Jackie Elridge   Ontario Institute for Studies in Education of the
                  University of Toronto
Milree Latimer   Brock University
Peggy Mason   Lakehead University
Lenore O'Rahilly Queen's University

We would especially like to thank the following reviewers who read through the draft chapters. Their feedback was insightful and constructive, and helped to shape the text that you see now. Moreover, their comments helped us to maintain perspective and reminded us of the needs of our teacher candidates.

Darlene Ciuffetelli Parker   Brock University
Yvette Daniel   University of Windsor
Rachel Heydon   University of Western Ontario
Jennifer Leclerc   York University
Christopher Milligan   McGill University
Betsy Reilly   University of Western Ontario
Melanie Tait   University of Ottawa
Marilyn Thain   University of Western Ontario
Pamela Toulouse   Laurentian University

Thanks go to all those at John Wiley & Sons Canada, Ltd. who worked on this book. In particular Michael Valerio, Acquisitions Editor, for his support in sharing our vision of what this book could be and facilitating its development; Daleara Hirjikaka, Developmental Editor, for her unfailing support and positive goodwill throughout the editing process; and Adrian So, Graphic Designer.

A special thanks to Michelle Daly for her research assistance and to Scott Maidens for his artistic representation of concepts.

Finally a heartfelt thanks to Dr. Helen Langford of Nipissing University for her shared vision of what this book needed to be, her ongoing support for this endeavour, and her personal integrity in making difficult decisions.

Wendy Frood Auger   Sharon J. Rich
Uxbridge, Ontario   Fredericton, New Brunswick

August 2006

BRIEF CONTENTS

CONTENTS

PART I

CHILDREN AND LEARNING:
How Does it Happen?

CHAPTER 1

LEARNING & TEACHING:
Charting the Course

" *All that is learned comes through the senses.*

~ Aristotle (384–322 BC) "

The purpose of this chapter is to
- examine characteristics of children's growth and development from the perspective of major theorists and researchers
- explore the basic notions of developmentally appropriate practice
- describe key elements which contribute to children's learning
- explain the teacher's role in creating effective learning environments

INTRODUCTION

This chapter establishes a foundation for understanding how children grow and learn by investigating principal beliefs about children and learning. Key aspects of cognitive, physical, and affective development are examined to establish an understanding of children's developmental patterns across various areas, and to identify those factors which influence effective learning. Characteristics of children's learning at various stages are outlined and key principles are established as an on-going reference for planning and teaching. The role of play and active learning, which are basic to children's learning, will also be examined briefly to determine developmentally appropriate practice. Various representations and models will provide some strong visual images to aid in understanding these concepts. Finally, the works of several major theorists are explored and linked to children's cognitive, physical, and affective development. The prime goal of this chapter is to create a heightened awareness of how theoretical concepts and practical ideas work together to create **PRAXIS**—the making of connections between theory and practice.

Theory + Practice = PRAXIS

THE SHIFT FROM BEHAVIOURISM TO COGNITIVISM TO CONSTRUCTIVISM

As the educational system has evolved over the last century and a half, it has been subject to the influence of many different views of learning. At times, various philosophical theories have come to the fore and others have faded to the background. The cyclical nature of developments in education continues to this day. Throughout the twentieth century, education was dominated primarily by three basic theories: behaviorist, cognitivist, and constructivist. Table 1.1, adapted from Glickman (1980; 2001), summarizes three of the main views of learning prevalent in the last half of the twentieth century.

Table 1.1 Views of Learning

	1 Constructivist (Piaget/Vygotsky)	2 Cognitivist (Bruner)	3 Behaviorist (Skinner)
Model of Learning	Constructivist (Piaget/Vygotsky)	Cognitivist (Bruner)	Behaviorist (Skinner)
Method of Learning	Self-Discovery— knowledge is constructed	Experimentation— mental processes are prime interest	Conditioning— learner adapting to external stimuli
Student Responsibility	High (Active)	Moderate (Active)	Low (Passive)
Teacher Responsibility	Low	Moderate	High

← A continuum from the "Guide on the Side" to the "Sage on the Stage" →

Adapted from Glickman, 1980; 2001

When the three approaches outlined on Glickman's chart are examined, the key features that stand out are the enhanced role of students in their own learning exemplified by the Constructivist approach and the more balanced roles of both teacher and student in the Cognitivist approach. While Behaviorist views were more prevalent in the 1950s and 1960s, they are not typically a strong influence in the modern classroom. It should be noted here that some aspects of Behaviorist theory are still evident, however, in programming for specific learning needs.

⭐ Examine Table 1.1—consider why Constructivist and Cognitivist views might be more popular in today's schools; also think of some of the drawbacks of these theories.

(handwritten) Pēe ajay

(handwritten) ⭐ Students are actively involved in learning, however lesson settings are less controlled.

Currently, the educational community has access to a wealth of information on child development, brain research, multiple intelligences, social issues, and cultural diversity, to name but a few. Cognitivist approaches seem to have evolved and been superceded by a Constructivist model of teaching and learning which has become more prevalent and influential since the 1990s. This latter approach will be dealt with in greater detail later on in this chapter and in the second chapter of this book.

> **MORE INFORMATION**
>
> For more information on comparing different theories of learning, see "Psychological Theories: A brief survey of the changing views of learning" on the companion website.

COGNITIVE DEVELOPMENT

> *Cognitive developmental* theory emphasizes the developing child's rational thinking and stages of thought.
>
> ~ *Santrock & Yussen, 1992, p. 258*

Research into the thinking of young children has shown that in the early stages, children's understanding of the world around them is dependent on the physical and social experiences they encounter (Santrock & Yussen, 1992; Berk, 1999). Initially, children's understanding is dependent on the development of inner frames of reference which are built up over time as a result of their experiences and their own actions on the environment. As children engage in physical actions upon objects they encounter, the results of these actions

> **GLOSSARY**
>
> **Cognitive development**—learning which occurs over a period of time and which involves changes in one's thinking.

Reactions to child's actions...

- become anticipated
- become rehearsed within
- provide a personalized basis for their thinking

For example, very young babies learn very quickly where their food comes from and begin to make sucking movements as soon as they see a nipple or a bottle or when they see their mother enter the room. This awareness results from their repeated and predictable experiences in relation to being fed.

Development involves the growth of children's thinking and emotions, and the expansion of their repertoire of strategies for coping with an ever-changing environment. These changes in mental structures occur as events in their environment interact with the ideas or notions that the child has already developed. Later, the meanings

Slotting,
Generalizing
Categorizing

"When I do X, then Y happens."

which children give to their experiences are derived from interpretations they receive from talking with others and the accumulation of knowledge from their own prior experiences.

Off to School

As children enter school, they usually do so with a spirit of hopefulness. They face a multitude of new experiences in this new environment, and their initial reactions are usually characterized by curiosity and enthusiasm. When these attitudes are reinforced and maintained by positive school experiences, cognitive growth is the result.

Since cognitive development is a very complex process and is unique to each individual, it serves no constructive purpose to compare children to each other solely on the basis of age. Such comparisons become even more of an issue with the current focus within the educational community on accountability and testing. One has to ensure that children are not judged or evaluated on something that has not yet developed! Development, by its very nature, cannot be rushed, remediated, or scheduled.

Complicating this issue is the realization that cognitive development, being less easily observable than either physical or language development, is therefore much more open to interpretation. Understanding how children think and reason or how they solve problems requires educators to involve children in activities that demonstrate these abilities, and to devise methods for assessing how children think and what they understand. This is a difficult task for teachers, since children do not always consistently demonstrate what they actually know—sometimes giving the impression that they know more or less than they actually do. For example children might be able to "count" to 100 without having a concept of the actual value of numbers. Therefore, they are calling out a sequence of number "names" without knowing the relative value of each number.

The Importance of Experience in Cognitive Development

Variation in life experiences can account for many of the differences seen among children, as can genetic and physical factors. The richness of the life experiences which children bring to school are of prime importance since these provide the basic tools for learning to occur.

rate of cognitive development is not consistent between children.

assessments are done with numerous problem-solving activities.

Differences in background experiences often present the teacher with unique challenges for meeting the diverse needs of all children in the class. As a result, many teachers begin by establishing a common base of experiences before some of the more formal aspects of teaching and learning can begin.

Find a Common Ground!

The Value of Play

Since the cognitive development of young children is so strongly tied to their senses and sensory input, on-going use of the senses as a prime means of learning is an essential component of programs for children throughout the primary and even into the junior years. The value of play in the life of young children is a basic need. As such, it must not be marginalized by adults, either teachers or parents, who feel more comfortable working and learning in the world of symbols and abstractions.

The research of Bodrova & Leong, (2003) linked play with the following:

- Advances in verbalization, vocabulary, and language comprehension.
- Increases in attention span and concentration.
- Enhanced problem solving strategies, imagination and curiosity.
- Improvement in impulse control, cooperation, group participation, and empathy.

MORE INFORMATION

For more information on how parents and teachers can become more aware of the value of play and the potential problems associated with too early an emphasis on formal learning, see "Too much learning damaging children's play" on the companion website.

Linked To Play!

A Look at Animals and Play

When considering different creatures in the animal kingdom, it is interesting to note that animals that play are perceived as being the most intelligent. The sophisticated communication systems of monkeys, apes, whales, and dolphins are but a few examples. This observation, then, begs the question, "Why would we do anything other than encourage our children to play?"

A sense of playfulness enables us to see new possibilities in situations and this, in turn, helps to expand our personal repertoire of strategies for dealing with life's experiences and challenges. What better preparation could there possibly be for dealing with the unknown aspects of the future than to play? Noted British educator, Alice Yardley, puts it succinctly:

Play lets Children act out and experience possible situations.

> *We learn through play what no one can teach us.*
>
> ~ Alice Yardley, personal communication, 1991

Unfortunately, some people perceive play as posing a threat or challenge to their adult sense of control or productivity. For some, the very word conjures up images of license and chaos. However, when observing the total absorption of a child at play, one must at least acknowledge the possibility of its intrinsic value. Play helps personal forms of perseverance to develop, as well as encourages the ability to explore deeply, to discover, and to make authentic, personal connections in learning.

Play is the highest expression of human development in childhood for it alone is the free expression of what is in a child's soul.

~ Frederick Froebel, 1782–1852

The Value of a Lengthy Childhood

Another factor that must be considered here is the relatively long period of time that children remain dependent upon adults. This must be recognized as a basic survival strategy within the human culture. By having close proximity to adult role models over a longer period of time, children have many opportunities not just to replicate what adults do, but to create new ways of doing things within a safe environment.

For example, a baby gazelle is on its feet and running within minutes of being born, but it is destined to always be a gazelle! Human beings, in contrast, have an extended period of exposure to a variety of experiences and are constantly organizing and reorganizing their thoughts in response to these experiences. As a result they can aspire to things beyond imaging—to be a doctor, an astronaut, an artist, a philosopher, etc.

Time and maturity, rich life experiences, and the creativity fostered by natural play experiences work together to facilitate the development of cognitive abilities in children. (Bredekamp & Copple, 1997; Caine & Caine, 1997)

KEY ASPECTS OF COGNITIVE DEVELOPMENT

The following provides a summary of key aspects of cognitive development during the elementary years:

• Children demonstrate increasing cognitive capacity to engage in more sophisticated learning activities and social relationships with thinking and reasoning processes showing major transformations around age 7, age 11, and age 15.

- Children must engage in active construction of their own understanding of concepts through handling real materials, interacting with others to clarify and extend their understandings, and verbally discussing/reflecting on their own experiences. As children act on physical objects in their environment, they become capable of thinking ahead and begin to anticipate the consequences of their actions.

- Primary-grade children increasingly become capable of understanding the viewpoint of other, to reverse their thinking—mentally go through a series of steps and then reverse them, and to focus on several aspects of a problem at one time.

- Children become much more capable of conceptualizing and solving problems about situations, objects, or symbols, but still must have a concrete referent for connecting the abstract concept to something real and familiar.

- A shift in cognitive ability affects every area of children's development. When playing, older children become able to engage in games with rules because now they can understand and apply these rules with consistency.

- Language usage becomes more complex as children realize that the same word can have many different meanings.

- Children's growing abilities in the social-emotional areas enhance their developing sense of self (Harter, 1990).

- Initially, attention and memory are not fully developed and children are often more distractible, especially when required to listen passively for extended periods of time or to work on a prescribed task chosen by someone else. Gradually, attention becomes more sustained.

- Social interaction plays a significant role in the child's cognitive development. Therefore, children need opportunities to challenge ideas, confirm or correct impressions, and extend their notions of the world through interactions with others.

- Children begin to apply memory strategies more systematically as the demands of school increase. As they accumulate knowledge and concepts, experiences and memories provide a greater range of categories or structures to which they can more readily connect new experiences.

- Children gradually develop their cognitive capacities. These processes take several years to become consistent and well developed.

(Berk, 1996; Bredekamp & Copple, 1997; Caine & Caine, 1997; Elkind, 1976; Gallagher & Reid, 1981; Healy, 1987)

Handwritten margin notes:
- Hands-on facilitates Learning.
- Can Rotate or Shuffle ideas"
- Concrete Referent
- Consistent with rules (older)
- ambiguous words
- Attn span ⊕
- Social Interaction
- eg: Chunking

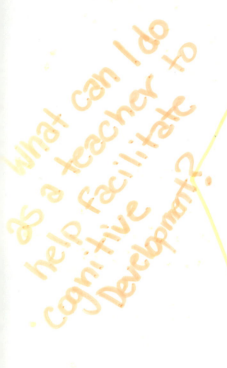

What can I do as a teacher to help facilitate cognitive Development?

Cognitive development does not happen in isolation. Skilled teachers can do a great many things to foster learning and promote cognitive development. They can

- play a facilitating role in the classroom
- ensure ample time for sustained play and engagement in learning
- foster children's interaction and collaboration with peers
- promote language development, problem solving, perspective taking
- promote children's thinking and acquisition of concepts and skills
- ask questions that promote further reflection or investigation to show connections
- facilitate children's involvement in challenging, meaningful problem solving
- encourage children to plan , review, and reflect on their work
- encourage children to represent what they know verbally, pictorially, and through varied modes and media
- encourage children to pursue interests or hobbies to support concept development

(Hewitt, 1995; Bredekamp & Copple, 1997; Gardner, 1999; Yardley, 1991)

Table 1.2 provides a summary and quick reference of cognitive development in the elementary years.

MAJOR THEORISTS

For more than a hundred years, the knowledge base about how children grow and learn has developed—and it is being added to even as you read this text. In order to understand basic notions about children and learning, it is necessary to examine some of the influences that have given rise to beliefs about children over the years. The following major theorists have contributed significantly to the understanding of child development and learning.

JOHN DEWEY (1859–1951; COLUMBIA UNIVERSITY)

John Dewey made one of the most significant contributions to the development of educational thinking in the twentieth century. His concern with interaction, reflection, and experience set him apart from many of his contemporaries. Indeed, his ideas provided the impetus for many writers who subsequently went on to influence the development of more informal and progressive forms of education

Cognitive Development in Elementary Years.

Table 1.2 *Cognitive development in the elementary years*

Early Primary	Late Primary/Early Junior	Late Junior	Intermediate
• use of movement and multi-sensory involvement are crucial	• begins to reflect consistently on past events	• sorts and classifies ideas and information as well as objects	• develops a greater capacity for abstract thought and for thinking in symbolic terms
• learns by manipulating and changing things	• continues to use real objects to assist reasoning	• focuses and sustains thoughts	• develops a greater capacity to make objective judgments
• uses a 'trial and error' approach	• enhanced and more objective use of language	• extends interests to many different areas	• develops a greater capacity to hypothesize
• often acts before thinking—'labels' things afterwards	• repeats experiences to verify ideas in various situations	• continues to need concrete referents to support ideas	• engages in scientific and philosophical discussion
• perceives from own point of view	• begins to coordinate and interrelate ideas	• refines notions about time and space	• develops a greater capacity to understand the past and plan for the future
• thoughts are governed by physical appearance of objects or situations	• becomes increasingly aware of patterns	• uses models, graphs, and symbolic forms to solve problems	• develops a greater capacity to combine information in a situation to make a decision
• has an extremely concrete orientation to learning	• begins to focus on more than one perspective or viewpoint	• begins to think in increasingly logical ways	• increased interest in social issues
• begins to make limited comparisons—initially limited to two objects	• increases ability to express and receive ideas in symbolic form	• reasons and explains ideas associated with change	• develops language skills
• links memory to particular experiences or actions (personal level)	• able to reverse thought	• thinks about different dimensions of a situation (whole, parts)	• increased questioning of values, attitudes, ideas
• listens for general rather than specific detail	• better able to predict change and anticipate outcomes in advance of action	• makes and carries out plans	• attempts to define relationship to perceived realities
• language meaning is clear to the child but not always to the listener		• becomes increasingly concerned with accuracy and realistic representations	• is preoccupied with self
• begins to develop awareness of space and time		• becomes consistently aware of how and why they learn (meta-cognition)	• is changeable in taking intellectual positions
• begins to develop 'reversibility' of thought		• uses language to develop and share ideas	• has rigid patterns in thinking on occasion
		• becomes more comfortable with abstract ideas	• has greater interest in organization
			• prefers group work, tasks
			• increased selectivity about preferences
			• is idealistic about life goals

(Berk, 1996; Caine & Caine, 2000; Gallagher & Reid, 1981; Healy, 1987; Hewitt, 1995; Jensen, 1998; Norris & Boucher, 1980; Santrock & Yussen, 1992; Wright, 1984)

© Wendy E. Auger, 1994. (Revised 2000)

John Dewey Cont'd

education is NOT prep for Life...

Education = Life

both in North America and in England. His philosophy of education and learning focused primarily on the link between democracy and education. For him, the ideal school represented a miniature society in which an individual's capabilities were used and not subordinated, and where cooperation and helpful living were the desired goals. He believed that education took place in response to active involvement and participation through play, construction, use of tools, contact with nature, expression, and activity.

For Dewey, education *was* life, not a *preparation for* life. He focused on the school as a social environment with cooperation and mutually helpful living as its goals. From Dewey's perspective, learning occurred through being involved, and initiative and originality were the desired outcomes, rather than obedience and submission. Learning, then, was an individual's representation of his or her experiences, which resulted when these experiences were talked about and reflected upon.

Basic Premises of Dewey

The following notions summarize some of the main aspects of Dewey's thinking about learning (Dewey, 1938):

- The purpose of education was to extend experience.
- Thinking and reflection needed to be explored and the associated role of the teacher defined in light of these two elements.
- Interaction and environments for learning needed to be considered within the context of practice.
- The purpose of education was so that all could share the benefits of democracy in common.

The on-going reconstruction and purposeful reorganization of experience were basic to Dewey's ideas about learning. (Dewey, 1938)

JEAN PIAGET (1896–1980; GENEVA, SWITZERLAND)

Our understanding of the learning process has been greatly enhanced by the research of Swiss psychologist Jean Piaget. His research spanned more than sixty years and the knowledge derived from his work continues to have a profound influence on the education of children around the world. A full understanding of Piaget's theory of cognitive development is essential for examining and understanding the **developmental needs** of children in their formative years. Even after his death at 84 in 1980, Piaget's learning theories have continued to dominate the field of cognitive development. Perhaps one of the most important ideas that Piaget put forth was the notion that children had to personally construct their own understanding about how the world works. He believed that children had to be actively involved in this process in order for lasting learning to occur.

Although some details of Piaget's theory have been modified over the years, constructivism stands as a fundamental principle governing his theory. It has been postulated that the concepts of **constructivism** and **autonomy** may ultimately be Piaget's main contributions to the educational community (Kamii, 1983). For Piaget, the developing child builds mental structures in response to experiences encountered in the child's environment. This forms an organizing structure which becomes more sophisticated with time.

Piaget was primarily interested in the development of knowledge. Since he felt that adults were not able to reconstruct their own cognitive development, he looked to children as an unbiased source of information for how this occurs. Thus, children's thinking became the prime focus of his research, and initially his own children were the subjects of his observations.

> *Development can no longer be an accumulation of pieces of learning … knowledge is never a simple copy of reality, but always results from a construction of reality through the activities of the subject.*
>
> ~ *Barbel Inhelder as cited in Gallagher & Reid, 1981, p. 38*

Adaptation as the Key

For Piaget, adaptation was the essence of intellectual functioning with direct observation of children facilitating his research. This was quite a revolutionary approach at a time when most theorists were basing their work on studies done in a laboratory setting or at least in very controlled situations, primarily with animal subjects rather than humans. His astute observations of children and the wealth of data gleaned from this approach enabled him to create a theory that, for the first time, had children at its centre.

Of particular note was Piaget's focus on the "mistakes" children made. He noted that children of like ages gave similar "wrong" answers (at least from an adult perspective), and they also justified their answers in very similar ways. These consistencies in the thought

MORE INFORMATION

For more background on Piaget, see "Genetic Epistemology (J. Piaget)", "Piaget's Stages: Inventions by Children" and "Papert on Piaget" by Simon Papert (1999) on the companion website.

Consistencies in types of mistakes.

processes of children of similar ages led Piaget to his theory of human **intellectual development** (Peterson & Felton-Collins, 1986). According to Piaget, the young child was neither a miniature adult nor an empty vessel that was gradually filled. Rather, Piaget (1969) viewed children, even from early infancy, as "active processors who struggle to understand the complicated world in which they find themselves."

Piaget believed that the spatial, sequential, and causal relationships that adults take for granted in their world have to be constantly created and recreated by each child through direct experiences.

As they experience their world directly, children construct meaning by conceptualizing, defining, classifying, making connections, discovering and creating patterns, and using their imaginations to build knowledge. They experiment, make discoveries, and form hypotheses that they then apply to new experiences and explorations. These processes, which are common to all forms of intellectual development, depend on enriched experiential and cognitive environments.

~ British Columbia Ministry of Education, 2000, p.24 †

The Processes of Adaptation

Piaget believed that three processes of adaptation are continuously in operation when examining thinking: **assimilation, accommodation,** and **equilibration.**

Assimilation

The process of taking in all forms of stimulation/information, which are then digested and reintegrated into existing forms/structures within the individual's thinking or mental structures; for example, "Four legs, animal = dog." (The assumption by the child is that all four-legged animals are dogs)

Accommodation

The process of adjusting the existing structures within an individual's thinking to fit new perceptions so that new information can be used; for example, "Four legs, animal, meows = cat." (The child has now created a new category)

Equilibration

Since learning cannot effectively occur when the individual is upset or in a state of disequilibrium, **equilibration** mediates between **assimilation and accommodation**, facilitating just the right balance between the two processes so that a sense of equilibrium can be maintained.

figure 1.1 *Assimilation and accommodation kept in balance through the use of equilibration.*

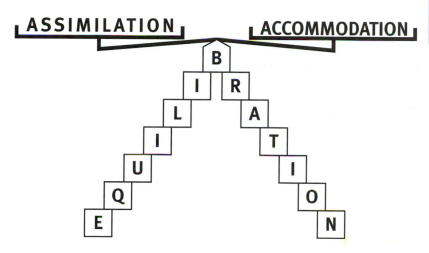

GLOSSARY

Equilibration—The on-going process of self-correction or self-regulation, keeping just the right balance between assimilation and accommodation, by which the individual strives to keep a feeling of balance or equilibrium as he or she makes sense of the world and changes his/her way(s) of thinking

When new information is taken in (assimilation) that doesn't fit the existing mental structures of children, they experience cognitive conflict, or a sense of **disequilibrium**. In order to counteract this feeling, they seek to acquire a state of **equilibrium** by using the process of **equilibration** to bring assimilation and accommodation into balance. This is accomplished by changing their thinking structures (accommodation) to fit the new information. It is this mechanism of adjusting or changing one's mental framework(s) that ultimately enables children to move from one stage of thought to the next. So, new learning can only occur when children

- are mistaken about their current notions
- are in a state of disequilibrium
- must reorganize their existing thinking

A need to create more rules of categorization

These points highlight the importance of risk-taking as an essential component in the learning process. Children must be able to risk being wrong and to state their current perceptions openly. Only then can these perceptions be adjusted to fit newer or deeper levels of understanding and incorporated into the newly adapted mental structures within the child. If children get the impression that they must always be correct, then they will play it safe, not take risks, and will offer little (or minimal) in return. Thus, learning can be seriously hindered by an overzealous focus on always being correct or by an adult model of perfection.

> Learning happens when children use assimilated information and accommodate new information into new ways of believing/thinking.

A Piagetian Perspective on How Concepts Develop

Using the processes of assimilation and accommodation, children create a schema (pl. schemata) or mental framework for how they perceive and/or interpret what they are experiencing. The early concepts of young children tend to be more global or general in nature.

Schemata are

- critically important building blocks of conceptual development
- constantly in the process of being modified or changed
- modified by on-going experience
- a *generalized* idea, usually based on experience or prior knowledge

At first, concepts may be highly generalized and even inaccurate, from an adult perspective. With added experience, interactions, and maturity these concepts become refined and more detailed. (Gallagher & Reid, 1981; Piaget, 1969)

All in all, making sense of the world from a child's perspective is a very complex and time-consuming process.

PERSONAL STORIES

"From Wow-Wows to Cows"

When my daughter was very young, she used to call every animal a "wow wow." This led to some interesting, delightful, humorous, and rather confusing conversations until she eventually figured out the distinctions. While she had to accomplish this for herself, it was not done in isolation. It resulted from many on-going interactions about animals with many different people.

The examples below illustrate the progression she went through as she refined these perceptions.

Generalizing:
"four legs = wow-wow"
(wow-wow = all animals—cat, dog, horse, cow, elephant ...)

Refining Concepts:
"four legs, long-haired, barks = dog"
and then later
"sheepdog = hairy dog;   or
poodle = curly dog, etc."

Refinement, Classification, and Creation of New Categories:
"four legs, large, eats grass, moos = cow"

Explanation:
Initially, young children take in information (by assimilation) and often over-generalize concepts. They may classify all four-legged animals under one general heading ("wow-wows")—usually stemming from personal experience with the family dog/pet.

With exposure to other animals over time and specific discussion about what different animals are like and what they do, children gradually begin to make refinements to their existing mental frameworks (by accommodation) to include a variety of categories based on finer and finer distinctions of what they are observing and discussing. The more experiences they have, the greater the number of potential categories they can form and the greater refinements they can make in their perceptions of the world.

Therefore, ongoing, varied experiences, interactions, and risk-taking are essential components in the learning process.

Conceptual development, then, proceeds from

- simple to complex
- general to specific
- vague to clear

"...learning is not merely an accumulation of information, but an adaptation and re-organization of the thinking process itself, with certain types of learning appropriate to certain stages of growth.

~ Piaget, 1969

"my P.O.V. is the only P.O.V."

Egocentrism

Another key concept for Piaget was the idea of egocentrism. Piaget regarded children as philosophers who perceive the world only as it has been personally experienced. Children see themselves as the centre of the universe, with everything revolving around them and occurring solely for their pleasure. Young children can understand only what they have directly experienced for themselves and expect everyone else to see things exactly as they do.

This aspect of Piaget's research helps us to understand how children perceive the world around them at different ages and why they ask questions and interpret information in ways that sometimes seem strange or illogical to us as adults (Peterson & Felton-Collins, 1986).

The Role of Reversibility and Conservation

There are two important ways in which children demonstrate changes in their thought processes as they progress toward developing understanding.

Reversibility

Reversibility refers to the realization that any change of position, shape, order, etc. can be reversed or returned to its original configuration, for example, five items can be rearranged and returned to their original configuration without affecting the quantity.

●●●●● can become ●●● ●● and then return to its original pattern of ●●●●●

Conservation

Conservation refers to the realization that a property such as the number of objects, length, or amount of a substance remains the same or is conserved even if its configuration, position, or shape is changed. For example, five items can be arranged in many different ways and still retain the same quantity.

●●●●● or ●●● ●● or ●● ●●● or ● ●●●● or ●●●● ● = 5

The attainment of these two concepts, *reversibility* and *conservation*, is an essential prerequisite for dealing with symbols and understanding abstract concepts in learning both language and mathematics.

PIAGET'S STAGES OF COGNITIVE DEVELOPMENT

Piaget believed that cognitive ability, which makes understanding possible, takes place in distinct stages. The stages are all subdivisions of a continuous pattern of cognitive development (Piaget, 1950, 1969).

Some key points of Piaget's stages are as follows:

- Each stage is unique.
- Each stage is necessary.
- You can't skip a stage.
- Progress from one stage to the other is gradual and continuous.
- Learning at each stage depends on both maturity and the opportunity to learn.
- What is learned in a previous stage forms the basis of learning for the next stage.

Piaget identified four stages of cognitive development, and in later years a fifth Piagetian stage was proposed by Patricia Arlin (1975).

Most children in the primary division will likely be represented in the first two of Piaget's stages, but a few might also be operating in Piaget's third stage of development. Most children in the junior and intermediate divisions will be operating in Piaget's third stage of development, and a few will be able to deal with abstract notions as evidenced by Piaget's fourth stage. Table 1.3 summarizes Piaget's stages.

> *The goal of intellectual education is not to know how to repeat or retain ready-made truths. It is in learning to master the truth for oneself.*
>
> ~ *Piaget, 1969*

Table 1.3 *Piaget's stages of development: The building blocks of learning*

5. Problem Finding/Seeking (15–30 years)
Additional stage proposed by Patricia Arlin (1975)
- inductive reasoning
- divergent thinking
- enhanced creativity
- problem seeking or finding approach to thinking

"How could we create shelters to live on Mars?"

4. Formal Operational (11–15 years)
- organizes and analyzes data
- uses reasoning, logic, and abstract thought
- generates and tests out hypotheses
- thinks about thinking (metacognition),
- sees own viewpoint as only one of many possibilities
- imagines possibilities inherent in a situation

"I could build a city of the future!"

3. Concrete Operational (7–11 years)
- sees cause and effect relationships (no longer dominated by perceptions)
- reflects on events in immediate past: focuses on detail and keeps the "whole" in mind
- shifts from egoncentrism to relativism
- predicts changes and anticipates outcomes
- seriation and classification develop fully
- expresses and receives ideas in symbolic form
- still needs concrete referents but relies less on actions

"I planned it and I built it"

2. Preoperational (Two Stages: 2–7 years)

(a) Preconceptual (2–4 years)	(b) Intuitive (5–7years)
• extremely concrete orientation to learning	• continued use of concrete objects to see relationships
• perception rules thoughts	• "reversibility" begins to develop
• tenuous notions of world (changes mind easily)	• rapid growth in language facility
• egocentric (difficulty in seeing another person's viewpoint)	• transition phase to next stage

" It looks like I can build a tower"

1. Sensory Motor (0–2 years)
- experience gained through movement and sensory involvement
- initiates action to discover properties of objects
- notion of " object constancy" develops
- actions develop in sequence (reflex-repetitive-deliberate)
- becomes capable of anticipation

"Everything goes into my mouth"

© *Wendy E. Auger. (Illustrated by Scott Maidens)*

Now that you have become acquainted with some of the specific information concerning Piaget's contribution to our understanding of how children learn, try the following task.

 # REFLECTIVE PRACTICE

A PIAGETIAN TASK FOR ADULTS
An adult exercise in conservation

Imagine you have a large glass of purple grape juice and a large glass of white grape juice which contain equal amounts of juice. Now, take one teaspoon of the purple juice, pour in into the white juice and stir it. Then, take one teaspoon from the glass of white juice, pour it into the glass of purple juice and stir it. Now for the classic question that would be posed by Piaget to determine conservation.

Think about the following question:

• Will there be more purple juice in the white juice or more white juice in the purple juice, or will the amounts be the same?

Do not read on until you have tried the task above and have had an opportunity to discuss your results with others!

Explanation

Once you put the teaspoon of purple juice into the white juice it becomes a mixture of purple and white juice, while the purple juice remains, at this point, totally purple in composition. When you take a teaspoon of juice from the white juice glass, it already contain some purple juice and is not in its original pure form. Therefore, when this task has been completed, there would be more purple juice in the white juice.

Significance

Piaget determined that the ability to hold a thought in one's mind and then operate on it was a prerequisite for many of the abstract tasks that we expect children to do in school. Successful completion of conservation tasks similar to the one described here would be an indicator of this enhanced capacity, and therefore would suggest readiness for more abstract/symbolic learning.

SOCIAL COGNITION AND SOCIAL CONSTRUCTIVISM

Social cognition is a process in which learning occurs through social interaction. This concept goes beyond how the brain processes information to examine the ways that learners make meaning or construct their learning from their experiences. Basically, there are two ways of thinking within the constructivist school of thought: cognitive-oriented constructivist theories and socially-oriented constructivist theories. While constructivism initially grew primarily out of the work of Jean Piaget, much of **social constructivism** is based on the work of Lev Vygotsky.

LEV VYGOTSKY (1896–1934, MOSCOW UNIVERSITY, RUSSIA)

The work of Russian psychologist Lev Vygotsky focused on learning as being primarily influenced by the culture or social environment of the child and mediated by the use of language. His theory stressed how the child's mind develops in the sociocultural world and termed this process the **social construction of knowledge** (Vygotsky, 1978; Santrock, 1992). According to Vygotsky, children learn from their own experiences and interactions, that other people have different points of view. For Vygotsky, language and thought develop independently initially, and then merge between 3 and 7 years of age. Interactions are seen as challenges which eventually prompt children to begin to change their egocentric perspectives. The highly integrated nature of development and learning is evident here as children's cognition affects their social interaction, and their social interaction, in turn, affects their cognition. These new developments within the experience of the child have important implications for social, emotional, and moral development.

> *...students actively construct their own knowledge and understandings. They do this by making connections, building schemata and developing new concepts from previous understandings. Instead of learning a set knowledge base, students develop evolving knowledge bases through interactions with others.*
>
> *~ Roehler & Cantlon, 1996, background section, para 2*

In his theory, Vygotsky emphasized the collaborative nature of learning and highlighted the importance of three main factors influencing the cognitive development of children.

GLOSSARY

Social Constructivism—the process by which knowledge is actively created through social relationships and interactions.

MORE INFORMATION

For more information on Vygotsky, see "Lev Vygotsky" by Solrun B. Kristinsdottir (2001) and 'Social Constructivism' on the companion website.

1. Culture and Society

- The child's mind develops within a social context.
- Social interaction is embedded within a cultural framework.
- Children are aided in their development by the guidance of more able or skilled individuals.
- Cognitive skills develop through interactions in a social and cultural setting.

2. Language and Thought

- Language and thought develop independently initially, and then merge some time between 3 and 7 years of age.
- They have their origins in a social context.
- Children use language and communicate with others before they focus inward on their own thought processes.
- Young children talk to themselves as a way of guiding their own behaviour.
- Eventually, children become able to act without verbalizing.
- The transition from external to internal speech/thought takes a long time.

3. Zone of Proximal Development (ZPD)

- The lower limit of ZPD is the level of problem solving reached by the child when working independently.
- The upper limit of ZPD is the level of additional skill the child can reach when assisted by an instructor.
- The relationship between the child and instructor is reciprocal and adjusts as interactions occur.
- Cues, questions, etc. provide a temporary "scaffold" for children.
- The instructor gradually reduces the cues and explanations until the child can perform independently. This becomes the new ZPD for the child.
- ZPD is a measure of learning potential.

GLOSSARY

Zone of Proximal Development (ZPD)—the range of tasks too difficult for children to master alone, but that could be mastered with guidance and assistance from adults or more highly skilled children (Santrock & Yussen, 1992, p.286).

> *Every function of the child's cultural development appears twice: first, on the social level and, later on, on the individual level; first between people (interpsychological) and then inside the child (intrapsychological). This applies equally to voluntary attention, to logical memory, and to the formation of concepts. All the higher functions originate as actual relationships between individuals.*

~ *Vygotsky, 1978 p. 57*

increases with scaffolding

GLOSSARY

Scaffolding—the skilful use of questions used by the teacher to enable children to understand and use concepts that would be beyond their level of thinking if they were doing this independently.

One of the major contributions of Vgotsky was the notion of **scaffolding**. This concept arose out of his work on the Zone of Proximal Development, where interaction between the child and someone who was more knowledgeable was an essential element. The opportunities presented by interacting with someone who is at a more advanced level of understanding can be limitless. The person who provides the scaffolding does not necessarily have to be the teacher—other adults or students who are at more advanced levels in their thinking, understanding, or interests can take on this role.

Initially in the scaffolding process, the more knowledgeable person or leader provides guidance and control of the learning through specific questions and prompts. Then, the leader gradually starts to share control of the learning with the students, and they begin to assume more responsibility for their own learning. The leader continues to guide the learners as their understanding emerges and provides assistance, as necessary. Eventually, the leader turns over complete control of the learning to the students. As this process evolves, enhanced information becomes part of the individual's changing base of knowledge (Roehler & Cantion, 1996). For Vygotsky, interactions within a social setting facilitate the development of thought and language, as children's understanding grows out of communication with others. The linguistic abilities—that people naturally possess—enable them to culturally make sense of and bring personal meaning to their perceptions of the world (Vygotsky, 1978).

According to Vygotsky the internalization of thought processes, which is facilitated by scaffolding, proceeds as indicated below.

figure 1.2 *The internalization of the thought process*

Begins on a **Social Plane** ⟶ Ends on an **Inner Plane**

Practical Implications of Vygotsky's Theory

• Encourage a social setting for learning with learners interacting among themselves as well as with the learning task.
• Encourage respect for the culture(s) of children by having them share and celebrate various aspects of their culture with others.

- Ensure children use language for a long time and communicate with others so they can learn to internalize mental processes (egocentric speech).
- Encourage self-talk (inner speech) in all aspects of the learning process. Teachers can facilitate this by expressing what they are thinking as they model certain aspects of their own learning (writing poetry on the board and expressing how they are doing this).
- Provide cues, questions, etc. to assist children through scaffolding, by creating a framework to help children to go beyond what they can do on their own in their thinking and in the expression of their ideas. This serves an additional purpose of promoting more independent approaches to problem solving.
- Encourage children to talk about their perceptions of what they know/understand. This encourages meta-cognition.

(Berk, 1996; Santrock & Yussen, 1992)

Differences Between Vygotsky and Piaget

In devising his theory, Vygotsky rejected the earlier assumptions of cognitivists that it was possible to separate learning from its social context. Instead, he argued that all cognitive functions could be explained by the social interactions in which they occurred. For Piaget, interactions with the environment were central to cognitive development, with the child engaged in learning, primarily, as a solitary pursuit. Piaget did acknowledge the social transmission of knowledge, however his research initially focused more on the actions in which children were engaged rather than on the context of these actions. In contrast, Vygotsky emphasized language and culture or the social context of children as being essential to cognitive development and to how they perceive the world. Vygotsky did agree with Piaget that learners responded not just to stimuli in the environment, but to their own interpretation of those stimuli (Vygotsky, 1978).

It should be noted that these two viewpoints are not necessarily mutually exclusive of one another. Rather, Vygotsky's ideas could be considered an extension or elaboration of Piaget's earlier work.

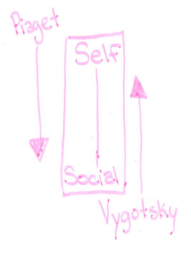

> "
> *While such an approach does not deny a Piagetian perspective, it also contains a major strength in that it can help to form learning as appropriate to the culture in which it is to be implemented.*
> "
>
> *~ Tudge (1990) as cited in McMahon, 1997, p. 4*

MORE INFORMATION

For more information on scaffolding, see "Scaffolding: A powerful tool in social constructivist classrooms" by Roehler & Cantlon (1996) on the companion website.

MORE INFORMATION

For more information on Social Constructivism, see "Social constructivism and the world wide web—A paradigm for learning" by Mark McMahon (1997) on the companion website.

THE THEORY OF MULTIPLE INTELLIGENCES

HOWARD GARDNER (1943– ; HARVARD UNIVERSITY)

In the mid 1980s, Howard Gardner proposed the existence of several rather than a single kind of intelligence. Gardner suggested that instead of asking, "*How smart are my students?*", teachers should be asking, "*How are my students smart?*" (1991). He introduced his theory of multiple intelligences and has continued to add to the repertoire of kinds of intelligences. To date, eight different intelligences have been identified and are commonly accepted within the research community. His theory continues to have far-reaching effects in classroom across North America as teachers work on practical applications of his theory.

Table 1.4 Gardner's Eight (Plus Two?)

Verbal-Linguistic	capacity to use language skillfully
Logical-Mathematical	capacity to use number patterns, problem solving, logic effectively
Visual-Spatial	ability to perceive the visual-spatial world accurately
Musical-Rhythmic	ability to perceive, discriminate, express, and transform music
Bodily-Kinesthetic	facility in using the body to express ideas and feelings
Interpersonal	ability to interact effectively with others
Intrapersonal	capacity for and use of self-knowledge
Naturalist	appreciation for and sensitivity to the environment
Existential (speculated)	the "intelligence of big questions"; contemplation of global or universal issues of importance to humanity
Spiritual (speculated)	appreciation of and focus on things of a more esoteric nature

Gardner stressed the following key points in his theory of multiple intelligences:

- All eight intelligences are present in everyone.
- Most people develop heightened use in two or three intelligences.
- These intelligences constantly interact with each other.
- People demonstrate their abilities within and between these intelligences in different ways.
- Facility in other intelligences can be developed.

(Gardner, 1983, 1991, 1999, 2005)

Today, teachers incorporate multiple intelligences into their classroom practice by presenting information in various ways and allowing students to demonstrate their understanding using different approaches. These include using pictures, developing 3-dimensional models, playing music, incorporating rhythms, using physical activity, encouraging discussion, planning for oral presentations, writing reflective journals, doing group work, and individual or group research projects, creating art work etcetera.

MORE INFORMATION

For more information on multiple intelligences, see "Howard Gardner and Multiple Intelligences" by M. K. Smith (2002) on the companion website.

REFLECTIVE PRACTICE

Re-examine Table 1.1; where would Gardner's Theory of Multiple Intelligences fit on the chart. Why?

Looking at the first eight of Gardner's multiple intelligences, consider how the following scenario could be adapted to incorporate as many of the different ways of learning as possible.

The Grade 6 students are beginning a study of "Flight." The culmination of this unit will be a visit to a local airport.

- List specific activities that students could use to demonstrate each of the eight multiple intelligences.
- See if you can come up with some additional ideas to incorporate the last two of Gardner's intelligences (speculated).

EMOTIONAL DEVELOPMENT

Today, children are confronted with a myriad of experiences, either first hand or secondary in nature, at progressively earlier ages. Unfortunately, some of these experiences are difficult for children to interpret and can also be of an inappropriate nature, which requires adults to guide children to a deeper understanding of and sensitivity to themselves and others.

Children make a gradual transition from self to others—they progress from being self-centred and egocentric in the early years of school to becoming more cognizant of and accepting of the viewpoints of others in later years. This shift comes about through experiences which foster cooperation, maturity in being able to consider the ideas of others, and a growing acceptance of being a member of a group.

ERIK H. ERIKSON (1902–1994)

Erik Erikson has greatly influenced our understanding of human emotions. He explored the ways in which society and culture affect personality development. His theory centres around eight psychosocial stages of human development that unfold as a person progresses along

Table 1.5 Erikson's eight psychosocial stages of human development

Crisis	Learning Basic Trust vs Mistrust	Learning Autonomy vs Shame and Doubt	Learning Initiative vs Guilt	Learning Industry vs Inferiority
Age	infancy; birth to 12–18 months	late infancy to toddlerhood; 18 months–3 years	early childhood to preschool; 3–5 years	middle and late childhood/ elementary school; 6 years–puberty
Characteristics	• child is almost completely dependent • caregiver represents the link to society • appropriate responses to needs result in feelings of trust toward the outside world • failure to respond to needs results in deep feelings of mistrust and fear	• child begins to develop some control (bladder, bowels) • demands begin to be imposed regarding socially acceptable ways to eliminate waste • if positive, will develop healthy sense of being in control • if negative, will feel out of control and develop feelings of shame and doubt	• child has alternating love-hate feelings for parent of the opposite sex • child tries to overcome feelings of powerlessness by engaging in various activities • if positive, a healthy attitude of being able to initiate actions will result • if negative, fails to discover appropriate outlets and feels guilty about being dominated by the environment	• child experiences expansive absorption of knowledge • child develops intellectual and physical skills • child is drawn into social culture of peers • child evaluates accomplishments by comparing self with others • if positive, feels basically competent and develops feelings of productiveness and industriousness • if negative, feels incompetent (especially with peers), unproductive and inferior
Possible Conflicts	if this crisis is not resolved, individuals will find it difficult to build trusting relationships with others and to engage in the necessary risk-taking that is an integral part of learning.	if young children are restrained too much or punished too harshly, this crisis will not be resolved and children will not only doubt their own capabilities, but also become overly dependent on adults.	if children are not able to expand their social skills or act irresponsibly, they may develop feelings of anxiety and fail to develop play skills and imagination.	if children do not resolve this crisis, feelings of being incompetent and unproductive may result.

the human life cycle. Each stage consists of a unique developmental task or crisis that must be resolved before moving on to the next stage. When these crises are resolved successfully, they form a solid foundation for personality growth and healthy emotional development.

Crisis	Learning Identity vs Identity Confusion	Learning Intimacy vs Isolation	Learning Generativity vs Stagnation	Learning Integrity vs Despair
Age	adolescence; 10–20 years	young adulthood; 20s–30s	middle adulthood; 40s–50s	late adulthood; 60s+
Characteristics	• stage centres on development of stable personal identity • child establishes a clear path toward a vocation • clear identification of role results in confidence and purposefulness • unclear identification results in feeling confused or troubled	• young adult focuses on forming intimate relationships with others • stage centres on "finding oneself yet losing oneself in another" (Erikson) • if healthy relationships are formed, intimacy will result • if not, then feelings of isolation will result	• adult develops and leads useful life • if positive, feelings of purpose and of helping the next generation will result • if negative, feelings of having accomplished nothing will result	• individual looks back and evaluates what he/she has done with his/her life • if positive resolution to most of the previous stages, then feelings of a life well spent will result; sense of personal satisfaction • if negative resolution to most of the previous stages, then feelings of failure will result
Possible Conflicts	if an identity is pushed or forced on adolescents by parents and they are not allowed to adequately explore many roles, a positive future path will not be identified and identity confusion will result.	if a person is unable to form meaningful friendships or to feel deeply connected to another person, the result is a feeling of isolation.	if this crisis is not resolved it results in feelings of self-absorption with a feeling of stagnation and isolation.	if this crisis is not resolved, the result will be a sense of despair and a life wasted. Without this final ego-integration, dissatisfaction and disappointment result.

It should be noted that Erikson did not believe that the solution to each crisis within these stages had to be completely positive in nature. Rather, he felt that some aspect of negativity was inevitable, and that this could result ultimately in the development of valuable insights. As long as positive resolutions dominated, however, the individual could end up having a positive outlook overall.

DANIEL GOLEMAN (1946–)

In recent years, the work of Daniel Goleman has added considerably to the knowledge and understanding of how emotions influence learning. The essential components of emotional health are not only to recognize, but also to manage emotions and social relationships. Goleman (1998) postulates that our view of human intelligence is far too narrowly defined, and therefore ignores a whole range of abilities that matter more when one ultimately considers life skills.

Goleman identifies five such pragmatic factors:

- self-awareness (recognizing feelings as they occur)
- mood management (reacting appropriately to situations)
- self-motivation (directing your emotions toward specific goals)
- empathy (recognizing feelings in others through verbal and nonverbal cues)
- managing relationships (handling interpersonal interaction effectively)

Goleman notes that all of these represent being smart in a different way: in other words, **emotional intelligence**. Goleman identified the following as being important dimensions of emotional intelligence that have the potential to impact on many different aspects of our lives.

- commitment and integrity
- the ability to communicate and influence
- facility in working with others to maximize group productivity
- the capacity to initiate and accept change
- maintaining a sense of curiosity and openness

Goleman proposes that skill in these areas is even more essential in today's ever-changing world. Fortunately, Goleman (1998) believes that emotional intelligence is not fixed at birth and can be nurtured and strengthened throughout one's life.

GLOSSARY

Emotional intelligence—the capacity for recognizing our own feelings and those of others, for motivating ourselves, and for managing emotions well in ourselves and in our relationships.

Applications Within the Classroom

Goleman refers to "emotional hijacking" as being the failure to maintain a sense of balance between behavioural/cognitive factors and the experiences of everyday life that can sometimes be overwhelming to people. Since children spend an extended amount of time in school during their formative years, the potential for influence on the part of the educational community is strong. At the very heart of this is the importance of encouraging enhanced levels of engagement in learning within a positive and supportive social setting.

Given the base that both Erikson and Goleman have established as a frame of reference concerning emotional development, it is important to explore how these can be translated into practice within the school setting.

Teachers can influence and foster the development of healthy levels of emotional development and emotional intelligence in the following ways:

- recognize characteristics of the students' emotional health
- be a good role model of emotional health for students
- create an environment where expression of emotions is valued
- establish a learning environment where trust and risk-taking are fostered
- encourage students to share their beliefs and feelings
- set up regular class meetings to discuss issues that arise
- involve children in decision-making in the class
- encourage children to self-evaluate honestly
- teach children how to evaluate their peers with sensitivity and directness
- model commitment
- have class meetings to discuss emotional issues openly
- ask more "why" and "how" and "what if" questions to encourage deeper thinking about issues
- teach children how to work cooperatively in groups
- teach children the specifics of peer evaluation
- express the value of honesty and integrity
- encourage variety in self-expression using art, music, drama, dance, and poetry

- use portfolios as a basis for teaching and establishing realistic self-evaluation
- create a warm and positive atmosphere in the classroom with colour, articles from home, objects of interest, cushions, stuffed animals, plants, art, etc.

(Sylwester, 1995; Goleman, 1998)

Goleman placed great emphasis on the importance of developing and addressing emotional intelligence issues.

Emotional intelligence is now as crucial to our children's future as the standard academic fare.

~ Goleman, 1998, p. 313

Table 1.6 provides a summary and quick reference of social and emotional development throughout the elementary years.

PHYSICAL DEVELOPMENT

Although physical development has been described by many theorists as a progression through a series of stages, in reality it is more of a gradual process of unfolding. In this process, children gradually move from the total helplessness of the newborn to relative independence in just a few short years. By the time children enter school, many already display overall smoothly coordinated gross motor movements as demonstrated by walking, skipping, running, etc. From this point on, it is a matter of refining these initial skills, a process that can continue throughout life. At the end of this section, a summary of characteristics evident at various ages throughout the elementary years has been included as a reference.

As children physically interact with their environments, they work toward coordinating eyes and limbs which, in turn, lead to more accurate approximations of movements. These efforts lead to greater facility and precision in handling objects and, ultimately, to the more intricate fine movements of the hands and fingers. Once this basic facility had been established, children then work on developing the strength and stamina that was not available to them earlier in their development.

Social/Emotional Development

Table 1.6 *Social/Emotional development in the elementary years*

Early Primary	Late Primary/Early Junior	Late Junior	Intermediate
• is more concerned with self than others	• is still concerned with satisfying own needs but is becoming more self-critical	• sees and respects the viewpoint of others	• demonstrates increased anxiety, mood swings, and impulsivity
• is more interested in the immediate time frame—not projecting into the future	• becomes more aware of self within broader contexts (family, friends, school, etc.)	• becomes aware of self within broader contexts (community, country, etc.)	• peers become the most powerful influence; replaces parental and even personal beliefs
• can appear very impulsive; rebellious if confined	• uses language more objectively	• is enthusiastic, competitive, can be somewhat moody at times	• shows increase in self-consciousness
• desires independence and autonomy yet doesn't know own limitations	• has more predictable behaviour	• assumes greater responsibility and perseverance	• shows increase in egocentric behaviour; sees the world in terms of immediate needs
• perceives from own point of view	• becomes more self-confident, outgoing, competitive, independent	• uses verbal skills rather than physical means to achieve ends	• has feelings of inferiority and anxiety about appearance; fear of isolation and rejection
• needs regular routines and reasonable, consistent guidelines	• is very imaginative; becomes aware of the ideas of others	• learns about self through peer interaction	• has anger and aggressive outbursts; these reduce with age
• finds it difficult to share and take turns	• becomes more settled and organized	• requires an inter-active learning environment	• dominant fears are related to social situations
• needs social contact to develop sense of self	• begins to focus on more than one perspective or viewpoint	• shows more sharing and co-operation	• affection becomes more intense: friends, pets, family
• develops autonomy through self-initiated tasks	• is better able to sustain interest and assume responsibility	• is better able to collaborate	• autonomy becomes a major need
• may prefer to play alone, beside others, or with special friends	• is better able to share and take turns	• may show leadership skills	• shows heightened emotionality (10–13 year olds)
• is dependent upon and seeks adult approval; enjoys learning from adults	• continues to need regular routines and guidelines	• develops close relationships with the same sex; "mini gangs" form	• increased emotional maturity around 13–14 years of age
	• may prefer to play alone, beside others, or with special friends	• may begin to challenge authority, debate ideas	• believes that sense of social identity rests with authority figures rather than a sense of justice
	• is better able to take part in group discussions; enjoys being with others	• peer relationships become dominant	• emotional maturity appears tied to intellectual development
	• considers adult approval to be important		• most frequent cause of anger is found in emotional relationships
			• has increased need for privacy
			• has increased sensitivity to and interest in social issues
			• has increased need for security and support
			• has tendency to live in the "moment"
			• has increased need to be accepted by a desirable social group
			• has increased concern with personal identity
			• has increased desire to learn within social contexts
			• obeys rules from fear or habit rather than from reasoning
			• has not formed life goals and ambitions

(Berk, 1996; Gallagher & Reid, 1981; Goleman, 1998; Healy, 1987; Hewitt, 1995; Norris & Boucher, 1980; Santrock & Yussen, 1992; Wright, 1984.)

© Wendy E. Auger, 1994. (Revised 2000)

PHYSICAL DEVELOPMENT IN YOUNGER CHILDREN

The amount and rate of physical growth in children varies considerably. It involves coordinating new physical capacities—resulting from the child's growth and maturation—with those physical skills that arise from experience.

Growth and Maturation, Sensation and Perception

As young children grow, they gradually change from being relatively top-heavy to having a more balanced proportion with respect to head and body size. This lowers the child's centre of gravity and gradually makes more steadiness in movement possible. Learning how to monitor their position in space is an on-going challenge for most children as they struggle to adapt to their ever-changing bodies.

The brain grows from 75 percent to 90 percent of its adult size during the primary years. Coordination improves gradually each year in response to maturation and experience. Hand preference is fairly well established by around 4 or 5 years of age, although the wrist contains some cartilage that will not start to harden into bone until after age 6. Since this places some constraint on fine-motor capacity (Berk 1996; Jensen, 1998; Shore, 1997), most children of this age should not be expected to do extensive seatwork which requires printing.

Most of the senses are well developed in this period. However, most young children tend to be naturally farsighted. They are still developing their binocular vision, which is why larger print is appropriate for this age group. While children's perceptual abilities are generally well developed by this stage, use of the incoming information is less complete because they have yet to develop some of the cognitive strategies and language refinements to interpret and communicate this sensory data. Information processing steadily improves throughout the primary years.

Gradually, children begin to recognize and then repeat and design visual patterns. Children continue to make letter reversals and often these may not be sorted out until well into the primary grades. Children will usually sort out the more obvious differences in letter formations first (discerning *b* and *p* or *d* and *q*—a mixture of vertical and horizontal planes determined by the position of the "stick" in each letter) before they sort out reversals on the same plane (*b* and *d*—horizontal plane). This confusion can be explained because in the physical world, an object has the same function and name regardless of its directional orientation, for example a favourite teddy bear is still the same teddy bear whether it is right side up or upside down.

Young children's sense of hearing is well developed by preschool age. Nevertheless, the ability to perceive subtle phonological distinctions in sounds, such as vowels and consonant blends (necessary for mastering all the phonetic combinations of language), is not well developed until after age 6 in most children (Bredekamp & Copple, 1997).

Perceptual development is influenced by experience, but is also dependent upon brain development. All young children need to handle an extensive array of concrete objects and explore their world through their senses to create these requisite neural pathways.

Gross-motor development includes increased use of limbs and variation in motor development. The sequence in which these skills are acquired remains constant. Physical development must be considered an essential aspect of learning, with physical activity a key part of every young child's day. Requiring young children to sit still for extended periods of time is at odds with their need to learn through active involvement.

Fine-motor Development

Younger children may experience frustration if they are often expected to perform tasks involving precise control of the hand muscles, careful perceptual judgement involving eye-hand coordination, and refined movements requiring steadiness and patience. They will benefit from activities that develop hand muscles and fine-motor skills, such as drawing and painting, working with playdough and sand, or constructing using a variety of building materials.

Physical Development in the Primary Grades

Children's physical growth and maturation during the primary grades interact with their experiences to produce major changes in gross- and fine-motor development.

Growth and Maturation, Sensation and Perception

Between the ages of 6 and 9, the rate of children's physical growth is slower but is relatively steady with occasional growth spurts. For instance, by age 8 or 9, girls sometimes experience a preadolescent growth spurt, overtaking boys in size but not in strength.

Much of children's growth occurs in the extremities, making children appear somewhat leggy in appearance. The face elongates to accommodate the growth of permanent teeth. The primary child is characterized by missing teeth. Progression of tooth development becomes a developmental milestone.

During these years, the brain reaches almost an adult size, and head growth is slower. The brain continues to become more efficient in its functioning. Coordination improves as lateralization (each hemisphere of the brain developing separate functions and interconnections) and myelinization (the process of insulating the nervous system) are nearly completed by about 7 years of age. Maturation of the corpus callosum, the broad band of tissue connecting the two halves of the brain, facilitates mental processing of information at this age level (Jensen, 1998).

By about age 6 or 7, binocular vision, the ability of the eyes to work together, is usually fairly well established, preparing the child for reading instruction and work that requires a closer focus. Children continue to demonstrate some farsightedness until around age 9, resulting in the necessity of continuing the use of larger print throughout the primary years.

Gross- and Fine-motor Development

Greater coordination of their bodies in space contributes to primary-age children's ability to control movement and to sequence or put together a series of movement skills. Their reaction time improves, making them more competent at throwing and catching a ball and other skills used in team sports. Improved physical coordination, combined with enhanced cognitive and social understandings, enables children to begin to accept and engage in games with rules and to cooperate as a member of a team. They remain, however, highly sensitive to comparison at this age, and it is especially difficult for them to cope when they lose. For this reason, competition should be minimized throughout the primary division.

At this age, children's fine-motor development continues to undergo refinement. Overall, girls are ahead of boys in fine-motor development at this age, while boys exceed girls in gross-motor skills requiring strength (Bredekamp & Copple, 1997).

PHYSICAL DEVELOPMENT IN THE JUNIOR AND INTERMEDIATE GRADES

Physical development at this age level reflects predictable patterns of refinement in response to a variety of challenges that older children will encounter. One cautionary note to consider is that full development of physical skills has not been accomplished by children in the junior division. There remains some fine tuning with respect to fine-muscle control at this age, and this is particularly evident in boys.

Growth and Maturation, Sensation and Perception

As with younger children, nerve pathways continue to grow in response to interactions with people and with concrete objects in the environment. Such experiences continue to facilitate learning by providing concrete referents to support concept development in both the junior and intermediate divisions.

Perceptually, children at this level have developed fully and are able to do a variety of pattern recognition tasks and extensions of many such tasks with relative ease.

Gross- and Fine-motor Development

Of prime consideration at this age level is the influence of more specified kinds of activity such as that which is required in team sports, experiences which are more competitive, and the impact of both physiological and hormonal changes that one sees in older children. Sensitivity to how the onset of puberty affects the children's perceptions of themselves must be of prime importance.

Finally, for students in both the junior and intermediate divisions, physical development continues to be a layering on and a refinement of skills developed at an earlier age. As children experience radical growth at certain times during this period of development, care must be taken to ensure correct nutrition and appropriate amounts of sleep. The school can play a central role in supporting these needs through sharing health information and providing opportunities for guidance in this important area.

Table 1.7 provides a summary and quick reference of physical development in the elementary years.

Table 1.7 *Physical development in the elementary years*

Early Primary	Late Primary/Early Junior	Late Junior	Intermediate
• child experiences rapid growth	• growth rate slows down	• growth spurt occurs before the onset of puberty, which is earlier in girls	• child emerges from latency to a period of rapid growth
• large muscles develop and child becomes more coordinated	• more even growth rate follows	• muscles are more coordinated	• arms and legs lengthen making the child feel awkward
• small muscles are less developed	• large muscles become stronger and more developed	• hand-eye coordination is well-developed	• increased weight gain
• muscles are not yet firmly attached to the skeleton	• large muscle development is more coordinated in boys	• wrist bones now fully developed with greater dexterity evident	• increased strength
• bones of the hand are mainly cartilage—very malleable	• small muscles are more coordinated	• sensory systems are coordinated	• wrists, ankles, ribs, shoulders, pelvis bones increase in density
• wrist bones are not fully developed in number	• fine muscle control is more evident in girls	• all aspects of development are generally coordinated	• facial features change: longer, more conspicuous nose; angular, more prominent jaw line
• uneven development in sensory areas (vision, hearing, touch, etc.)	• some wrist bones still not fully formed	• child continues to build new nerve pathways within the nervous system throughout life	• strong influence of hormones with the onset of puberty
• child is naturally far-sighted; random eye movements	• uneven sensory development continues	• child expends tremendous amounts of energy and is often hungry	• increased body hair, menstruation, breast development, voice changes, skin problems
• nerve pathways develop in response to interactions with people and with objects in the environment—active involvement is crucial	• most develop normal vision but some remain far-sighted	• boys develop better overall coordination	• metabolic rates fluctuate, leading to extreme hunger
• child has high energy levels yet tires easily	• more systematic scanning in eye movements (7 yrs. +)	• general growth pattern of girls remains ahead	• wide variations in energy levels, from restless energy to extreme lethargy
• there are no differences in muscle development between boys and girls	• nerve pathways grow in response to interactions with people and with objects in the environment		• wide range of sleep needs
• general growth patterns of girls are more advanced	• nerve pathways within the nervous system develop primarily in response to movement (up to 7½ years of age)		
	• child becomes stronger but still tires easily		
	• general growth patterns of girls remain ahead of boys		

(Berk, 1996; Caine & Caine, 2000; Healy, 1987; Hewitt, 1995; Jensen, 1998; Norris & Boucher, 1980; Santrock & Yussen, 1992; Santrock, 1992; Wright, 1984.)

© Wendy E. Auger, 1994. (Revised 2000)

SUMMARY

Throughout this chapter, you have been exposed to the ideas of several different theorists and to the practical ramifications of their ideas. This chapter provides an opportunity to become more conversant with various aspects of the developmental growth patterns of children in the elementary years. The importance of having this strong base of understanding cannot be overemphasized. Such understanding has the potential to take teachers to an entirely different level of professionalism and to truly meet student needs by being knowledgeable about not only the curriculum, but also the clientele. This is the starting point!

Once this understanding has been established, it is then appropriate to delve more deeply into various aspects of learning. In this chapter the charts on Cognitive, Social/Emotional, and Physical Development are intended to be used regularly as on-going checklists to see how children are progressing in their development. Therefore, it is recommended that teachers copy them and place them at the front of the planning binder as a quick reference.

The teacher as Janus

These charts highlight the need for teachers to have the information that will enable them to be able to look back at where children have come from and project where children will go as their development proceeds. It requires teachers to be rather like the two-headed, Roman god, Janus, who guarded the gate of the new year and was able to see in both directions—back over the last year and forward to the next. The older face in the drawing represents the old year that had passed and the youthful face represents the new one to come.

 ## CHAPTER 1 ACTIVITY

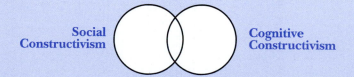

Create a Venn diagram and use this to record your ideas on comparing and contrasting the ideas of cognitive constructivism as represented by Piaget and social constructivism as represented by Vygotsky.

Social Constructivism   **Cognitive Constructivism**

Pay particular attention to the areas of overlap between these two related theories.

CHAPTER 2

CONSTRUCTIVISM: Making Connections, Risk-Taking, and Other Sundry Bits

" *Students must be permitted the freedom to think, to question, to reflect, and to interact with ideas, objects, and others—in other words, to construct meaning.* "

~ Brooks & Grennon Brooks, 1999, p. 24

STUDY OBJECTIVES

The purpose of this chapter is to
- explain the principal beliefs about how children construct their own understandings from physical and social interactions
- describe the basic concepts inherent in holistic learning and teaching
- examine the role of play in learning

INTRODUCTION

This chapter builds on Chapter 1, which established a theoretical foundation for understanding about how children grow and learn. The focus of Chapter 2 is on the principal beliefs about how children construct their own understandings through active engagement and involvement. It will examine constructivist theory and place the theory within a context of understanding how this can be represented within the classroom. The chapter will also discuss the importance of educating the whole child and propose a model for ensuring balance in children's learning. In addition, it will establish the role of play in learning and a rationale for active learning. Other areas explored in the chapter include principles of adaptation as demonstrated in the prediction learning cycle, and the spiral of knowing.

WHAT IS CONSTRUCTIVISM?

This theory was first introduced by Kant (1724–1804), who proposed that knowledge was not solely based on innate qualities or on environmental experiences but on interaction between these two factors. Constructivism is an approach to learning and teaching which focuses on how people learn. According to research on this topic, individuals construct their own knowledge and understanding rather than receive them "ready made" from someone else. This does not preclude the importance of interactions with others when engaged in learning experiences, but rather it emphasizes the importance of the individual's role in creating his or her own unique interpretations of the world. The foundation for this belief is the notion that knowledge is gained through individual exploration and active engagement in the learning process. This is accomplished through the use of "hands on" materials and through interactions with the physical environment as well as with others in the child's social environment. In the process of learning, individuals are encouraged to reflect on and explain their thinking. Information is integrated across subject areas so that interconnections and relationships become obvious, rather than dealt with in isolation.

BRUNER THINKS ABOUT THINKING

Jerome Bruner was one of the major researchers in this area. He perceived learning as an active process in which learners construct their new views of the world based upon their prior knowledge and experiences (Bruner, 1966). In recent years, Bruner has expanded his basic constructivist theory to encompass both social and cultural aspects of learning (Bruner, 1996).

Some of the basic principles of Bruner's work include the following:

- Instruction should focus primarily on the experiences and contexts that prepare and motivate students for learning.
- Instruction should be structured so it can be easily grasped by the students.
- Instruction should be challenging and facilitate going beyond the information that is given.

One of the lasting points taken from Bruner's research is the notion of the spiral organization of learning and teaching, also known as the "spiral curriculum". In applying this approach, students are exposed and then re-exposed, at regular intervals, to specific aspects of the curriculum. In this way, greater depth and breadth of study and understanding is possible as the child re-encounters this knowledge from a more mature standpoint. This model of learning and teaching will be elaborated upon later in this chapter.

> *Learners control their learning. This simple truth lies at the heart of the constructivist approach to education.*
>
> ~ *Brooks & Grennon Brooks, 1999, p.21*

HOW CHILDREN CONSTRUCT KNOWLEDGE

While this quotation might, at first glance, appear to be somewhat at odds with our perceptions of who is in charge of learning, in actuality it makes perfect sense. No matter how skillful, no one can force another individual to do something he or she doesn't want to do or is not ready to do. In learning, children control what they take in or discard, what they attend to or ignore, and what they become engrossed in or find irrelevant. The challenge for educators is to tap into what is of interest to children at different ages and stages and to incorporate this into rich and meaningful learning experiences.

In order to understand the role of constructivist theory in children's learning, teachers must understand what it is. The following list summarizes how children construct knowledge.

- Children cognitively seek to organize their experiences from a very early age.
- Continual refinement of this organization is an inherent part of development.
- Children continually integrate and coordinate many branches of knowledge that often develop independently.
- There is considerable movement between states of cognitive equilibrium and disequilibrium as assimilation and accommodation work in concert with one another to produce cognitive change.

(Berk, 2000; Santrock & Yussen, 1992)

Social Constructivism

While children play a major role constructing their own understanding, this does not happen in a vacuum. Interaction with others is a vital component in becoming thinking and knowledgeable human beings who reflect on and represent the culture in which they function. For social constructivists, both the **physical context** in which the learning occurs and the **social context** which the learners bring to the learning are essential for learning. (Gredler, 1997) Therefore, there is a need for collaboration among learners. According to Vygotsky (1978, p. 57)

> Every function in the child's cultural development appears twice: first, on the social level and, later on, on the individual level; first between people (interpsychological) and then inside the child (intrapsychological). This applies equally to voluntary attention, to logical memory, and to the formation of concepts. All the higher functions originate as actual relationships between individuals.

Vygotsky provided much of the foundational thinking for social constructivist theory. He did most of his research in the early part of the twentieth century and focused primarily on the collaborative nature of learning. He argued that learning originated from social interactions and that these interactions, in turn, enabled the child to be integrated into a "knowledge community" (Vygotsky, 1978). For social constructivists, language and culture play an essential role in intellectual development. The context in which the learning occurs is central to the learning itself (McMahon, 1997).

Within the constructivist classroom, learners are given some measure of control over their learning and, because of this, the importance of the social and cultural environment of individual children must be kept in mind. Society and culture tend to shape the overall receptiveness that children have toward learning, their personal interests, how they will interact with others, and the kinds of responses they will make when demonstrating their learning.

Social constructivism is based on certain assumptions concerning reality, knowledge, and learning. (Kim, 2001)

1. **Reality** is constructed through human activity, and therefore

   - it cannot be discovered,
   - it is created out of social interaction,
   - it implies shared understanding among individuals.

2. **Knowledge** is a product which is constructed both socially and culturally, and therefore

- it is created through interactions with each other,
- it is created though interactions with the environment,
- it is influenced by cultural and historical factors within a community,
- it is shaped by negotiation within communicating groups.

3. **Learning** is a social process, and therefore

- it does not take place only within the individual,
- it is not passive,
- it is meaningful when it occurs in the context of social activities,
- it shapes personal meanings through experiences with others,
- interaction with more knowledgeable members of the society is important.

(Kim, 2001; Gredler, 1997; McMahon, 1997; Vygotsky, 1978)

MORE INFORMATION

For more information on social constructivism in learning, see "Social Constructivism" by Beaumie Kim on the companion website.

PRINCIPLES OF CONSTRUCTIVIST THEORY

Given the rich background of research provided by both the cognitively-oriented constructivist theories and the socially-oriented constructivist theories, it is now appropriate to examine how both of these can be incorporated into a broader context of constructivist theory.

> *Hands-on materials are used instead of textbooks, and students are encouraged to think and explain their reasoning instead of memorizing and reciting facts. Education is centred on themes and concepts and the connections between them, rather than isolated information.*
>
> *~ McBrien & Brandt, 1997*

Gallagher & Reid (1981) outlined some basic principles of cognitivist theory which formed a foundation for further work on this topic. Some of these beliefs are outlined below.

- Learning is an internal process of construction.

Children's own activities determine their individual reactions to environmental stimulation, both in a social and a physical sense. They do not learn merely by being told about something, but rather by being actively engaged in physically handling objects and in relating their understanding directly to their own actions as they interact with others.

• Learning is subordinated to development.

Awareness and competence are preconditions for learning. This lends credence to the expression, "You can't put an old head on young shoulders." If certain requisite development has not yet occurred, then more sophisticated levels of learning will not happen at this particular time. Rather, it is more important that children be engaged in a variety of activities to develop the necessary background experiences. These experiences will form an appropriate foundation and ultimately stimulate and facilitate development and learning.

• Children learn by observing objects or people, by interacting with their physical and social environments, and by reorganizing their thoughts.

As children learn, they are engaged in a continuous process of change. New information is tested and retested against preconceived notions of how the world works. If the new information is consistent with existing ideas, it is noted and stored for future reference. While this may feel comfortable, it is just an affirmation and no new learning has occurred. New learning can only occur when incoming information is *not* consistent with the child's current world views. When this happens, existing thoughts have to be changed or modified so that the child's understanding or perceptions can be brought back into a more balanced state. Therefore, it is only when a child is wrong that the impetus for change and growth can occur. Real learning occurs when current thinking needs to be reorganized to a higher mental level.

• Growth in knowledge is often sparked by a feedback process.

Changes in thinking are prompted by questions, contradictions, and consequent mental reorganization. One of the most important skills that a teacher can develop is providing the appropriate scaffolding of questions to lead children to deeper awareness of relationships and to facilitate their understanding. When children encounter contradictions and new information does not fit their old world view, this feedback prompts them to change their thinking through adjustments and modifications.

• Questions, contradictions, and the consequent reorganization of thought are often stimulated by social interaction.

Children need to engage in ongoing interactions not only with their peers, but also with more knowledgeable individuals. These interactions stimulate their thinking to undergo the necessary changes that will indicate learning has occurred. As they test their ideas with their peers, they receive feedback and may begin to reorganize their thinking. When they test their ideas with older or more knowledgeable individuals, the potential for more reorganization of thought is possible.

• Since awareness (or conscious realization) is a process of reconstruction rather than sudden insight, understanding lags behind action.

The research of Brooks and Grennon Brooks (1999) takes a more pragmatic view of constructivist theory and melds it into practical applications for the classroom. Their research has extended these basic principles by challenging teachers to have "the courage to be constructivists." Some of these basic ideas are outlined below.

• Teachers need to seek and value students' points of view. Incorporating this information makes student learning more meaningful and relevant.

For example, check for perceptions by surveying students at the start of a unit to find out what they already know about the topic.

• Plan lessons that challenge the students' suppositions. Asking students to justify their beliefs causes them to examine their own thinking more critically.

For example, ask, "Why do you think that?" or "Tell me why you did this in that way!"

• Students must attach relevance to what they are learning. Interest in learning grows when students can relate to the curriculum on a more personal level.

For example, have the students share personal stories that relate to what they are doing.

• Students need to initially focus on "big ideas" rather than small bits of information. This helps them to establish a meaningful context in which to place related parts of a topic being studied. Their knowledge of various components of a topic will then have a relevant place in which to be considered as they refine their understandings.

For example, use "mind maps" at the start of a unit to set the context for learning and add more details as the unit/topic progresses. This also provides a strong visual example as an on-going student reference.

- Assess within the context of daily classroom experiences as students demonstrate their understanding in a variety of ways.

   For example, encourage the use of daily journals; collect samples of work regularly (date stamped); take photos of larger items that cannot be stored easily.

Both of these groups of researchers have contributed considerably to our knowledge base in different ways, one more theoretical and the other more practical, and, in the end, producing a greater sense of praxis!

   One of the things that teachers must be aware of is the inherent danger of their adult preconceptions (or perhaps, adult ego-centrism?) when looking at the learning process. Sometimes teachers ascribe thinking to children that is far beyond their capabilities. Adults often make connections quickly when faced with new information, due to the broader range of experience they have and which they automatically bring to any new learning situation. The same, however, is not true for children. Children are constantly in the process of constructing more and more refined perceptions of the world based on their everyday experiences. They may need to repeat an experience many times before they truly accept what it is demonstrating to them on a personal level. Accordingly, teachers must learn to observe and interact carefully with children to determine whether or not an experience has actually been internalized.

   Development is not a static process. Rather, it is dynamic as it changes daily due to the experiences and reorganization of thought occurring within different individuals. Awareness of different aspects of child growth and development, therefore, is a prime source of information for determining where young children are in their particular patterns of development and understanding. Due to these differences, teachers need to internalize this knowledge so that accessing it becomes automatic. In this way, this knowledge base becomes a part of their repertoire of information that they can subsequently apply in their on-going observations of and interactions with children.

   While there is no absolute when it comes to identifying the different levels of development in individual children, there are some predictable patterns of growth and development which will apply to all children.

 **REFLECTIVE PRACTICE**

Given the work of researchers like Gallagher & Reid and Brooks & Grennon Brooks, consider how constructivist theory could be put into action in the following scenario.

The grade five students are beginning a study of Early Civilizations: Ancient Greece. The teacher has assembled relevant materials to support their learning in this topic.

Think about the following questions:

- How could the teacher introduce this topic?
- How could the teacher make the topic more relevant to these 10-year-old learners?
- What kinds of activities/experiences would facilitate their learning?
- How will the teacher assess for understanding during the study of this topic and at the end of the unit?

EDUCATING THE WHOLE CHILD

There is a growing body of research that supports looking at all aspects of the child's development and educating the whole child. Eisner (2005) challenges educators to consider the following:

- Educators need to recognize, encourage, and support the unique talents that all children possess. It is essential that teachers assist children in realizing their potential.
- Educators need to focus on the various ways in which students respond to what the teacher has planned—emotionally, socially, and imaginatively.
- Educators need to look beyond that which is measurable when assessing children's learning. Assessment should provide a more comprehensive picture of development that is not limited solely to the academic or cognitive areas.
- Educators need to ensure that addressing the social and emotional life of the child be given as much emphasis as the child's academic achievement.
- Educators need to encourage the integration of the Arts into the whole curriculum and all aspects of classroom life. This strengthens the relationship between thinking and feeling.

" *Not everything that matters is measurable and not everything that is measurable matters.* "

~ Elliott Eisner, 2005, p. 16

All aspects of development must be emphasized in conjunction with the cognitive domain. To do otherwise would abdicate teachers' collective responsibilities in optimizing children's learning. It particular, it is imperative that teachers address moral, social, emotional, physical, as well as cognitive issues, since these can have such a far-reaching influence on whether or not children can even hope to experience success in other aspects of their lives. Attention to aesthetics within the classroom is another important area of concern, and it can be integrated into all aspects of the curriculum. When children are encouraged to represent their understanding in many different ways, it becomes an integral part of what they do in school and addresses individual needs and learning styles. (Gardner, 1999; Eisner, 2005; Miller, 1993; Noddings, 2005)

"*...students are whole persons – not mere collections of attributes, some to be addressed in one place and others to be addressed elsewhere.*"

~ Nel Noddings, 2005, p.9

If teachers focus on developing the whole child, then children will be encouraged to be healthy in a physical sense, knowledgeable in a cognitive sense, confident in a social sense, motivated in an emotional sense, and ultimately, engaged in all aspects of their learning.

EXAMINING THE 3 CS: A RATIONALE FOR TEACHING THE WHOLE CHILD

Recognizing that teaching in today's schools is a complex and multi-faceted task, let's now examine how this connects with teaching the whole child. There are several key elements that must be considered in order to provide meaningful and balanced learning experiences for children:

• knowledge of the individual child (variable)
• understanding of patterns of child growth and development (somewhat variable)
• the curriculum (predetermined)

The following section presents a series of visual models to convey more clearly the intended meaning and significance of how these three factors interrelate and affect learning.

The following diagram illustrates a Utopian scenario where all three of these elements work in harmony to provide optimum meaningful and balanced learning experiences for all children. This model emphasizes the connectedness of all three elements, where none is given priority over the others and where all are given equal weight in the contribution that they potentially make to children's learning.

figure 2.1 Maintaining balance in the child's learning

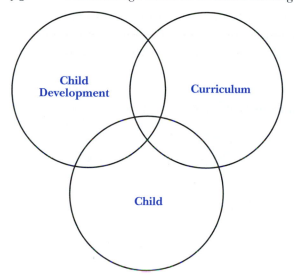

If any one of these elements becomes a central focus at the expense of the other two, student learning will potentially lose its sense of balance and the teacher will be less effective at meeting the diverse learning needs of children. For example, if curriculum becomes the dominant focus, the result would be learning experiences that operate in isolation from children's individual needs as well as from the teacher's professional knowledge about patterns of child growth and development—physical, social, emotional, cognitive, and spiritual.

Similarly, if the focus is primarily on the individual child, the contribution of having an established set of curricular expectations that builds a common base of knowledge for all children would not be addressed appropriately. Since this is undoubtedly a societal goal, it would not be acceptable.

Additionally, if the teacher's knowledge of child growth and development is the main focus. Then the teacher would use highly theoretical approaches that do not focus enough on the practical aspects of either meeting individual needs or establishing a common curriculum.

In each of these three instances, the emphasis has shifted so that one aspect of the child's learning experience receives undue importance at the expense of the other two. Such an imbalance does not promote educating the whole child.

Overlapping of Factors

In addition to seeking a sense of balance with respect to different aspects of children's learning, as described previously, several important issues become evident when examining the areas of overlap in each part of this model.

figure 2.2 Balanced learning

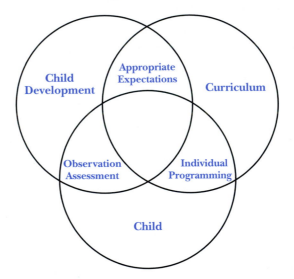

The overlap between knowledge of patterns of child growth and development and the curriculum leads to an examination of whether or not the curriculum expectations are appropriate within the context of overall patterns of child growth and development for particular age groups (see Figure 2.2). This provides educators with valuable information to use as an on-going method for assessing the appropriateness of the expectations within the curriculum, and for making the necessary changes to meet students' overall learning needs.

Similarly, when the area of overlap between the individual child and the curriculum are examined, this leads to an examination of individual programming. Here, individual interests, needs, and capabilities are identified and checked against the expectations for covering the common curriculum.

It should be emphasized that whenever there is a mismatch in this area, the needs of the child should take precedence. Children are entitled to be who they are as a result of the life experiences that they have had to date, and that must be the starting point. Since children bring a great deal of variation in their experiential backgrounds to any learning experience, the curriculum can and should be adapted to meet the needs of the child rather than the child's needs changed to meet the demands of the curriculum.

The area of overlap between knowledge of the patterns of child growth and development and the particular needs and talents of the individual child can lead to an examination of the information obtained from observation and other forms of assessment. This can become a touchstone against which to do on-going checks to ascertain whether or not children are developing in predictable ways. Knowledge of child development then becomes the professional standard for assessing expected or anticipated patterns of growth within individual children. By truly looking at the individual interests, needs, and capabilities of children, learning can be made more meaningful and the curriculum more personalized to meet these needs.

Lastly, when all three of these elements are in balance and working in harmony with each other. The result can be balanced support for active and child-centred learning in the richest sense.

INCORPORATING STUDENTS' INTERESTS INTO LEARNING

Teachers must strive to incorporate children's interests when devising activities for a topic of study. Many teachers find that starting a unit by surveying what the students already know about the topic is an appropriate place to begin. Recording these ideas on a chart to use as an on-going reference for the students as they proceed through the topic is of tremendous value in that:

- it honours where the children are coming from in terms of their prior knowledge and experiences
- it provides a relevant context for new learning
- it demonstrates a dynamic example of reflective practice

A practical example of this would be the use of a KWL chart.

K: what the students already *know* about the topic (written on a chart at the start of a unit).

W: what the students *want* to know about the topic (written after the initial chart has been developed and added to as the study progresses).

L: what the students have *learned* at the end of studying the topic (checked at the end of studying the topic).

When a sense of balance is accomplished and maintained, our knowledge of the individual child, understanding of patterns of child growth and development, and the curriculum are all taken into consideration,and the learning of the whole child then becomes the heart of the learning process. The result is enhanced learning experiences and quality of understandings for all children.

THE REGGIO EMILIA APPROACH

An interesting application of seeking balance in teaching and learning can be seen in the Reggio Emilia approach which arose out of early care and education programs in the city of Reggio Emilia in northern Italy (Allen, 2001; New, 2003; Turner & Krechevsky, 2003). This is essentially a project focused approach, with the curriculujm not being either child-centred or teacher-directed. Rather, the curriculum is developed cooperatively between the children and the teacher. The children initially generate the topics of interest to be studied in the curriculum under the guidance of the teacher and the teacher then steps in to frame the curriculum to suit the direction and needs from the broader perspective of the school system.

According to Allen (2001), there are three phases involved in this approach which encourages children to engage in exploring a topic of interest.

Phase 1: Developing questions to be pursued by sharing ideas, experiences, and information about the topic.

Phase 2: Gathering and representing data from first-hand experiences.

Phase 3: Debriefing and sharing what has been learned.

In the second phase of this approach, a key feature was to have the children engage in making predictions so that they could make distinctions between what their initial perceptions were and the changes in their thinking that resulted in their final conclusions. The value of encouraging children to engage in prediction in the learning process cannot be over emphasized.

SETTING THE STAGE FOR USING PREDICTION: ADAPTATION REVISITED

Before proceeding further with how children construct individual understanding, it is important to revisit some basic concepts involved in the process of adaptation. Piaget believed that three processes of adaptation are continuously in operation when examining thinking: **assimilation**, **accommodation**, and **equilibration** (Gallagher & Reid, 1981).

Since **equilibration** mediates between **assimilation** and **accommodation**, it facilitates just the right balance between the two processes so that a sense of equilibrium can be maintained. It is important to remember that as the individual processes new information, there is a continuous flow back and forth between states of equilibrium and disequilibrium. It is an on-going process that repeats itself continuously. For a visual review of this concept, see Figure 1.1 in Chapter 1.

ADAPTATION IN ACTION: THE PREDICTION LEARNING CYCLE

In order to learn something new, children need to reflect on their prior experiences to determine what they already know and to identify the schema that they have already created within their minds. If their life experiences have been extensive and varied, they will be able to use these experiences to create a variety of categories that represent their changing notions about how things work. These categories become an individual organizing structure that helps children make sense of their world. Their notions about how the world works are in a constant state of modification to fit new and different circumstances.

As children compare new information with their existing understanding (categories), they begin to make predictions about how they think something will work. The feedback that they get, either through direct experience and/or from interactions with others, enables them to see if their prediction was correct (and can be assimilated), or if they will have to change their existing mental structures (and accommodate this new information). Figure 2.3 provides a diagram of this process.

figure 2.3 The prediction learning process

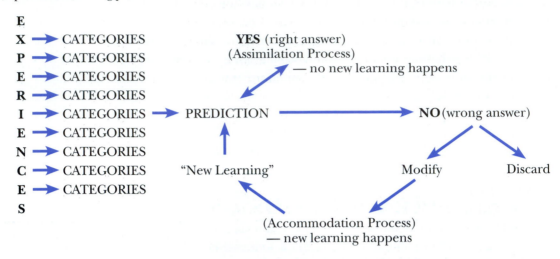

SUMMARY OF HOW THE PREDICTION LEARNING PROCESS WORKS

1. Experiences begin in the real world and the child creates categories to try and organize incoming information. If it does not fit with their current levels of understanding or mental structures, they will experience a sense of "disequilibrium."

2. In order to deal with new information and to bring about a sense of equilibrium, the child begins to form a hypothesis about what is happening by searching among existing categories or mental frameworks (schema) for information that is similar or that matches.

3. Then the child makes a prediction by generating a reasonable idea for why and how things are working the way they are.

4. The child tests out the prediction/idea physically, verbally, etc.

5. The child receives feedback on how accurate the prediction was. Based on this new information, the child must now either *confirm* (assimilate) if the prediction was right and incorporate the information into existing frameworks, or *correct* (accommodate) if the prediction was wrong by either discarding the hypothesis as being unworkable or by modifying it so it will now fit within a new or adjusted mental framework.

Since assimilation means that new information is incorporated into existing knowledge and therefore doesn't require making any changes to existing mental structures, learning may appear to happen very quickly. In the process of accommodation, new learning can only occur when the prediction is wrong and the mental structures have to be changed or modified. In the accommodation process, learning will often appear to happen at a slower rate due to the changes being made to these mental structures. This process highlights the importance of active involvement and risk-taking in the learning experience.

PERSONAL STORIES

Making Constructivism and the Prediction Learning Cycle Come to Life

At the beginning of a lecture on constructivism, the professor asked the teacher candidates to raise their hands if they had never eaten an apple. No hands were raised, so the professor could then assume that everyone had eaten an apple at some point in their lives and that a common base of experience had been established for the group.

Next she asked the students to name their favourite kinds of apples. In response to this, individuals initially mentioned common types of apples such as Granny Smith, Red Delicious, MacIntosh, and then went on to name some more uncommon types such as Courtland, Empire, and Russet.

When the number of responses started to diminish, the professor announced that her favourite apple was a "Love Apple." This pronouncement was greeted with absolute silence, some frowns, and a sense of puzzlement from the group. She went on to explain how she liked to eat her favourite "apple." She stated that she liked to slice a love apple thinly and make a sandwich of it, served between slices of whole wheat bread, topped with a bit of mayonnaise. At this description, several of the group started to make faces, to look very confused, and even look a little ill. But she noted that a few students realized what she was talking about and started to nod and smile at her description. She then announced to the group, "If I tell you that a love apple is another name for a tomato, does that make you feel any better about what I just said?" To this additional piece of information, the entire group smiled and nodded their approval.

Analysis from a Constructivist Perspective

Initially, the professor had established a common base of understanding that everyone in the group had a mental framework (or **schema**) for what an apple was. This schema was further activated by asking the group to name different types of apples. In doing this, the members of the group had to access the **sub-categories** they had already formed about different kinds of apples (Granny Smith: firm, green apple category; Red Delicious: somewhat heart-shaped and very sweet category, etc.). These kinds of distinctions would have required

Personal Stories continues...

personal experiences of eating different kinds of apples as the basis of this understanding—you don't know what Granny Smith tastes like by having it described to you or by seeing a picture!

Next, the professor named a different kind of "apple" (the love apple) which was not familiar to the group and, in doing so, caused the group to be somewhat puzzled, unsettled, and at a loss for what was being presented. This puzzlement resulted in a state of **disequilibrium** since the group did not apparently have a category to fit this particular kind of apple. The members of the group searched their individual schema to find a way to make this information fit with what they knew about apples by hypothesizing/predicting what it could be. However, they could not assimilate the information because they did not have any existing structures to fit this particular piece of information.

When the professor described how she liked to eat her apple, the clues provided enough additional information so that at least some of the group began to realize what was being discussed and their change in demeanor reflected this awareness. Some of the students had deduced that it was a tomato based on feedback provided by the professor, and were somewhat relieved of the tension that had built up when they had been in a state of disequilibrium.

When she told the students what a love apple really was, the tension dissipated and the feelings of the group returned to a level of comfort with the topic under discussion. A state of **equilibrium** had been re-established and a **new category** for the apple schema had been learned. Existing schema had to be reorganized and expanded to create a new category (through accommodation). In essence, new learning had only been able to happen as a result of being wrong!

Importance

Everybody goes through this same process when confronted with something that they do not initially understand and they have to work actively to construct the new understanding. A serious issue is that a person can never learn too far from his/her existing schema since these are the mental frameworks against which he/she will check all incoming information! In this scenario, the group of adults experienced firsthand many of the same frustrations or feelings of discomfort that students experience in the classroom when they do not have sufficient background information or prior knowledge when learning something new. Therefore, teachers need to be sensitive to and attend to the different background experiences that their students bring to any learning experience. The more experiences students have, the more categories they will have constructed, and therefore the more refinements they will be able to make to their existing schema.

THE IMPORTANCE OF RISK-TAKING

Since changes are only made to the existing mental structures during accommodation, one can only learn something new if one is prepared to be wrong! Risk-taking is an essential component in the learning process.

Risk-taking is an essential component in the learning process, and is at the heart of true learning. Children have to be actively engaged in the learning process and able to risk being wrong in order to learn something new. Only when they are wrong and have to make adjustments to existing mental structures can new learning occur. Learning environments where risk-taking is fostered and valued are places where learning can occur naturally. If the focus is narrowed to always finding one definitive "right answer," then the learning process can be seriously compromised as children play it safe and give only a minimal "correct" response.

To ensure that children think deeply, care passionately, and respond expressively, teachers need to establish emotionally safe learning environments where children are encouraged to

• try out new ideas without fear of being judged
• view wrong answers as positive approximations and springboards to new ideas
• be receptive to a variety of possible ideas and answers
• be supportive to the attempts and viewpoints of others
• view learning as a journey, not just a destination
• remember that a mistake is evidence that someone has tried to do something
• be creative and unique in expressing their ideas

With respect to the prediction learning cycle, there are some additional factors that need to be taken into consideration. The following factors will influence how children are able to respond to learning.

Maturation

> **Prior experience**

>> **Prior knowledge**

>> **Self-confidence**

>>> **Innate intelligence**

>>> **Chronological age**

The teacher needs to consider that when children are slow to grasp a new concept, it could be due to lack of experience rather than lack of ability. Piaget also noted that children may have to repeat an experience as many as two hundred times before they fully accept what is happening as a fact and therefore predictable. This relates to what is often referred to as the "magical thinking" of young children, where they do not see cause and effect situations in the same light as adults due to their extreme ego-centric nature (Gallagher & Reid, 1981).

 # REFLECTIVE PRACTICE

All of the following questions present some serious ramifications and raise some important questions for teachers to consider if they are tempted to rush children through the curriculum.

Think about the following questions:

- As a profession, do teachers build in enough opportunities for children to go back and revisit their learning? What are some of the problems associated with neglecting to do this?
- How can teachers provide enough opportunities for children to reach conclusions about their understanding that are natural for them and within a timeframe that is flexible enough to reflect the needs and capabilities of the individual?
- How might teachers encourage children to be reflective about what and how they have learned? What specific strategies could be put in place to ensure this?
- Do teachers make the mistake of always moving forward? How can teachers show that consolidation is valued and supported within the classroom setting?

These issues lead to another serious aspect of encouraging a learning environment where children actively construct their understandings of the world—the issue of play!

THE SERIOUS BUSINESS OF PLAY

We do not cease to play because we grow old but rather we grow old because we cease to play.

Many researchers have concluded that play is something that children must be allowed to do if cognitive growth is to be facilitated (Eisner, 2005; Bredecamp & Copple, 1997; Fine, 1987). More specifically, educators must accept that play is a necessary part of the learning that will take place within the school setting. Through active involvement and play, children create and recreate new mental structures that will be used as a base of comparison for all future learning. They must be allowed to "mess around" with real objects to find out the latent possibilities in the learning materials before teachers start to impose specific curriculum content into their play/learning. Teachers play a central role in providing the necessary materials, interactions, and support for children to optimize their learning through play. Indeed, it becomes a professional responsibility to develop deeper levels of understanding about the role and value of play and to make a commitment to share this knowledge with parents so that children's learning can be supported by all parties.

Over the years, many theorists have presented ideas about the value of play in children's learning. The following is a summary of some of the key factors which make play such a beneficial part of children's learning experiences.

KEY CHARACTERISTICS OF PLAY

- Play is not work. Work is something that people engage in when directed to do so by someone else.
- Play facilitates intense levels of involvement that can promote longer attention spans.
- Play helps children to learn to persevere—a valuable life skill.
- Play is spontaneous, self-initiated, and self-directed.
- Play is sometimes engaged in for sheer pleasure.
- Play enables children to make choices and to become more autonomous.
- Play is active involvement in one's own learning.
- Play focuses primarily on process, but can focus on a finished product as well.
- Play is an intrinsically motivating and rewarding activity.
- Play helps children to make sense of new information.
- Play can help children search for solutions to personal inquiries.
- Play helps children to make closer approximations to real life situations and to find personally relevant solutions.
- Play enables children to explore, test out their ideas, and see limitless possibilities in their learning.
- Play enables children to be in control of and to gain mastery over their own their learning.

- Play enables children to see connections between and among ideas.
- Play develops problem solving abilities through trial and error and the testing out of ideas.
- Play is a natural way in which children try to make sense of their physical, social, emotional, cultural, and intellectual world.
- Play encourages children to be flexible in their thinking.
- Play shows variation from one child to another and from one situation to another.
- Play can express some element of pretending, fantasy, or imagination.
- Play emphasizes means rather than just ends, showing less concern with a specific goal than with the various means of reaching it.
- Play with objects contributes to success in tasks requiring multiple solutions.
- Play is facilitated within a rich physical and social setting.
- Play provides opportunities for teachers to observe the intellect in operation.
- Play provides opportunities for teachers to participate closely in children's learning both as observers and as participant-observers.

(Alderson, 1985, Fine, 1987,
Smilanski & Shafatya, 1990; Yardley, 1991)

Since play can take many forms, it has also been described in various ways. Over the years, play has come to be linked to some degree or another with the following terms: active learning, thematic instruction or theme-based learning, the integrated day, or learning activities, to name but a few.

PLAY: IS IT A VALUABLE AND VIABLE PART OF LEARNING?

The term play has often been perceived as something that is done as part of a recess break, as a reward after the "real" work of the classroom has been accomplished, or as something that children do outside of school hours. The controversy about play focuses on whether or not play can be used as an effective teaching strategy within the regular functioning of the classroom.

What can children learn through play? They can learn many skills that will form the foundation to the skills they will use throughout their entire lives.

> " *Children learn through play what no one can teach them.* "
>
> *Alice Yardley, personal communication, 1991*

In order to ascertain when and how these skills are developing, the teacher needs to become an astute observer of children's behaviour to determine in which stage of play individual children are operating. Although systematic anecdotal notes of observations provide an on-going, tangible record upon which to base conclusions about stages of play, the teacher must ensure that the children are engaged in meaningful activities/experiences that provide sufficient opportunities for the teacher to observe natural play in action.

The different levels of play in which children engage are of particular interest to teachers. Awareness and knowledge of the characteristics evident in each stage of play are a vital part of the professional skills that all teachers must have to identify, plan for, and facilitate the learning needs of children through play.

Figure 2.4 provides an overview of the developmental stages of play which focus on social development.

figure 2.4 *Otto Weininger's developmental stages of play (F.W.T.A.O., 1986)*

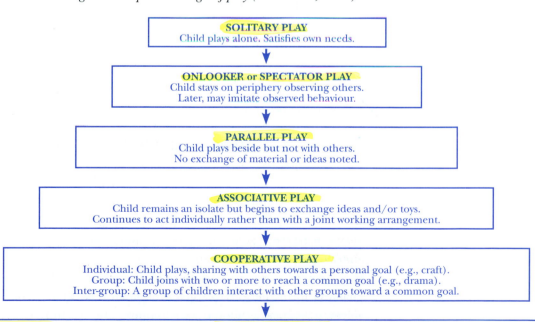

SOLITARY PLAY
Child plays alone. Satisfies own needs.

ONLOOKER or SPECTATOR PLAY
Child stays on periphery observing others.
Later, may imitate observed behaviour.

PARALLEL PLAY
Child plays beside but not with others.
No exchange of material or ideas noted.

ASSOCIATIVE PLAY
Child remains an isolate but begins to exchange ideas and/or toys.
Continues to act individually rather than with a joint working arrangement.

COOPERATIVE PLAY
Individual: Child plays, sharing with others towards a personal goal (e.g., craft).
Group: Child joins with two or more to reach a common goal (e.g., drama).
Inter-group: A group of children interact with other groups toward a common goal.

COMPETITIVE PLAY
Individual: Child competes with herself/himself to improve skill.
Group: Two or more children cooperate in a group effort.
Inter-Group: Groups of children compete for superiority.

Figure 2.5 shows the different types of play in which children will engage.

figure 2.5 Opper & Ginsburg's developmental types of play

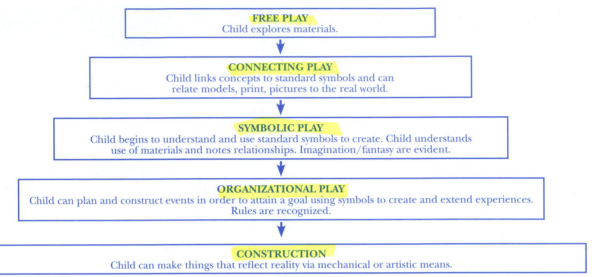

FREE PLAY
Child explores materials.

CONNECTING PLAY
Child links concepts to standard symbols and can
relate models, print, pictures to the real world.

SYMBOLIC PLAY
Child begins to understand and use standard symbols to create. Child understands
use of materials and notes relationships. Imagination/fantasy are evident.

ORGANIZATIONAL PLAY
Child can plan and construct events in order to attain a goal using symbols to create and extend experiences.
Rules are recognized.

CONSTRUCTION
Child can make things that reflect reality via mechanical or artistic means.

(Opper & Ginsburg, 1969. Adapted by permission of Pearson Education, Inc., Upper Saddle River, NJ)

HOW CHILDREN USE PLAY

In each of these stages, the child uses play to acquire social skills and to develop or refine emotional maturity.

Play enables children to

- explore different problem solving strategies
- develop an understanding of social relationships
- develop individual creativity
- facilitate language development
- represent their ideas and understandings in various ways
- extend their thinking abilities (both divergent and convergent)

Symbolic play has been described as "pretending behaviour in which children re-enact real-life situations" (Fine, 1987, p. 1). This form of play relates to cognitive learning by linking it to creative thinking, problem solving, and language development. Socio-dramatic play involves at least two children and "requires the learning of roles and rules about roles, more complex social interaction, and extensive verbalization" (Fine, 1987, p. 1). Socio-dramatic play is considered to be a mature form of play that eventually leads students into participating in games with rules, such as sports or board games, and ultimately opens them up to considering the viewpoints of others. Achievement of this level of play can then be considered a prerequisite for being able to do more formalized aspects of school work. As a result, the characteristics indicating a transition into this level of play are of particular importance to the teacher.

Piaget and Vygotsky were among the first to identify play as a generator of cognitive development for children. They suggested that play was a powerful learning tool that helps children develop "verbalization, vocabulary language, attention span, imagination, concentration, impulse control, curiosity, problem solving strategies, cooperation, empathy, and group participation"(Bodrova & Leong, 2003). Mature play involves the characteristics of incorporating imaginary situations, playing multiple roles, accepting clearly defined rules, being receptive to flexible themes, progressing in language development, and sustaining length of play. These characteristics explain how mature play can be such an effective aid to learning in a more formal sense.

The following definition of play highlights not only the key characteristics of play, but also focuses on the value inherent in the process of play.

> *Play… is spontaneous, a self-initiated, and self-directed search or inquiry that leads us through a labyrinth of trial and error toward a solution to some puzzle or problem of personal interest.*
>
> *~ Sue Alderson, 1985, p.8*

PLAY AND OLDER STUDENTS

Since play has been historically and culturally designated as something that is done primarily by the young, the notion that older children can and should engage in play can be an unsettling thought for many adults. But the use of play can be adapted to facilitate learning in older students as well. Since higher levels of involvement or engagement tend to enhance learning, it naturally follows that any pursuits that foster this will contribute to student learning (Cambourne, 1988; Torp & Sage, 2002). In older students in the junior and intermediate divisions,

GLOSSARY

Cooperative small group learning—an approach which focuses on small groups of students working together to solve or resolve a common problem. Individual group members are responsible for their own learning and for facilitating the learning of other group members. This approach is characterized by positive interactions, individual account-ability, equal participation, and shared social skills (Johnson & Johnson, 1991).

Problem-based learning—experiential learning which is organized around investigations of real-world problems (Torp & Sage, 2002).

this can be accomplished by using such strategies as **cooperative small group learning**, peer socialization experiences, research/project work, and group **problem-based learning**, to name but a few (Hewitt, 1995). These kinds of approaches reflect the needs of this age group to be involved in social interactions as they learn to discuss and begin to accept the perceptions/viewpoints of others. As students engage in problem solving activities, they

• identify root problems
• discover the conditions that promote good solutions
• pursue meaningful questions and solutions
• become more self-directed learners

Teachers who espouse this approach

• become problem solving colleagues by modeling problem solving strategies
• facilitate interest and enthusiasm in learning
• become cognitive coaches
• encourage open inquiry in their students

(Torp & Sage, 2002)

It should be noted that if older students are not used to being involved in active learning situations, these approaches need to be implemented slowly. Since this age level is more capable of following specific instructions, the procedures they will need to follow must be taught in a concerted way to optimize their learning during these experiences.

Play can be a powerful force that enhances children's motivation and ability to learn. Therefore, it is the educator's responsibility to promote the enjoyment of learning through meaningful, varied, and exciting learning/teaching strategies. In this way, play can provide a wealth of learning opportunities for children of all ages.

You can learn without playing, but you cannot play without learning! *end*

Regardless of how often educators debate the value of play as an effective learning strategy, it is important to keep in mind that learning shouldn't always be dependent on such narrow views as rote memorization and learning primarily from books. Children can and must be

MORE INFORMATION

To learn more about play, see "Too Much Learning Damaging to Play" by Sue Rogers (2005) and "Active Learning Through Play" by the Iowa Department of Education on the companion websites.

allowed to explore new concepts through a variety of experimentation and problem solving techniques—they need to CONSTRUCT their own understandings of the world!

PIAGET'S STAGES REVISITED

At this point, it is appropriate to take another look at Piagetian stages, but this time from a slightly different perspective. Figure 2.6 presents an overview of the percentage of children who are at a particular stage in Piaget's sequence of development, based on their age. Of significance is the length of time it takes most children to make the transition fully into the next stage. Piaget assumed that, given the right set of circumstances, all children had the potential to make the transition automatically to the next stage of development as they matured.

figure 2.6 Comparison of achievement of Piagetian stages by age (Huitt & Hummel, 2003)

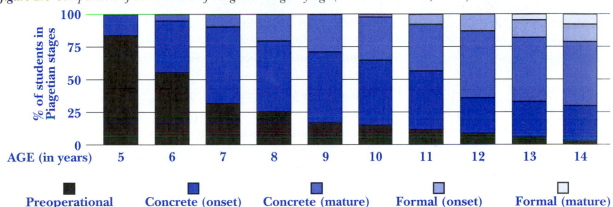

These findings provide an interesting challenge to some beliefs that educators have long held concerning expectations for functioning at certain grade levels. These findings should prompt educators to re-examine and rethink just how much children can be expected to handle cognitively in the curriculum at various ages. It is of particular interest to note that about 80 percent of students will remain in the Concrete Operational stage of thinking into the secondary school level.

It is also interesting to note that not all children will make the transition through all of the stages. Indeed, research findings indicate that only between 30–35 percent of adults attain the cognitive stage of Formal Operations (Kuhn, Langer, Kohlberg & Hann, 1977 as cited in Huitt & Hummell, 2003).

MORE INFORMATION

For more information on this topic, see "Piaget's Theory of Cognitive Development" by Huitt & Hummel (2003) on the companion website.

The Spiral of Knowing

Piaget used **the Spiral of Knowing** model as a way of describing the dynamic nature of learning central to constructivist theory. In this model, the child starts out with some basic experiences which are subsequently revisited and elaborated upon in more sophisticated ways as the child matures. These early experiences form the foundation for the development of basic mental frameworks (schema) and the initial attempts to establish a preliminary set of categories for organizing information. As the child has more experiences, the categories are expanded to fit new information.

In Figure 2.7, this model is illustrated by the following diagram: an inverted cone "**A**" with a peripheral "envelope" "**E**", surrounding the main spiral.

- The envelope (**E**) represents interactions with the environment.
- "**a**" represents the successive, hierarchical levels of the cognitive structures that are developed over time.
- "**b**" represents the changes due to the effect of the environment and the resulting sense of "disequilibrium".
- "**c**" represents explorations leading to partial reorganization or to a complete revamping of mental structures.

figure 2.7 The Spiral of Knowing model

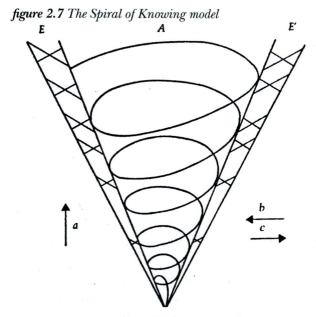

Piaget (1974) as cited in Gallagher & Reid, 1981
© Hermann éditeurs des sciences et des arts; www.editions-hermann.fr

The Spiral of Knowing model illustrates the openness and dynamic nature of Piaget's stages: they are a continuous process that is ever-expanding with no rigid breaking points to separate one stage from another. For example, looking at the bottom the spiral, early experiences would be represented there. When the child encounters a similar experience later on, reference would be made to prior understandings (lower on the spiral), predictions would be made, feedback would be received from the environment, and modifications or totally new mental structures created in response to this feedback (Gallagher & Reid, 1981). Some basic concepts include the following:

- everything students have ever experienced is contained within their spiral of knowing
- students are always learning since they are constantly reorganizing their spiral
- students must construct new meanings from prior knowledge as this is the basis of their own comparisons
- students need to repeat experiences because their spiral becomes different with the passage of time and subsequent experiences
- students must reflect on an experience to bring new associations to their spiral
- the strongest reflections involve prior experience
- the whole is greater than the sum of its parts as feelings, associations, and relationships trigger other thoughts
- interactions transform students' spirals and personalize them
- students' spirals are self-regulating—they can never learn too far away from their current understanding
- students' spirals are self-preserving—defense mechanism activate if they are threatened
- active involvement is crucial: "Teaching is neat. Learning is messy!"
- learning moves from the familiar to the less familiar and in doing so establishes a richer context
- accurate forms follow meaning and function—whenever students add a requirement of form, they reduce fluency
- students learn things as a whole first, and then they break it down as they establish a context
- error is crucial to learning since it results in reorganizing thinking
- students' feelings are important springboards for learning—the learning environment must be nurturing and supportive

(Mary Poplin, personal communication, May 1987)

The process of constantly changing one's spiral of knowing does not operate only within the domain of young children, but rather the process relates to all human learning. Indeed, this process goes on throughout life; people are always in the process of refining their spirals of knowing (Bruner, 1966; Gallagher & Reid, 1981).

Piaget's model demonstrates the interactive nature of learning and how previous knowledge forms the foundation for the next level of understanding. The significance of the dynamic, open, and ever widening mouth of the spiral is summarized as follows:

" Any knowledge raises new problems as it solves preceding ones. "

~ Piaget, 1977

If teachers are to optimize the experiences that children have on their journey toward deeper levels of understanding, then they must serve as a pivotal point around which appropriate and effective teaching and learning coalesce. Teachers have a prime responsibility for knowing where to guide children in their learning, and for providing not only the rich learning experiences that will enable children to enlarge their current world views, but also the supporting structures that will facilitate all aspects of development. It is the teacher who provides the modelling, the appropriate learning materials, and the scaffolding of questions that will help children to clarify and extend their thinking.

ORGANIZING THE CONSTRUCTIVIST CLASSROOM AND THE ROLE OF THE TEACHER IN CONSTRUCTIVISM

Since children bring many prior experiences with them to any learning situation, the teacher's main responsibility is to help students connect their previous learning to the new learning. According to Brooks and Grennon Brooks (1999, p. 22), "Initial relevance and interest are largely a function of the learner's experiences, not of the teacher's planning. Therefore, it is educationally counterproductive to ignore students' suppositions and points of view."

The following are some ideas about how teachers can apply/facilitate constructivist theory in their classrooms:

- Help children attach new information to their spirals through direct experience and multi-sensory experiences, for example, "hands on" or active learning
- Recognize that when teachers add a requirement of form, they will reduce fluency as children will tend to focus on one aspect of learning at a time. For example, there will be a reduction in the amount that a child will write when a definite focus is placed on neatness in handwriting.
- Encourage connectedness by emphasizing associations, integrating various aspects of curriculum, and using real-world situations and problems.
- Encourage penalty-free errors (risk–taking).
- Emphasize language development by encouraging discussion and an exchange of ideas; this can also be used as a diagnosis tool for individual needs.
- Use and respect humour since it encourages more associative thinking.
- Celebrate diversity as this enhances students' understanding and level of tolerance.
- Share interests with the children so that it is part of a sense of connectedness within the classroom community.
- Allow children to have choices as this fosters autonomy and independence; it ensures a stronger commitment to learning.
- Draw out information from children's spirals. This requires that the teacher know child development in all of its dimensions.
- Keep relevant facts, information, and skills at the forefront of planning and when discussing bigger ideas with the class.

(Mary Poplin, personal communication, May 1987;
Brooks & Grennon Brooks, 1999;
David Perkins, 1999; Cunningham & Allington, 2003).

Basically, it is important for educators to offer a variety of learning strategies for students, all of whom have unique and different combinations of learning styles. Above all, it is essential to make learning an enjoyable process for the student. If teachers model enthusiasm and optimism about new concepts being presented, then this motivation will transfer to the students and inspire them to explore and learn new things in a positive spirit. The learning process is also seriously impacted by the teacher knowing

MORE INFORMATION

For more information on Constructivist classrooms, see "Design of constructivist learning environments" by D. Jonassen (2001) on the companion website.

the strengths, weaknesses, and interests of each individual student and by incorporating these into the children's learning experiences.

The following description outlines the personal thoughts of a kindergarten teacher and the journey of some young children in using the power of constructivism in the classroom.

 # PERSONAL STORIES

A Teacher's Voice on Constructivism: Schema Creation in Action

I find the kindergarten program is a natural place to begin working with children to help them grow in their awareness of their personal schema and an exciting venue for showing them ways to expand their existing schema. These children use their schema daily when role playing in the drama centre, working with a friend to present a puppet play, using Lego to build a hydro truck, and in a variety of other tasks. The children are excited to give important labels to their activities, and after a few lessons were verbalizing their awareness of when they needed to draw on a schema to work through a task!

We began by defining schema so that the children knew that they gain information whenever they use any of their five senses, and that everything they remember from their experiences is joined together to create their schema. To make this very abstract idea more concrete for these young children, we created a collective schema about an animal—specifically a dog. We put on paper, using words and pictures, every idea that the children had in their heads. The children could see that this was our schema on paper, and that each of them had all of that stored within their own minds. And from that day on, they were using the word schema with a good understanding of its meaning.

Next we looked at how we can create a picture in our minds using our schema, and we call it our mental image. To experience this, the children were asked to lie on the carpet, close their eyes, and listen to a song about a familiar topic—dogs. When they were finished, they were asked to show me what they saw in their minds as the song played. This was difficult and some of the children honestly saw nothing. With lots of sharing and practise with a variety of songs, all of the children were able to give a representation of their mental image in a very short time.

I then began to discuss the fact that our schema changes. We talked about the different opportunities and experiences we have as we get older—beginning to read books, staying up later to watch different T.V. shows, learning to use the computer—and how this means we have more to add to our schema. Again, to make this idea more concrete for the children, we performed an experiment. The children had a short passage that described a rainforest scene read to them by their learning buddy. While being read to, the kindergarten children closed their eyes and tried to create a mental image of the rainforest. They were then asked to draw their image on paper. Even though the passage talked about the large tropical trees and exotic animals of the jungle, the children's pictures contained apple trees, dogs, and horses along with the tall grass and the tigers.

Personal Stories continues...

Over the next four weeks, I completed many activities using wild animals (sorting zebras, locating tigers and gorillas on a grid, counting spots on hippos, and matching rhyming alligators). I helped the children complete a research project (kindergarten style—with headbands and collages) on their favourite wild animal and had each child present their project to the class. I facilitated the creation of jungle bulletin boards with painted tropical birds and large paper palm trees. At the end of the four weeks, the children again closed their eyes and created a mental image of the jungle as I read the story "Little Polar Bear." The children then put their image on paper. The use of colour, the choice of animals, and the background scenery in the illustrations was clear evidence to all of us that their schema of jungle life had changed since the beginning of our topic. These little ones were well on their way to developing and understanding their schema.

Cheryl Dakin, JK/SK Teacher

SUMMARY

In conclusion, the following ideas outlined in an Ontario Ministry of Education document (1995) support the concept of a classroom where students work to construct their own understanding of the world. The following principles indicate that:

- Learning involves developing values as well as knowledge and skills.
- Students learn in different ways and at different rates.
- Students learn by asking questions and making connections.
- Learning requires effort and self discipline.
- Students must see the relevance of what they are learning.

CHAPTER 2 ACTIVITY

What should the constructivist classroom look, sound, and feel like?
Teachers need to encourage the following kinds of activities in their classrooms:

- handling learning materials so that relationships become more obvious
- seeking connections/relationships between and among ideas
- organizing ideas by creating more and more categories
- verbalizing current understandings
- sharing thoughts and predictions with others
- testing out ideas with others
- verbalizing changing perceptions

Using the ideas summarized above, create a collage of pictures, images, quotes, and inspirational sayings to show what an ideal constructivist classroom would be like.

CHAPTER 3

AUTONOMY:
A Self-Starter is Born

*" There is growing awareness that of all the per-
ceptions we experience in the course of living,
none has more profound significance than the
perceptions we hold regarding our own personal
existence—our concept of who we are and how
we fit into the world. "*

~ William Watson Purkey, 1984, p. 25

STUDY OBJECTIVES

The purpose of this chapter is to
- examine key elements contributing to the establishment of an effective climate for learning
- explore how the development of autonomy (moral and intellectual) influences the lives and potential learning of children
- explore the impact that self-concept and self-esteem have on children's learning

INTRODUCTION

This chapter builds on information from the two previous chapters and explores the underlying factors which can facilitate or inhibit the development of an effective climate for learning. Connections between constructivist theory, self-concept, and the development of autonomy will be examined in depth. The chapter develops the contributions of self-concept and self-esteem to learning, along with the effects of establishing a mutually supportive classroom environment. The chapter also explores the long-term influence of developing autonomous thinking, both in a moral and an intellectual sense. These concepts are elaborated upon in terms of practical applications within the classroom setting.

INVITATIONAL LEARNING

Invitational learning focuses on four basic principles:

1. People are able, valuable, and responsible. They should be treated accordingly.
2. Teaching and learning should be a cooperative activity.
3. People possess relatively untapped potential in all areas of human development.
4. This potential can realized by inviting development to occur and by providing people who are personally and professionally inviting to themselves and others.

Even the words used to label this approach are positive and welcoming! To invite can mean "to offer something beneficial for consideration." According to Purkey and Novak (1984, p. 3) "… invitational education is the process by which people are cordially summoned to realize their relatively boundless potential."

This approach encourages teachers to perceive children in positive ways and to have high expectations for how they will respond. When children are treated as being able, capable, and responsible, they can approach their own learning in positive terms and in a spirit of hopefulness. In doing so, they can become more personally engaged in the learning process. When this approach is planned thoroughly and implemented in a concerted way, a cooperative classroom community can result (Lewis et al, 1996). With students truly engaged in and committed to working with others, the scene can be set for developing their interpersonal and intrapersonal skills even further. This leads to the role of autonomy in learning.

AUTONOMY

Autonomy has been defined as "acting independently" or "being governed by oneself" and, therefore, it is the opposite of **heteronomy**, or being governed by someone else. Why then is the whole issue of autonomy so important? To understand the vital role that the development of autonomy plays in learning, it is essential to examine how it evolves and how it can be encouraged within the learning environment.

The concept of constructivism, as outlined in the previous chapter, is central to the development of a sense of autonomy. For Piaget, the true aim of education was not only the development of intellectual autonomy, but also of moral autonomy. It follows that if these two components

of autonomy are to be developed and are to occur within individuals, then ultimately they will potentially manifest themselves within society as a whole. He believed that it is essential for children to construct their own understanding of the world in personal ways rather than be given ready-made "truths" created by others (Piaget, 1969). Through direct experience in solving a variety of problems in different situations, children begin to develop a sense of what it means to be responsible for their own actions and thoughts. Piaget believed that when there is direct personal involvement, children are encouraged to respect rules that they have helped formulate and work harder to achieve goals they have set for themselves. Therefore, with respect to the development of autonomy, active learning is an essential component of the learning process.

> *The teacher's responsibility is one of facilitating children's discovery of knowledge through their spontaneous activity and by organizing encounters."*
>
> ~ *Piaget, 1969*

Since teachers play such a major role in the lives of school children, Piaget felt they could play a similar role in the development of autonomy, both in a moral as well as in an intellectual sense.

The following diagram illustrates a continuum of dependency from being totally dependent to totally independent. Naturally, this will vary from person to person, and the degree of learner autonomy will shift given certain circumstances or events. It is important to realize that there needs to be some balance in the degree of dependency that will be encouraged in students and that teachers will play a major role in assisting their students in becoming more autonomous learners. The goal, ultimately, is to support students in being more independent by guiding them toward more autonomous ways of thinking and learning.

figure 3.1

MORAL AUTONOMY ("FREE WILL")

Given the many examples seen daily in the news media, there would appear to be an urgent need for society to develop a stronger sense of moral autonomy, integrity, and ethics. This does not start, however, when people become adults, but instead has roots in the experiences of childhood.

Individuals demonstrate moral autonomy when they choose to do the right thing, no matter how strong the pressure is to do otherwise. The influence of rewards and punishment play a key role here. For example, children may have learned that stealing is wrong, but because they don't like the punishment of being grounded and they like the reward of having money to buy something, they learn that they had better not get caught.

On a different level, adults participating in "reality" TV shows are well aware that lying and cheating are wrong in a moral sense. However, in the context of the game in which they are involved, devious behaviours suddenly become permissible or even encouraged because of the monetary reward. What confusing messages children must derive from seeing adults engaged in this kind of behaviour!

The Subtle Influence of Rewards and Punishments

The examples above may seem obvious, but there are more subtle forces at work when children are rewarded or punished, especially in the long term when it comes to relationships. The opposite of autonomy is *heteronomy*, or being governed by others. When adults use rewards or punishment in responding to children's behaviours, they reinforce the development of heteronomy (Kamii, 1984, 1991).

Rewards are usually perceived as being positive, especially on the part of those receiving them, but there can also be a negative side to using rewards. When children consistently receive rewards for everything they do, they become more dependent upon extrinsic recognition to motivate their actions. When this happens, the reward can become the central focus of the experience rather than the act for which the reward was received (Kohn, 1996). Over a period of time, the pattern of being rewarded can make the child dependent on receiving rewards before experiences are even attempted. It is interesting to note that this kind of dependant behaviour can often be seen in children who constantly seek to please the adults in their lives, both teachers and parents.

Over the years, educators have shared varying views on this topic, with many expressing frustration at the perpetuation of practices which encourage children to be overly dependent on adult praise for their motivation. An obvious example, seen in many classes, is the practice of giving stars to children in recognition of good work. This practice might seem to be rather innocuous, but consider, for a moment, any practice that does not ensure (at some time or other) that everyone will receive

such positive attention. What happens to those children who never get stars on their work? Or even worse, what happens to those children who have their apparent inadequacies posted on a spelling chart on the wall of the classroom, minus any stars, for all to see and even ridicule?

The following quote rather caustically sums up the beliefs of those educators who do not support the use of such extrinsic rewards in dealing with children's learning.

There is a special place in Hell for the teacher who first gave stars to children!

~ Leland Jacobs, personal communication, February 1972

Perhaps it is possible to achieve some middle ground in relation to this issue, with stickers used to identify completion of work rather than as a summative judgment of its value, for example, used as an indicator of completing a workbook or unit before it is sent home. In this way, everyone will eventually receive some form of tangible recognition or reward, but of a kind that is not so overtly or publicly judgmental. The purpose of the reward, in this case, has shifted to one of recognition that is within the reach of all students.

Punishment, on the other hand, can also elicit strong responses from children. If children are regularly confronted with their own limitations, they may seek to avoid being exposed for judgment by lying to protect themselves. On the other hand, they may demonstrate absolute conformity and compliance. Sometimes, what appear to be children's limitations are instead expectations that are too narrowly defined or behaviours that are beyond the control of an individual at a certain point in their development, for example, it is unfair to be censured for untidy work when small muscle control is not yet fully developed, or for spilling something when children are not strong enough to effectively handle a large container of liquid. It should be noted that children do not always choose their behaviours. Either way, a negative confrontation in situations such as these does little to promote either personal responsibility or self-governance.

Adults often inadvertently reinforce contradictions in children's responses by making such statements as, "Don't let me ever catch you doing that again!" When this happens repeatedly, children may learn to become more secretive or devious, or to blindly accept the ideas or control of others. The latter can be especially disturbing when

MORE INFORMATION

For more information on the importance of autonomy in learning, see "What does research on Constructivist Education tell us about effective schooling?" by Rheta DeVries on the companion website.

considering the inevitable role that peer pressure will play in children's lives as they get older (Coloroso, 1994; Kamii et al., 1994; Kohn, 1996).

If we want children to develop the morality of autonomy, we must…encourage children to construct moral values for themselves. It is possible for a child to think about the importance of honesty…only if he or she is confronted with the fact that other people cannot trust him or her.

~ Constance Kamii, 1984, p. 411

The following real life example illustrates how a young child responded in a self-initiated autonomous experience.

 **PERSONAL STORIES**

Autonomy in Action

A kindergarten teacher noted that one of her little girls was missing when the children came in after recess one afternoon. Arranging for another teacher to look after her class, the teacher went out to the playground and found the little "prodigal" standing in the middle of the playing field with a look of absolute rapture on her face. On seeing her teacher, the little girl ran over to her with a big smile and, excitedly, she burst out, "I was out here all by myself."

Her teacher calmly reminded her that as soon as the bell rang, she needed to come in with the other children. On hearing this, the little girl ignored this gentle admonishment and persisted in sharing her own personal enlightenment by saying, "No! No! You don't understand! I was out here all by myself and I could have 'scaped!"

Explanation:

While this example has obvious charm, the underlying message is that this little girl was engaged in a totally autonomous experience. For a brief period of time, she was in total control of her own personal universe. Her reaction indicates that this experience had a powerful impact on her. This is understandable, since once children come to school, they are subjected to rules, forms of control, and the ongoing problem of competing with their peers for the attention of their teacher.

One can only imagine the feeling of absolute bliss this little child experienced in being by herself and able to choose whatever she wanted to do. Autonomy, indeed!

How can Autonomy be Facilitated?

A major way that adults can stimulate the development of autonomy is by encouraging children to exchange points of view. Through regular discussions of various scenarios, children come to see the value of being honest and straightforward in their dealings with others. A positive result is that children typically learn to correct themselves autonomously as points of view are exchanged (Kamii, 1991; 1994). Ideally, children will construct their own set of personal beliefs from their interactions within the learning environment and with others.

Children are not merely empty vessels to be filled with discrete bits of factual information. Instead, they are active processors who compare what they already know with what they are currently experiencing. In doing so, they derive deeper levels of understanding about connections, relationships, and how things work in the world. If they are encouraged to have these kinds of experiences, they will be enabled in constructing their own personal belief systems. Since learning is not simply a matter of accumulating bits of information, this prompts teachers to consider what they do with what they know, and this leads to the issue of intellectual autonomy.

INTELLECTUAL AUTONOMY ("FREE CHOICE")

Intellectual autonomy means being governed by oneself and not blindly accepting the ideas of others without questioning their veracity. Given the number of compelling visual images and persuasive verbal messages to which children are exposed every day in the media, this particular form of autonomy has potentially far-reaching effects on children's lives. Intellectual autonomy invites children to

• question what they are told rather than just accepting it as the truth
• find their own truths whether they are the same as others or not
• re-examine their beliefs on an on-going basis
• interact and discuss their ideas with others
• approach their learning in the spirit of inquiry

 REFLECTIVE PRACTICE

"Is Santa Real?"

This question will inevitably arise when teaching/interacting with young children. The classic question from children, about whether or not Santa Claus is "real," presents an interesting example of how teachers and parents can foster intellectual autonomy. Over time, children formulate and ask more elaborate questions about this issue and eventually arrive at the true answer. In the process of doing so, teachers and parents alike can experience some rather tense moments. If this is handled with sensitivity, most children will ultimately conclude that Santa is a symbolic ritual that adults play out with children. Other more intellectually autonomous individuals might eventually conclude that Santa does exist in "the spirit of Christmas."

Think about the following question:

• How can the development of autonomy be facilitated through this situation?

Questioning to Facilitate Autonomy

Having children debate and discuss different points of view—rather than simply labelling things "right" or "wrong"—not only helps develop autonomy, but also aids in the development of students who are confident and secure in their thinking. By allowing them to work through ideas and concepts, they are provided with a sense of accomplishment that they would not have had if their ideas were simply dismissed as being wrong. Such approaches encourage students to develop confidence in their own learning as they become less afraid of being singled-out or embarrassed by the "wrong answer," and more willing and comfortable in opening their ideas to debate and discussion. Being open to the ideas of others is a major contributor to intellectual autonomy (Kamii, 1991). Through ongoing exposure to an accepting and supportive atmosphere where various responses are encouraged and multiple answers sought, children learn that it is perfectly all right to have ideas that differ from their peers (Lewis et al, 1996). Indeed, intellectual autonomy can be attained by defending one's ideas.

Teachers who consistently use leading questions risk undermining the development of intellectual autonomy. This occurs when children give responses based on what they think the teacher wants to hear as the teacher plays the game of "Guess What's In My Mind". In doing this, children often give an expected answer and not an answer that could necessarily solve a particular problem. It is interesting to note that when questioned on how they "arrived at their answer," children who have been exposed to looking for one definitive right answer will typically try to correct their response before even attempting to explain their reasoning (Kamii, 1991). This would appear to denote a certain degree of basic insecurity about their own thinking (Kohn, 1996; Chilton Pearce, 1992).

For intellectual autonomy to develop, children must be supported in their learning so they will trust their own thought processes. In the following example, the child has written a solution to a mathematical question:

$$4 + 2 = 5$$

A typical response would be to say that the child is wrong. But how does this help the child become an independent thinker? The following response demonstrates how intellectual autonomy can be fostered in such a scenario (Kamii, 1984, p. 413):

> The wise teacher refrains from correcting a child who says that $4 + 2 = 5$. A better reaction is to encourage two children who arrived at different answers to explain their thinking to one another. Alternatively, the teacher can ask the child "How did you get 5?" Children often correct themselves autonomously as they try to explain their reasoning to someone else. In the process of explaining, they have to decenter—that is, try to coordinate their points of view with those of others. In doing so, children often recognize their own mistakes.

Teachers, by virtue of their position, are already viewed by children as people in authority and therefore very knowledgeable. If the teacher consistently reinforces that a response is either right or wrong, children may cease to look within themselves for answers and will look to others to provide them with the expected answers. If this happens repeatedly, the teacher can be perceived as being the prime source of all correct answers and the "font of all knowledge." This perception could ultimately lead children to doubt their own abilities.

Instead, children need opportunities to uncover their own errors for themselves and to learn to see these as springboards to deeper awareness of what they know. When this is encouraged consistently within the classroom environment, it can lead to the development of metacognitive skills where children understand *how* they know

MORE INFORMATION

For more information on Kamii's views on autonomy, see "Teachers need more knowledge of how children learn mathematics" by Constance Kamii on the companion website.

something. This development is essential if children are to become independent learners with a strong sense of trust in their own abilities, understanding, and thoughts.

Since intellectual autonomy frees people to have faith in their own thinking, those with a strong sense of intellectual autonomy will be less susceptible to being lead by others, less willing to accept the views of others without question, and less likely to believe propaganda on blind faith (Coloroso, 1994; Kohn, 1996; Chilton Pearce, 1992). Having these skills becomes particularly important when considering the proliferation of questionable input in the information age.

The Importance of Choice

One of the most important things that teachers can do to facilitate the development of autonomy is to provide children with choices. If everything is always laid out for children, then their decision-making capabilities will not be challenged, encouraged, or exercised. There are, however, some preconditions that need to exist before choices can be provided within the learning environment. Many of these are reflective of the values and beliefs that teachers themselves have.

- Teachers must value the importance of choice within the classroom.
- Teachers must provide a variety of activities from which children will choose.
- Teachers must be open to providing more child-centred approaches.
- Teachers must commit to providing more play-based or active learning programs.

MORE INFORMATION

For more information on the role of choice and how this facilitates the development of critical thinking, see "Choices for children: Why and how to let children decide," by Alfie Kohn on the companion website.

What does choice provide for children? It gives them a feeling of control over some aspects of their learning and, in the process, helps them develop their sense of self-esteem. Children, by their very immaturity, cannot be left totally in control of what happens in their lives. However, whenever feasible, choice has the potential to enhance their view of themselves, both as individuals and as members of a group. Most children are aware of and accept at least some of the limitations placed on them by virtue of their size, age, or lack of experience. It follows then that when choices can be made available, they will respond in a positive manner.

Becoming autonomous and self-reliant learners requires that children be allowed to make choices, be independent, and work through problems that arise from their own decisions.

This does not happen in a vacuum, but instead necessitates on-going social interaction. In order to understand this concept, it is important to be fully conversant with different aspects of social development and how autonomous feelings can have a strong influence on people throughout various stages of their lives.

Erikson's Contributions to Autonomy

Erik Erikson's stages of social development provide some valuable insights into the importance of choice at all stages of the life cycle. He believed that in each of his stages, there needed to be a healthy resolution of a crisis and that this would enable the individual to move successfully to the next stage. Ultimately, from Erikson's perspective, the end result would be a positive retrospective of one's life (Santrock & Yussen, 1992; Berk, 1996). For a description of Erikson's Stages of Social Development, see Chapter 1.

In each of these stages, people are confronted with choices that will enable them to resolve different crises, and the choices they make can have far reaching effects on all aspects of their lives. It would seem logical, then, that providing children with on-going opportunities to practise making appropriate choices, even from an early age, would ultimately be a positive step in helping them to become more productive and autonomous decision-makers. In doing so, they would become more adept at resolving many of the crises to which Erikson referred.

PRACTICAL APPLICATIONS OF AUTONOMOUS TEACHING

The following are some ideas which teachers can use to help children become more autonomous learners:

- Encourage discussion of different points of view.
- Encourage children to coordinate their viewpoints.
- Use group work to promote the exchange of ideas.
- Establish an atmosphere of mutual respect where all ideas are valued.
- Encourage children to think by having them confront the ideas of their peers.
- Accept varying interpretations of a common experience.
- Use appropriate questioning to encourage children to share what they think.
- Encourage children to make choices in what they learn, how they learn it, and how they represent their knowledge.

If teachers want to encourage autonomous learning, then it is important to re-examine what they do with children and what they provide for children's learning. An ongoing message that persists in current research is that teachers must, above all, be concerned with educating the whole child (Bredekamp & Copple, 1997; Eisner, 2005; Miller, 1993; Noddings, 2005). Promoting autonomous thinking, both morally and intellectually, provides the necessary vehicle for facilitating this important endeavour.

> *Exchanging points of view contributes to children's social, affective, moral, and political development.*
>
> ~ *Constance Kamii, 1984, p. 414*

Teaching strategies that encourage children to coordinate viewpoints are far more effective than methods which aim only at getting the students to give "right" answers. Thinking is stimulated when teachers ask children what they think about different interpretations of the same event. Such discussions lead to greater intellectual autonomy and better comprehension of specific content, since children are not only actively relating their own ideas to the discussion, but are also simultaneously evaluating the various perspectives of their classmates.

Autonomy Revisits Constructivism

The concept of autonomy leads to a fundamentally different approach to teaching. Autonomy requires that children be active participants in their own learning and, similarly, constructivism demands that learners control the learning.

The following points demonstrate the connectedness between autonomy and constructivism. Constructivist teachers

- seek and value students' points of view
- structure lessons to challenge students' suppositions
- recognize that students must attach relevance to the curriculum
- structure lessons around big ideas, not just small bits of information
- assess student learning in the context of daily classroom investigations and not just as separate events

Therefore,

- Learning should take place within a social context.
- Provisions for group learning should be evident.
- Students should be encouraged to challenge each others' opinions.
- Students should build on one another's ideas.
- Students should assist each other in drawing conclusions.
- Students should support one another in the learning process.

(Kamii et al., 1994)

Kamii's ideas provide teachers with guidelines for creating and encouraging autonomous, constructivist approaches in their classrooms. The points outlined above raise important issues with regard to making learning meaningful, relevant, and interactive. Learning must incorporate the personal interests and experiences of the children. It must be set within an environment where ongoing communication is facilitated. It must occur in an atmosphere of mutual support and respect for the ideas of all learners and for various learning styles (Lewis et al, Kohn, 1996). According to Kamii (1984, p. 411),

> Learning is non-linear because research illustrates that instruction based on drill and practice of isolated facts and skills does not foster student learning. Facts learned out of context are hard to organize and retain.

AUTONOMY AND PLAY

The teaching style that promotes the development of autonomy, in turn lends itself well to the idea that play is a powerful tool for learning. Teachers and researchers alike have discovered that learning is a complex, active process and that using play in learning can be an integral part of the learning process (Bennett, 1997; Alderson, 1985; Fine, 1987; Yardley, 1991). According to Sue Alderson (1985, p. 8),

> Sometimes play is engaged in for the sheer joy of mastery, but usually there is a drive to find out, or a trying-on component that is most personal, creative and imaginative. It's a *let's see if,* or a testing-out of little theories and assumptions about how something works, how things mean and make sense. Play is active involvement in one's own learning, with progressive and successive *hmms* and *ah-ha*'s along the way.

Many teachers have come to realize that "*Hmms* and *ah-ha*'s" can be the best forms of learning. Students can be formally introduced to a topic from the curriculum and then be given the opportunity to play with it, reflect on it, and internalize it in ways that have personal meaning to them.

Play provides opportunities for students to play together, exchange points of view, and challenge one another's ideas.

In doing so, students are provided with a positive learning environment where more autonomous thinking can be facilitated.

Constructivism dictates that learning should be active and interactive, with the learners in control of their learning. What more appropriate way to provide for this type of learning than through play? Active involvement, meaningful experiences, interaction with others, along with a healthy self-esteem, all blend together in the ultimate goal of producing autonomous learners.

Peer interactions and exchanging points of view help students

- develop a social conscience
- develop critical thinking
- become aware of connections and interrelationships in learning
- participate more fully in a democratic society

… we owe to our children … a supporting context of wholeness and unity … where success is measured by the completeness and richness of human experience.

~ Bob Samples, 1987, p. 253

REFLECTIVE PRACTICE

Choice and Exchange of Ideas

Two major factors that contribute to the development of autonomy are **choice** and **exchange of ideas.**

Think about the following questions:

- How could the classroom setting be planned to foster autonomy in learning?
- What might be some appropriate strategies to encourage exchange of ideas within the classroom?

What does an autonomous learner look, sound, and feel like?
As an autonomous learner, I:

- dramatize my favourite part of a story!
- paint a picture!
- make choices!
- write an original poem!
- laugh with my classmates!
- build a model of a bridge!
- write a list of supplies needed for a project!
- am happy!

- help my classmates learn something!
- discuss ideas!
- create a costume!
- become engrossed in a story!
- make up a song and sing it!
- work in a small group!
- research my favourite animal's habitat!
- choose a project of my own!

- play a game with my group!
- finish a project!
- share ideas with others!
- am responsible!
- present my ideas to the class!
- feel confident!
- want to come to school!
- see connections between and among ideas!
- learn with my friends!

A major aspect of educating children is responding to their needs and interests, not just covering the prescribed curriculum. Providing the full range of experiences and subjects must be taken into consideration so that all aspects of their interests and needs can be stimulated. By promoting autonomy, teachers can help students realize the value of their own ideas as well as the ideas of others, and the contribution that these ideas can make to everyone's learning.

SELF-CONCEPT & SELF-ESTEEM

What makes things significant for the learner? The answer lies in each individual's search for identity and meaning in life. **Self-concept** is a fundamental need that must be nourished to achieve the attitudes and values that will support lifelong learning. Self-concept is comprised of two different parts:

- **Self-confidence**—the belief in one's own capabilities
  For example, "I am capable and able to do certain things."
- **Self-esteem**—the way one feels about oneself, or basically how much one likes oneself; it is the positive regard or good opinion that we have about ourselves.
  For example, "I believe that I am likeable and worthy."

The feelings people have about themselves are commonly referred to as self-esteem. An understanding of self-esteem and its relation to learning is essential so that teachers can optimize students' learning.

You know where self-esteem comes from? It comes from being liked, accepted, and connected.

~ Roger & David Johnson, 1987

When people experience success in what they attempt and receive positive responses from others to what they do, they begin to feel more confident, capable, and likeable. This is an on-going process that continues throughout their lives. Feelings of self-confidence and self-worth have a strong influence on how people behave as individuals, how they interact with others, and how they view the future.

People who have a strong self-concept approach new experiences expecting success. If people have a positive self-concept, they will be more willing to attempt new things and will not feel defeated by the occasional failures which are a part of everyone's life experiences. In turn, they will be more likely to think and act independently than those who do not have as much confidence in themselves and their abilities. Most importantly, people with a healthy self-concept will be less likely to be influenced by pressure from others—a key factor in the development of autonomy.

Self-esteem is the experience that I am competent to live and worthy of happiness.

~ Nathaniel Branden, 1983, p. 5

Figure 3.2 summarizes key components associated with the development of self-concept.

figure 3.2 Self-concept: the foundation for independent thinking

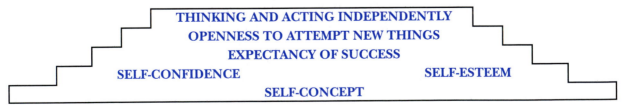

THINKING AND ACTING INDEPENDENTLY
OPENNESS TO ATTEMPT NEW THINGS
EXPECTANCY OF SUCCESS
SELF-CONFIDENCE   SELF-ESTEEM
SELF-CONCEPT

Starting with self-concept, self-confidence and self-esteem are the two major components of this essential factor. If experiences are positive, the following develop from these two components: an expectancy of success, openness to attempt new things, and, finally, thinking and acting independently. All of these lead ultimately to more autonomous thinking.

SELF-ESTEEM

Self-esteem differs from self-concept in the following ways:

• It is not primarily dependent upon the approval of others.
• It is a gift we give to ourselves.
• It is one of our most basic needs.
• It impacts every major aspect of our lives.
• It has a profound effect on our thinking, emotions, values, choices, and goals.
• It is important to our mental health.

(Branden, 1994)

How Self-esteem Develops

As children interact with the world in a physical sense, they develop notions about how objects in the environment work in relation to one another and they begin to anticipate patterns of behaviour. The same is true in their social interactions. In response to social experiences, they develop either a sense of feeling in control of a situation if it is a positive one, or feelings of being overwhelmed or helpless if the experience is negative. Children encounter this early in their lives and it can have long-lasting effects on the development of a healthy self-esteem.

Self-esteem in Preschoolers and Early Childhood

Very young children do not have a very well-defined sense of self-esteem (Berk, 1996). They tend to base their social acceptance by other people on how "good" they are at doing certain tasks. Prior to seven years old, when they are still very egocentric, they tend to overrate their abilities and capabilities and underestimate the difficulty of a task (Berk, 1996). This can often get them into situations where they don't know how to deal with the consequences of their actions. Since this period is characterized by exposure to many skills in all areas of development—physical, cognitive, social, and emotional—young children will naturally require the patience and support of encouraging adults as they work to construct their own notions of the world (Canfield & Wells, 1976; Kohn, 1996).

Self-esteem in Middle Childhood

Around seven years of age, there is a major shift in self-understanding. While in transition, children initially engage in generally positive descriptions about themselves. Then they begin to make more comparisons between themselves and their peers and start to become more self-critical. Finally, they begin to examine the potential reasons behind their own strengths and weaknesses (Berk, 1996). This gradual transformation is the act of **decentering** (Piaget, 1969). Since this period is characterized by both consolidation and transformation of a lot of earlier perceptions about themselves, they need opportunities to express their viewpoints in relation to their peers within an environment that provides a lot of teacher and peer support (Lewis, 1996).

Self-esteem in Early Adolescence

Significant cognitive changes during this period strongly influence adolescents' perceptions of themselves. Over time, they begin to see themselves as being more organized, complex, and consistent in their views. This, in turn, provides the foundation for a more unified personal identity (Berk, 1996). Since conformity is a strong factor in this period, adolescents seek to be liked and approved of by their peers. While providing the necessary experiences in peer interactions, the teacher must pay close attention to ensure the emotional and social safety of all students (Coloroso, 1994; Hewitt, 1995).

The Gift of Self-esteem

A healthy self-esteem is accomplished over a period of time. When people are allowed to work at their own individual pace, at things that are of interest to them, and at appropriate levels of functioning, they will have a greater chance of achieving success. Self-esteem is reinforced every time new things are attempted and success is experienced. As self-esteem develops from a solid base of personal strengths, it becomes a valuable springboard for encouraging individuals to attempt a variety of more challenging tasks.

Self-esteem is a result of the actions and interactions which arise from people's view of themselves. To trust in their own mind and to believe they are worthy of happiness is the essence of self-esteem (Purkey and Novak, 1984). It is a powerful motivating force which influences how people act. In turn, how they act influences their level of self-esteem. The difference between a person who perseveres and one who gives up is often a reflection of that person's self-esteem.

When people have a strong sense of who they are and what they stand for, they will have strong expectations not only for themselves, but also for what they will tolerate from others. This becomes a prerequisite for having a healthy respect for others as a base in any effective relationship. People with a strong sense of self-esteem treat others respectfully and expect the same treatment in return. So, a healthy self-esteem doesn't just encourage positive feelings about oneself; it enables people to live a more positive life in conjunction with others (Coloroso, 1994).

The ultimate source of feelings of self-esteem is internal. Therefore, it is impossible to teach self-esteem in a direct or external manner. Rather, positive self-esteem can be fostered by creating a learning environment that is supportive of those experiences that will lead to success, and by encouraging interactions that will create feelings of mutual respect. In doing so, self-esteem will be strengthened in all participants (Lewis et al, 1996). Teachers have the potential to exert a critical influence in the development of healthy self-esteem.

Canfield and Wells (1976) believe that positive self-esteem can only be taught if teachers model it in the classroom by acknowledging themselves and their strengths, by admitting their mistakes, and by being confident enough to laugh at themselves. It is also important that teachers display self-esteem by nurturing their bodies and by taking good care of themselves.

On a cautionary note, there is an inherent danger in overemphasizing experiences or feedback that focus on the actions and responses of others as a base for self-esteem. This can result in students becoming overly dependent upon the approval of others for their sense of self-esteem, and it does little to encourage independent thinking, self-reliance, and autonomy.

Healthy self-esteem is highly dependent on the quality of the relationships children have with the people around them. In these relationships, self-esteem increases when

- children are completely accepted for who they are, not what they do
- children have clear expectations which are enforced fairly and consistently
- children are respected
- children are provided with choices
- teachers have high expectation for behaviour and performance
- teachers have a high level of self-esteem themselves

(Kamii et al., 1994)

Since teachers spend relatively large amounts of time daily with their students, they can play an essential part as significant role models, particularly in the elementary grades. It is therefore essential that teachers become strong role models for high self-esteem. It is widely known that "...foster(ing) a self-esteem building environment results in higher levels of productivity for both students and teachers" (Lewis, 1996).

Opportunities for children to contribute to and promote other children's learning should be facilitated by allowing children to work in pairs and small groups, solicit opinions from other students, and engage in thorough discussions to clarify their thinking. Ultimately, the focus should be on ensuring success. Since cooperative small group learning strategies are success-oriented, these should be encouraged regularly within the classroom.

It has been said that, "If at first you don't succeed, you don't succeed." This statement speaks volumes about the need for success-based learning and the development of a healthy self-esteem, from the earliest experiences that children have in the school system. Whenever possible, it is imperative that the teacher build in opportunities for praising the efforts and approximations that children make as they work toward understanding concepts. The connections between success-oriented approaches and the contributions of autonomy become even more obvious when considering the overall learning potential of children as they progress toward full understanding of their world, both in a social and an intellectual sense.

When children discuss differing viewpoints, rather than simply accepting things as being "right" or "wrong," they develop not only a stronger sense of their own autonomy, but also confidence in expressing their own ideas. When children are encouraged to work through ideas and concepts for themselves, they develop a stronger sense of accomplishment than they would otherwise develop. Positive and validating experiences help children develop confidence in their own abilities and they become less fearful of being embarrassed by giving a "wrong" answer. As a result, they become more willing to risk being wrong, more open to various possibilities, and more engrossed in the learning process.

As stated previously, risk-taking is an essential ingredient in the learning process. To become independent, autonomous thinkers, children have to be able to try out new ideas, risk being wrong, reorganize their thinking, and express their expanded world views within a safe and secure learning environment. Open interaction within an atmosphere of trust is an essential component if this is to happen.

> **MORE INFORMATION**
>
> For more information on self-esteem, See "Review of Self-Esteem Research" by Robert Reasoner on the companion website.

What would a learning environment that fosters self-esteem look like?

Non-judgmental · Respectful · Secure · Caring · Interesting · Accepting · Trusting · Inviting · Comfortable · Calm · Supportive · Warm · Encouraging · Positive · Predictable · Exciting · Safe

REFLECTIVE PRACTICE

What is the teacher's role in establishing a learning environment that encourages and supports the development of healthy self-esteem in all students in the class? What is the student's role?

Think about the following question:

- How could teachers engage parents in supporting this idea?
- How could teachers celebrate the success of this kind of approach in their classrooms and on a school-wide basis?

CREATING AN ATMOSPHERE FOR LEARNING

Students work harder, achieve more, and attribute more importance to schoolwork in classes in which they feel liked, accepted, and respected by the teacher and fellow students.

~ Lewis et al, 1996, p. 18

The following ideas outline some of the essential points necessary for establishing a positive learning environment where children can flourish in their development. Catherine Lewis provides some valuable insights into the five principles for fostering a caring classroom environment (Lewis et al, 1996).

1. **Children need warm, supportive, stable relationships.**
   This is not something that teachers can accomplish alone. To paraphrase a well known quote, "It takes an entire school and a supportive home environment to educate a child." Those involved need to clearly share their beliefs and support one another in this important endeavour. All parties need to model the necessary degree of consistency and strong commitment that will facilitate a learning atmosphere to ensure success. To do this, there must be a shift from competitive to more cooperative approaches. Because of this need, the following question takes on particularly strong relevance:

Do students view their classmates primarily as collaborators in learning or as competitors in the quest for grades and recognition?

~ Lewis et al, 1996, p. 16

2. **Children need to be engaged in constructive learning.**

   It takes time and creativity on the part of the teacher to make learning as engaging as possible for the learners. Children need opportunities to explore using materials and then using and applying ideas. They need to discover answers on their own and test out their ideas with others. They need to be exposed to multiple possibilities and open to creative alternatives. All of these approaches lead the intellect forward to deeper levels of understanding and connections between and among ideas as they construct their own views about how things work.

   Good teaching fosters these efforts to understand…helping children become ever more skillful, reflective, and self-critical in their pursuit of knowledge.

   ~ Lewis et al, 1996, p. 18

3. **Children need an important, challenging curriculum.**

   While teachers don't have a lot of control over what they teach, they still have control over how they teach. It is the teacher's responsibility to present curriculum content in ways that are developmentally appropriate, challenging, and exciting for their students. It is essential that the teacher assist the children to make connections, see relationships, and identify the personal relevance of what they are learning.

   …certain skills and habits are likely to remain important—thoughtful reading, self-critical reflection, clear communication, asking productive questions.

   ~ Lewis et al, 1996, p. 19

4. **The focus needs to be on intrinsic motivation.**

   Instilling intrinsic motivation in students can be a difficult task. Offering rewards or prizes gives an immediate response to a short-term goal, but it fails to teach the child the value of long-term motivation. Since this practice appears to be so ingrained in the school system and in many homes, minimizing extrinsic rewards can be a difficult task. It is, however, one that is well worth the effort. Intrinsic rewards focus on the more long lasting effects of doing something for the sheer joy of doing it and on the feelings of personal accomplishment which result.

To minimize extrinsic rewards, educators need a curriculum that is worth learning and a pedagogy that helps students see why it is worth learning.

~ Lewis et al, 1996, p. 19

5. **Attention must be paid to the social and ethical dimension of learning.** This must become part of the daily routine in the classroom. Most teachers teach in schools that have a mix of social, economic, and ethnic diversity. It is important to expose their students to this diversity through open discussions about personal concerns and different viewpoints. They need to realize that not everyone feels exactly the same about all issues and they need a regular forum in which to share their ideas freely.

Everything about schooling—curriculum, teaching, method, discipline, interpersonal relationships—teaches children about the human qualities that we value.

~ Lewis et al, 1996, p. 19

These ideas relate strongly to the concepts introduced earlier on both constructivism in general, and social constructivism specifically. There is a strong body of research which is now calling for recognition of the importance of these ideas and for implementing them in classrooms in a concerted way.

While everything really begins and ends with the child, the teacher has a major role to play. Basically, the teacher's attitude is the key factor that will make a difference or not. Teachers model and implement new innovations in teaching. Through positive attitudes and continuous learning, teachers facilitate not only their own professional growth, but also promote change on a broader level. To accomplish this, the teacher is responsible for seeking out appropriate resources, being conversant with new developments in teaching and learning, sharing these with others who are involved in educating the children, and using all of these resources, both personnel and material, for the benefit of students.

There can be no significant innovation in education that does not have at its centre the attitude of teachers.

~ Neil Postman & Carl Weingartner, 1969, p. 33

SUMMARY

As a profession, it is important to keep in mind what teachers want their students to learn and to be like. The teacher's prime goal should include the development of autonomy, both in a moral as well as an intellectual sense. Educators need to emphasize the use of approaches which help to create autonomous learners, since this provides a worthy long-term goal of educating children for the future.

Constructivism provides a way to attain autonomy, and play can add important dimensions to student learning which can facilitate the achievement of that goal. Approaches consistent with constructivist thought must be incorporated into classroom practices to optimize children's involvement and, ultimately, their learning.

Educators must pay close attention to fostering healthy self-esteem in children since this provides the basic framework from which children will proceed in their understanding of the world.

CHAPTER 3 ACTIVITY

Since feelings and perceptions will influence how teachers will respond in any situation, this activity provides an opportunity to engage in some personal reflection. Respond to the following three questions to see how autonomy is or can be manifested in your own life.

Fostering autonomy

1. What are some examples of moral autonomy evident in your own life?

2. What are some examples of intellectual autonomy in your own life?

3. How could you personally facilitate the development of your own sense of autonomy?

Write a metaphor for how autonomy is exemplified in your own life. For example, "Autonomy is like a garden that needs to be carefully nurtured before it will produce" or

"Autonomy is like underwear. The more you use it, the more comfortable and supportive it becomes."

(This can be done with humour or sensitivity, etc.)

Note: You may wish to illustrate your metaphor using whatever medium is most appealing or comfortable for you (photography, paint, pastels, torn paper collage, etc). You might also consider placing your finished metaphor in the front of your daily planning binder as a personal inspiration for your own future growth.

CHAPTER 4

THE BRAIN IN A PLAIN BROWN WRAPPER:
Everything You Ever Wanted to Know About the Brain and Might Be Afraid to Ask

"Cogito, ergo sum. (I think, therefore I am.)"

~ Descartes (1596–1650)

STUDY OBJECTIVES

The purpose of this chapter is to
- examine basic structures and specific functions of the brain
- relate brain functioning to key aspects of learning
- explore how learning can be enhanced through the development of brain-compatible classrooms and practices

INTRODUCTION

THE HISTORICAL CONTEXT

Although the study of the human brain has held the interest of people for centuries, and in spite of advances in our understanding over the last few decades, many mysteries remain to be solved and things to be learned about this enigmatic topic. Indeed, it seems that the more you learn, the less you know! Initial perceptions of the brain and how it works arose in response to observations of brains that were not functioning normally, either through injury or some form of defect. Hence, the foundations of brain research began as a deficit model.

Over the years, people have formed various hypotheses about how the brain works. It is interesting to note that society's perceptions of the basic functioning of the brain have regularly paralleled the prevalent technology of the time. For example, in the 1800s, the brain was perceived as being like a pump which duly pumped information to all parts of the body. Later, when electricity became the technology of choice, the brain was compared to a giant switchboard which transmitted messages by throwing switches, rather like a "neurological Ma Bell." In recent years, the human brain has been likened, predictably, to the computer. In truth, all of these descriptions fall short of the mark since the human brain has capabilities that go well beyond relating it to current forms of technology. While these technologies are dependent upon someone either priming or operating them, the human brain has talents and generative capabilities that make it unique.

> It is primarily in the areas of creativity, flexibility of thought, and the ability to generate new and wonderful ideas that the human brain excels. This generative quality makes the human brain not solely dependent upon that to which it is exposed.

An important distinction to remember is that while the brain is the organ that supplies the physical venue for our thinking, it is the mind that determines what we do with it. Over the last four decades, there has been a growing body of research on how the human brain develops, matures, functions, and influences all other aspects of growth and development. Educators have viewed this research with great interest since it, in turn, has a strong influence on what they can do to optimize learning when children come to school. Before we can begin to understand how the brain works and how we can use that understanding, a preliminary look at the basic structures of the brain is essential to establish a context for further learning.

THE HUMAN BRAIN

KEY BRAIN STRUCTURES

When first confronted with the term "brain," many different images may arise. Some might imagine something that looks rather like a head of cauliflower. Others might see an image resembling a shelled walnut. Whatever image is conjured up by the term, there are certain features that stand out. The brain is a rounded form that has deep folds, or convolutions, and is comprised of two asymmetrical halves (Figure 4.1). If you make a fist with each hand and put them together at the knuckles, you have something that closely resembles the human brain both in size and in shape.

The human brain has evolved from our earliest ancestors, both in size and in complexity. In response to challenges faced in their daily living, our ancestors had to reorganize their thinking and ways of doing things in order to survive. If their adaptations were successful, they lived and subsequently used this enhanced base of thinking to apply to similar or new situations. If the changes they made were not sufficient to enable them to master a problem, they usually didn't survive. As new strategies were successfully tried out, new nerve pathways were created and there was a gradual change in both the size of the human brain and in the degree of complexity of which it was capable. A graphic example of how convolutions characterize the physiological structure of the modern brain, is evident in the following diagram. It is interesting to note that the further down the phylogenetic scale one goes, the smoother and less convoluted the brain.

figure 4.1 *Top view of the human brain*

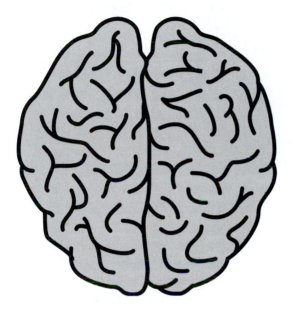

The deep convolutions on the brain surface have developed in response to a "folding over" process as the brain increased in size while being restricted to occupying a relatively confined container, the human skull. This folding over process of the cerebral cortex onto itself has served to provide a greater surface area and hence a greater number of brain cells and nerve pathways available to humans for future adaptations and modifications. For example, if you try to put a sheet of computer paper into your pocket, it won't fit. If you crumple it up, however, it will easily fit into your pocket. You could even put a much larger piece of paper into your pocket once it is crumpled.

The same principle applies to why the human brain has folded over on itself as it has evolved. If you were able to flatten out the convoluted outer surface of the human brain, it would cover an area approximately the size of a full two-page newspaper.

The following diagram illustrates key areas of the brain surface and their general functions.

figure 4.2 Side view of the human brain

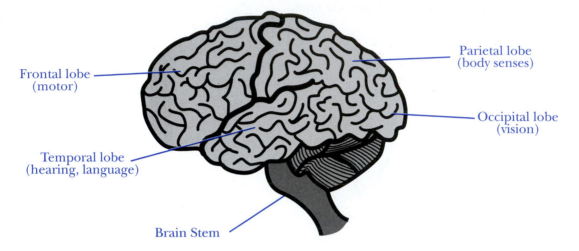

Frontal lobe (motor)

Parietal lobe (body senses)

Occipital lobe (vision)

Temporal lobe (hearing, language)

Brain Stem

The brain is composed of two hemispheres, each having four lobes. Different parts of the brain control different functions.

• Frontal lobe—located in the forehead and temples; controls the motor area of the cerebral cortex
• Parietal lobe—located behind the frontal lobe and above the temporal lobe; controls sensory information from the skin and muscles
• Occipital lobe—located in the lower back portion of the head; receives visual (light) information
• Temporal lobe—located just above the ears; receives auditory information and is associated with hearing, speech, and language

Looking Within the Brain

In order to establish a meaningful context for understanding how the brain works, it is important to understand some of the key structures within the brain: the spinal cord, the brainstem, the limbic system, the cerebral cortex, the corpus callosum, and the right and left hemispheres. These structures will be discussed in the order in which they evolved through the development of the human brain. The following diagram illustrates a cross-section or midline view of the brain.

figure 4.3 *Cross-sectional view of the human brain*

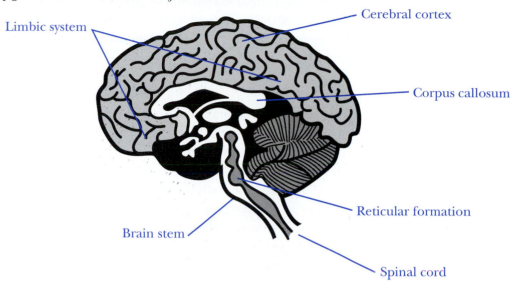

Spinal Cord

The first area on our neurological tour is one that is probably the most familiar: the spinal cord. The diameter of the spinal cord is roughly the size of a finger and it contains ascending and descending nerve tracts, as well as large and small neurons. Messages to and from the brain are conveyed through the spinal cord, eventually connecting with all the muscles of the body. As it ascends, the spinal cord connects with the brainstem. All vertebrates have a spinal cord in common, but the level of development of this structure varies from species to species (Sylwester, 1995; Wolfe, 2001).

Survival

One of the most primitive parts of the brain, from an evolutionary perspective, is the brainstem. This area controls the basic functions that enable a person to live. It regulates and monitors such basic functions as maintaining an optimum body temperature, correct salinity levels in the blood, appropriate blood pressure, respiration, organ functions, etc. (Santrock & Yussen, 1992). Since this is the innermost part of the brain, it is also the most protected. This is why individuals, even with extremely severe head injuries, are often able to survive for a long time although they might not have any cognitive functioning. Within the brainstem is a special formation known as the reticular formation.

This is a powerful regulator of wakefulness or alertness, and it controls the functional state of the brain from moment to moment. The cells in this formation are designed to spread excitation rapidly throughout the entire brain (Restak, 1993; Wolfe, 2001).

Emotions

Capping over the end of the brain stem is a closely interconnected group of structures known collectively as the limbic system. The structures within this part of the brain process information and regulate internal body states such as motivational, emotional, and sexual behaviour (Restak, 1993). These are controlled by the release of hormones into the bloodstream and through nerve connections to other parts of the nervous system (Jensen, 1998). Since emotional responses are processed here, this part of the brain is of particular interest to educators. Attitudes toward learning can be seriously influenced or seriously compromised by negative emotional states (Kohn, 1993, 1996; Goleman, 1998). This is also the part of the brain where the "flight or fight" response is initiated, so educators must be cognizant of the importance of fostering a positive emotional learning environment. Keeping learning experiences positive is a major goal since emotions provide the vitality which motivates children to want to learn.

Higher Level Thinking

The cerebral cortex forms the upper portion of the brain. This is the newest part of the brain, in an evolutionary sense, and this part of the brain has undergone the greatest change in the evolution of the mammalian brain (Jensen, 1998). The cerebral cortex is essentially involved in higher level cognitive functions such as perceiving, thinking, planning, and reasoning. It also directs the activity of most of the other parts of the brain (Restak, 1993; Jensen, 1998). This part of the brain involves very complex processing which enables individuals to decide how to respond to a given circumstance, plan for future events, use language, and even examine their own thinking (metacognition) (Fogarty, 1997). Logically, it would follow that a primary goal of educators would be to encourage the kind of functioning present in the cerebral cortex. Although each area of the brain has been described separately here, it is important to remember that all parts of the brain act in concert with one another and are highly interdependent.

Downshifting in the Brain

When an individual is confronted with a highly stressful situation, functioning in the cerebral cortex shuts down and processing shifts into the limbic area of the brain where emotions are processed. Then, the brain automatically directs the body to respond in different ways by flooding the body with hormones to increase alertness (Jensen, 1998). If an experience is particularly stressful, the chemicals released at this time can even set up a permanent chemical blockage which can prevent a similar message from being transmitted in the future (Shore, 1997). This explains how a situational experience can be manifested in a physiological response. It could also account for the negative feelings that some students seem to perpetuate toward certain subjects. When a threat is perceived, negative feelings follow and can persist. Perhaps "math phobia" has its beginnings in such hormonal or neurological reactions.

> *Emotions are the chemistry to reinforce an experience neurologically. We remember things that are more heightened and more emotional, and that's the way it should be.*
>
> *~ Joe Dispenza, in Arntz et al, 2006, p. 159*

Brain Terminology

The following terminology associated with brain structures may be useful in understanding how the human brain functions as messages are transmitted within the nervous system.

Axon: Also known as a nerve fibre, it is the major communicating link between neurons. There is only one axon per neuron, and it connects with dendrites of other neurons. The axon carries outgoing messages away from the cell body to other neurons. It conducts messages by electrical energy within the cell and stimulates chemical substances at the end of its length so that messages can be transferred across the synaptic gap to the dendrites of other neurons.

Cerebral Cortex: This is the outer surface of the brain. The colour of the "grey matter" results from a greater density of blood cells. It contains 75% of the brains total neurons. The cerebral cortex is concerned with integration of information from several different senses and higher levels of cognitive functioning/thinking.

Corpus Callosum: It is a compact bundle of nerve fibres (axons) connecting the right and left hemispheres. The corpus callosum allows the two hemispheres of the cerebral cortex to communicate directly with one another and exchange information. Myelination of the corpus callosum is completed by about 7 years of age.

Dendrites: These are hair-like extensions growing outward from the cell body. There are many dendrites extending from each neuron. Dendrites receive and carry incoming messages from other neurons to their neuron cell body in the form of electrical energy.

Myelination: This is the process by which fatty insulation is formed around an axon. Development proceeds on nerves from the head outward to the extremities. It speeds up electrical transmissions and reduces interference from nearby reactions. Myelinated fibres are at least 10–12 times faster at transmitting messages than non-myelinated fibres.

Neuron: A neuron is the nerve cell and basic functional unit of the brain or central nervous system. Neurons make up about 10% of the cells in the brain and consist of a cell body, usually one axon, and numerous dendrites. They are responsible for passing along information within the entire nervous system. Messages within the neuron are electrical in nature.

Neurotransmitters: These are chemicals that facilitate the transmission of messages within the nervous system. They are released at the end of the axon and allow electrical impulses carried from the axon of one neuron to be transmitted across the synaptic gap to the dendrites of another neuron.

Synapse: A synapse is the communication point where neurons interact. The synapse is the space at the end of an axon where chemicals (neurotransmitters) are released and carry the message from one neuron across the synaptic gap to the receiving dendrites of another neuron.

(Diamond, 1998; Jensen, 1998; Restak, 1993; Santrock & Yussen, 1992; Shore, 1997; Wolfe, 2001)

The following diagram illustrates the function of some of the structures within an individual neuron or nerve cell, defined above.

figure 4.4 The structure of a neuron

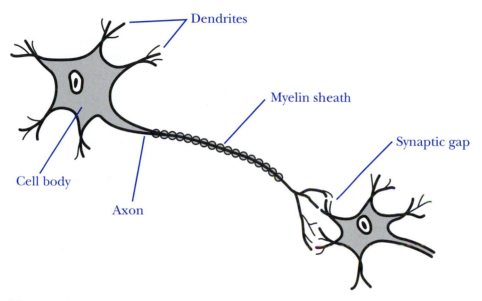

HOW A MESSAGE IS TRANSMITTED

The prime function of a neuron is to make connections within the nervous system. A signal or message originates in the **neuron** and is carried as an electrical impulse down the **axon** to be passed on, chemically, across the **synaptic gap** to the **dendrites** of another neuron. The **myelin sheath**, which insulates the axon, facilitates this process by ensuring that the message is transmitted speedily with no part of the message being lost. When the signal reaches the end of the axon, chemicals are released as neurotransmitters which allow the message to cross over the **synaptic gap**. On the other side of the synaptic gap, dendrites from another neuron receive the message and these, in turn, pass it on as an electrical impulse to the nerve cell or neuron (Jensen, 1998; Diamond, 1998; Wolfe, 2001). It should be noted that if there is extreme stress associated with a particular experience, at this stage of the process the neuron can actually set up a chemical blockage by not allowing the appropriate chemicals to be released as neurotransmitters. This can effectively stop a message from being sent across the synaptic gap and, subsequently, on to other neurons (Jensen, 1998).

In summary:

- Axons assist in sending messages out of the neuron.
- Dendrites assist in receiving messages into the neuron.
- Myelination insulates the axon and facilitates effective transmission of messages.
- Chemical neurotransmitters are released at the end of an axon and ensure the passage of a message across the synaptic gap to another neuron. Stress can impede this process.
- Messages are transmitted electrically within the neuron and chemically as they cross the synaptic gap to another neuron.

(Jensen, 1998; Restak, 1993; Shore, 1997; Diamond, 1998; Wolfe, 2001)

MORE INFORMATION

For more information on brain structures and functions, see "Brain facts and figures" by Eric Chudler on the companion website.

> "*The brain acts as a laboratory. It's an architect. It designs models, and it puts the pieces together.*"
>
> ~ *Joe Dispenza, in Arntz et al, 2005, p.143*

BRAIN DEVELOPMENT IN YOUNG CHILDREN

One of the most important areas of physical development occurring in early childhood is the rapid development of the brain and nervous system. The brain and head grow more rapidly than any other part of the body during these early years. At birth, the human brain is about 25 percent of its adult weight. By 5 years of age, children's brains are already nearly 90 percent of their adult size and weight (Shore, 1997). The potential for brain growth is influenced by a number of factors. The human brain develops primarily as a result of the interplay between the genes a child is born with and the experiences the child has in the environment. Firstly, there is the influence of the basic genetic blueprint that each individual carries from birth. At specific times, chemicals that trigger brain growth are released in waves, causing certain parts of the brain to develop in a predictable sequence. In addition, interactions with the environment initiate processes which cause further brain development (Shore, 1997). When fully grown, the human adult brain weighs approximately 3 pounds or about 1.3–1.4 kilograms. (Jensen, 1998; Wolfe, 2001).

At birth, most of the brain's 100 billion neurons are not connected into networks and the major task in the early years is to build and connect these basic structures. This process of laying down ever-increasing numbers of nerve pathways is repeated throughout the first decade of life and continues until at least adolescence (Jensen, 1998; Santrock & Yussen, 1992; Shore, 1997; Diamond, 1998). More recent research suggests that the human brain may even be capable of rewiring itself throughout life (Jensen, 2005; Arntz et al, 2005).

Since the number of neurons that an individual has at birth will remain relatively stable, the increase in size of the human brain during childhood is due primarily to an increase in the number and complexity of nerve pathways within, between, and among different areas of the brain. Neurons become larger, heavier, and produce more dendrites in response to a growing repertoire of experiences derived from interaction with the child's natural environment. Up until 7 ½ years of age, this growth happens primarily in response to movement (Hebb, 1970, as cited in Restak, 1993). During this time, the child's brain creates trillions of connections or synapses.

Another factor contributing to the brain's increase in size is the process of **myelination**, by which well-used axons are covered and insulated with a layer of fat cells called the myelin sheath (Jensen, 1998; Santrock & Yussen, 1992). As the brain processes information, the development of myelination within the nervous system adds to the speed and efficiency of messages as they are transmitted. It is interesting to note that major areas of the nervous system become myelinated around 2 years of age and 7 years of age, corresponding to two of Piaget's major stages in early childhood when definite shifts in thinking become evident.

THE ROLE OF ACTIVITY IN BRAIN GROWTH AND DEVELOPMENT

The increase in the number of nerve pathways and interconnections within various areas of the brain occur as children interact with their environment, both in a physical as well as in a social sense. New physical actions promote the development of new pathways within the brain and, with subsequent use, these pathways become strengthened and more efficient in transmitting messages within the nervous system. The brain takes in sensory input—the smells, sounds, sights, tastes, and touch of the surrounding world—and reassembles this input into countless neural interconnections. By doing this, the brain begins to make sense of the world and creates an enhanced neural network that will support future development and communication. So, the early interactions and experiences of the child directly affect the way the brain is "wired" (Shore, 1997; Jensen, 2005). As a result, learning, in a neurological sense, is dependent upon both physical and social interactions.

> *What makes synapses and neural networks form?... Active interest and mental effort by the child is key. Every response to sights, sounds, feelings, smells, and tastes makes more connections...The weight and the thinking power of the brain increases in an elaborate geometric progression. The more work the brain does, the more it becomes capable of doing.*
>
> ~ Jane M. Healy, 1987, p. 19

MORE INFORMATION

For more information on the role of active learning, see " Why hands-on tasks are good" by Kathy Nunley on the companion website.

As the brain matures and children are exposed to a wider range of physical and social experiences, children's cognitive abilities continue to grow accordingly. Throughout their childhood years, children use direct experiences to build on the potential that exists in their genetic neurological framework and customize these neural networks to match the world they encounter (Jensen, 2005). They learn to coordinate sensory input, test out their growing awareness about how things work, try out new ideas and modify old ones, and make sense out of an ever-changing world. This highlights the necessity for children to have learning environments where activity is a prominent feature, play is encouraged, and social interaction is actively valued and supported. Children must not be considered as being passive receptors where learning is concerned—learning is definitely not a spectator sport! Children's learning will only be neurologically enhanced if they are encouraged to be active participants in the learning process.

An interesting finding with respect to brain growth is that the brains of young children are twice as active as the brains of adults, with neural activity levels dropping during adolescence. Previously, the reverse of this belief was the norm (Shore, 1997).

> *Making sense out of experience is the key to early learning. The necessary tools are the body, the hands, and the senses, which bring new learning into the brain. Children at play are working hard at brain building.*
>
> ~ Jane M. Healy, 1987, p. 43

IF YOU DON'T USE IT, YOU'LL LOSE IT

Initially, children's brains form many more connections than they will ever need. It has been estimated that the average 3 year old has about 1,000 trillion synapses, or about twice as many as the average adult. This number holds constant during the first decade of life (Shore, 1997; Wolfe, 2001). This "built-in" form of neural redundancy provides a wealth of potential for the growing child and is believed to be, in part, a survival mechanism. Initially, the brains of young children are in a very labile state in that they are not yet specifically committed to a particular function. With so much potential brain power uncommitted in the early years, the brain is free to develop in many different ways. If pathways are subsequently used and prove to be useful, they are strengthened and become part of the brain's permanent circuitry. If they are not used often enough, they will atrophy and eventually be eliminated. This "pruning" process continues throughout life (Shore, 1997; Wolfe, 2001; Nunley, 2004). So, the statement, "If you don't use it, you'll lose it" certainly applies, in a neurological sense.

> *The number of nerve cells in our brain peaks prenatally and then they start to prune themselves out, one by one, through childhood. By the time we enter adolescence, our brain has chosen the final select neurons it will keep throughout our adult life. The decision is based on which cells we use and which we do not. The cells we do not use are pruned away leaving more room to add branches, or dendrites to the nerve cells that we do use. New branches are added as the brain receives and processes any new information.*
>
> *~ Kathie Nunley, 2004*

Throughout life, there is a purposeful reorganization of the brain occurring in response to real-life experiences. Jensen refers to the brain as being a "system of systems" which is influenced by these experiences. He views the brain as being " a dynamic, opportunistic, pattern-forming, self-organizing system of systems" (Jensen, 2005). The benefit of such a hopeful view is that it is founded on the belief that every person has the potential for neurological change.

MORE INFORMATION

For more information on the pruning of unused/underused pathways within the brain, see "Brain Biology: it's basic gardening" by Kathy Nunley on the companion website.

NOVELTY, LAUGHTER, & LEARNING

Some interesting and somewhat perplexing aspects of how the brain functions are found in its natural ability to form new connections, and its relative plasticity or capacity to be malleable (Diamond, 1998). These characteristics, also known as **neuroplasticity**, provide the human brain with enormous potential to change and adapt throughout a person's lifetime.

One of the findings in recent research is how the brain attends to novel things or situations.

"The brain likes surprises. After a surprise, the neuroplasticity of the brain goes way up…Your brain has to immediately go into high gear to work out a way to deal with a new situation. Connections have to fire instantly to link up all possible solutions and help you choose among them. You have to process the information very quickly in order to survive. Neuroplasticity also increases after laughter. And since neuroplasticity is the prime ingredient for learning, you learn better after a good laugh."

~ Arntz et al, 2005, p.151

THE FAR SIDE® BY GARY LARSON

"Mr. Osborne, may I be excused? My brain is full."

Over the years, many effective teachers have made use of humour in their teaching perhaps because they sensed, intuitively, that it was an effective strategy to motivate students and to facilitate learning. Practical examples of this are evident in the school system, with teachers who share their sense humour being perceived as good teachers. Whether this is because students find these teachers more approachable, or because students can relate to them better on a neurological level, remains to be seen.

"FOOD" FOR THOUGHT

Awareness of the need for good nutrition is of prime concern today for many reasons. The importance of correct nutrition, from a neurological perspective, cannot be overemphasized during children's formative years. An appropriate diet provides the basic building blocks and chemical requirements that enable the brain to grow, function, and flourish. (Shore, 1997; Jensen, 1998, 2005) This is true from the time that children are conceived. Since attention to correct nutrition affects babies right from conception, parents need to be informed of the potential neurological impact of this important information.

The sole responsibility for this doesn't rest only with the parents, but is part of society's collective responsibility. Once children come into the school system, teachers are in a unique position to be able to monitor and provide valuable input into this important aspect of children's lives. Optimizing nutrition should be a shared responsibility of all participants so that children have every opportunity to grow and develop to their full potential in all aspects of their lives (Bredekamp & Copple, 1997; Shore, 1997).

 # REFLECTIVE PRACTICE

Think about the following questions:

- Why is correct nutrition important in a neurological sense?

- What specific strategies can teachers implement, with students and their parents, to ensure that children have optimum nutrition?

HEMISPHERIC SPECIALIZATION

The following diagram presents a comparative overview of the types of thinking processes occurring in the right and left hemispheres of the human brain.

figure 4.5 *Hemispheric Specialization*

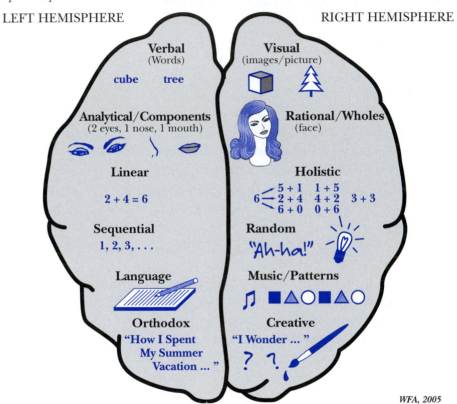

LEFT HEMISPHERE   RIGHT HEMISPHERE

WFA, 2005

HOW THE HEMISPHERES OF THE BRAIN WORK

In very basic terms, the left hemisphere appears to be more specialized for dealing with discrete pieces of information, putting things in order sequentially, labelling, and using language to represent this kind of processing. In contrast, the right hemisphere seems more specialized for taking in information randomly and synthesizing it into an integrated whole, within a spatial context. While each hemisphere is described separately, this does not imply that they operate apart from each other. Instead, recent research suggests that both hemispheres are constantly engaged in ongoing communication and coordination as information is being processed (Jensen, 2005). When processing information, individuals tend to use the kind of thinking that is a personal *preference* for them, with linear processing occurring in the left hemisphere and more random processing occurring in the right hemisphere. Each type of processing outlined in Fig. 4.5 will be discussed, in turn.

Verbal (Words) versus Visual (Images/Pictures)

The left hemisphere processes information in ways that are quite different from the right hemisphere. The left deals with information in a more "bits and pieces" approach, dealing with components. It cannot deal with information holistically. For example if someone were to examine a face using only the left hemisphere to process the incoming information, he/she would see each eye individually, then the nose, then the mouth, etc., but would be unable to put all the pieces together and recognize the individual's face.

This kind of processing also relates to the ability to label items accurately. This could explain why people who are more oriented to the kind of processing which occurs in the left hemisphere tend to be better at remembering names.

In contrast, the right hemisphere only deals holistically with incoming information and relies on pictorial images to provide the necessary data that can be placed in relation to other existing information. Returning to the example of looking at a face, the right hemisphere, in contrast, cannot analyze the component parts that make up the face. The person would primarily see the whole face and not focus on the details or parts that make up the face.

This could explain why individuals who have a strong preference for the kind of processing which occurs in the right hemisphere are often good at remembering faces but are often not particularly good at remembering names.

Some research seems to suggest that females have language more generalized between both hemispheres, while males tend to have more specialized brains (i.e., each side of the brain deals mainly with specific functions for each half). This could explain why females, in general, have a better recovery rate from strokes than do males (Russell, 1979). Admittedly, this is a relatively simplistic description of a very complex issue. As stated earlier, the two different kinds of processing previously described are not really operating totally in isolation. There is a lot of intercommunication going on all the time between the two hemispheres. Simultaneous activity in each hemisphere is also evident as information is being processed, with each side attending to the kind of processing required of it by individual circumstances (Jensen, 2005; Russell, 1979; Sylwester, 1995). So, words and images are not always handled separately but in a more interrelated manner, as seen in the following descriptions.

Verbal Language versus Eidetic (Image) Language

It is interesting to note that language can be present in both hemispheres, but the way in which language is processed reflects the orientation of the hemispheres as outlined previously.

The following descriptions highlight some of the differences between verbal and eidetic language.

Description 1:

Four wheels, steering wheel, fenders, chassis, windshield…

The topic of this description is immediately obvious: a vehicle of some kind. However, although the words used are very specific, the reader does not get a clear picture of the kind of vehicle. Therefore, many interpretations are possible—is it a Model T? a Ferrari? a truck? The language, as it is presented, doesn't elicit images to enable the reader to "see" the vehicle in his or her head.

Description 2:

Long green spikes
Reaching for sun and water
Seeking fulfillment
A cascade of babies
Tumbling down.
                    WFA, 1981

In contrast, the language used in the second description is quite different. The reader can judge quite quickly that the topic is a plant of some sort. Clues such as green spikes, sun, and water are descriptors that provide strong images to guide the reader to this conclusion. On closer examination, other clues become apparent and the reader begins to narrow the predictions (for example, "cascade of babies"). Some might even come to the conclusion that the title for this piece is "Spider Plant."

When comparing the two samples of language, the first is more succinct. It limits the description to nouns and doesn't provide any verbs or adjectives to add to basic, factual information. In contrast, the second description is more poetic and uses verbs and adjectives to create images which the reader can then relate to personal experience. In the latter example, the reader might sense more of a flow to the language and might feel this kind of language elicits a more emotional response.

Each form of language has its strengths and is valuable in its own right; one is not better than the other. In practical terms, people need to be able to make a specific list of attributes, but they also need to be able to write vivid descriptions that will capture imaginations, create images, and stir emotions. Additionally, people need to consider how each form of language augments the other. One provides a starting point and the other enhances the capacity to go creatively beyond the ordinary. Accordingly, teachers and parents need to expose children to both kinds of language—that which is factual as well as that which generates powerful images in their minds. These examples highlight the importance of sharing with children different genres of language, and poetry in particular, on a regular basis.

Analytical/Component Parts versus Relational Wholes

The left hemisphere is concerned with sorting things out in terms of increments or "bits and pieces." So, attention to discrete pieces of information and categorizing them by topic is processed by the left side of the brain. The right hemisphere, in contrast, deals with information in a more holistic way and determines its relevance in terms of how it fits within the general scheme of things. It should be noted that total communication between the two hemispheres is not accomplished until around age 11, when the corpus callosum has fully matured (Jensen, 1998). As a result, younger children will tend to look at the world more holistically since analysis will not be readily accessible to them until closer to that age. Often, teachers will begin to note a gradual transition toward more analytical thinking beginning around 7 years of age (Jensen, 1998).

Once more, it must be emphasized that the two sides of the brain act in concert with one another. For example, when categorizing an item by narrowing its characteristics and finding a distinct category for it (a left hemisphere function), the mind also has to put this information into some kind of broader context so it can be related to what is already known generally about the item or topic (a right hemisphere function) (Sylwester, 1995; Wolfe, 2001; Erlauer, 2003).

Linear versus Holistic

Another example of how language can be used to highlight the differences in how the two hemispheres work can be seen daily in the lectures that teacher candidates attend at the university. For instance, when a professor starts to give a lecture, the fact that he or she can put a string of words together in a logical, sequential order that makes sense is a function of that person's left hemisphere. The fact that the professor can make the verb tenses agree, however, is a function of the right hemisphere.

This ability to coordinate the functions of both hemispheres results from a process of "to-ing and fro-ing" that goes on continuously between the two hemispheres. People must be able to project ahead and "see" the whole context in order to deal effectively with component parts. In doing so, they are able to think about what they plan to say and, keeping that in mind, come up with the appropriate verb to match the circumstances and the content of the words being spoken. Thus, the two sides of the brain are constantly communicating with one another, via the corpus callosum, to ensure a smooth and comprehensible result.

The left hemisphere strings letters together to make words and words together to make sentences. The right hemisphere's role in this scenario is to add the texture and components that have it make sense as it relates to what is already known about a given subject or topic.

Another example of this can be seen in music. We may know people who can play the piano with technical precision, but it is far more interesting to listen to someone who adds that textural, emotional component. When the two sides of the brain work together, each doing what it does best, the result is indeed something that is much greater than just the sum of its parts.

Therefore, when someone plays the piano, that fact that the notes are played in the correct sequence is a direct result of left hemisphere functioning. The ability to think ahead and anticipate how certain sections of the musical piece will be treated with respect to how softly or loudly he or she will play it (the texture of the musical interpretation) is under the control of the right hemisphere.

In problem solving, a distinct symbiosis between the functioning of the two hemispheres is evident. Initially when a problem is presented, processing starts in the right hemisphere, as if to establish a broader context for the problem. Then activity switches to the left hemisphere where the information is broken down and dealt with in smaller, more manageable increments that can be categorized and refined. This switching back and forth continues throughout the problem-solving process as ideas are tested and reconsidered. At the end of the problem-solving cycle, activity again returns to the right hemisphere, as if to verify how the newly-processed conclusions fit into a context which has now been altered (Sylwester, 1995; Erlauer, 2003). It is interesting to note here that this process parallels the prediction learning cycle mentioned in Chapter 2. As children work at solving problems and begin to think about things differently or try out new alternatives, they are building an enriched array of neural pathways which can subsequently be used in the future (Jensen, 1998; Wolfe, 2001; Arntz et al, 2005).

Sequential versus Random

The sequential nature of left hemisphere functioning represents a linear form of processing. The information is laid out according to a specific sequence and is processed in a predetermined fashion. For example, counting requires saying number names in a predictable sequence (1, 2, 3…), or certain stories have the same beginning ("Once upon a time…"). The kind of activity associated with this kind of functioning includes making lists, crossing things off as they are completed, putting things in order, and categorizing items. When engaging in this kind of activity, the left hemisphere is in control.

In contrast, the right hemisphere is much more random in its processing. It likes to reflect on several things, look for patterns, and mull things over before coming to conclusions. Unlike the left hemisphere, the right hemisphere can engage in simultaneous pattern recognition where awareness of and connections between or among things becomes suddenly apparent—those "Ah-ha" experiences! These kinds of serendipitous events then are primarily the domain of the right hemisphere.

 **PERSONAL STORIES**

Looking for Patterns in Learning

The following number stories were done by two 6-year-old boys, Michael and Greg. Each was given 10 counters, a placemat for placing and organizing their counters, and a blank piece of paper to record their "Stories for 10." Although they worked together, discussing their findings and having ample opportunities to "copy" one another's work, the order/pattern of their number stories was quite different.

Michael's Recording Sheet

Stories for 10
10 − 1 = 9
10 − 2 = 8
10 − 3 = 7
10 − 4 = 6
10 − 5 = 5
10 − 6 = 4
10 − 7 = 3
10 − 8 = 2
10 − 9 = 1
10 − 10 = 0
10 − 0 = 10

Greg's Recording Sheet

Stories for 10
10 − 9 = 1.
10 − 1 = 9.
10 − 8 = 2.
10 − 2 = 8.
10 − 3 = 7.
10 − 7 = 3.
10 − 6 = 4.
10 − 4 = 6.
10 − 5 = 5.
10 − 10 = 0.
10 − 0 = 10.

Though the boys were "best buddies" and were inseparable in all activities, it was interesting to note the differences in the ways they processed information as they worked beside each other doing a math task. These two examples of their work on reviewing subtraction facts for "10" were very revealing.

Michael
- systematic
- pattern awareness (counting)
- linear approach
- more left brain approach

Greg
- appears more random at first
- pattern awareness (relational)
- looking at number "pairs"
- intuiting the commutative property?
- more right brain approach

Orthodox versus Creative

The functioning of the left hemisphere focuses on orthodox thinking and is characterized by maintaining the status quo and working toward a predetermined outcome. Thus, familiar approaches and thought patterns are reinforced and perpetuated. This is fine if one can be content with having the same experiences repeated over and over, but perhaps we need to be more receptive to new challenges if we are to deal with an ever-changing world.

> *Do we only want children to learn that which is already known?*
>
> *~ Jean Piaget, 1969*

The right hemisphere deals with information in unique and creative ways, seeking to make connections and interconnections that are less obvious. Pattern recognition is the domain of right hemisphere thinking as ideas are organized and reorganized to make clusters that show relationships. Novelty is also a characteristic of creative thinking and the right hemisphere seeks this out as a means of stimulating new thoughts (Jensen, 2005; Arntz et al, 2005). For many years, behaviourist theory assumed that learning always depended on rewards. However, new information on how the brain works suggests that not only does the human brain find novelty itself rewarding, it also appears to have an inner drive to search out new or unique experiences (Caine & Caine, 1997; Jensen, 1998; Shore, 1997; Arntz et al, 2005).

 # REFLECTIVE PRACTICE

Make a list of behaviours that would characterize left-brain functioning.

Now, make a list of behaviours that would characterize right-brain functioning.

Think about the following questions:

- What are some of the strengths and weaknesses of each?
- How would using a balance in the two kinds of functioning make learning more beneficial and meaningful to students?

"Handedness"

Up until this point, the descriptions for the functions of each hemisphere have been very straightforward—left is linear and right is holistic. Now that a basic foundation of understanding has been established, it is appropriate to clarify that the differentiation between the two hemispheres is not that simple. There are, however, certain specific patterns that can be identified relating to how the brain functions.

Human beings are cross-wired neurologically. That is, a specific side of their body is controlled by the opposite side of their brain. For example, if someone raises his or her right hand and waves, the left hemisphere determines and controls that particular action. Conversely, if raising and waving the left hand, the right hemisphere is in charge (Wittrock, 1977; Restak, 1993). Since approximately 85 percent of the world's population is right-handed, the configuration of hemispheric specialization illustrated in Figure 4.5 would typically represent the brain organization of most right-handed people. This configuration is supportive of many of the tasks people are required to do in our left hemisphere culture—those which involve writing something down or putting something in the form of a list. In this instance, it is an advantage to have the language side of the brain opposite (and in control of) the dominant hand.

To explain this concept further, the kind of task associated with writing (writing one word after another in a linear, sequential fashion) is processed primarily in the left hemisphere. As the right-handed person starts to write, the messages travel through nerve impulses up the right arm and cross over into the left hemisphere (due to cross-wiring). Since the left side of the brain is ideally suited to process the kind of information needed to deal with linear tasks such as writing, the messages would be processed quickly and sent back and forth by a relatively direct route (due to cross-wiring) between the dominant hand and the hemisphere best suited for the nature of the task, on the opposite side of the body.

If the individual is required to do a different kind of task that requires processing that is the domain of the right hemisphere, however, the messages would have to travel further before they would be processed. This can be especially problematic for young children who do not have a fully developed or myelinated corpus callosum (which allows for ease and speed in communication between the two hemispheres), as discussed previously.

To continue the previous discussion, if the same right-handed person wanted to draw a representation of a three-dimensional cube, the messages would again travel through nerve impulses, up the right arm and arrive in the left hemisphere (due to cross-wiring), but now the kind of processing (spatial) required to complete this task cannot be accomplished on this side of the brain. So the message would have to cross over the corpus callosum into the right hemisphere where it can now be readily processed. Once processed, the message would then have to cross back over the corpus callosum again and proceed from the left side of the brain directly (due to cross-wiring) back down to the right hand.

Simply put, information given to/by the right hand is sent first to the left hemisphere and then, depending on the nature of the information, it may be sent on to the right hemisphere to be processed. Since messages are continually flowing back and forth between the brain and the muscles, the extra distance across the corpus callosum could be significant, especially if the corpus callosum and myelination of that structure have not fully developed. This is especially true for younger children.

The Problem with "Lefties"

The profile represented in Figure 4.5, Hemispheric Specialization, is basically that of a right-handed person with language or linear processing in the left hemisphere, opposite the dominant hand. Due to the cross-wiring nature of message transmission, this would not be a problem for right-handed people. Potential problems arise, however, when looking at left-handed people.

Approximately one-third of left-handed people also have language or analytical processing opposite their dominant hand (Restak, 1979). That is, they have the reverse of the diagram in Figure 4.5: in this case linear processing is in the right hemisphere, and holistic processing is in the left hemisphere. These are "true lefties"—they have the linear processing side of the brain opposite their dominant hand. Since messages are transmitted in a cross-wiring manner, this reverse configuration will not be problematic for them.

The potential for problems arises for the remaining two-thirds of left-handed people. These individuals have the same configuration as right-handed people, as shown in Figure 4.5—but in this case, linear processing is not opposite their dominant hand. For these people, the potential problems with messages, as described in the previous example, would be an on-going issue since longer distances would have to be covered for each task. In addition, if they are young, the corpus callosum and myelination process might not have fully developed. Full communication between the two hemispheres is not complete until around 11 years of age. This has serious implications for some of the expectations for younger children doing tasks that require a lot of analysis or linear processing. It is also interesting to note that among students who have been identified as having a learning disability, a very high percentage of them are left-handed.

The "Eyes" Have It

Just as people are cross-wired in terms of how their bodies are controlled by the opposite hemisphere, the same holds true for how the eyes are structured. The only difference is that there is an element of cross-wiring in each eye. That is, the information from the right visual field of *both eyes* is wired the left hemisphere and, conversely, the information from the left visual field of *both eyes* is wired to the right hemisphere. Even though each hemisphere receives information from both halves of the visual field, an individual will tend to have a dominant eye, due to a greater percentage of visual information being sent to the dominant hemisphere. Thus, the left eye sends more information to the right hemisphere and the right eye sends more information to the left hemisphere (Wittrock, 1977; Restak, 1979; Meister Vitale, 1982).

As a result, right-eye dominant individuals have an "edge" in reading print since they are perceptually set up to begin visual processing in the left visual field of both eyes. Because we read print from left to right in our culture, these children are already set up perceptually to process information visually from left to right.

REFLECTIVE PRACTICE

The Eyes Have It:
Are You a "Lefty" or a "Righty"?

Just as people are right-handed or left-handed, so too are they either right-eyed or left-eyed. Try this informal test to determine whether your right or left eye is your dominant eye.

1. Make a circle with your index finger and your thumb, holding it about 30 cm in front of your face. With *both eyes open,* focus on an object on the opposite side of the room. *Do not move your hand from this position for the remainder of the test!*

2. Now, close one eye and, without moving your head or your hand, look through the circle. Note what happens.

3. Now, close the other eye and look through the circle using the eye that was previously closed, without moving your head or your hand. Note what happens.

If you have done this test properly, the object would seem to have shifted when looking through the circle with one eye but not for the other one. This is because, when you had both eyes open, you automatically set the initial view of the object to favour your dominant eye. So, if the object can be seen through the circle by your right eye, then you are right eye dominant. If, on the other hand, the object can be seen through the circle when your left eye is viewing it, then you are left eye dominant.

Reread the initial section on The "Eyes" Have It. Now, think about the following questions:

- What might be some problems associated with being left-eye dominant?
- When might it be advantageous to be left-eye dominant? (Think sports!)

ADAPTABILITY AND FLEXIBILITY

One of the most interesting considerations arising from current brain research is the realization that the human brain, at birth, is one of the most immature in comparison with other animals. The human infant is basically helpless, and this period of extreme dependency is prolonged for several years. Since patterns of growth and development occur for good reasons in terms of survival, what benefit is there for the prolonged period of dependency seen in immature humans?

The answer lies in the degree of plasticity evident in the human brain. People are wired neurologically to be incredibly adaptive and flexible right from birth. Therefore, a large part of the human brain is largely uncommitted to specific tasks, and most of its 100 billion neurons are not yet connected into neural networks. It is the major task of early brain development to create, strengthen, and extend these networks (Shore, 1997; Jensen, 1998; Diamond, 1998; Wolfe, 2001).

Many animals are up and running within minutes of their birth because their very survival depends on the ability to run away from prey. Indeed, if an animal cannot keep up with the adults of the species right from birth, it will not likely survive. No matter how beneficial this capability might seem, it is also limiting in an evolutionary sense because the potential for dramatic change has been greatly reduced by the very characteristics that promote its survival. The human baby, in contrast, remains relatively helpless, spending long periods of time in association with its parent(s). This extended time frame of dependency, however, allows the human infant more opportunities to observe, explore, and learn various coping or problem-solving strategies while experiencing the environment from a position of relative safety. The more and varied the experiences young humans have, the more adaptive and flexible their thinking and problem solving abilities will become (Shore, 1997; Jensen, 1998; Arntz et al 2005). Their potential, then, is limitless!

IMPORTANT CONSIDERATIONS FOR LEARNING

Given all of the information about the human brain that has been discussed so far, it is now possible to raise some important points that teachers should take into consideration when planning appropriate programs and determining effective strategies to use with children at the elementary level.

- Learning environments which include a wealth of sensory experiences encourage optimum brain growth and build a vital foundation for a lifetime of learning (Wolfe, 2001).
- Emotions play a key role in determining how receptive children are toward learning. Fear, threats, or stressful situations reduce or impede brain function and, in turn, can short-circuit the whole learning process (Sylwester, 1995; Fogarty, 1997).
- Intelligence is not a function of how many neurons people have, but rather it is a function of the number of connections and interconnections that exist between and among other neurons. Physical movement and social interactions increase the number of these interconnections (Diamond, 1998).

- Through direct physical and social experiences, children ultimately develop firsthand, concrete knowledge and the ability to manipulate this knowledge mentally. Opportunities to repeat experiences are essential to brain growth since pathways in the nervous system become strengthened through repeated use. Those pathways which are not used are subsequently "pruned out" and eliminated (Diamond, 1998).

- Through play with others, children expand their mental frameworks, learn to go beyond their own perspectives, and, as they did earlier with real-life objects, begin to use language to manipulate their world. Social settings for learning are essential to brain development (Caine & Caine, 1997).

- Early experiences directly affect how the brain is wired, both in a quantitative and qualitative sense. The quantity of nerve pathways is increased through varied sensory experiences, and the quality of these experiences provides a richer background of comparisons which affects understanding and future potential (Wolfe, 2001).

- "Hands on" active learning approaches are essential to facilitate brain growth and development. Nerve pathways grow in direct response to interactions with people and with real objects (Diamond, 1997).

- Until 7 1/2 years of age, nerve pathways grow primarily in response to movement (Hebb, 1970). This makes a strong case for active learning environments and approaches as well as planned physical activity on a regular basis.

- The nerves in the corpus callosum, the broad band of connective tissue running across the brain and connecting the brain's two hemispheres, become myelinated between 7 and 11 years of age. The completion of this process facilitates communication between both hemispheres (sides) of the brain and enables children to begin to use analysis more effectively in their thinking (Sylwester, 1995; Jensen, 1998). This occurs at about the same age that Piagetian "conservation" and "reversibility" are starting to be achieved.

- Until at least 7 years of age, children view their world more holistically and primarily use the right side of their brains to process information. This tendency to deal with learning more holistically rather than engaging in analytical thinking could explain why primary age children are better able to engage in spatial reasoning (Bredekamp & Copple, 1997).

- Setting learning within a challenging problem-solving context aids in the creation of new dendritic connections that, in turn, make even more neural connections and interconnections. Variation in approaches to solve problems results in the creation of more neural pathways which can subsequently be used for similar challenges (Wolfe, 2001).
- Inclusion of the arts, in all of its various dimensions, builds a strong foundation for later academic success. (Jensen, 1998; Sylwester, 1995).

"

It's the arts that lay the foundation for later academic and career success. A strong art foundation builds creativity, concentration, problem solving, self-efficacy, coordination, and values attention and self-discipline.

"

~ Eric Jensen, 1998, p. 36

COGNITIVE THEORY AND THE HUMAN BRAIN

In order to have a relevant context for the practical applications of current brain research, it is appropriate to re-examine the basic tenets of cognitive learning theory. Cognitive learning theory identifies learning as

- an active process
- non-linear
- multi-dimensional
- set within a social context
- influenced by the affective domain
- concerned with cognition and metacognition

LEARNING IS AN ACTIVE PROCESS

Learning is not finite. Rather, it is an ongoing process in which students are continually receiving information, interpreting it, connecting it (through assimilation) to what they already know (prior experience), and reorganizing and revising (through accommodation) their internal understandings of their world. As mentioned previously, these internal conceptions are called "mental models" or "schemata." These schemata are constantly being revised and elaborated upon each time the child encounters new experiences. In doing this, children create their own unique understanding of the world, interpret their own experiences and knowledge, and subsequently use this knowledge to solve more complex problems. So, in a neurological sense, the brain/mind is constantly working to build and rebuild itself as it takes in, adapts/modifies new information, and enhances understanding.

A related consideration is the brain's propensity to deal primarily with the "process" involved in learning rather than just the "product" of the learning experience. Jensen probably explains this best.

> *Humans have survived for thousands of years by trying out new things, not by always getting the "right" tried-and-true answer. That's not healthy for growing a smart, adaptive brain... Surprisingly, it doesn't matter to the brain whether it ever comes up with an answer. The neural growth happens because of the process, not the solution. A student could go to school for 12 years, rarely get right answers, and still have a well-developed brain.*

> *~ Eric Jensen, 1998, pp. 16 & 36*

LEARNING IS NON-LINEAR

Learning is a very complex process that can proceed in a variety of ways, depending on individual differences, strengths, and interests. It is not acquired by merely assembling various bits and pieces of simpler learning into larger portions. Indeed, research suggests that instruction based on structured drill and practice of isolated facts and skills does not foster effective learning because information learned out of context is difficult to organize and therefore retain (Gallagher & Reid, 1981; Sylwester, 1995; Jensen, 1998; Arntz et al, 2005). Since people are constantly refining their understanding, relevant contexts are essential. As a result, learning sometimes involves spontaneous recognition of relationships, awareness of patterns, and integration of understanding into broader contexts—definite aspects of right hemisphere functioning.

LEARNING IS MULTI-DIMENSIONAL

Learning involves the use of a variety of talents and abilities. Traditionally, schools primarily recognized only two kinds of capabilities: verbal-linguistic and logic-mathematical. The research of Howard Gardner alerted us to the existence of many other kinds of "intelligences." Currently, eight kinds of intelligence are widely recognized by the educational community, but two more are beginning to gain acceptance. Basic to this is the assumption that all people are capable of learning, that people acquire knowledge in various ways and at different rates, and that they bring their own personal experiences to each learning situation. Gardner believes that individuals usually have strengths in two or three of these areas. Using the different strengths of each of the brain's hemispheres is an obvious connection to Gardner's work (Gardner, 1991; 2005).

LEARNING IS SET WITHIN A SOCIAL CONTEXT

Human beings do not learn in a vacuum. They are programmed to participate within an interactive setting as social beings, and the interactions in which they engage enrich and enhance them neurologically (Jensen, 1998, 2005). Various groupings are used in schools today to facilitate more effective interactive learning. Peer coaching and assessment add to the sense of a community of learners in the classroom, and life skills are learned within meaningful frameworks. As ideas are shared, concepts are questioned and new positions or understandings are established. In this way, students consolidate their current understanding and use the ideas of others as springboards for further insights. As this process is repeated, within an interactive environment, the neurological pathways within the brain are extended and strengthened (Caine & Caine, 1997; Shore, 1997; Jensen, 1998; Arntz et al, 2005).

LEARNING IS INFLUENCED BY THE AFFECTIVE DOMAIN

Emotions play a major role in a person's receptivity toward learning. As students work collaboratively, they are affected by working with others who think differently and who bring different strengths and experiences to the task. In this way, they gain insights into the importance of cooperating with others. They learn to develop respect for another's ideas and to challenge opinions that are not supported by evidence. Many life skills are acquired as children interact with one another. They learn to listen respectfully, to help one another clarify their thinking, to draw conclusions, to challenge the ideas of others, to solve problems and make decisions, and to express their own thoughts and feelings. All of these factors play a major role in brain development (Jensen, 1998; Goleman, 1998; Arntz et al, 2005).

LEARNING IS CONCERNED WITH COGNITION AND METACOGNITION

As children learn, they experience a wide range of thinking strategies and develop skills that enable them to use constructive feedback. In order for this to happen, children need to have appropriate role models whom they can emulate. They need to be provided with relevant and meaningful examples of what constitutes exemplary practice in real-life contexts.

Some specific strategies to encourage this development include the following:

• Encourage students to engage in regular reflection of what they produce, so that they are able to understand, internalize, strive for appropriate standards of excellence, and set realistic goals for themselves.
• Provide students with practice in using appropriate thinking skills through on-going decision- making, both within the classroom setting and in out-of-school experiences.
• Set their learning within a problem-solving context whenever possible.

(Caine & Caine, 1997; Healy, 1987; Jensen, 1998; Nunley, 2004)

ATTENTION AND THE BRAIN

Major systems devoted to attention are located throughout the brain. This is a complex system that involves many different factors. According to Jensen (1998, p. 42) we know "that contrasts of movement, sounds and emotions consume most of our attention, that chemicals play the most significant role in attention and that genes may also be involved."

While we are awake, the brain is constantly making decisions and is always paying attention to something. When teachers talk about attention, however, they are usually referring to externally focused attention, which implies that the student is looking at the teacher and thinking only about the material being presented during a period of direct instruction. What the teacher expects the child to pay attention to assumes that the child's brain has found the material interesting enough to focus his or her attention. In reality, the brain is more likely to focus on something for which it has been primed to look. Students who succeed academically have the ability to "tune in" to what is being learned (Jensen, 1998; Arntz et al, 2005).

Sometimes our assumptions about what attention is can get in the way of really understanding the factors that influence attention. One such assumption on the part of many adults is that young children naturally have short attention spans and that as they grow older, their attention span will increase. Given that kind of logic, one could postulate that by the time a person is quite old, attention span would be limitless! Through the many personal experiences that we all encounter, we know that this is just not the case.

When considering the whole issue of attention span, we must consider the influence of interest, motivation, and choice. When choosing to do something and setting about to do it without being hindered by imposed timelines, the results can indeed be quite amazing! The following anecdote points out not only the importance of allowing choice in learning, but also the need for teachers to pay attention to process as well as product.

 # PERSONAL STORIES

The Misshapen Ball of Clay

A four-year-old child worked diligently for two solid hours, with no divergence from the task and ignoring distractions within the regular classroom atmosphere, to produce a misshapen round ball made of clay. At first glance, it was unremarkable to the extreme! But when examining the process the child went through to create this object, the results were truly astounding.

This young child, with fine motor coordination not yet fully developed, had laboured long and hard to produce a hollow ball of clay! The problem solving ability, trial and error learning, physical restrictions, level of involvement, and persistence demonstrated by this very young child were truly awe-inspiring and humbling.

Can you imagine how difficult it would be to do this? No doubt most adults would have difficulty doing this task and would probably give up long before it was done.

Young children have short attention spans? Indeed!

Misconceptions about attention persist, in spite of examples like the one above; and that is where research can provide valuable insights to guide practice. Research has found that the brain requires novelty in order to learn and is, therefore, relatively poor at engaging in activities that require nonstop attention (Jensen, 1998). Specifically, student attention is difficult to sustain for long periods of time especially during direct instruction, when the motivation for the learning is provided externally by the teacher. In response to this, Jensen suggests the following guidelines as being more neurologically compatible and developmentally appropriate for timeframes set for direct teacher input at different grade levels.

• Kindergarten to Grade 2: 5–7 minutes
• Grades 3 to 7: 8–12 minutes
• Grades 8 to 12: 12–15 minutes

A device for remembering appropriate timing for direct input sessions could be: One minute for each year of age!

At first glance, these guidelines may appear to be very limiting, especially when compared with usual classroom practice, where direct instruction normally extends for much longer periods of time. Indeed, when implementing these guidelines, many teachers may feel pressured about the time needed to cover all of the curriculum content. In response to these concerns, the shorter times for direct instruction can be extended somewhat by breaking them into smaller sessions where more active involvement and small group processing are incorporated within the time periods designated for specific teacher input. Therefore, instruction can be adapted to be more appropriate for meeting the learning needs of children while still being more manageable for meeting the curriculum goals of the teacher.

" *In most spheres of knowledge, what we don't know far exceeds what we do know. Brain research is no exception.* "

~ *Rima Shore, 1997. p. 57*

SUMMARY: DEVELOPING THE BRAIN-COMPATIBLE CLASSROOM

" *Education is more than reaching certain standards of learning; education is developing a desire to learn, knowing how to learn, and implementing teaching practices based on how the brain actually functions.* "

~ *Barbara Given, 2002, p.1*

In order to foster a strong brain-compatible classroom, the human brain needs learning environments where

- risk-taking and prediction are encouraged
- the program involves active learning as a vital component
- play is encouraged and valued
- problem-solving and decision-making are an integral part of learning experiences
- expression of emotions is supported and encouraged
- diverse learning styles are addressed and integrated into the program
- multiple/diverse responses to learning are encouraged
- opportunities are available to work individually as well as in various groupings
- imagery and visualization are encouraged
- real objects, pictures, and symbols are used in conjunction with one another to facilitate the understanding of concepts through "hands on" activities
- discussion and informal talk are encouraged to facilitate the consolidation of existing understandings and to use the input of others as springboards for understanding new ideas
- art, music, and drama are integral parts of the program
- integration across subjects is encouraged to show connections between and among ideas
- the teacher facilitates learning by "scaffolding" and promoting awareness of connections between and among concepts
- information is presented through various sensory modes—concrete, visual, and auditory
- teachers make concerted use of charts and graphic organizers to show connections and interrelationships in learning
- applications are relevant, authentic, and are connected to real life experiences
- individual interests and opinions are incorporated into the learning process
- mutual trust and a sense of belonging are fostered
- learning environments are enriched with various learning materials
- age-appropriate choices are provided to promote intellectual and moral autonomy
- appropriate amounts of time and flexibility are provided so that students become fully engaged in learning

(Caine & Caine, 1997; Fogarty, 1997; Given, 2002; Erlauer, 2003)

As we come to the end of this chapter, here are some final thoughts that may convey some images about the brain and how it functions.

THOUGHTS

Sparking and sparkling,
Rushing and leaping,
Pirouetting and connecting,
In a magical maelstrom,
A cranial mind storm
Of wondrous delights!
WFA, 2005

CHAPTER 4 ACTIVITY

"Using Your Noggin"

Draw a T-chart on your page and label each of the two columns as indicated on the diagram below. Identify some potential obstacles that you might encounter in setting up a "brain-friendly" or "brain-challenging" learning environment – list these points in the left-hand column and be sure to leave space between each one. Now brainstorm some strategies that you might use to provide solutions to these problems and record them in the right-hand column. Share your ideas.

Obstacles	Strategies

Note: It is interesting to see how even the way that this graphic organizer has been set up will facilitate both left hemisphere functioning and right hemisphere functioning.

PART II

CREATING THE ROAD MAP
FOR TEACHING & LEARNING

CHAPTER 5

PLANNING:
The Itinerary

"A new idea is an unsettling of received beliefs;

otherwise it would not be a new idea.

~ *John Dewey, 1991 [1927], p. 59*

STUDY OBJECTIVES

The purpose of this chapter is to
- understand a learning framework
- recognize differences between novice and expert learners
- learn how to complete a lesson plan within a framework for learning
- learn how to complete a unit plan
- relate the lesson and unit plan to the curriculum as a whole
- understand the role of learning centres within the curriculum context
- develop a plan for a learning centre

INTRODUCTION

The focus of this chapter is organizing for learning and teaching in the classroom. One of the most challenging activities for new teachers is developing a framework that allows the days, weeks, months, and academic year to be placed in a context. When faced with a class full of students at the beginning of the year, teachers have to begin to shape the daily learning experiences. Indeed, some would suggest that it is the nature of teachers' work to address a range of educational issues through the planning process in the preparation, development, and implementation of any program. In most instances, teachers have some curriculum documents at hand for which they are responsible. Their task is to consider these documents and begin to parallel the **curriculum expectations** with the teachers' own intimate knowledge of the students. The task of planning seems onerous and impossible at first, but over time, as teachers recognize the value of talking with colleagues, sharing ideas, and observing the students they teach, what seemed impossible becomes much simpler and more manageable. According to Van Manen (1986, p. 43)

> If a teacher competently adheres to a set of curriculum objective, but in a deeper sense does not know where he or she is going, ...then the observable teacher behaviour, what the teacher is doing overtly is a profound contradiction of the way he or she exists in the world, or better, in the school, in this classroom with these young people. Or maybe we should better say that when the teacher fails to be what he or she ostensibly does, then that teacher is really an absence, and is not at all genuinely present to those kids.

GLOSSARY

Curriculum expectations— These are listed within curriculum documents and outline what students are expected to be able to know, do, or understand at the end of each year.

GETTING STARTED: THE "HOW PEOPLE LEARN" FRAMEWORK

The National Academy of Science (National Research Council, 2000) developed a framework to organize what is known about learning and teaching. Some aspects of this framework have been discussed in other chapters, but it is worth reviewing them here as a starting point for considering the organization of curriculum. In the framework, the authors identify assumptions that are held about the following:

- Knowledge—what is to be taught and why it is important
- Students—who is to learn the material
- Communities—how communities/environments enhance learning
- Evidence—what counts as evidence of learning (assessment)

Most teachers have some conception of a framework for learning as they engage in the planning process. This framework is shaped by their reading, by their prior experiences as students, and by their understanding of what it is to learn and to teach. The next sections highlight some aspects of learning frameworks to help teachers identify their own conceptions and to help them examine the curricula that they are to teach.

KNOWLEDGE

Teachers who are aware of all aspects of the framework and who understand their assumptions about what constitutes teaching and learning are better able to create an effective classroom environment. One of the most important assumptions is the way in which knowledge is organized differently for the experienced learner and for the novice learner. For example, think about entering a classroom for the first time. What does an observer notice? The teacher seems to be in control and the students seem to be learning. How does an observer know what to look for? For the novice learner in any area, the level of skill development necessary to foster learning is simply not there. The repertoire of skills available to enable the novice teacher to look for the various aspects of a fine teaching performance has not yet been developed. However, over time, as attention is focused, the novice teacher begins to see a pattern in the lesson. Links are made between prior knowledge and what students are expected to learn in today's lesson.

Questions that help focus the students' attention on the topic at hand are asked. There is a follow-up to the questions and the basic lesson that allows for practice. Bruner (1969, p. 31) noted "teaching specific topics or skills without making clear their context in the broader fundamental study of a field of knowledge is uneconomical..."

Thus, when teaching and organizing to teach, teachers must give attention to those big ideas that are fundamental and enduring to a particular discipline. In understanding the student and the relationship to subject knowledge, the teacher has to think about the type of learning that needs to be fostered. Schwartz, Bransford, & Sears (2006) have developed a map of expertise that helps to understand the nature of expert/novice learning and enables development of appropriate planning for transfer of learning (see Figure 5.1).

Figure 5.1 *Map of expertise*

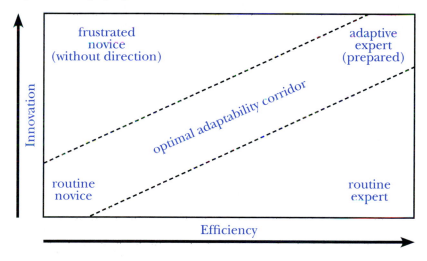

Note that some experts are very good at repetitive tasks, while others have to be adaptive and innovative. The task for teachers and indeed all educators is to decide what type of expert learner is needed. For example, adaptive experts demonstrate a realistic self-assessment and demonstrate self-checking behaviours. They are aware of the environment and can define questions as well as seek answers. One of the notions inherent in this model is that there are two types of transfer of learning that must be accounted for: one is horizontal and focuses on developing efficiency; the other is vertical and focuses on adaptability and innovation.

In planning lessons teachers need to think about the learner and the nature of the skill or content that is taught. Is the lesson the first in a sequence? Are the learners familiar with the topic? Have they been exposed to such content before? Answers to questions like these will help the teacher to determine the approach to take and enable the development of a more effective lesson plan.

STUDENTS

It is almost a truism that one cannot speak about knowledge without also considering the student and what the student brings to the task. When teachers consider the student during planning, they take into account the learner's developmental stage, background knowledge, and social context. All of these factors play a role in establishing or enhancing the student's relationship to knowledge and the curriculum. In short, attending to the student means that the teacher takes into account the student's prior knowledge because this will influence what students learn and what they attend to in the classroom context. It is important that teachers understand their students' histories and help them make connections between who they are now and what they might become. In addition, it is important that teachers attend to other aspects of the students when planning, including their motivation and their prior assumptions about what they can and cannot do. For example, girls who believe they cannot do math may be more likely to give up once the subject becomes challenging. Their belief in their lack of ability in the area causes them to withhold the effort needed to understand the topic or to subvert the efforts that they make. Lack of motivation in a specific subject area may cause students to become disinterested in a lesson or a subject.

COMMUNITIES

The notion of **community** has been popularized in recent education literature, as well as in the business world. Some have suggested that "community" is simply a code for helping students feel good without imposing challenges; yet in any community there are challenges and failures, as well as success, that make students feel good about themselves. In an earlier chapter, Vygotsky's notion of the Zone of Proximal Development was discussed. It is important to note that Vygotsky's notion of ZPD enables the use of yet another lens to view the concept of community. If students learn with the assistance of others, then their

GLOSSARY

Community—A group of people with a common focus or vision. In classroom learning, communities consist of people who are learning together. Learning is the common purpose.

ability to learn in that context may be even more indicative of what they can do independently (Vygotsky, 1978). The challenge for the teacher is that unlike the home, where caregivers can give attention to one or two children, the classroom teacher has several ZPDs, all of which are likely to be different. The implication is that, as noted later in this text, there are many co-learners in the classroom. All students can become responsible for assisting peers to achieve different levels, and if challenged by an appropriate teaching model, they can move forward. Both knowledge and the learner must be considered within a social context that extends beyond the walls of the classroom into the school and beyond.

From the perspective of planning, it means that teachers will think about the ways in which they are motivating or engaging students in learning. Motivation toward learning will help construct a community, and students will come to appreciate the ways in which they are all participants in the learning task as a community.

EVIDENCE

In today's era of **high stakes curriculum and testing**, it seems at times that the test is really the only measure of learning that counts. As noted in Chapter 9, there are different types of assessment for different purposes. What constitutes evidence that children have learned depends on the nature of the assessment and whether or not the assessment fits the content that has been taught. As teachers plan, they consider what will be used as evidence both at the end of a unit and as the unit progresses. All effective planning should then consider how the lesson or unit is to be evaluated; although attention should also be given to those moments of spontaneous learning along the way. The lesson becomes a road map that teachers use to determine whether a destination is reached.

> **GLOSSARY**
>
> **High Stakes Curriculum and Testing**—Testing that is standardized and administered to groups of students on a systematic basis. Results are used to compare groups of students across the country. This term also encompasses the influence of test results on the curriculum whereby the curriculum is designed to produce good test results rather than good learning outcomes. The assumption here is that only knowledge and skills that can be measured are worthwhile.

 # REFLECTIVE PRACTICE

Consider what you have just read about knowledge, the student, the community, and evidence.

Think about the following questions:

• How does it fit with what you have already been thinking about?

• What surprised you?

• In what ways will this information be applicable to your context?

PLANNING TO ACCOUNT FOR KNOWLEDGE, STUDENT, COMMUNITY, AND EVIDENCE

Wiggins and McTighe suggest that to plan effectively, teachers need to think about where they want to go; in short, they suggest that planning begins with the end in sight. They call this **backwards design**. Think of it as planning a trip with a specific destination: there are many potential routes to get to the final destination, but having a destination means that ultimately there is a goal. Wiggins & McTighe (2001) suggest that there are three stages to this planning:

1. What is worthy of understanding? (What is the destination?)
2. What is evidence of understanding? (How will I know I have arrived?)
3. What experiences will promote understanding and interest? (How do I keep busy during the trip or how will my experiences enhance my appreciation of the destination?)

Alternatives to backwards design include teaching for understanding (Blythe, 1998) and integrated inquiry (Murdoch, 1998). Table 5.1 below highlights the similarities and differences between each planning model.

GLOSSARY

Backwards Design—Planning with the assessment measures decided before the unit/lesson begins.

MORE INFORMATION

For more information on Teaching for Understanding, see "Introducing TFU: What is the teaching for understanding framework?" on the companion website

Table 5.1 Similarities and differences between various planning models

Backwards Design or Design Down (Wiggins & McTighe)	Teaching for Understanding (Blythe & associates)	Integrated Inquiry (Murdoch)
Stage 1. What is worthy?	• Through lines (over-arching goals)	• Tuning in
Stage 2 What is evidence?	• Generative topics (ideas that keep us going; central to the discipline)	• Finding out
Stage 3. What experiences are needed?	• Understanding goals (identify the processes and skills we want students to acquire)	• Sorting out
	• Understanding performances (tasks that indicate/demonstrate learning)	• Extending
		• Conducting
	• On-going assessments	• Acting

Integrated inquiry accepts the notion that students are capable, actively involved in their learning, and can reconstruct their own understanding as they gain new knowledge. The process begins by providing a focus for students' prior knowledge and experience, and then extending into new knowledge by challenging and refining it.

One of Murdoch's contributions to the understanding of planning is distinguishing between a teacher's educational and pedagogical intentions. It is useful to think about these distinctions before beginning any planning exercises.

Table 5.2 *Distinguishing between educational and pedagogical intentions*

Teacher's Educational Intentions	Teacher's Pedagogical Intentions
• What key ideas do I want students to develop?	• How will I introduce these ideas to students?
• What information do I need to help me clarify these ideas?	• How do I find out what students already know?
• What skills do I want students to develop?	• Which ways of working together will I introduce?
• What focus/topic/unit will help provide a context meaningful to students?	• How can I cater to all learning styles? Have I accounted for a range of teaching approaches? How will I form students into groups?

Note the differences between pedagogical intention and educational intention. Effective teachers constantly reflect on both sides of the table, since effective planning requires teachers to think about topics from both the student's and the teacher's perspective. Murdoch's approach helps teachers to clarify the ways in which their knowledge differs from that of someone who is simply a subject specialist. In short, the focus on pedagogical intention highlights the specialized knowledge of the professional teacher.

No matter what planning outline is used, there are some key principles that cross all subject and grade areas. Each of the models reflected above includes big ideas or overarching goals, i.e., the ones that all children will have mastered once the unit or grade level is completed. Big ideas include concepts like: "What does it mean to say that all living things change?" These big ideas are at the heart of what is valued in society and reflect what a student needs to know. Further, they have the potential to engage students because they are big ideas. To get the big idea, students have to be challenged to explain, interpret, apply, empathize, or demonstrate the way in which this idea relates to ongoing learning, and teachers need to keep track of and plan experiences that will allow students to demonstrate that they are indeed making progress toward acquiring the idea.

The key difference between Wiggins and McTighe's backwards design model and the other planning models is their emphasis on assessment and evidence building. This model reflects the high stakes curriculum discussed in Chapter 9 and, depending on the school board, may be the most appropriate for planning. Nevertheless, the other models that are discussed are also appropriate for working with and organizing activities for student learning.

REFLECTIVE PRACTICE

Think about the following questions:

• Which of the above planning processes make the most sense to you?

• What are the strengths and limitations of each process?

• What assumptions are embedded in each process?

GETTING STARTED

To plan for any classroom, teachers need to first be aware of the curriculum documents that are in place. These documents provide the framework for organizing each subject. Although these documents can guide and inform the planning process, planning must reflect the needs and character of the individual school. Though novice teachers may plan from lesson-to-lesson and from day-to-day, long-range planning ideally creates balance and an enhanced use of resources. Further, if the school year is considered as a whole, the task of teaching that year seems more manageable when using long-range planning. It is also helpful for novice teachers to plan with others who work in the same division or grade level. In this way, novice teachers benefit from the expertise of others, and although the plans themselves may be implemented differently, at least some of the concern about whether or not all the topics are being covered is alleviated.

It is important to recognize that effective planning takes time—it does not all happen the night before school starts. Effective teachers take time to reflect on the curriculum as a whole and then begin to sequence it. Long-range planning, done in the months before school starts, provides an overview of the year; but all teachers know that this overview changes as they become acquainted with the students in their class. All planning is informed and modified by individual students' interests, needs, and learning styles. A key question in any planning experiences has to be, "Why am I doing this? And how does it fit with the other things I am doing in the classroom?" Over time, as teachers gain experience both with planning and with teaching, they are able to acquire and use resources that fit with the ways in which they teach. As they teach units, they gather and store resources together so they will be readily available when a unit is taught in another year.

Table 5.3 *One way of planning for the academic year*

Learning outcomes (organize by month)	Performance measures	Target	Key strategies/themes/tasks
Reference Curriculum Document (e.g., Language Arts)	What students will do (assessments)	Level of expectation	What theme/skills in each subject

Once an overview of the school year has been developed, the teacher can then begin to concentrate on individual subject areas and start to plan. Different stages in planning have different levels of specificity. Many teachers find it useful to send home a school year planner; this is also a good way to communicate with parents. This planner provides the broad strokes so that parents are aware of what is likely to happen in the year. See the example below.

Table 5.4 *A sample of a school year planner*

What to Expect This Year

September: Getting acquainted month. We will be reviewing basic addition and subtraction in math. In language arts and social studies we are studying the neighbourhood. Science is also about the community.

October/November: Literacy focus with theme of folk and fairy tales. Science looks at the theme of change. Art will be about mapping changes.

November/December: First reporting period and interviews. Physical education theme is movement through dance.

Note that the outline only briefly highlights issues to be covered. Details will follow, as weekly newsletters keep parents up-to-date with classroom activities.

THEME PLANNING

One of the most effective ways to think about planning is to use themes that evoke the big ideas discussed earlier. Broad-based themes allow for big ideas to be developed more fully, and also provide opportunities for students to have their own input into the ways in which the theme is developed. In short, when the theme is organized around a big idea, there are more opportunities for student ownership. In planning any unit, teachers follow the following sequence of steps:

1. Read the relevant curriculum document and become familiar with the content. Also read the relevant texts that students will be using. Select a theme based on what students of this age/grade level are interested in.

2. Consider the students' prior learning. What assumptions have been made about what students already know? Do the students have gaps in knowledge that will need to be filled?

3. Research the theme topic to determine what resources are available. What do you have to learn to be able to teach this theme?

4. Divide the theme into sub-topics. How does the theme fit into different curriculum areas? Decide whether the theme has to cross all areas, or whether it fits best into one or two areas.

5. What are the essential learning outcomes of this unit? Consider the subject areas being integrated into the theme. Which outcomes from each subject area will be articulated in this unit? Note that trying to make a theme "fit" all subject areas can lead to surface learning. It is better to make sure that the unit has a logical cross-curricular fit. Having a page of seat-work with houses containing mathematics questions is not thematic integration.

6. How will you assess and evaluate students throughout the unit? How will you know when students have acquired the learning outcomes?

7. How will you accommodate students' interests and learning styles throughout the unit?

8. What is the focus of the learning? Will this be an inquiry-based unit or will it be more delivery of information? Why?

9. How will you organize for learning? What pedagogical strategies will you use? If you are using learning centres, decide what they will be.

10. What materials do you need to gather for this unit? How will you use them?

11. What provisions will need to be made for remediation (an alternative way for students to gain knowledge and skills that were not acquired when the lesson was first taught) and enrichment (value added activity)? What strategies will you use to enhance this? In short, how will you plan for whole class, small group, and individual activity?

12. How will you inform parents about the theme? Is this necessary? (To some extent, this depends on the grade level. In early years, for example, it is useful to inform parents and potentially involve them in the development of the theme.)

13. Decide whether you will include a theme bulletin board in the classroom. Decide how permanent centres will be accommodated/modified for the theme.

14. Include both theme related and non-theme related activities in daily activities.

Different approaches to unit planning are introduced below:

Table 5.5a *A sheet like the one below might help teachers as they begin to think about unit planning.*

Unit name: Subject area: Grade level:		Anticipated duration:		Unit organized by theme: type of instruction:	
Learning outcomes:					
Resources	**Instruction mode**	**Activity**	**Time**	**Assessment**	**Notes**

Table 5.5b *An alternative approach to unit planning*

Theme: <u>Fairy and Folk tales</u>

Duration: <u> </u>

Level: <u> </u>

Instructional Focus (Learning outcomes)	Methods (What I will use to teach)	Assessment Strategies	Resources (Books, DVDs software, trips, etc.)
Develop social responsibility and understand diversity	Conduct a whole class discussion about *Beauty and the Beast* and *The Jungle Book*		Books Video
Understand that stories have messages	Write or draw character from stories Have a pre- and post-discussion on the text	Have learners make a story map Note the type of comparative adjectives and descriptors they use	
Understand how to critically reflect on images presented in stories	Activity with two packages: one wrapped in newspaper the other in decorative wrapping. Invite learners to discuss which one is most appealing. Relate this to stories.	Note whether students refer to books or videos in their discussion.	

Table 5.5c *Yet another way to organize for teaching. Note that the following sketch of learning needs to be accompanied by a more detailed unit plan.*

Month: October

Theme: Growth and development

Subject Areas: Health, Science, Language Arts, and Social Studies

Goal: Develop an understanding that all living things grow and change

Outcomes: Read books about change (*Big Sarah's Little Boots, The Fall of Freddy the Leaf, On the Day You Were Born*)

• Recognize that all living things grow and change
• Plan for a healthy diet
• Map growth and development

Calendar of Activities

Week One:

• Introduce theme
• Establish centres: Growing beans, measurement centre
• Add relevant books to library area
• Introduce concept of growth and development charts
• Lessons on what is needed for growth (plants, animals)
• Develop comparison charts
• Language arts (compare/contrast), vocabulary building

Table 5.5c continues...

Week Two:

- Visit from a physician or nurse
- Draw sketches of changes in the environment; chart on calendar
- Map students' own growth
- Language Arts focus is record-keeping and extension of vocabulary in science and social studies

Week Three:

- Develop booklets on growth and change (can use growth of bean plants *or* changes in trees outside the classroom)
- Height growth charts posted
- Application of skills across subject areas

Week Four:

- Plan for culminating activity
- Take plants home to families; keep one or two in class to chart progress
- Share booklets—student publishing—add booklets to class library
- Have students share what they have learned about growth and development
- Post-learning charts (plan to revisit at end of year to determine how humans grow)

Yet another way to think about theme planning is to use a web.

Figure 5.2 *Planning web*

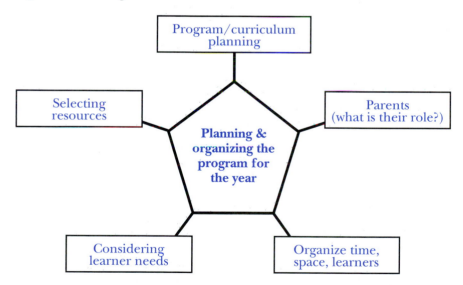

Regardless of the type of planning that occurs before the unit, teachers must be prepared to think about and plan for the unexpected.

For each type of plan, the teacher may wish to develop two checklists: one for the teacher and one for the students. The list for the teacher will likely include things that are needed for the purposes of instruction during the whole unit. The one for the student will include things students will need during the course of the unit. Thinking through these things ahead of time will make teaching the unit that much easier. In addition, the teacher may develop a list of teaching strategies that will be used during the course of the unit. If these are systematically recorded over the course of the unit, the teacher can determine at a glance what learning styles have been accommodated and what might need to be included in another unit. In each unit, the teacher will want to have a balance between whole class, small group, and individual activities. Each student needs time to practise what has been taught, and also needs time to talk with others to consolidate learning.

In all the examples above, the outlines provide only a brief overview of the kinds of activities that will take place in the classroom. From the overview of the theme or the year-long plan, teachers have to break the larger goals into smaller units. These units are the daily lesson plans that organize each day. Each lesson, like each unit, has a rhythm that begins with a motivation and connection to prior learning. The unit then introduces new information or skills, and goes on to give students an opportunity to practise. Finally, student learning is evaluated. In essence, each planned lesson becomes a part of the jigsaw puzzle that makes up the entire unit. The following chart presents one way of thinking about a lesson plan. Beginning teachers often need more detailed plans to help them establish the cycle and flow of teaching/learning.

Table 5.6 *Creating a lesson plan*

Topic:	*Theme or unit of study*
Subject:	*Specify subject area/curriculum outline*
Time:	*Duration of the lesson. You may specify where the lesson falls in a sequence.*
Objectives/Outcomes/Expectations:	*(What students will be able to know/do after the lesson is taught. Think about how you will know whether learning has taken place. This relates to the assessment of learning. Many of these will be drawn from the curriculum documents for specific subject areas.)*

Action	Material Needed *(Resources)*	Time Allocated
Motivation and connection to prior learning	*List resources that both the student and the teacher will need at each stage of the lesson*	*Suggest how much time will be needed for each step in the process*
Sequence of steps in the lesson (body)		
Seat-work/activities (what will students do to reinforce learning?)		*Decide how much time students will need to practise*
Assessment (how will you know what has been learned?)		*What will serve as evidence that students have learned?*

Planning a lesson takes time and effort. At the beginning of their careers, many teachers spend much of their time planning lessons and relating them to the curriculum documents. As teachers gain experience, however, the rhythm of teaching becomes more intuitive and lessons may not be as detailed.

REFLECTIVE PRACTICE

Think about the classrooms that you have visited. Consider the following questions:

• To what extent did you detect the pattern of lessons noted above?

• What were the deviations?

• Why might those deviations have occurred?

Shulman (1992) suggests that teachers' pedagogic content knowledge is a key factor in helping them to plan lessons and units. Think about your own experience.

• In what subject areas do you feel most comfortable as a teacher? Why?

One of the ways to determine what constitutes a lesson plan is careful observation. Mrs. Crawford's grade 8 students were asked to present their findings from a history unit on famous Canadians. Mrs. Crawford had introduced the unit to the students, then used a jigsaw plan to have various students research different personalities from history. The research portfolio in Figures 5.3a and b was developed by one of the students who was studying the medical researcher, Sir Frederick Banting.

MORE INFORMATION

To view a student developed lesson plan see "A sample lesson plan: Preservation of Westminister Ponds" on the companion website.

Figure 5.3a Example of student research

Figure 5.3b Example of student research

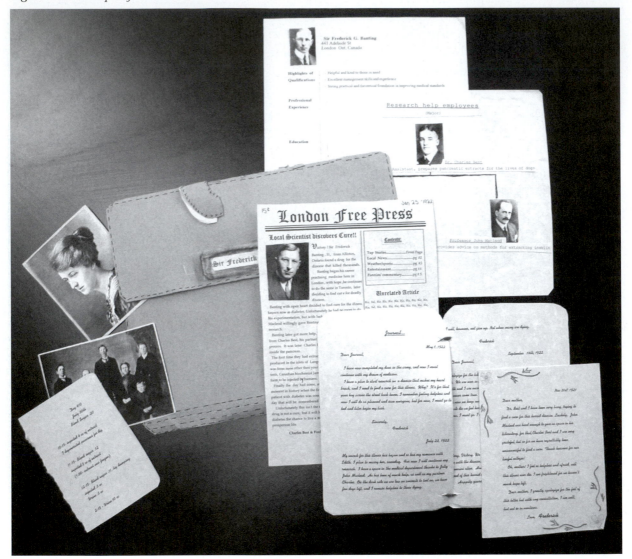

Some questions to consider include:

• What have these students learned from observing their teacher?
• What differentiates the students' research plan from the one that the teacher imposed?
• How might a research portfolio be incorporated into a lesson plan?

REFLECTIVE PRACTICE

Oops. What Happens Now?

Keisha Chan was an eager student teacher who was very enthusiastic when Mr. Dudley invited her to plan a unit for his grade 1 class that involved making use of the very wintry weather that North Bay usually has in January. She had many ideas from her work at the Faculty of Education and her grasp of the science and language arts curriculum documents. It was relatively easy for her to develop a unit plan that involved students at centres completing independent activities as well as reading and recording the results of the many science activities she had planned. She convinced the public library to provide her with a box of books, both fiction and non-fiction, on snow and winter. She planned a week of activities ranging from making ice cream with plastic bags, snow, condensed cream, chocolate, and salt, to snow shoeing and tracking animals in the woods behind the school. Mr. Dudley reviewed her plans on the Friday before the unit was to start and with only a few minor changes suggested that on Monday the students and Ms Chan would be ready for their first day of what looked like a great unit.

Keisha worked on the weekend to set up the centres, after first obtaining permission from Mr. Dudley and the custodian to be in the school. By Saturday evening all was in place: the writing centre, the reading corner, the science centre, and the physical education centre with appropriate activity cards. All that was needed was the children who would arrive at 8:50 am Monday morning.

At 6 am Monday morning, Keisha awoke to the sound of rain against her window. She thought at first it was freezing rain, but soon learned it was a steady, wet rainfall, unusual in many seasons, but with the strange weather lately not a real surprise. By the time she arrived at school there was nothing but slush in the playground and around the school. The activities so carefully planned for the day would have to be modified.

Think about the following questions:

• If you were in Keisha's place what would you do?
• What are the key issues?
• What might be salvageable from her plan?
• What does this scenario indicate about planning?

PLANNING FOR CENTRES: IS IT NECESSARY?

Most elementary school classrooms have some type of centres for student activities. At times these centres are simply supplementary to the program, but at other times—especially in primary classrooms—they are essential for program delivery. Regardless of the nature of the centre, supplementary or essential, there should always be a rationale and a plan for the use and development of the centre. Indeed, some have argued that every aspect of the classroom context should relate to some aspect of student learning. The teacher articulates how and why each element in the classroom is there. In short, planning for learning centres is necessary.

It is also important to distinguish between permanent centres and those that may change over the course of the year. Permanent centres are those likely to be found in every classroom from the early years through to secondary school. These centres may be considered supplementary but essential to the program. They will likely include some of the following, although the exact composition of the centres may vary from classroom to classroom:

• library or research centre
• technology resource area
• writing centre

In some primary classrooms, these will be supplemented by the following:

• creative centres
• science and mathematics centres

Teachers need to consider the purpose of each centre as it is planned. For example, what materials should be included in the library/research centre? Why should they be included? Table 5.7 outlines some of the purposes of a library/research centre. Think about the ways in which the purpose might change over the course of the year.

Table 5.7 *Library/research centre*

Purpose	• To provide further reading material for students to complete during independent reading time. • To provide further reading on themes developed in class. • To develop research skills. • To foster independent reading and research.
Skills to be developed:	• Silent reading practice • Skimming and scanning for information • Expand reading interests
Materials	• Selection of fiction both at and above grade level • Reading material that is inclusive and not geared to one gender or group • Selection of magazines and articles related to themes on which the class is working • Reference material, including texts • Student-written texts • Materials will change over the course of the year and relate to different units in the classroom
Space organization	• Comfortable area for reading • May include couch, comfortable chair, different lighting

At other times, centres may be the basis of a portion of a unit or, as in kindergarten classrooms, may be the foundation of the program. In these cases the teacher needs to be able to articulate how and why each centre contributes to the child's learning. Learning centres have carefully planned activities and materials that foster specific learning outcomes and provide for active learning and problem solving. They can be used for reinforcing or introducing new concepts and they allow the teacher to organize learning so that different achievement levels can be accommodated. It is not sufficient to say that students will go to the creative centre or the writing centre. There needs to be a plan for the activity and the teacher should be able to determine how the activity fits within the overall yearly learning activities. To develop learning centres, think about the following questions:

• What curriculum objectives will this centre address?
• What materials are needed?
• How will the materials be organized according to complexity? Which ones might be more difficult for some students?

• Decide how the materials will be used. Will students be able to follow directions and work independently or will the activity require assistance? If students are involved in recording the results of an experiment, can they conduct the experiment alone? What is the experiment? If it is a creative activity, what are the steps? Does it involve paper folding, gluing, writing, drawing, or are there other steps involved in the process? What is the purpose of each step and how does it relate to the curriculum?
• Does the centre activity involve more than one centre? If the activity is a reading response activity that starts at the creative centre, will it also require that students proceed to the writing centre at some point? How will this movement be managed?
• Finally, how will the teacher know that students have acquired the expected skill/knowledge? What is the assessment?

In centre-based learning, the assessment is often derived from observing students' activities at the centre and from the artifacts they produce. Teachers may wish to think about developing observation sheets for each centre that will allow them to determine at a glance what learners are doing. For more information about observation, refer to Chapter 9 of this text.

PROFESSIONAL PLANNING

Just as teachers have to plan for their classroom, many teachers will also develop a plan for their professional development. Indeed, such plans can work well to supplement on-going teacher assessment. Having a plan for personal professional development will ensure that teachers remain up to date in their practice and remain aware of new developments in their specific field. The following are the kinds of professional development plans that new teachers may have:

- New teachers may wish to begin their career by focusing on professional planning, and they may organize their professional development focus around that.
- Teachers in Ontario may want to master the electronic curriculum planner in their first year of teaching.
- Science majors assigned to a grade 1 class may decide to develop their skills and knowledge about the primary age learner or acquire more information about language and literacy development.

> **MORE INFORMATION**
>
> Many provinces have developed electronic curriculum planners to assist teachers with planning units. For more information on curriculum materials and resources for teachers across Canada, click on 'The curriculum foundation' on the companion website.

The plan that teachers develop for their professional practice will demonstrate their commitment to the profession and can become a part of their professional portfolio. Like most plans, teachers' learning plans may change over time as their professional needs grow.

If a teacher competently adheres to a set of curriculum objectives, but in a deeper sense does not know where he or she is going,…then the observable teacher behaviour, what the teacher is doing overtly is a profound contradiction of the way he or she exists in the world, or better, in the school, in this classroom with these young people. Or maybe we should better say when the teacher fails to be what he or she ostensibly does, then that teacher is really an absence, and is not at all genuinely present to those kids.

~ M. van Manen, 1986, p 43

REFLECTIVE PRACTICE

Courtney's Professional Growth Plan

Courtney, a lifelong resident of a small urban centre, is a graduate of a four-year honours program in Geography. She worked at a gym as a personal trainer before entering a faculty of education, where she completed her degree and is now qualified to teach grades 7–12. Her subject specializations are Geography and English. In her first year teaching, she was fortunate to gain employment at a large school in downtown Toronto teaching a grade 8 class in which over 60 percent of the class are recent immigrants.

Courtney developed the following professional learning plan:

Long-term goal: *Teach Geography and Guidance in a secondary school*

Short-term goal: *Learn more about teaching students for whom English is a second language*

Strategies for short-term goal:

1. Take courses in teaching English as a second language offered through OISE/UT
2. Become involved in school board level professional development for ESL teachers.

3. Attend workshops on cultural awareness sponsored by the local centre for new Canadians.
4. Meet with each student's parents on an individual basis to determine more about their individual history.

Strategies for long-term goals:

1. Enroll in courses on teaching guidance in the second year of teaching. Relate these to second language courses taken last year.
2. Seek out leadership opportunities in the school board that will help me learn more about education in general and our board specifically.
3. Accept a role to assist with ninth grade orientation.

Think about the following questions:

- What do you notice about the Courtney's learning plan?
- How will Courtney know when she has achieved her goals?
- What would your professional learning plan look like?

SUMMARY

This chapter began with an outline of learning frameworks in order to remind teachers of the ways in which pedagogic knowledge is distinct from other forms of knowledge. These frameworks then provided the foundation for considering various ways to plan units and lessons and provided a rationale for planning the curriculum. A number of alternative approaches to planning were introduced, and it was noted that backwards design is but one way to approach a design for the curriculum. Key points from the chapter include the notion that teachers need to understand the way in which curriculum is constructed and need to see evidence of learning. In addition, all activities in the classroom should be related to some particular student outcome.

Many practical examples of ways to plan units and lessons were introduced; teachers should determine which method best suits their style. Although much of the chapter may seem to reflect the notion that teaching and learning can be reduced to technical design, it is recognized that the individual teacher, students, and their interaction together in the classroom will take precedence over pre-planned outcomes. In short, teachers have to plan so that they can deviate from the plan. Knowing the destination means that teachers and students can take side trips that make learning much more exciting and worthwhile.

 ## CHAPTER 5 ACTIVITY

Select a theme that could be taught in either grades 1–3 or grades 4–6. Decide what subject areas could be taught through this theme. Use the outline suggested in "Theme Planning" to outline a unit that would take one month to complete.

In addition to the overarching unit plan, develop a detailed lesson plan for each of the curricular areas that will be covered by the theme.

Suggest at what point in the theme these lessons might be appropriate. Make sure that you also indicate resources.

Share your unit plans with two peers to gain feedback. Invite them to suggest what has been done well and to make suggestions for ways in which the unit can be further developed.

CHAPTER 6

STARTING WITH WHAT YOU HAVE: Organizing Time, Space, and Materials

"The teacher's role is to make sure that learners have the opportunity to clarify the problem, to make observations in potentially profitable areas, to form and test hypotheses, and to reflect on the results. To omit any of these opportunities would be to jeopardize the learning.

~ Garth Boomer, 1983 in Goswami and Stillman, p 12

STUDY OBJECTIVES

The purpose of this chapter is to
- develop a plan for organizing space in the classroom
- recognize and implement a grade appropriate timetable
- learn how to organize storage for accessibility in the classroom
- learn how to design learning centres
- conduct an inventory of classroom space and materials

INTRODUCTION

One of the most important activities for any classroom teacher is organizing the classroom in terms of time, space, and materials. Although it may seem to be taken for granted, careful planning can make the whole year much more effective. A well-planned classroom has an impact on behaviour management and student achievement. This chapter suggests ways to establish different types of learning environments and discusses the strengths and limitations of each. While reading through the chapter, think about the classrooms in which you have spent time as a student or as a student teacher. What made them effective? What factors contributed to a lack of effectiveness?

STARTING WITH THE SCHOOL: DESIGN PRINCIPLES

From the early days when schools were first structured as learning institutions, the school's design seemed to reflect the outlook of society toward the curriculum and learning. For example, the design of schools in Upper Canada was heavily influenced by Edgerton Ryerson's notion of form and function working together. Deputy Superintendent George Hodgins translated Ryerson's ideas about the design of schools in a book called *The Schoolhouse, Its Architecture.*

Early twentieth century schools tended to look more like factories and reflected a concept called daylighting, a bank of windows along one side of the long axis of the classroom to produce light over the student's left shoulder (Rafferty, 1969). Look at Table 6.1 and note the way in which the school's architectural design reflects the approach to teaching and learning and includes the concept of **daylighting**.

In this era, schools tended to be organized in tightly structured groups, often with the vocational courses located at the back of the school on the first floor. Academic subjects like arts and sciences were grouped together on the floors above with each subject discipline clustered together. In the elementary school of the day, primary children were grouped in one area of the school while the more senior classes were located away from them. Even playground time was structured to keep primary children way from other students.

Later, as progressivism became a part of the philosophy of schools, the design of schools changed and they were often constructed around large resource areas that opened into open-concept classrooms, where again all primary classes were together. Today, as new schools are constructed, they often resemble shopping malls with glass, large open areas, and large resource centres that are well-equipped to bring the larger world into the school through the Internet.

There is a body of literature in architecture that considers school design as the beginning of the creation of a learning environment. Lackney (2003) suggests 33 design principles that should be incorporated into the development of any school. While reading through the table below, think about the degree to which these principles are applicable at the classroom level. Some implications have been provided. What can you add?

GLOSSARY

Daylighting—Daylighting is the concept that classrooms should have natural light that falls over a student's left shoulder.

MORE INFORMATION

For more information on classroom design see Blackstock school smart classroom designs on the companion website.

Table 6.1 *Design Principles*

Principle to be Applied in Designing a School	What It Might Mean in the Classroom
Maximize collaboration in planning the building. There is a need for the community to feel they have ownership of the space.	Students should have some say in developing the learning environment in the classroom.
Build a proactive facility management program. That is, make sure the decisions made facilitate custodial care and ease of maintenance.	Custodians need to be able to access the room for cleaning. What steps will have to be taken to ensure accessibility?
Plan schools as neighbourhood community learning centres.	In what ways can the community be drawn to the school or the classroom?
Consider home as a template for school.	
Meander circulation to ensure supervision.	
Design for safe schools.	Create an environment in which students feel safe to take risks.
Cluster instructional areas.	
Provide space for sharing instructional resources.	
Design for a variety of learning activities.	Consider three types of activities: whole class, small group, and individual
Provide resource-rich activity pockets.	
Integrate early childhood education into the school.	Create a buddy system with younger students.
Provide a home base for every learner.	
Provide a place for a community forum.	
Provide a conferring space as well as individual spaces.	
Weave together virtual space and face-to-face space.	
Provide a parent information centre.	Provide a parent information bulletin board and a lending library.

SO WHAT? CLASSROOM DESIGN

The previous section noted that the school's design has an influence on the construction of classrooms. In addition, with open area schools and changing schools into designs with moveable walls, the principle of daylighting that was seen as essential during Ryerson's time seemed to have disappeared as schools were modernized. Yet today there is a movement to try to reconnect with the outdoors, at least in parts of the school. Natural lighting is finding a place once more, especially with the movement toward education linking physical needs and learning spaces.

MORE INFORMATION

For more information about these design principles and to discover the research base from which they have been developed, see "33 principles of classroom design" by Jeffery A. Lackney on the companion website.

Lackney's research conducted in 1999 examines the ways in which the design of physical space can enhance brain-based learning. He suggests that much of what we know about the brain and the ways in which it operates has been articulated by designers and urban geographers who understand the meaning of place and the ways in which place can inform learning. Lackney (2003) suggests that brain-based design for physical space includes the following:

- providing rich, stimulating environments in which displays are created by the students rather than the teacher
- including places for group learning that enhance social interaction (in short, making the classroom like a home)
- linking indoor and outdoor spaces, ensuring that learners have the opportunity to move
- having corridors and public places that remind students of the school's purpose
- including safe spaces in which all students can be who they are
- providing a variety of spaces for different types of activities and to accommodate different learning styles
- having resources available
- having a personal space
- having both active and passive spaces for learning

These principles should also be reflected in the ways in which classrooms are organized. The organization of the classroom should be appropriate for the age of the students, and at the same time provide opportunities for children who are at different developmental levels to find a place. Early years classrooms (junior and senior kindergarten) will be primarily organized through centres that in many ways reflect different aspects of the home environment; in the upper grades, classroom organization may be more formal and the day itself timetabled differently. The next section discusses the different aspects of organization in each division.

PRIMARY AND UPPER ELEMENTARY CLASSROOM ORGANIZATION: THE SAME OR DIFFERENT

There is a well-documented relationship between the physical learning environment and instructional design and activity (McGuffey, 1982;

Lackney & Jacobs, 2005). The organization, cleanliness, as well as the temperature of the classroom can all have an impact on students' ability to learn and focus on the task at hand. The issues related to classroom organization and management are similar in both the elementary and secondary school contexts. The key to effective classroom organization at any level is ensuring that the arrangement of space and the organization of time suit the particular activities in which students are engaged. All too often, new teachers assume there is little to think about when organizing furniture in the classroom, and may simply place student desks and materials where it seems to be convenient. Yet organization of space not only assists in fostering student learning, but also facilitates behavioural management. Think about the following questions while considering classroom organization:

• Where will you put your desk? (Or do you want one?)
• Do you prefer tables for students or do you prefer individual desks? (Do you have an option about either since the furniture already exists and there is no money to purchase new materials?)
• What learning centres will you have? Here there may be some real differences depending on the grade level: a kindergarten classroom may have sand and water tables as well as housekeeping and block centres; the middle years classroom may have a reading and writing centre as well as a computer area; and the secondary classroom may have reference material and a student organization area containing common material such as staplers and paper.
• Further, whether there are centres in the classroom or not, decisions have to be made about storage of materials and their accessibility. Certainly bookshelves may be necessary, but how will they be organized? Will all shelving hold books or will some be storage places for bins that hold paper?

Any classroom at any level needs to be organized so that students can be quickly organized into three basic settings: whole class teacher-directed, independent small groups, and individual workstations. One space should allow for large group or whole class instruction; the second should be a location in which students can be involved in small group instruction. These two spaces might be considered **areas of primary instruction**.

Teacher proximity and sight lines need to be considered as well. This is critical in the primary classroom for purposes of supervision and safety, but it is equally important in the later grades when it enables the teacher to keep track of whether or not students are on task. If teachers decide to have a desk in the classroom (and they may indeed want to since, like students, they too need their own space), where will it be located? Many teachers spend little time at the desk during the day, but it is important to remember that at all times they will want to position themselves so that they have proximity to the largest possible number of students. Management by proximity can help to eliminate many issues created by students who have difficulty maintaining their behaviour during independent work periods.

Another key issue is that of traffic patterns. The quiet study space in a classroom should not be in the path of traffic in the room. Similarly, safety issues require attention for both traffic patterns and general location; for example, it makes sense that frequently used materials and centres should be placed away from doors. Student desks can be organized in small groups or other patterns as necessitated by the particular activity and subject area. Social Studies and Language Arts teachers may prefer small groups, while Mathematics teachers may prefer a horseshoe arrangement. If teachers decide they want as much flexibility as possible in terms of individual student desk arrangement, they should think about a process for having students move their desks as quickly and efficiently as possible from one organization to another. If the process for changing desk arrangements is decided ahead of time, there is less likely to be confusion and management problems when it occurs.

Finally, especially in a primary setting, activity boundaries need to be outlined. Some teachers use low bookcases to mark out a library or writing area, while others use tape on the floor to help students decide where they should be. One of the key issues in establishing boundaries in the classroom is to be sure that sight lines are maintained; for example, a bookcase that towers over primary children blocks the teacher's view and can be a safety hazard if it should topple on youngsters. Similarly, from a safety perspective, it is important to know where electrical outlets are located since their location can have an impact on room arrangement and design.

REFLECTIVE PRACTICE

Mrs. Beasley had been teaching grade 1 for a number of years, but this year she decided to implement an activity-based program since she had a number of young boys in the classroom who had been identified as potentially benefiting from a more active environment. Accordingly, she arranged for a water and sand table as well as for some blocks for a block centre. She organized student desks into groups of six and placed the library at the back of the room. At the front near the door, she had an area for small group instruction. The children were very responsive to the change in her classroom and the centres themselves evolved well. Children signed in to the centres and the products they produced were related to the language activities she introduced in the classroom. Mrs. Beasley was quite concerned, however, that when she attempted small group reading instruction with her group of five young boys, they most often would begin to fidget, look around the classroom, and try to crawl away from the instructional area. She also noted that when she worked with small groups there seemed to be large quantities of water on the floor.

Look at the diagram of Mrs. Beasley's classroom in Figure 6.1. Think about the following questions:

• What do you think the problem might be?
• How would you organize the classroom differently?

Figure 6.1 *Diagram of Mrs. Beasley's classroom*

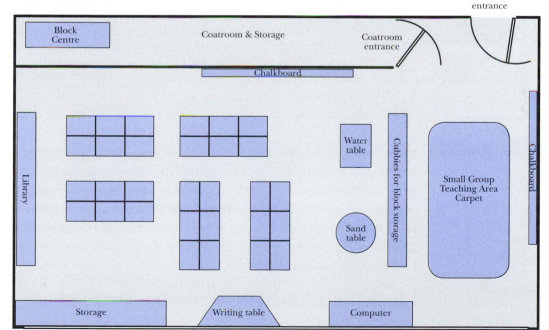

In addition, it is important to ensure that the ambiance of the classroom reflects the needs and the developmental levels of the students. In traditional primary classrooms, for example, the alphabet is often placed on cards that are fastened to the border above the chalkboard. However, primary children may have difficulty seeing these cards or tracking individual letters from the posted cards. It would be a better use of resources to have the alphabet posted at a child's eye level, or even better to have alphabet strips fastened to children's desks where they can see and be better able to track individual letters.

REFLECTIVE PRACTICE

If you teach primary or early years, track your classroom from a child's eye view. Bend down so that you are the height of a child at a primary school level.

Think about the following questions:

- In what ways does this change your perspective of the classroom?
- What seems obvious from an adult perspective but not from a child's?
- If the physical environment of the classroom were designed for children, how would it be organized differently?

Similarly, if you teach at the secondary school level, track your classroom by thinking about the following questions:

- What size of furniture is appropriate?
- What are your expectations vis-à-vis student activity levels?
- Remember that the typical adolescent's biological clock starts later in the day than the typical adult's. What are the implications of this for designing programs and classroom activities?

GLOSSARY

Progressivism—is an educational philosophy that assumes that humans are interactive, social beings. Relying on the notions of John Dewey, **progressivists** believe that students learn by doing and involve students in activities that require that they make decisions and evaluate their learning.

It has been said that the design of the classroom reflects the teacher's philosophy of teaching and learning. Primary classrooms that tend to be more informally organized with space for small groups and activity centres certainly seem to reflect the **progressivist** notion that children learn by doing. At the late elementary school level, the more formally organized classroom could be said to reflect a more abstract notion of knowledge as transmission.

MATCHING CLASSROOM DESIGN AND TEACHING PHILOSOPHY

Conflicts and management issues often arise when the classroom design and layout do not reflect the orientation of the teacher toward teaching and learning. Similarly, students learn more effectively when the classroom environment is one in which they feel comfortable and in which they find a reflection of who they are as learners. Purkey (1999) talks about invitational approaches to teaching and learning and suggests that everything in and around schools contributes to or subtracts from students' abilities to grow intellectually, physically, spiritually, and psychologically. There are four central tenets to Purkey's notion of **invitational learning**.

1. **Respect**: people are able, valuable, and responsible
2. **Trust**: collaboration and cooperation are key elements in learning and process is as important as product
3. **Optimism**: all people have untapped potential in all areas of human endeavour
4. **Intentionality**: human potential can best be developed by creating and maintaining places, policies, processes, and programs to invite development, and by people who are intentionally invitational with themselves and others both personally and professionally

For Purkey and John Novak (2003), this meant designing classrooms and school environments in which care is taken to make sure that students, teachers, and all who enter the school are welcomed. It means paying attention to details such as keeping the environment tidy. It also means ensuring that there are pleasant spaces for visitors to the school and greeting students at the door each morning.

CLASSROOM DECORATION? YOURS, MINE, AND OURS

Many teachers look forward to getting their first classroom and are eager to decorate the classroom so that it welcomes the students. Indeed, some teachers with an eye for decoration completely decorate the classroom before the students arrive. However, the classroom environment is not just the teacher's space; it also belongs to the learners and they too need to have some stake in its organization. Ideally, all classrooms have spaces for students only (yours), spaces for the teacher only (mine), and spaces that are shared (ours). When planning the classroom environment, think about visual aids and the ways in which they can assist with teaching specific concepts within a unit.

Bulletin boards and posters should be colourful and appealing, but most importantly they should reflect the current work of the classroom.

GLOSSARY

Invitational learning—A phrase coined by William Purkey, invitational learning suggests planning the teaching and learning activities and space so that students are welcomed into the environment. Inviting schools are places where students are welcomed and respected.

MORE INFORMATION

To read more about invitational learning, see Invitational education on the companion website.

Student work related to the theme or unit should also be posted to facilitate learning and demonstrate the value of the work. Thus all boards should be rotated frequently to reflect OUR classroom activities. It is especially important that classrooms take into account the diverse populations served by the school. If the classroom has a large multi-cultural, multi-ethnic community, one way to ensure that all children are welcome is to provide some evidence of their culture and language in the classroom or at the entry to the classroom. Having "welcome" in many languages is a good start. Students have their personal space in their desks, lockers, or cubbies, but it is also appropriate to provide them with some specific display space in the classroom for events in which they have an interest (e.g., schedules for school teams, advertisements for the local dog show if someone is showing their puppy for the first time). Posting a daily schedule in a clearly visible and accessible area of the classroom helps students organize for the day and can also be a reminder for homework at the end of the day. An assignment schedule for a middle years' classroom might look like the one in Table 6.2.

Table 6.2 *Assignment Log*

Today's objective(s)	Begin the new unit on space in science Finish our art project in collage
Today's homework	Mathematics—page 45 Language Arts—read book for the book report
Reminders	Book reports and oral presentation are due on Friday

STORAGE: THINGS TO THINK ABOUT

All classrooms need storage space for both student work and instructional materials of various types. At all grade levels, decisions have to be made about how items will be stored and where they can be accessed. Also, if the goal of classroom instruction is to foster independence, then storage should be organized so that there is logic to it and a process for using materials. All classrooms need the following:

• a place for books and other informational material
• a place for writing material such as paper and pencils
• a place for returned student work
• a place for submitted student work

• storage for personal items (coats, boots, physical education equipment)
• storage for instructional materials (notebooks, writing folders)

Primary classrooms may also need storage for blocks, material for activity centres, dress-up costumes, art supplies, and various sizes and types of paper. Upper elementary and secondary school level classrooms may need places to display student projects.

Many teachers find using transparent or open-sided plastic bins a good way to store material such as personal items or material from activity centres. These bins enable both teacher and students to readily see what is in the bin. Other teachers use such bins to store books on a similar theme so that all books about mammals, for example, are stored together then removed from the classroom once a unit is finished. To enhance literacy development in primary classrooms, labelling these bins helps children associate what is in the bin and the label for it.

Figure 6.2 *Labelled storage bins for personal items*

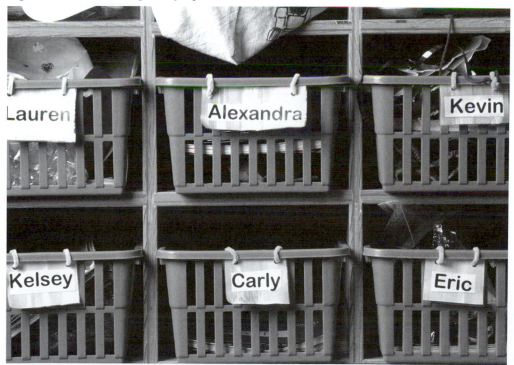

Many teachers also use bins to organize materials for thematic units. They put worksheets, literature, activity materials, and even samples of student work in the bin to use as demonstrations for other classes. The bins can be stored in the teacher's home once a unit is completed, then used again another year with a different group.

Also in primary classrooms, if open shelving is used to store materials, labelling the space on shelves with the name of the item to be placed in an area, along with the shape of the item, can help children become more independent and take responsibility for tidying the classroom. Although Judith Schikendanz (2003) suggests this for early years, children who use the same type of labelling in middle and upper elementary can assist those who have learning difficulties to take responsibility for managing their own materials and space.

New supplies such as notebooks and paper of various sizes for different types of activities should be stored in a space in the classroom to which students do not have daily access—it does not take long for eager students to quickly use consumable classroom material. Once notebooks and so forth have been distributed, students may store them in their desks (if they have them) or in open bins or cubbies, each labelled with the students' names. Again, routines and classroom rules need to be established for accessing the bins and maintaining personal space and materials.

 # REFLECTIVE PRACTICE

As you work in schools, you will notice that some teachers have developed very creative and inexpensive ways to store student material. Listed below are a few that work well for teachers. What are the advantages and disadvantages of each? Add some of the unique storage systems that you have seen to the list. What works well and what has limitations?

- A clear shoe holder hung over a cabinet door to store items that constantly disappear, like scissors and tape.
- A multi-layered skirt hanger to clip on clear plastic bags filled with manipulatives for mathematics.
- To hide messy shelves, sew some Velcro onto a short curtain and fasten the curtain above the shelf.
- To store writing folders or notebooks, cut the top from cereal boxes and have children decorate them.
- Bankers boxes with hanging files to store student work for assessment.
- Tool caddies from the local hardware store to store basic materials such as pencils, crayons, scissors, and glue; this way there are always materials available and no one can say, "I don't have a pencil!"

WHAT WILL YOU DO ALL DAY? THINKING THROUGH THE TIMETABLE

One of the challenges for a new teacher is thinking about the structure of the school day and making decisions about what that day will look like for both teacher and students. All teachers need to address some principles when organizing the day, yet in school these principles may be overtaken by organizational needs outside the control of the classroom teacher. For example, time for physical education in the gym may be slotted on a school-wide basis, as a result the period may interfere with a large block of time that would be ideal for language arts. Alternatively, some schools have specialty teachers whose time is also slotted into the day. One of the things that becomes apparent is that teachers generally have to learn to be flexible with their structure because the school day, and even the school year, never seem to have the routine that some might enjoy. Teachers need to take into account both the biological and physical needs of students, as well as the conceptual demands of the subjects, when planning timetables.

BIOLOGICAL ISSUES

It is important to remember that assumptions about the prime time for particular age groups may not correspond to the students' biological rhythms. For example, some students in upper elementary school may have biologically moved into the periods when their biological clock dictates staying up late and sleeping in—for these students, early morning is not the ideal time for conceptually demanding activities. Very young children in the primary grades may not be as alert in the afternoon, especially if they do not have a regular bedtime at home. Providing time for a healthy snack in the middle of the morning or afternoon may enable some children to better focus. Similarly, ensuring that there is adequate time for children to meet their needs for a washroom break can facilitate concentration. Most teachers recognize that a change in the weather can have an impact on student behaviour and may necessitate a change in routine. However, it is also important to note that the security of a regular routine can help all students anticipate the day ahead. When students are not fretting about what will happen next in the classroom, they are more likely to be able to attend to the task at hand. Thus many teachers have the timetable posted in the classroom, and some send a copy home with students so that parents are aware of the daily routine.

SUBJECT AND DIVISION ISSUES

In general, large blocks of time are ideal in the early and primary years' divisions, especially with language arts. These large blocks give teachers the opportunity to incorporate many aspects of language and provide activities that range across the curriculum. Some school boards may designate the amounts of time required for each subject area, as determined by the curriculum. Curricular activities such as art may also need a large block of time, as well as time within the period for cleanup. In general, Friday afternoon as a time for art activities does not lend itself well to a focus on art. Instead, if the school has a **five-day cycle**, that period may become one for recreation after a busy week. To avoid this, some teachers use a six-day planning cycle. A **six-day cycle** avoids some of the issues created by holidays that fall on Mondays and also avoids the Friday afternoon issues for other subjects.

Table 6.3a *Five-day cycle timetable*

Time	Day One	Day Two	Day Three	Day Four	Day Five
8:50 – 9:00	Opening Exercises				
9:00 – 9:35	Physical Education	Language Arts	Language Arts	Language Arts	Physical Education
9:35 – 10:00	Language Arts				Language Arts
10:00 – 10:30		Math	Math	Music	
10:30 – 10:45	Recess				
10:45 – 11:15	Math	French	Physical Education	Math	Social Studies
11:15 – 11:45	Music	Language Arts	Mathematics		
11:45 – 12:50	Lunch Break				
12:50 – 1:30	Language Arts	Music	Art	Science	Language Arts & Social Studies
1:30 – 2:00		Physical Education			
2:00 – 2:30	French	Social Studies	Physical Education	French	Science
2:30 – 2:45	Recess				
2:45 – 3:30	Science	Social Studies	Art	Language Arts	Science

Table 6.3b Six-day cycle timetable

Time	Day 1	Day 2	Day 3	Day 4	Day 5	Day 6
8:50 – 9:00	Opening Exercises					
9:00 – 9:35	Language Arts	Science	Language Arts	Language Arts	Language Arts	Language Arts
9:35 – 10:00		Physical Education				
10:00 – 10:30		Science				
10:30 – 10:45	Recess					
10:45 – 11:15	Math	Math	Physical Education	Math	Physical Education	Math
11:15 – 11:45		Music			Music	
11:45 – 12:50	Lunch Break					
12:50 – 1:30	Physical Education	Language Arts	Math	Art	Math	Science
1:30 – 2:00	Social Studies					
2:00 – 2:30			French		Social Studies	
2:30 – 2:45	Recess					
2:45 – 3:30	Social Studies	Social Studies	Music	Physical Education	Science	Social Studies

REFLECTIVE PRACTICE

Look at the two timetables. One illustrates a simple five-day cycle, the other a six-day cycle.

Think about the following questions:

- What are the advantages and disadvantages of each?
- What assumptions seem to be embedded in each timetable?

Two areas that are always offered each day at any grade are mathematics and language arts. In many school boards, physical education has also been added to the list of subject areas that must be delivered daily.

Think about the following questions:

- Why have these subject areas been privileged over others?
- What might that suggest about society's values?

Ask for a copy of the daily timetable when you are in schools. Compare the timetables for primary classes with those for the middle years and upper elementary classes. Think about the following questions:

- What do you notice about them?
- What stays the same?
- What is different?

ORGANIZING UNITS

From the general timetable, teachers move to thinking about the organization of various units that they plan to teach, and determining how the units will fit within the daily time allotment. For example, if a teacher plans an integrated studies unit in social studies, he or she will have to think about how much time is available in a month for teaching the unit. If the unit is designed to be taught over a month with daily, one-hour classes, it might have to be modified to meet the teachers' timetable. Alternatively, some teachers alternate large units and focus on science for one month, for example, then focus on social studies for the next month. These decisions should have a specific articulated rationale so that students, their parents, and the school administration understand why the decision to alternate subjects was made.

DAILY SCHEDULES

Teachers move from the general timetable to the daily schedule that is organized in their **daybook**. The daybook provides an opportunity for teachers to specify what will happen in the classroom during each period of the day. Many new teachers take for granted that they can simply "wing" their planning, but successful teachers think through the implications of a daily schedule. The written detail may disappear over time, but all teachers need to establish a "natural" rhythm to both their lesson planning and to the day.

Chapter 5 considered lesson plans, while this chapter considers aspects of the day itself. For example, in the timetables above, there is a simple notation that there are opening exercises, yet in a teacher's daybook this might be written as indicated below:

OPENING EXERCISES:

1. Students pick up book to read when they enter classroom
2. Students put book down and stand for national anthem
3. Students listen to opening announcements
4. Take attendance
5. Gather together for the first lesson.

Similarly, the language arts designation will be followed by an outline of what is to be done during that period. For example,

GLOSSARY

Daybook—The teacher's record of what is to happen each day of the school year. It will contain daily lessons and schedules.

Language Arts (first half):

    Group 1—shared reading activity, introduce new novel *Up to Low*

    Group 2—continue writing activity with reader response to short story

    Group 3—teach directed reading thinking strategy; have students apply this strategy to the short story from reading anthology

Language Arts (second half):

    Model writing—story outline format; have all students develop an outline of the text they are reading

Figure 6.2 *A teacher's daybook might look like this*

Monday, Sept 12, Day 2

Opening exercises: quiet reading, announcements, anthem, attendance

Science: Introduce new unit on weather. Use Smartboard to visit http://www.theweathernetwork.com/ to explore range of forecast in Canada.

Key outcome: Ability to predict

Physical Education

Science: Recall range of weather with students. Introduce short story on weather patterns in local area. Develop prediction chart with students that will be filled in during next month. Plan for weather station in schoolyard.

Recess

Math: Introduce concept of multiplication. Use manipulatives. Text page 45. Groups work with manipulatives to complete challenge sheet.

Lunch

Language Arts: Introduce stories in which weather plays a role. Teach strategy for report writing. Individual reading/writing conferences.

Social Studies: Discuss impact of natural disasters on human activity. Focus on topic related to local area. Present a case study of a problem created by a weather related disaster.

Note that many teachers supplement the daybook with detailed lesson plans that outline how they will develop each lesson or group of lessons. As a new teacher, the amount of planning can seem overwhelming; but soon the rhythm of the curriculum and the day will be established.

Organizing for Instructional Groups

One aspect of organizing for group work that some teachers find problematic is deciding how to meet the instructional needs of various groups in particular subject areas during a specific time period. Many teachers find it useful to think of large blocks of time and the organization of the classroom simultaneously. The plan shown below is an assignment log which indicates one way of organizing for instructional groups in the classroom. Note that this plan is for language arts. In what ways might it be adapted for other subjects?

Table 6.4 *Assignment log showing organization for instructional groups in the classroom*

Whole Class: Conduct a shared reading activity with all students. Read part of a chapter or short story. Challenge students to write an ending. Specific skill developed—prediction derived from facts in short story

Group 1:	Group 2:	Group 3:
Teacher action: Introduce an "asking questions predicting answers" strategy using a short story. Challenge students to use strategy in novel they have been reading independently. Suggest that they should be able to complete learning chart for next group session.	Work on activity from whole class lesson.	Complete activity assigned during whole class.

Take a few moments to ensure that there are no significant issues with students' independent work.

Group1:	Group 2:	Group 3:
Complete question strategy.	Teacher action: Follow up with hypothesizing activity introduced a day earlier. Challenge students to share their hypotheses about characters in novel they are reading. Encourage students to provide evidence to support hypotheses.	Journal writing activity—students write a response to a chapter from a novel they are reading.

Take a few moments to ensure that there are no significant issues with students' independent work.

Group 1:	Group 2:	Group 3:
Complete the specified activity from whole group work that initiated the session.	Journal writing in which students write a response to the novel they are reading. This reader response activity extends their learning.	Share written responses. Teacher Action: Introduce a cloze activity developed from a text students have read. Challenge students to complete the cloze independently then share their answer with two others. Have students work in triads (groups of three) to decide on the best word. Compare student decisions with those of the author (vocabulary development).

Whole class: Have each group share their key learning from the morning activity.

Note that each block of time with a group of students is only about 10–15 minutes, and that time is taken between each instructional block to ensure students are on task. Some teachers who have used this squared format for organizing groups find that they need to alternate which group they work with first each day. One of the key issues with this organizational format is that if the group that is instructionally weak is always left as the last group in the cycle, the teacher and the students are tired by the time they reach the instructional period; changing the organization is often appropriate. Other teachers find they prefer to work only with two groups each day. In these instances, the plan become a four square block. Note that organizing groups like this can be useful in multi-age or split-grade classrooms because the scheme keeps the teacher and students on track in terms of what will happen at various times during the day.

In any day planning, as has been noted before, the move between whole class, small group, and independent work is critical to maintain student interest and provide the necessary opportunities for practice. Independent work ideally should be within the students' ability and skill level, while instructional activities should be designed to help students move to the next level of development.

TIME MANAGEMENT

Time management is a major concern for teachers in any classroom. Teachers recognize that work has to be done within set time limits, on hourly, daily, weekly, and year-long basis. In schools, time itself is marked by reporting periods that tend to influence the ways in which the school year is structured. Many researchers including Rae Raphael (1985) have commented on the structure of the school year as having a rhythm like the one noted in Table 6.5.

Table 6.5 *The school year*

Period	Characteristic
Late August	Anxious preparation and anticipation as the teacher begins to think about the year ahead. How will I organize the classroom? How will I plan the day?
September	The year has started and I have to get to know these students. What are their strengths, their needs? How will I get routines established? What do I have to modify to meet their needs?
October–November	A rhythm has been established. We know each other well. I think that they are progressing well in ____. We have to work on ____. It's almost time to report to parents. What will I say about ____ ?
December	Time to ease a bit. The weather is changing and routines are well established. Students are set in a pattern and we can be creative.

January–February–March	The class has settled in for the long haul. This is the time when we can really focus on the curriculum and building skills. Students are focused and the curriculum itself is the key element in the classroom.
March Break	A much-needed breather for students and teachers.
April–May	The end is in sight. This is another time for reporting and reflection. What remains to be covered? How will those who have not yet mastered the curriculum fare? Work begins to intensify as the pace picks up toward June. In some classrooms, attention is given to standardized testing as students and teachers feel increased pressure.
June	Final evaluations and reporting. How far have students moved in their learning? Anticipation and worrying about the next year and the next class becomes a part of teachers' and students' lives.
July	A much needed break or perhaps summer courses to increase skills. In the first weeks of July during classes, teachers celebrate being away from students and enjoy the company of peers. But by August, once again there is nervous excitement as the first back-to-school ads appear.
August	Nervous anticipation of another first day.

Yet for all of the rhythms that have been documented, teachers also have to be prepared to modify their organization of time. Teachers are under constant pressure created by classes full of lively learners whose needs must come before those of the teacher. Targets set at the beginning of the day or of the term may not be reached, and most teachers learn to expect the unexpected, as indicated in the following scenario.

REFLECTIVE PRACTICE

Mr. Farnal decides to start his grade 3 class with a few challenging problems on the chalkboard. As he enters the classroom, ready to put the first problem on the board, he is met by a bitterly weeping girl accompanied by six of her closest friends who are all talking at once, trying to comfort their friend while at the same time explaining the situation to Mr. Farnal. He has to decide whether the girl is hurt or upset, and at the same time decide how to cope with her as the rest of the class enters the room. Mr. Farnal copes with the upset girl. Meanwhile, the rest of the class discovers there is no "board work" to start the day. The students begin to engage in a number of activities, ranging from quietly chatting, to showing each other work they had done the night before, to gathering around Mr. Farnal's desk to share their versions of the story and/or to simply bear witness. In no time the six girls who came in with their friend are shouting at the other students. Then a student from another class appears with a request from the teacher down the hall for some coloured paper and several children who are not occupied offer to help find the paper. The announcements begin and all classes are to prepare to go to an impromptu assembly in the gym.

Think about the following questions:

• How might you handle time in this instance?
• What would have been a more appropriate routine for the beginning of the day?

MANAGING RESOURCES

Along with managing time, all teachers have to be able to manage classroom resources. The ability to keep track of classroom supplies and materials develops over time, but all teachers need to think through how they will store materials and then distribute them in the classroom as lessons are taught. In most classrooms, teachers face a key challenge when organizing for an art lesson, as often they may need to reorganize furniture, distribute supplies, cover desks with paper to protect them, and so forth. The teacher needs to ensure sufficient time to organize the materials and resources, which is why most teachers arrive at school well before the opening bell and return from lunch early.

Teachers do not have to organize all the materials themselves. Indeed, it is preferable to assist the students to become independent and able to organize their own material. However, to ensure they can achieve this independence, teachers need to think about the routines for each lesson and be able to communicate the routines to students. For example, the teacher may prepare a list on the chalkboard indicating what each student will need for an art lesson. In addition, routines for getting paint or paper ready could become part of classroom management.

CENTRES IN THE CLASSROOM

Centres in classrooms are not just places in which material is stored; each centre should be relevant to the teaching and learning activities. Teachers also need to know why the centre is used in a unit, and in what ways the centre will contribute to student learning. In designing centres for the classroom, think about the following:

• What types of centres will the classroom have? What is the purpose of the centres and what access will student have to them? Will all students have the chance to use each centre, or will they be reserved for only a few? Note that the answers to these questions will determine to some extent the degree to which the centres are successful.
• Where will each centre be located? Earlier in this chapter, there was discussion about centres and safety. How will the positioning of the centres relate to the curriculum and to student needs? Also think about the form of the centre: will it be located on a table, in a box, or on a bulletin board? The physical shape of the centre can contribute to its invitational appeal, as well as to its accessibility and use by students.

- Will the centres be theme-based or will they relate to an on-going aspect of the curriculum?
- Are there instructions for the centres and how might students determine how to use them? Complete a task analysis of the activities students are to compete at the centres. (This is critical in primary classrooms since time at the centres may be limited.)

Any learning centre should be attractive and include both teacher- and student-made materials, as well as commercial ones when appropriate. There should be choice in the tasks at the centre and they should fulfill a teaching role. It is equally important that centre activities be evaluated. Learning centres are seen as places where learning is less formal, and as such they can be good sites for students to practise skills. They tend to be motivational because students view them as a break from the regular routine of the classroom, while at the same time they provide a good supplement to more traditional activities.

In many classrooms, teachers draw a distinction between so-called permanent centres and others that are introduced to support a theme or unit. Permanent centres at all grade levels might include:

- Library reading corner: A place for reference materials, books, and magazines related to themes that are studied in the classroom; usually has comfortable seating and is separated from the mainstream of the classroom.
- Writing centre: Contains a variety of writing material and implements as well as a computer for word processing; also includes thesauruses, dictionaries, and other types of reference materials; in primary grades, may include booklets for children to complete.
- Mathematics centre: A place for challenging activities in mathematics; manipulatives may be stored here as well.
- Theme centre: An opportunity to extend learning in the thematic unit studied in the classroom; may alternate between science and social studies or other thematic activities.

There are other permanent centres in the kindergarten classroom. Early years' programs tend to be established around less formal opportunities for learning. The permanent centres shown in Table 6.6 are often included in the kindergarten classroom.

Table 6.6 *Essentials for Kindergarten*

Type of Centre	Materials Needed
Blocks	• Large and small blocks in a variety of shapes • Space for storage and toys such as cars/trucks to be used in play • Small blocks such as Lego for use in smaller construction projects
Housekeeping/dress-up	• Child-sized furniture, fridge, stove • Clothes for dress-up • Dolls, dishes, utensils • Can be modified to become a restaurant, store, hospital, etc., depending on the theme
Sand and water	• Containers for sifting, pouring, measuring
Library	• Area for reading books • Many books at children's level • Comfortable seating
Writing and computer	• Materials for writing • Computer(s) with programs designed to facilitate mathematical and literacy development
Discovery	• Science-oriented materials • Magnifying glasses • Reference books
Creative area	• Painting and craft materials • Materials for construction

Note that in kindergarten, all centres can and should be modified as themes are introduced in the classroom. There are also opportunities at each centre to involve children in literacy. For example:

• in the block centre, children can make diagrams and label their constructions
• in the house centre, children can record grocery lists and take phone messages
• at the sand and water tables, children can record their measurements (e.g., how many cups fill a litre container?)

SUMMARY

As can been seen from the information included in this chapter, teachers must cope with many practical issues on a daily basis. Lortie (1979) speaks of classroom teaching as a lonely profession in that teachers work on their own in classrooms without the contact of other professionals, while at the same time they have to make hundreds of decisions each day that have an impact on the lives of their students. Although we speak of schools as learning communities, there is at times a reluctance to share uncertainties and a lack of confidence in the work. Most teachers have backgrounds in specific disciplines and have obviously successfully coped with school, yet there is little to really prepare a teacher for the reality and responsibility that comes with the classroom. A difficult child, for example, either because of behaviour or because of not achieving well, can cause any teacher to have feelings of self-doubt. Yet there is a reluctance to share those feelings or to ask for assistance. All teachers need to remember that talking through these issues can provide advice and insights into different ways to organize and structure the day. At times, inviting a colleague to visit the classroom and provide advice can enable the teacher to see the classroom in a different way. Like the observer in Mrs. Beasley's classroom, colleagues may be able to note something that has remained invisible to the teacher.

Key issues to remember from this chapter are that all classroom organization and management should start at the level of the individual learner. Because the teacher is responsible for all of the students, the teacher's task is large. Organization of time in the classroom is perhaps one of the most critical issues for teachers, yet it can be the issue most often disputed. Finally, when a teacher is well organized, many of the issues that create behavioural problems in the classroom are resolved because the teacher has thought ahead to see when issues might arise.

CHAPTER 6 ACTIVITY

Planning your first classroom

You have been assigned either a grade one or a grade 6 classroom for the coming year. Your principal has allocated $500 to your classroom for purchase of teaching materials and you have just been told that you will be teaching 28 students in a classroom that has space indicated in the diagram below.

You have a choice of 10 small tables and chairs or 28 desks. You have a desk and a filing cabinet. There are no bookcases in the room.

Your task is as follows:

1. Design a classroom plan that makes effective use of space.
2. Suggest how you will use the money the principal has allocated.
3. Develop a wish list for other materials/furniture for the classroom. Have a rationale for your list and prioritize items on it.
4. Outline how your plan relates to effective teaching and learning.
5. Identify the issues that will have an impact on your students from a time and space management perspective.
6. Share your list with a colleague for comments and suggestions.

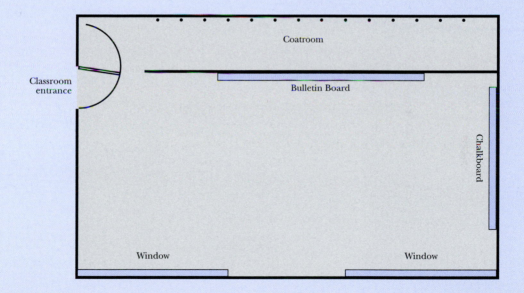

CHAPTER 7

STRATEGIES FOR TEACHING:
The Teacher's Tool Kit

"

What we need is a generation of students who

are fearless in the face of the tentative.

~ *Bob Samples, 1987, p. 222*

"

STUDY OBJECTIVES

The purpose of this chapter is to
- gain knowledge of the skills and strategies associated with effective teaching
- examine the underlying principles of effective classroom management
- explore various dimensions of the questioning process
- help teachers incorporate effective learning and teaching strategies into their classroom practice

INTRODUCTION

This chapter deals with many practical elements that play a part in making the learning environment run smoothly. Attention is paid to classroom management, the development of effective questioning skills, how the classroom can be organized to promote appropriate learning conditions, and instructional strategies and techniques that facilitate teaching and learning. Finally, a detailed description of the integrated day approach is provided to demonstrate how many of these elements can be combined within an effective, active learning environment.

TEACHING STRATEGIES

Teachers require an extensive repertoire of skills to be able to meet the diverse needs of children in the modern classroom. All of these skills work in concert with one another to produce a dynamic pattern that is unique to each teacher and to each classroom. Indeed, this mixture will vary not only from teacher to teacher, but also with individual teachers from year to year.

Some of these factors include:

- personal attitude and management
- classroom management
- questioning skills
- organization strategies
- cooperative learning

PERSONAL ATTITUDE AND MANAGEMENT SKILLS

The Teacher as Leader: Setting and Maintaining the Tone

In any classroom situation, the teacher is ultimately responsible for ensuring that learning occurs for all students. Teachers manage this by thoroughly planning for student involvement, by continually refining their communication skills, by monitoring the teaching–learning process as it occurs, by assessing how well students have learned at the end of the process, and by reflecting on the effectiveness of their role at each stage of this process.

One of the key factors in being an effective teacher is demonstrating a strong commitment to the teaching profession by being enthusiastic toward students and the learning process. Students quickly pick up on whether or not this is evident in the class and reflect this attitude back in their interactions, both with their teacher and with their peers. The powerful impact of a positive learning environment has been well documented, and the teacher plays a crucial role in setting the tone for this to happen (Lewis et al, 1996). Crucial elements such as courtesy, respect, sincerity, acceptance, and enthusiasm can be highly contagious within the classroom setting! The teacher's attitude can have far-reaching effects on how students perceive themselves and how they relate to the learning process in general. When teachers

MORE INFORMATION

For more information on the effect of teacher attitude on learning, see "Student behaviours and teacher approval versus disapproval" by Dan Laitsch (2006) on the companion website.

reflect a more approving attitude toward their students, more positive learning environments result (Laitsch, 2006).

Communication Skills

Since it is the teacher who takes the lead in the teaching–learning process, it must be the teacher who ensures effective communication skills. Some of these include:

- using an effective tone of voice which is varied, well-modulated, clear, and confident
- having clear enunciation and patterns of speech to ensure that intentions are fully understood
- having the ability to focus and sustain attention easily
- using effective language which is appropriate to the age level
- speaking expressively and in an animated fashion to hold interest
- having an overall interactive communication style which encourages active student participation and engagement

Transitions

Another major skill that teachers must develop is the ability to manage the many transitions that occur throughout the school day. Students need specific guidance to manage transitions effectively and smoothly, as topics or subjects change, as activity shifts from one area to another, and as classroom/school schedules intervene. Consistent rules and routines are essential for this to happen. Another key factor in how smoothly transitions are handled is whether or not both the teacher and the students are absolutely clear on what is expected, not only in expectations for behaviour, but also in terms of the procedures to follow. The importance of clear instructions cannot be underestimated. Providing an agenda at the start of the day and charts outlining procedures to follow are strong visual references that will facilitate smooth transitions throughout the school day.

Timing and Pacing

Timing and pacing have powerful effects on how efficiently the classroom functions. Appropriate pacing can set the tone for the effectiveness of any lesson. If students are presented with information that is relevant, and are given opportunities to process it and interact with it, then authentic learning is more likely to occur.

When teachers use effective timing and pacing, lessons flow more smoothly and teachers are able to cover the intended material in the allotted time. When this happens, students do not feel rushed or overwhelmed by the content. It should be noted that the age and stage of the learners influences appropriate timing.

As a practical guideline, try to limit teacher-directed input sessions to a total of 10 to 15 minutes. After this time has elapsed, more and more students will pay less attention to the input and will start to become distracted. Children may learn to be less attentive when they are expected to listen to another person for extended periods of time which are far beyond their natural capacity. In general, the younger the children, the shorter these input sessions should be, since extended sessions run counter to their egocentric nature.

Active Learning

Although this topic has been previously discussed, it is appropriate to mention it again briefly within the context of this topic. Teachers are naturally responsible for establishing the physical layout of the classroom. Encouraging an active learning environment is an important part of their duties. Awareness of student needs and capabilities at various ages and stages provides valuable guidance. Since children in the primary and junior divisions are still very much in their formative years, they need to be actively engaged in many learning activities that will facilitate various aspects of their development; appropriate learning materials are essential to support this. Even older students benefit from "hands on," real-life learning experiences since many of them will not reach a stage of being able to deal with abstract concepts in the absence of concrete referents until much later (Hewitt, 1995).

In addition, setting children's learning—at any age or stage—within a problem solving venue that encourages them to interact with one another and make decisions will enhance their thinking skills (Jensen, 1998; Gardner, 1999). Effective teachers will plan for many of these opportunities at all grade levels.

The Role of Direct Instruction

There is a definite place for direct instruction within the many different approaches that teachers use in their classrooms. When new information is presented and a common base of understanding is required, direct instruction is the mode of choice. All of the skills mentioned previously remain as the foundation to effective direct instruction. Communication skills, organization, timing and pacing, and handling transitions all play a crucial role in providing effective direct instruction.

An effective introduction is one of the most important things to use at the start of a teacher-directed lesson. Sometimes this is referred to as a "hook" or a "grabber." It need not be a lengthy process, but can be accomplished by using a visual image, playing some music, reading a passage of text, or posing a problem to be solved. The purpose of this strategy is to capture the students' attention right from the start and provide them with an anticipatory mindset or context for their new learning. It should serve to capture their interest, activate prior knowledge on the topic, and initiate new thoughts about what is being learned.

The teacher should then present new information in a systematic way so that concepts are clearly and thoroughly developed. Appropriate sequencing of concepts is vital at this step in the instruction. Using visual aids or concrete materials is still a necessary part of instruction so that concepts can be fully understood by students. While not everything can be learned through individual discovery, teacher guidance and the use of concrete materials/examples should still be part of the direct instruction process. Teacher modelling and demonstration can be powerful teaching and learning tools as the teacher gives specific direction to the learning. At various points in the lesson, the teacher can use "scaffolding" to focus attention on specific ideas and develop these further through adroit questioning skills.

At various points throughout the presentation of concepts, the teacher should monitor students and question them carefully to ascertain their level of understanding. Before the students are sent to do some form of independent follow-up or application of the new knowledge at the end of the lesson, it is important to summarize the new content to bring about a sense of closure to the topic. This summary can also help the teacher ascertain the students' readiness to do a task independently.

It is important to mention that teachers will use many of the skills mentioned here not only during sessions with small groups, but also in whole class instruction, and while working with or instructing small groups.

CLASSROOM MANAGEMENT

In recent years there has been a shift away from teachers being primarily disciplinarians within the classroom, toward teachers modelling and teaching students about self-control. One of the most important factors that affects **classroom management** is the relationships that exist within the classroom. In general, teachers set the tone within individual classrooms as they consider how their classroom will function on a day-to-day basis, but the students also contribute to this dynamic. A smooth-running classroom is one in which learning can more readily occur. This does not happen by chance, but demands considerable forethought, planning, and commitment on the part of the teacher, as well as involvement and cooperation on the part of the students. Teachers who are effective classroom managers

- use time as effectively as possible
- implement group strategies with high levels of involvement
- choose lesson formats and tasks conducive to high levels of engagement
- communicate expectations clearly
- implement a system right from the beginning of the year

(Curwin & Mendler, 1999)

Curwin & Mendler's research provides teachers with some interesting insights into student behaviour: (1999). According to their research,

- 80 percent of students will routinely behave properly, no matter what teachers do
- 15 percent of students will misbehave, from time to time
- 5 percent of students will chronically misbehave and respond poorly, in general

The issue for teachers, then, is how to get the potentially wavering 15 percent to join with the behaving 80 percent, rather than with the more predictably rebellious 5 percent.

> *Our challenge is to provide enough structure for the 15 percent, without alienating or over-regulating the 80 percent, or backing the 5 percent into a corner.*
>
> *~ Curwin & Mendler, 1999, p. 28*

GLOSSARY

Classroom Management—a multifaceted process which depends upon an engaging curriculum, student responsibility, appropriate teacher modelling, effective instruction, and management skills to work toward conflict resolution with individuals and the whole class.

Mendler felt that if teachers use an obedience model for addressing classroom management, they risk having the 80 percent lose interest and the 15 percent only temporarily adjusting their behaviour. To accomplish a more positive result, one of the most important things for a teacher to do is to treat the students with respect and work consistently to win them over. This can be accomplished by

• modelling appropriate and desired behaviours
• being open to student input and ideas
• using humour in the classroom to set the tone and diffuse problems
• being consistent in monitoring acceptable behaviours

Why Do Students Misbehave?

The research of Rudolf Dreikurs (1971) provides some interesting insights into the basic reasons why children misbehave. He felt that most reasons behind misbehaviour could be classified under four "Goals of Misbehaviour": attention seeking, power seeking, revenge, and assumed disability. The following section provides brief descriptions of the kinds of behaviour associated with each of these goals.

1. **Attention**: This form of misbehaviour is one that many teachers will face from time to time during their careers. Many children exhibit some form of attention-seeking to some degree or another. It is one of the most common types of behaviour problems, but it is also one of the easiest to rectify.

   Example: Amy constantly engages in behaviour which prompts the teacher to give her repeated reminders of what she should be doing even though Amy is a very capable student. When she is checked on this, the behaviour stops, but only temporarily.

2. **Power**: This kind of misbehaviour can be difficult to deal with in the classroom situation. Children who are seeking power have had their power taken away from them and will typically respond in defiant ways.

   Example: Cameron's mother has a newborn at home and his father is out of the country on a prolonged business project. When Cameron comes into the classroom, he immediately starts to direct the other children in what they should be doing. The children complain to their teacher that Cameron is being very "bossy." When the teacher reminds Cameron of his behaviour, he responds defiantly and a confrontation ensues.

3. **Revenge**: The child who exhibits this kind of misbehaviour may only feel significant when able to hurt others. This is one of the most serious forms of misbehaviour and, in all likelihood, some professional help will be needed to deal with this problem.

   Example: Sean is 9 years old and has a history of confrontations with others. At recess, he goes out to the edge of the playground, takes a small branch from a shrub, and proceeds to sharpen the stick by rubbing it back and forth in the mortar grooves of the brickwork on the school building. He then threatens to stab everyone in the schoolyard.

4. **Assumed Disability** or "**Learned Helplessness**": In this situation, the child's basic self-esteem is at issue. The child has come to feel defeated by whatever he or she is asked to do and perceives himself or herself as a failure, and so gives up trying.

   Example: Bekka gives up easily when a task is even slightly challenging even when it is still within her capability. She ends up taking a long to time to even start a task and, as a result, rarely finishes any assignment. She appears to be very lethargic.

Of these reasons for misbehaviour, the first two, attention and power seeking, are the most amenable to change once the teacher puts consistent responses in place. The last two, revenge and assumed disability or learned helplessness, can be very resistant to change since there are often serious underlying emotional issues that need to be faced first. Most often, the latter two reasons for misbehaviour require professional support and assistance beyond the classroom level for change to be effective and lasting.

Table 7.1 summarizes some key points and appropriate responses for resolving Dreikurs' types of misbehaviour.

Table 7.1 Dreikurs' types of misbehaviour, underlying reasons for the behaviour, and the teacher's responses

	Characteristics	Underlying Reasons	Teacher's Response
Attention	Engaging in repeated forms of inappropriate or annoying behaviour which deliberately calls attention to oneself.	Feels annoyed; lacks confidence and seeks constant boosts to ego to relieve levels of anxiety.	Never give attention when the child is demanding it. Give attention before it turns to attention seeking. "Catch a kid being good!"
	Perception of the child: *"Nuisance."*	Message from the child: *"Look at me."*	*"I like the way you came in so quietly and were kind to…"*
Power	Similar to attention seeking but has greater overall frequency and intensity. Defiant responses from child. Challenges the teacher's authority.	Feels disempowered, angry, defeated, and out of control. Wants others to feel this way too.	Don't argue and don't give in! Give some legitimate or controlled power to the child before it is demanded.
	Perception of the child: *"Stubborn."*	Message from the child: *"I am in charge and you can't stop me."*	*"Would you please do the helper job for me today?"*
Revenge	Deliberately hurts or plans to hurt others, either emotionally or physically.	Deep psychological problems. Has been deeply hurt and lashes out in retaliation.	Never say you are hurt by what the child does. Often outside expertise is needed to make real changes in this behaviour.
	Perception of the child: *"Vicious."*	Message from the child: *"I hurt and I'm going to make you hurt, too."*	*Alert administration early to the need for help.*
Assumed Disability or Learned Helplessness	Passive responses to requests. Feels overwhelmed, helpless, or discouraged.	Basically a serious issue of self-esteem.	Work on building self-esteem. Break tasks down into smaller, more manageable pieces.
	Perception of the child: *"Hopeless."*	Message from the child: *"Don't expect anything of me. I am a failure."*	*Focus on being "success oriented."*

> *Punishment can control misbehaviour, but by itself, it will not teach desirable behaviour or even reduce the desire to misbehave.*
>
> ~ *Faber & Mazlish, 1995, p. 102*

The Importance of Being Proactive

In any classroom management situation, teachers can basically respond in one of two ways: by being **reactive** or **proactive**. Since reactive responses tend to be more emotionally charged and can therefore put one at a distinct disadvantage when dealing with students, it is best to think things through beforehand and have a workable plan for responding to most circumstances. By doing this, teachers are less likely to get drawn into experiences that escalate beyond their control. The key is to deal with an issue or challenge before it becomes a problem; to be proactive rather than reactive.

Proactive teachers are more in control of situations because they

- anticipate potential problems
- involve the students in setting reasonable and manageable guidelines for behaviour
- have a plan of appropriate action to follow
- have alternate approaches to try if certain ones are not effective
- consistently monitor and follow through on potential problems

> *The secret in education lies in respecting the student.*
>
> ~ *Ralph Waldo Emerson*

The statement above highlights one of the most important things that a teacher can do: If teachers treat children with respect, children will give it back tenfold! When teachers model mutual respect in the classroom and it is expected of all parties, more productive levels of learning will result (Lewis et al, 1996). Modelling a respectful, polite tone in interactions, showing compassion and consideration when students are unsure of how to respond, and being enthusiastic about one's profession can go a long way in preventing the development of management issues within the classroom right from the start.

Anticipating Potential Problems

Having an anticipatory mindset is a valuable starting point for planning effective classroom experiences and dealing with classroom management issues. By anticipating potential problems, teachers can predict which areas are most likely to be of concern, and have a workable plan in place to deal with potential problems. This process enables teachers to be proactive in approaching classroom management.

Involvement of Students

One of the most effective and yet easiest strategies to implement in the classroom is to involve the students in devising the rules for how the classroom will be managed. If students are directly involved in creating the rules, they will be more likely to follow them. As suggestions are given by the students, teachers should record them on a chart which can subsequently be posted in the classroom as an ongoing visual reminder and reference. This strategy relates strongly to the whole issue of developing and encouraging autonomous behaviour in students (Kamii, 1991).

Another important aspect of classroom management is Kounin's "ripple effect" (Kounin, 1970). Jacob Kounin, one of the earlier researchers to systematically examine the issue of classroom management, noted that when the teacher focuses attention on the inappropriate behaviour of one student in a straightforward manner and the message is clear that such actions are not acceptable, the behaviour of the whole class is affected. One of Kounin's greatest contributions, however, was his focus on the importance of "withitness"—the degree to which a teacher has a keen awareness of and ability to sense potential issues or behaviour problems in students (Kounin, 1970).

In more recent years, the focus has shifted to address the importance of establishing an atmosphere where there is positive cohesive bonding and a sense of community within the classroom. Relationships within the classroom are recognized for the powerful role they play in determining how smoothly the daily business of the classroom can be accomplished. When all students feel a sense of belonging, they work harder and accomplish more (Lewis et al, 1996).

Having a Plan of Action: Dealing Proactively with Classroom Management Problems

When dealing with classroom management issues, it is essential that teachers have a plan of action for dealing with problems that arise; this is an important part of having a proactive management style. When dealing with problems within the classroom, teachers begin with milder forms of action and gradually increase their responses until a level of success is reached to manage the misbehaviour. Table 7.2 outlines a comprehensive list of strategies to guide teachers in managing student behaviour from the very beginnings of misbehaviour, through the development of persistent patterns of misbehaviour, to misbehaviour that requires more formalized, documented responses.

Table 7.2 *Strategies to guide teachers in managing student behaviour*

The Problems Begins	The Problem Persists	The Problem Escalates
Action: Low Key Responses	Action: The Teacher Focuses	Action: Things Become Formalized
When behaviour first starts to become a problem, the teacher responds initially using low key responses that do not overtly interrupt the progress or flow of the lesson.	When low key responses do not work, more specific strategies must be brought into use.	When all previous attempts fail, an even stronger response is required to bring the situation back under control
Some of these responses include: • Ignoring the behaviour (it may self-correct) • Pausing briefly to focus attention • Pausing and giving 'the Look" • Moving to closer proximity (beside the student) • Making a gesture to indicate what is expected (hand signal) • Saying the student's name	Some of these responses include: • Directing attention to the problem (limited verbal interchange) • Offering a choice (participate or withdraw; now or later) • Applying an implied choice (you mean what you say) • Defusing the power struggle (never argue; your agenda; both save face; time out) • Setting an informal agreement (private chat) • Set boundaries and have an agreement by the end of the meeting.	Some of these responses include: • Formalizing of a contract (outlines specific expectations) • In-school Suspension (Administration takes over)—supervision done by administration staff • Out-of school Suspension (very serious level of response)—results in a specified time away from school • Expulsion (most serious response)—lengthy duration or permanent removal from school
These strategies are not arranged in any hierarchical order but are used according to the individual circumstances.	These strategies demonstrate an increase in the amount of interaction and specificity of instructions. Alert Administration to persistent problems.	These responses are reserved for the most serious behaviour problems. Decisions are made by senior administration.

Guiding principles: It is important to say, "Thank you" to each positive response on the part of the student. It is important for students to be able to maintain their dignity!

Adapted from Dreikurs, 1971; Bennett & Smilanich, 1991

Teacher Responses: Some Basic Tenets of Classroom Management

• **Always treat students with dignity and respect:** Without dignity, students learn to reject school and learning. Teachers might be able to get them to follow the classroom rules, but lose them to anger and resentment. Above all, teachers must maintain or enhance their self-esteem, for example, there should be no sarcasm, put-downs, criticism, scolds, or threats delivered publicly.

- **Engage in and model active listening**. Teachers need to be open to feedback from students and to use "I-messages" to communicate their feelings to students. These messages tend to be less accusatory and reduce the pressure on students, thereby enabling them to "save face," for example, "I prefer that you listen quietly when others are presenting."

- **Keep the lines of communication open**. Teachers should explain why they want something done in a certain way and how students will benefit. Give students some say in the decisions that govern the running of the classroom, for example, "If we all put things back where we found them in the first place, then there would be no missing parts of the game."

- **Teachers should never try to discipline a child when they are angry**. When teachers are angry, it is particularly important to remain calm and keep their dignity. If they react, the situation will likely escalate and the ensuing power struggle will only get worse. Think of this as an opportunity to model appropriate behaviour for the students, for example, "I will talk to you right after class when you have had a chance to think about your behaviour."

- **Use the PEP strategy (Privacy, Eye contact, Proximity) to deliver a corrective message**. Comment quietly (where only the teacher and the student can hear) while maintaining eye contact (subject to culture considerations), in close proximity.

(Curwin & Mendler, 1999)

> **MORE INFORMATION**
>
> For more information on classroom management, see "Rewarding democracy/ class management" by Constance Kamii on the companion website.

REFLECTIVE PRACTICE

Allan has been experiencing some difficulty for about a week in managing his behaviour. Today his anger spills over when he is questioned about why his homework is not done (again). He throws his notebook on the floor and tells his teacher to "get out of my face."

Put yourself in the role of the teacher in this scenario. Think about the following questions:

- How would you interact with Allan?
- What strategies would you introduce to defuse the situation?
- How would you seek to discover the underlying reasons behind his behaviour?
- How would you ensure that this kind of response does not spread to other class members?

QUESTIONING SKILLS

Being good at questioning is one of the most important skills that a teacher must possess. Indeed, most teachers continue to work on this skill throughout their professional careers. Looking at this from the teacher's perspective, or even from outside the profession, the need to focus on this particular skill might seem to be obvious but, due to its powerful influence on student learning, it must be emphasized. No matter how well-prepared teachers may be or how interesting the curriculum, their teaching will not be as effective unless it is accompanied by appropriate questioning techniques to facilitate learning during discussions.

As a profession, teachers are aware of the need to use different kinds of questions as they interact with students. For several decades, Benjamin Bloom's (1956) work has been a definitive guide to assist teachers in this area.

Bloom's Taxonomy

Bloom and his associates identified the following cognitive levels or levels of thinking in hierarchical order (from lowest to highest):

- **Knowledge Level**—able to recognize and recall facts and symbols
- **Comprehension Level**—able to understand, interpret, or summarize ideas in own words
- **Application Level**—able to apply an abstract idea in concrete situations, solve a problem, and relate it to prior experiences
- **Analysis Level**—able to break down a concept into its component parts; able to identify relationships among components; sees cause and effect; sees similarities and differences
- **Synthesis Level**—able to put components together in new and original ways; creates patterns or structures that were not there before
- **Evaluation Level**—able to make informed judgments about the value of ideas or materials; supports opinions and views using standards and criteria

(Bloom et al, 1956)

Questioning and Bloom's Taxonomy

Bloom's research highlighted how the different types of questions that are asked, in turn influence the kind of thinking that is generated in children. A rather disturbing finding from his research indicated that more than 70 percent of the questions that teachers ask on a daily basis are at the lower levels of his taxonomy (Bloom et al., 1956). Thinking at a basic level is encouraged if children are primarily exposed to lower level questions. This kind of questioning can obviously influence whether or not children are able to see beyond simple interpretations of factual information.

Teachers can enhance their questioning ability by becoming skillful at using "scaffolding" techniques as part of their questioning repertoire. In doing so, they enhance children's understanding and assist students in becoming more aware of the interconnections between and among ideas. Through skillful questioning, teachers help students to focus their attention on details, call forth expertise, and see more global connections in their learning. In short, the right kinds of questions and questioning techniques naturally energize the entire learning and teaching process.

Bloom's levels represent the full range of cognitive functioning, up to and including adult levels, and are not necessarily demonstrated by all children. For example, younger children, due to their highly egocentric nature, relatively narrow range of experiences in comparison to older students or adults, and relatively incomplete neurological development, initially focus more on the lower levels of Bloom's Taxonomy. This does not mean that teachers should not ask higher level questions of younger students. It just means that teachers must be sensitive to the fact that younger students will only be able to respond to questions on the basis of their own personal experiences which are, naturally, more limited in this age range. This is, once more, an example of "you can't put an old head on young shoulders." In the later primary grades, complex questions can be included to be applied with greater consistency to more difficult concepts.

The following chart provides an effective reference for teachers to use in improving their questioning skills. It outlines not only the different levels, but also indicates what both the teacher and student should be doing.

Table 7.3 Bloom's taxonomy of cognitive objectives

AREA OF TAXONOMY	DEFINITION	WHAT TEACHER DOES	WHAT STUDENT DOES
KNOWLEDGE	Recalling specific bits of information	Directs Tells Shows Examines	Describes Selects Remembers Recognizes
COMPREHENSION	Understanding material communicated without relating it to other material	Demonstrates Restates Questions Compares Examines	Explains Summarizes Demonstrates Concludes
APPLICATION	Using methods, concepts, principles and theories in new situations	Shows Facilitates Observes Organizes	Solves problems Demonstrates use Constructs Reports
ANALYSIS	Breaking down information into its component parts	Probes Guides Observes Role plays	Discusses Classifies Lists Dissects
SYNTHESIS	Putting together component parts to form a comprehensive whole	Reflects Extends Reorganizes Analyses Evaluates	Discusses Generalizes Relates Compares Contrasts Predicts
EVALUATION	Judging the value of materials and methods; applying standards and criteria	Accepts Reveals criteria Concludes Harmonizes	Judges Disputes Debates Critiques

While each of these levels has a definite role to play in the cognitive functioning of the individual, Bloom felt that problem solving was best suited to the higher levels of application, analysis, synthesis, and evaluation levels.

More Views on Questioning

In many classrooms, teachers use standard questioning triggers such as the "5 Ws" to guide and remind them about varying the types of questions they use with students.

| Who? | Where? | When? | What? | Why? |

MORE INFORMATION

For more information on useful questioning techniques, see "Maximizing learning for all students" by Kathy Checkley on the companion website.

Indeed, these are important elements to remember. All too often, however, the questioning of students stops at these five. Close examination of these types of questions reveals they have mainly one thing in common: With the exception of "Why," the rest of these questioning triggers focus primarily on factual responses. This kind of questioning focuses on **convergent thinking** and on usually eliciting one expected response or "right" answer. If memorizing factual information was all there was to learning, this might be considered an effective strategy. However, since the type of questioning used with students determines and even generates the kind of thinking in which they will engage, it is imperative that teachers be familiar with using higher levels of questions to elicit higher levels of thinking. Therefore, teachers need to ensure that students are challenged, not only to seek out factual details to use as a common base of information, but also to search for different interpretations in giving responses to questions; in other words, to incorporate **divergent** as well as **convergent** thinking into their problem solving repertoire.

As well, teachers need to ask more "process" questions, which are much more divergent in their orientation. For example,

How?	Why?	What if?

The benefits of using these kinds of questions are listed below.

- **"How?"** focuses on the process that is happening.
- **"Why?"** focuses on the reasons behind something or the interconnections between and/or among ideas.
- **"What if?"** focuses on various possibilities if things are tried in different ways.

Convergent questions are not superior or inferior to divergent questions. Rather, the important thing is to ensure that teachers regularly use both kinds of questions in the classroom. Convergent questions serve an essential role in providing students with a common base of specific, factual information from which to pursue their learning in greater depth. Divergent questions serve an equally vital role, however, in providing students with greater insights into the range of relationships and connections that exist between and among ideas. The following example illustrates how using more "process" types of questions can be beneficial to students' learning.

 # PERSONAL STORIES

Enhancing Questioning Skills

A grade 6 class was given the task of designing and making a robot as a follow-up to a unit on "Motion". The robots were to be made from various scrap materials, including gears, springs, washers, screws, nuts, and bolts from the class "Take Apart Centre".* An additional requirement was that the robot had to incorporate some form of motion, tying it to the curriculum unit being studied.

When the robots were completed, each student presented his or her robot to the class, explaining the design and the function of the robot. At the end of each presentation, the class was given an opportunity to ask questions of the presenter. When the presentations began, the class asked very simple and predictable questions of the presenter:

> "**What** job does your robot do?"
> "**Where** would you use your robot?"
> "**When** would you use your robot?"
> "**Who** would use your robot?"

After a couple of presentations, the teacher became frustrated at the lack of depth to the questions being asked, and she called the students' attention to the need to ask more processing questions. They discussed how the questions being asked only required a simple answer, and how these questions could be expanded to promote even higher levels of thinking. The teacher then purposefully demonstrated the use of more divergent questions. Within a very short time, the students were asking more thought-provoking questions and the level of thinking as well as discussion appeared to increase dramatically:

> "**Why** did you design your robot that way?"
> "**How** did you make your robot so it would move back and forth?"

Since they still had some problems generating even more abstract kinds of questions, the teacher demonstrated the following:

> "**What if** your robot had to work in a temperature of 200°C?"
> "**How** would you modify it?"

*The "Take Apart Centre" was an activity provided to give older students experiences to stimulate problem solving and generate interest in individual projects, while enhancing their fine muscle control (a common need for this age level, particularly among boys!). The teacher provided simple tools such as a hammer, pliers, wrenches, screwdrivers, clamps, and safety glasses to assist the students as they dismantled various small appliances or motors. The teacher clipped any appliance cords for safety's sake and provided various containers to hold the inevitable stray pieces to facilitate sorting and organizing the materials. The teacher initially introduced the centre by providing an old alarm clock; from then on, the students provided a wealth of things to work on through the school year.

The examples above illustrate how much more thought is required on the part of both the people asking the questions and those providing the answers when using process-type questions. This also highlights the fact that there are many possible answers for each question, and that the students are required to justify their responses more when they are responding to more complex questions.

In response to this experience, the teacher realized she needed to post reminders—in the form of visual clues—within the classroom to help students remember to ask different levels of questions. This helped promote more student metacognition about their own questioning skills as they became more aware of what they were doing.

It is interesting to note that the teacher also reported enhanced questioning skills on her own part, since she also used the visual reminders to help her vary the kinds of questions she asked.

Another simple strategy that can facilitate appropriate discussions in response to presentations is the use of "Two Thumbs Up and a Wish." This strategy works well for all ages, and requires the students to respond to a presentation by telling the presenter two things that they liked about what was presented and telling the presenter one thing that they wish had been included. This strategy also enables them to be more critical in their thinking while still being positive and supportive of the efforts of their peers.

The Importance of "Wait Time"

Adults spend nearly ninety percent of their time in the interrogative when they are around children—the questions are non-stop.

~ *Bob Samples, 1987, p. 168*

Mary Budd Rowe's (1974) contribution to the whole area of questioning has been invaluable to teachers. Her concept of "wait time" had an immediate effect on the quality of teachers' questioning. According to her research, the average teacher waits less than three seconds after asking a question before asking another question on the same topic. She found that when teachers waited or extended this time frame by as little as from three to five seconds, more students were able to answer the questions and the quality of their responses improved dramatically (Rowe, 1974). Her research is consistent with what is currently known about how the brain functions—the preference on the part of the brain to "mull things over" in its search for meaning and to establish a meaningful context for remembering (Jensen, 1998). In response to this important research, teachers need to

- refrain from rushing in to ask auxiliary questions or "stacking" questions when answers are not immediately forthcoming
- allow for more thinking time for students in the questioning process
- develop more of a tolerance for "dead air" once a question has been asked

Incorporating Cooperative Learning Strategies into Questioning

Today, many teachers incorporate cooperative learning strategies into their repertoire of skills to enhance their questioning even further. For example, by using such effective techniques as **Think–Pair–Share**, teachers are able to focus the students' attention specifically on the question being posed and, in doing so, enhance the responses that students make (Lyman, 1992). This strategy is most effective in that not only does it incorporate appropriate levels of "wait time," but it also encourages greater involvement on the part of the students. The Think–Pair–Share process is as follows:

• Initially, students are asked to **think** about a question individually and are given a short period of time to ponder it on their own.
• Then, they discuss their ideas quietly with a **partner**, who is sitting close by.
• Lastly, they are given opportunities to **share** their ideas with the rest of the class.

Teachers find that using just this simple strategy ensures that no one is left out, that greater attention is focused on the task, and that enhanced involvement is facillitated. Many teachers report that using this strategy virtually eliminates the common response of "tuning out" once someone else has raised their hand and volunteered an answer.

REFLECTIVE PRACTICE

According to Bob Samples, (1987, p. 106) "Children never give a wrong answer... they merely answer a different question. It is our job to find out which one they answered correctly and honour what they know."

Form groups to discuss the merit of Samples' observation. Next think about the following questions:

• How might a teacher identify such a question—i.e., a question that is answered correctly but is not the one that had been posed?
• How could this be explained to the other students?
• This statement may seem to be a contradiction. Why might it be important to address this issue?

ORGANIZATION STRATEGIES

In classrooms today, many different things happen at the same time and classrooms function far more fluidly compared with their earlier counterparts. Less and less classroom time is dominated by the teacher as the central focus at the front of the room—"the sage on the stage" approach. In contrast, many classrooms operate in an atmosphere similar to a busy workshop, with students engaged in small group work or individual projects while the teacher circulates, giving individual or small group instruction and support—"the guide on the side" approach.

This provides a more dynamic flow for how the classroom functions throughout the school day. At times, these changes can generate many questions or even concern on the part of some parents, because these approaches are far removed from what they may have experienced in their own schooling. Therefore, it is essential that teachers ensure parents fully understand these changes, how they are being used, and what the benefits are to the students. As parents become aware of the reasons behind these changes, they develop understanding and, what they understand, they can begin to support.

Teachers recognize that learning happens in a variety of contexts, students need elements of choice in their learning, and individual learning styles must be incorporated into the classroom structure. This leads to an examination of some of these organizing structures.

Different Organizing Structures

Despite changes in how education is handled in various classrooms, some elements remain the same. The important factor is that students need to experience balance in the ways that they learn. Within a balanced approach, students still have information presented to them from time to time as a whole class, they have opportunities to work in small groups, and they have a chance to become engrossed in individual projects. It is important, therefore, to understand some of the different curricular and instructional contexts in which learning can occur.

The Three Ts: Transmission, Transaction, and Transformation

J.P. Miller outlined three different positions for describing curriculum and instruction practices (Miller, 1993).

1. **Transmission**: The transmission approach is typically associated with traditional teaching practices. It has been described as a mechanistic view of teaching and learning which is reminiscent of Skinner's behaviourist views. Within this approach, the student is perceived as a passive receptor of information presented by an outside source or authority. Information is separated into discrete bits and is presented in isolation with little attempt to show any connections between or among ideas. This approach is attractive to some educators since acquisition of knowledge using this approach is more easily measured, tested, and verified. Factual information is the order of the day in this position! The following diagram illustrates the one-way nature of this method of instruction.

Figure 7.1 *Transmission*

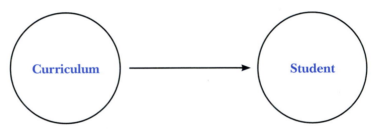

2. **Transaction**: The transaction approach, in contrast, is much more focused on the role of the individual in his or her learning. The focus in this approach is on interaction between the students and the curriculum through problem solving, inquiry, and reconstruction of knowledge. Since interaction with the curriculum is important in this position, the teacher's role is as the conduit for the exchange of information between the child and the curriculum. Assessment involves both awareness of and facility in social interactions, as well as problem solving ability. The following diagram illustrates the interactive nature of this approach.

Figure 7.2 *Transaction*

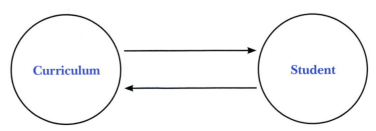

3. **Transformation**: The transformation approach is focused on personal and social change. The child and the curriculum are seen as connected in a holistic manner. Miller saw two strands within this position: humanistic and social. The humanistic aspect is concerned with individual growth and the social is concerned with social change. Thus, growth of self and self-actualization are key components. Assessment in this position is expanded to include self- as well as peer-evaluation, and using reflection as a valuable skill. The following diagram illustrates the dynamic nature of this position.

Figure 7.3 *Transformation*

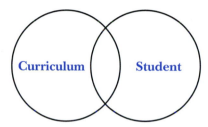

Miller did not intend that these three positions necessarily be exclusive of one another, but rather that each one be more inclusive than the previous one(s). For example, the transmission position of basic recall of knowledge could be incorporated into the transaction position as a necessary part of the problem solving process, and the more holistic transformation position could incorporate the transaction position into a broader context or world view. The following diagram illustrates the interrelated nature of Miller's three positions.

Figure 7.4 *Interactive nature of the three positions*

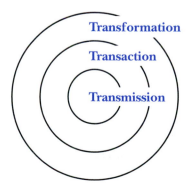

Miller's research provides teachers with an important backdrop against which to consider different methods of instruction: whole class, small group learning, cooperative learning, and individual learning.

Whole Class Instruction

Presenting information to an entire class at the same time does have some obvious benefits, in terms of delivery.

- It is a fairly efficient means of presenting a common message to a group of students within a relatively short time frame.
- It can serve to give the appearance of covering a lot of information quickly.
- It can be perceived as an effective use of the teacher's time since lessons, in theory at least, are considered to be covered and therefore will not have to be taught again.

There are, however, some limitations to using this approach, especially if it is used as the primary source of teaching instruction in the classroom. Of prime importance is the fact that such an approach does little to meet the different needs of individual students. This approach makes several serious assumptions.

- It assumes that all students are ready to receive the same information at the same time.
- It assumes that the students all have similar background experiences in terms of having already established a meaningful context for their learning.
- It assumes that all students learn in exactly the same way.

In addition, there are other potential areas of concern.

- Problems with classroom management are more likely to arise when students are sitting passively and are not actively involved in the learning process.
- Attention to the content will not be as keen when students are only asked to answer the teacher's questions instead of generating some of their own.
- Individuals may be more able to hide their lack of understanding when working in a large group setting.
- A few students can dominate and leave other students out of the class discussion.

All of these problems are more likely to arise when the instruction takes place in a whole class setting, where students play a much more passive role. When information is delivered in this manner, it is reflective of the "Transmission" position (Miller, 1993).

Small Group Learning

Learning in a small group setting has some obvious benefits in terms of student learning.

- Students are called upon to participate more frequently within a smaller group.
- Students feel less threatened working within a small group.
- A spirit of cooperation and support is facilitated more easily.
- More direct involvement in the learning is enabled.
- More problem solving is encouraged.
- Better use of learning materials is evident since these can be shared more equitably.
- Opportunities are provided for different strengths to be developed and validated.
- Leadership skills are facilitated and developed.
- Social skills are practised and learned as students interact with one another.

This approach is not used all the time, but is incorporated to address those learning experiences that can benefit from small group interaction. It is particularly noteworthy that this approach provides many instances where individual needs, strengths, and interests can be accommodated.

Some areas that need to be considered so that small group learning function effectively include the following:

- Expectations for behaviour must be absolutely clear.
- The group's task must be carefully explained.
- Appropriate learning materials must be available and accessible to the students.
- Careful, consistent monitoring and interacting on the part of the teacher must be a prominent feature.
- Social skills must be taught and modelled before small group work begins.

Within a small group setting, students are engaged in more interactive learning. When learning occurs in this manner, it provides an appropriate focus for the development of the "Transaction" position (Miller 1993).

COOPERATIVE LEARNING

There can be several different responses in terms of interaction. Basically, interaction can be competitive, individualistic, and cooperative. (Johnson & Johnson 1991)

While most adults would support a competitive learning environment, **competitive** interactions do not always result in positive outcomes since there is usually only one winner, and therefore many losers. A major difficulty with competition is that, inevitably, competition can produce conflict (Yardley, 1991).

Individualistic interactions occur when individuals pursue personal goals on their own. While this can result in individual excellence for some, it does little to foster the necessary interactions and cooperation that expose learners to the ideas of others and develop the social skills that enable all people to function better in society.

Cooperative interactions, in contrast to the other two, promote interdependent goal achievement and foster concern for the well-being of others (Johnson & Johnson, 1991).

It is alarming that, in the current educational scene, more emphasis is being placed on the delivery of a very specific curriculum and the high levels of narrowly focused accountability that accompanying such approaches. As a result, many classrooms are organized primarily for competitive-individualistic learning. The challenge, then, is for educators to balance this situation by incorporating a wider range of experiences to enhance children's learning through character development and encourage development of broader world views.

What is Cooperative Learning?

One of the major characteristics of cooperative learning is that it provides a planned situation in which students are helped to cooperate with and support one another in their learning. In addition, when people work together, they learn different kinds of communication skills—those which have more of a process orientation. Cooperative learning is characterized by the following features:

- It is organized in mixed ability (heterogeneous) groupings.
- Students work toward a common goal.
- It is success-based (for all).
- The overall focus is on academic improvement.

Skills that are taught in cooperative learning include

- leadership
- decision-making
- trust-building
- communication
- conflict management

(Johnson & Johnson, 1991)

Johnson & Johnson (1991) proposed the following mnemonic device to help people remember the necessary components of a cooperative learning experience.

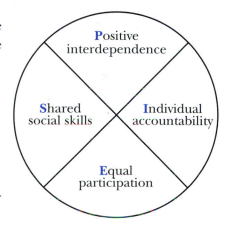

Positive interdependence
Individual accountability
Equal participation
Shared social skills

As an addendum to this reminder, Spencer Kagan, cooperative learning guru, quipped, "Everyone loves **PIES!**"

To facilitate cooperative learning in the classroom, experts recommend that about 25 percent of class instructional time be devoted to cooperative learning (Kagan, 1992). It should also be noted that unless these four main characteristics are in evidence, then the experience may be group work but it is not cooperative small group learning

The following are but a few examples of some cooperative small group learning strategies:

- Round Robin—students give input, in order, by proceeding in a specified direction around a group.
- Jig Saw—students start out in home groups where they assume a role of becoming a specialist in one aspect of a topic, on behalf of their group. They move to a mixed group with representatives from all other groups where they receive specific input and become

specialists in one area. Then they return to their home group to teach their home group members about this part of the information from their area of expertise. Other group members share until everyone has learned all information from all the experts in their home group.

• Numbered Heads Together—a group is established and members number off. Sharing is done on the basis of calling out random numbers of group members.

What Does Cooperative Learning Look, Sound, and Feel Like?

- sitting close to one another

- feeling responsible for myself and others

- discussing a task together

- sharing learning materials

- trying out different roles

- working toward a common goal

- being accountable on an individual basis

- using social skills

- feeling good about myself and my contributions

- sharing leadership

- helping others and being helped

- sharing responsibility

- caring about my classmates

- helping everyone learn

- recognizing that we all have different strengths

Benefits of Cooperative Group Learning

A growing body of research has identified the many benefits to student learning when cooperative learning approaches are used. In particular, low-achieving and average students seem to derive the greatest benefit (Kagan, 1992; Johnson & Johnson, 1991; Bennett et al, 1991). In addition to achievement, there seems to be a basic need that is answered by using cooperative learning approaches.

The following benefits can be derived from using cooperative learning strategies in the classroom:

• Improved academic achievement
• Greater motivation to learn
• More effective problem solving strategies
• Curriculum related to interests, life experiences, and values
• Development of communication skills
• Use of higher levels of thinking

- Greater acceptance by peers
- Awareness of own strengths and weaknesses
- Enhanced active involvement in own learning
- Development of more positive attitudes toward self and others

(Johnson & Johnson, 1991; Bennett et al, 1991)

> Schools should be a place where students help one another to become who they are, to achieve all that they can, and to accomplish this in an atmosphere of caring and support.

The Goals of Cooperative Learning

Within cooperative learning groups, students engage in interactive learning which often replicates real-world experiences and, in doing so, facilitates the development of heightened social responsibility. When learning occurs in this manner, it provides an appropriate venue for the development of Miller's "Transformative" position (1993). Learning where transformation is the goal can be incorporated into many different learning environments and approaches. Sometimes, this requires great patience on the part of the teacher since this degree of change may be difficult to ascertain within the confines of a single academic year. In some cases, it may take years for this kind of change to become evident.

MORE INFORMATION

For more information on cooperative learning, see "Cooperation works!" by Dianne Augustine on the companion website.

Individual Learning

In addition to learning in both large and small groups, students need to spend time following their own interests and working independently. This will provide them with opportunities to delve into areas of specific interest, to develop perseverance in pursuing learning to a degree that reflects not only each individual's temperament but also their preferred learning style, and to bolster individual self-esteem and level of confidence. Often this can be effectively accomplished by using individual written contracts made between the student and the teacher which outline specific goals, timelines, and expectations for both parties.

When students work on individual projects, some form of monitoring system must be put in place so that steady progress toward goals and timely completion of all work can be ascertained. Often teachers

develop a tracking sheet which can be quickly checked by both the student and the teacher. Individual work also provides unique opportunities for students to engage in meaningful self-reflection, and the provision of forms, prepared by the teacher in conjunction with the student, become valuable tools to facilitate awareness of strengths and areas for improvement.

The important thing to remember is that all students benefit from having balance in the kinds of groupings they experience. In this way, their learning styles, interests, and preferences are all taken into account in the teaching-learning process. Jot down the advantages and disadvantages of whole class, small group, and individual learning. Share your ideas with members of your class.

THE INTEGRATED DAY APPROACH

It is important to consider how these ideas and approaches can be combined and demonstrated in a practical sense within the classroom. Over the years, many different approaches have been experimented with to determine methods which enable students to become more involved in their learning, more independent in their thinking, more empathetic in their interactions, and more creative in their problem solving. One approach that has met with success is the integrated day.

In the integrated day approach, the flow of the day centres on children

- making choices about what and how to learn
- asking and pursuing their own questions and interests under the guidance of the teacher
- working cooperatively with others in a workshop atmosphere
- tracking their own choices throughout the day
- taking responsibility for their learning
- reflecting on their own learning as well as the learning of others

When teachers make a concerted effort to involve students as active participants in how the classroom functions and in becoming a community of responsible learners, the integrated day can be an exciting next step. In addition to fostering autonomy, this approach sets learning within a more meaningful context where all aspects of learning are seen as being interconnected. Many different life skills can also be learned within the integrated day approach.

RATIONALE FOR USING THE INTEGRATED DAY

When teachers set out to plan what they will do with the learners in their classrooms, the instructional approaches they select are related directly to the individual teacher's own metacognitive processes. How a teacher thinks, conceives, and organizes knowledge is reflected in the interpretations and assumptions that underlie the actions taken within the classroom.

The content of planning activities must be based on a philosophy of how children learn, for they are the starting point. Regardless of how much time has been spent on developing a curriculum document or how much detail has been put into the topics for each subject area, if it is not developmentally appropriate, personally meaningful, or inherently interesting to a particular age level, it will not be effective and will not truly be learned.

A well-grounded, working philosophy of education enables teachers to coordinate and integrate all the planned activities so the learners perceive them as being useful, relevant, and interconnected. Once this context for learning has been established, the philosophy leads to consistent approaches used across all curriculum areas. Consistency is essential for successful learning over time since this is the framework that makes learning predictable and stable. Such an approach focuses on a holistic philosophy of learning that facilitates the development of the whole child. The whole child is considered to include all aspects of human growth and development (Eisner, 2005; Miller, 1993; Noddings, 2005).

> *Just what does it mean to care for the whole child? The term is partly metaphorical but the implications are clear. First, it means that those of us in education try to recognize the talents that individual children possess and to create an environment that actually fosters potentialities. We are not in the business of canning beans. We are interested in helping them become who they are.*
>
> ~ *Elliott Eisner, 2005, p. 16*

The integrated day approach has been used successfully in many classrooms across the country. It embodies many of the precepts already discussed earlier in this textbook. The basic philosophy of the holistic curriculum is evident in the practical ideas described, and it provides a working example of how such philosophy can be put into action—in short, it demonstrates Praxis (the connection between theory and practice)!

The following description outlines, in detail, one teacher's attempts to implement an integrated day approach to facilitate children's learning, growth, and development across various dimensions, and to bring current research to life in the classroom setting.

PLAN SHEETS: A METHOD OF PLANNING, IMPLEMENTING, ADJUSTING, AND TRACKING IN THE INTEGRATED DAY

The planning/tracking sheets in figures 7.8 and 7.9 were initially developed and used in grades 1 and 2 to facilitate learning in an integrated day approach. As time went on and different approaches were tried, discarded, or adapted, modifications were made to the original sheet and it was adapted for use by other teachers at the grade 2 and grade 3 levels. Eventually, it was even expanded to serve as daily planning sheets for use in the junior division—with more detailed information added to account for the more specific curriculum load or content covered with older students.

Evolution of the Plan Sheets

At the beginning of the school year, when the children came in on the first day, they were asked to look around and see what activities were available in the classroom for them to do. This provided the children with an opportunity to familiarize themselves with the layout of the classroom and to begin to think about what activities might be of interest to them. Once this familiarization was completed, they were directed to sit on the carpet at the front of the classroom.

The teacher proceeded to lead a discussion of what they had observed and, cooperatively, they created a "To Do" chart outlining all the activities they thought were available in the classroom. As each activity was recorded on a chart in word form, the teacher also quickly drew a picture to symbolize each activity. Thus, the children had not only a word to represent the activity, but also a picture clue to help them "read" the list of activities. In addition to the word and picture, the teacher elicited input from the students about how many students they thought could comfortably work at each activity and stick figures were drawn beside each item on the chart as a further visual reference. Incorporating input from the children was essential to ensure they had some ownership of the rules governing use of the activities. The chart was done on a long narrow strip of chart paper which could be added to as new activities were introduced throughout the school year. It also provided the children with a quick visual reference to reinforce the routines for each activity (see Figure 7.5).

It was interesting to note how many children, even from the very first day of school, began to use this list as a source of words in their early ventures into reading and writing. These words and pictures were part of the overall philosophy for the classroom where children were immersed in a language-rich environment which they had helped to create.

Figure 7.5 *Chart of available choices and activities*

- **word label**
- **pictorial clue**
- **number at each centre**

The weekly planning sheets were ultimately derived from this initial list (see figure 7.5). After a few days of using the group chart as a reference, and once the teacher was sure the students were confident in using the reference chart, the teacher transferred the information from the chart onto a single page. This became the individual plan sheet, and the children were then taught specifically how to use it. Since the children had been part of the process of creating the initial categories from which the plan sheets were ultimately derived, they had strong feelings of ownership and personal connections to the sheets right from the start. Therefore, use of plan sheets became a natural outgrowth of what had been initiated from the first day of school.

The basic plan for use of the daily plan sheets was as follows:

- The teacher distributed individual plan sheets at the start of each day.
- Students took their plan sheet with them to various activities throughout the day and marked off activities as they were completed.
- Plastic sleeves were used to protect the plan sheets.
- Plan sheets were collected at the end of the day and the teacher entered new selections in preparation for the next day.

Some Specific Points on the Use of the Plan Sheets

1. The teacher partially filled out the plan sheets the night before, indicating the "musts" or required tasks for the day, from the teacher's perspective (see Figure 7.6).

These tasks were indicated in ink so that the tasks assigned by the teacher would be distinguishable from the choices that the children made (indicated in pencil). Once the children completed a task set by the teacher, they took the sheet to the teacher to be checked off and initialed. The following checking system was used.

Figure 7.6 Variation in use of check marks

 checkmark in ink = assigned by teacher as a "must"
checkmark in pencil = chosen by the student

 checkmark cross-checked by the child or the teacher = task completed

 checkmark cross-checked and initialized by the teacher = checked by the teacher

This method worked well since the plan sheets provided a strong visual indication of what had been completed. The teacher could tell at a glance which required tasks had been completed, which had been checked, and which were still incomplete at any given point during the school day. The teacher could also quickly tell if a child needed to be reminded to work at specific tasks at various points during the day, for example, some children needed to be prompted to complete at least one task before recess.

This approach also enabled the teacher to fill out the plan sheets with each child's particular learning needs in mind. For example, if a certain child had poorly developed fine muscle control, the teacher could subtly direct the child to those activities that would provide the necessary background experiences to encourage development in that particular area, for example, activities with sand, clay, blocks, puzzles, etc.

2. Plan sheets were given out first thing in the morning and assigned tasks and possible choices for tasks were discussed.

The children were assembled on the carpet at the start of each day and all of the possible choices were discussed. Any new activities or additions to the program were discussed and routines explained/re-iterated carefully at this time before the children went to their first activity for the day. They were taught that they could either start with a "must" or with a choice of their own for their first activity. The teacher found it particularly beneficial to have the children commit verbally to where they would start their day. This served to emphasize to the children that decision making was an integral part of the program and that it was valued. This also provided the teacher with the opportunity for some form of input in case too many children wanted to start at the same activity. A gentle reminder of the number of people allowed at each activity was often enough to divert a potential problem.

Since the children had participated in establishing these guidelines, they were more amenable to following their own rules. Another key factor that emerged for the children was that since these activities were available to them throughout the day, there was less pressure for them to get to a specific activity right away. In this way, a calm flow to the school day was established and reinforced.

As well as taking their plan sheets with them to each activity, the children had a "tent" name card. In a setting where all of the work surfaces were used in common and no one had their own desk, this designated their own personal working space on a temporary basis, and resulted in fewer problems over territory. The name cards served a dual purpose in that they were used to save a space at a specific activity if the teacher called an individual to a small group session. Children were less likely to be upset at being called away from an activity they had chosen if they knew their place would be saved for them when they returned. Figure 7.7 indicates how these name tents changed over time, from name, to phrase, to sentence.

Figure 7.7 Evolution of name tents

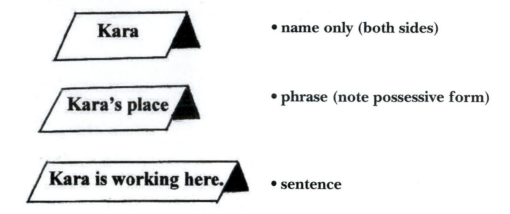

• **name only (both sides)**

• **phrase (note possessive form)**

• **sentence**

As the children began their initial tasks, the teacher circulated and carefully monitored the beginning of the day, noting which children were able to handle choices wisely (with respect to time as well as type of activity) and which children needed more guidance or direct assistance. When some children were reluctant to choose or didn't stay very long at an activity, the teacher quietly limited some of the choices until they felt more comfortable in making choices for themselves. This raises another important issue. If children are not used to making choice for themselves, it is wise to limit the number of choices available until they are more comfortable with choosing from a full range of activities.

Figure 7.8 shows what a plan sheet looked like when the children received it at the start of the day. It contains checkmarks written in ink by the teacher, indicating tasks that must be completed at some point during the school day. This provided the children with a clear framework to guide their activities and choices.

3. Once things were running smoothly, the teacher would call small groups or individuals to meet for specific curriculum input or to hear individuals read.

As the children independently worked on their tasks, the teacher made observations and recorded information about various children.

At intervals, individual children would come up to the teacher to have their work or plan sheet checked, to ask for assistance on a task, or to check on a choice. The teacher was able to accommodate these ongoing interruptions by requiring that

- no more than two children come up at a time
- they wait quietly until a child has finished reading aloud to the teacher or the teacher has finished interacting with/teaching a group
- they whispered their request in her ear so that the group or individual was not disturbed (except for urgent requests)

At regular intervals, the teacher would break from the teaching tasks outlined above and check on the progress of the whole group, as well as that of individuals. In this way, the children did not have to wait too long for attention to their needs, and the teacher could monitor their choices on a regular basis throughout the day.

Just before recess, the teacher did a quick check of plan sheets to see who had completed at least one of their "musts," who had not started any yet, or who had forgotten to record what they had done so far. Gentle reminders to individuals about requirements were given at this time so that things could continue to progress appropriately right after the recess break. See Figure 7.9 for a sample of a plan sheet where the children recorded their choices and indicated tasks they had completed.

The same procedure continued throughout the rest of the day. Sometimes the teacher might call the entire class to the carpet and do a teacher-directed lesson—for example, story reading, introduction of a new activity and appropriate routines to accompany it, specific curriculum content, etc.

4. At the end of the day, the children reassembled on the carpet to discuss how the day had gone and hand in their plan sheets. The teacher did a final check to ensure that all "musts" had been completed for the day.

After the children left for the day, the teacher reviewed the plan sheets to see the choices that the individual children had made and checked the "musts" (indicated by an asterisk on the plan sheet) for the next day, based on whether or not the children had chosen a balance from the kinds of activities available. In this way, the teacher was made aware of, and was able to quickly address, individual needs. For example, if a child consistently chose just one kind of activity, the teacher would select an activity of a different type as a "must" for the next day so the child's learning would be more comprehensive; for example, if a child had chosen sand as an activity for two days in a row, the teacher might check the listening centre as a "must" (and vice versa). This "checking" process was not particularly burdensome, and usually only took about 15–20 minutes to complete at the end of the school day.

On the sample planning sheet that follows, there are numbers listed after the headings for **Language Arts (2), Mathematics (1), and Creative (1)**. These numbers indicate the minimum number of activities the students were expected to do/choose in each of those subject areas each day. In addition to these, regular scheduling of topics in Science and/or Social Studies were checked in the section at the bottom of the plan sheet.

Two of the planning sheets illustrate the process used in a grades 1 and 2. The first one has been filled out by the teacher in preparation for the start of school day (Figure 7.8). The second one illustrates the range of activities assigned, chosen, and completed by a grade 1 child (Figure 7.9), and indicates what the typical input and choices by the student and the teacher would look like at the end of the school day/ week. A third planning sheet is also included that was developed for use at the junior level (Figure 7.10). Regardless of which grade level is using the plan sheets, the basic principles remain the same. Children are guided to make choices and take responsibility for recording what they do and what work has been completed. By using a flexible yet consistent framework such as this, even very young children can learn to make appropriate choices and track them while older students can develop autonomy in being almost totally responsible for their own learning. It should be noted that using plan sheets in the junior grades requires providing more teacher input and structure, especially at the beginning, due to the heavier content load and increased expectations evident at the junior level.

Figure 7.8 *Plan sheet (Grade 1): Set up by the teacher for the first day of the week.*

NAME:			WEEK OF		
Daily Work	Monday	Tuesday	Wednesday	Thursday	Friday
Helper Job ☺					
Library 📚					
Gym 👟🏓🕐		✓		✓	
Music ♫	✓	✓	✓	✓	✓
LANGUAGE ARTS (2)					
language lesson*					
silent reading ☺📖					
reading to … 👤📖👤					
story writing 📄✏	✓				
printing/writing 📖✏					
language games 🔤⌨					
book corner 📖🐛					
puzzles 🧩					
listening centre 🎧	✓				
puppets 👥					
computer 🖥					
filmstrip 🎞					
word hospital 📦					
MATHEMATICS (1)					
math lesson*					
math games 🎲📖					
centre work ⊙⊙	✓				
paper/book 📄✏					
CREATIVE (1)					
lessons (techniques)*					
painting ✏🖼					
cut and paste ✂					
picture making ✏📄					
plasticene ☁	✓				
chalkboard AaBb					
blocks ⬜⬜					
LEGO 🧱					
toys 🚂					
sand/water					
SOCIAL SCIENCES					
lesson/discussion*					
centre work 🔍📺					
paper/book 📄✏					
walk/excursion 👫					
Comments:					

Figure 7.9 Plan sheet (Grade 1): Selections by the teacher and the student completed by the end of the week.

NAME: WEEK OF

Daily Work	Monday	Tuesday	Wednesday	Thursday	Friday
Helper Job ☺	X				
Library 📚		X			
Gym		X		X	
Music 🎵	X	X	X		X
LANGUAGE ARTS (2)					
language lesson*		X ✓		X ✓	
silent reading ☺📖	X	X		X	X
reading to …		X ✓	X ✓		X ✓
story writing	X ✓		X ✓		X ✓
printing/writing					
language games			X		X
book corner		X		X	
puzzles			X		
listening centre	X			X	
puppets	X				
computer					
filmstrip			X		
word hospital	X	X	X	X	X
MATHEMATICS (1)					
math lesson*		X ✓		X ✓	
math games			X	X ✓	
centre work	X ✓			X ✓	X ✓
paper/book		X ✓	X ✓		
CREATIVE (1)					
lessons (techniques)*		X ✓		X ✓	
painting		X			
cut and paste	X				
picture making				X ✓	
plasticene	X		X		
chalkboard					X
blocks			X		X
LEGO	X				
toys		X			
sand/water				X ✓	
SOCIAL SCIENCES					
lesson/discussion*	X ✓		X ✓		X ✓
centre work		X		X	X ✓
paper/book	X ✓			X ✓	
walk/excursion			X		

Comments: *Choosing broad range of activities— follow through*

© Wendy Auger, 1980.

Figure 7.10 Plan sheet for use at the junior level.

Name:					Week of:					
Reading					Writing					
M.					M.					
T.					T.					
W.					W.					
Th.					Th.					
F.					F.					
Conference:					Conference:					
Mathematics: $2\overline{)486}$ $\frac{1}{6}$					Language Skills:					
M.					M.					
T.					T.					
W.					W.					
Th.					Th.					
F.					F.					
French: oui non aujourd'hui					Music: ♫					
M.	T.	W.	Th.	F.	Art:					
					Phys. Ed:					
Social & Environmental Studies:					Activities:					
M.					M.					
T.					T.					
W.					W.					
Th.					Th.					
F.					F.					

© *Wendy E. Auger, 1983.*

5. Assessment: The information was used to provide a very comprehensive look at how the children were progressing in their overall development.

It is important to look at how to manage the data generated by the plan sheets. At the end of each week, the plan sheets were filed in the children's individual files—the children were taught how to do this task for themselves! By the end of the month, there was a collection of at least four plan sheets, per student, in each file. In addition, samples of typical work, photos of three-dimensional constructions, and artwork were included in each file. All work samples were dated using a date stamp (another task the children enjoyed doing).

Analyzing the Data

At the beginning of the last week of each month, the teacher would take home five or six files every night and examine them in detail to note any issues, problems, or patterns of behaviour that were evident in the plan sheets or work samples. By following this process, all of the children's files were examined, in detail, by the end of each month. The plan sheets were examined in terms of

• patterns of behaviour
• specific choices
• range of choices
• responsibility in recording and completing all tasks

Work samples were examined with respect to

• indications of developmental progress
• quality of work
• indication of understanding
• creativity and uniqueness

The teacher recorded information from the sheets and samples, in point form, in the individual learner profiles. This information was combined with the teacher's anecdotal notes from observations to form a comprehensive picture of overall patterns of growth and development. It also provided information on how the children were functioning within this particular format.

At the beginning of the next month, the plan sheets for the previous month were put together and, if necessary, the teacher copied any sheets she wanted to keep as an ongoing reference for specific purposes (for example, unusual patterns of growth, development, unique responses, evidence of a major breakthrough in learning, etc.). Then, the plan sheets for the month were sent home to the parents in a special envelope. These sheets provided the parents with tangible evidence about what their children were doing at school on a daily basis, and also provided an opportunity for the parent and child to discuss progress on a regular basis.

The parents really enjoyed this form of ongoing communication and became a lot more supportive of active learning approaches, in general, once they had a deeper understanding of what was happening in their child's classroom. They found the pictorial record of what their child was choosing to do particularly enlightening, and commented that they learned a lot about their child as they talked about what they had been doing each day and how they had made specific choices. Many parents shared the sentiment that, "It is like getting a report on my child's progress every month… and it is outlined, graphically, in terms that I can really see and understand."

BENEFITS OF THE INTEGRATED DAY APPROACH

By providing an easily-managed structure for the children to operate within, the teacher was free to

- work with individuals and address individual needs
- observe and record evidence of the children's learning
- have tangible proof in visual and written form of what the children were choosing to do
- learn firsthand how responsible the students were at making their own choices and at handling tasks set for them by others

All of this became part of the record-keeping process and development of learner profiles which were ultimately shared with parents at regular interviews. The children's own plan sheets presented a wealth of information about their strengths, needs, choices, and patterns of growth over time.

Some Final Thoughts on the Integrated Day

The development of this system or process did not happen overnight, but took specific teaching, consistent monitoring, and ongoing guidance in order to run smoothly. It was, however, initially surprising for the teacher that a relatively simple procedure could result in such incredible results, even initially with this group of young learners. Indeed, all parties involved in this process derived enormous benefits from this approach.

The children rapidly became independent, responsible, and confident learners. As they exchanged ideas and made choices, they became more aware of the interconnections between and among ideas to which they were exposed. This was a real life example of what Constance Kamii described in her work on autonomy (Kamii, 1991).

The teacher became re-energized and excited about teaching in a way that was truly addressing individual learner needs. In the process of doing this, she found that she had developed greater insights into the subtleties of the teaching–learning process itself.

And finally, the parents became more aware of what was happening in their children's classroom, more conversant with the benefits of active learning approaches, and more supportive of their children's overall learning.

All in all, everyone came out a winner when using this approach. Children felt secure working in a predictable framework, and the teacher had an enhanced awareness of what her students were doing and learning.

 # REFLECTIVE PRACTICE

A Relevant Myth

According to Greek mythology, there was a very cruel innkeeper by the name of Procrustes who compelled weary travellers to stay overnight at his inn with the promise of good food and a sleep in a special bed. Procrustes told them that the bed had the remarkable quality of being able to match the length of whoever slept on it. In actuality, the iron bed was adjustable and he would arbitrarily determine how long or how short the bed would be for each person. If they were too short, then he would have them stretched to fit the bed and if they were too long, he would amputate their appendages until they did fit. In the end, Procrustes met his end when Theseus, as one of his challenges for becoming a hero, fatally adjusted him to fit his own bed.

Think about the following questions:

- If an arbitrary standard is set for all children to reach within a narrowly defined time frame, are we, in effect, engaging in Procrustean bed tactics?
- For children, what are the potential problems associated with this approach?
- Does a "one size fits all" approach work if the ultimate goal of educators is to have all children succeed in their learning?

SUMMARY

This chapter presented some interesting challenges to teachers' perceptions and beliefs about teaching and learning. Basic notions about proactive classroom management skills were explored. The importance of appropriate instructional techniques such as questioning skills, different orientations to teaching and learning, the use of various groupings, and the overwhelming benefits of cooperative learning were examined. Lastly, a detailed example of the integrated day was presented as a practical alternative for bringing to life many of the ideas presented both in this chapter and in the initial section of this text.

Above all, it is important to remember that just as children will differ greatly from one another, so will the programs that they need to optimize their learning, including the teaching strategies that are used.

© Wendy Auger 1981. (Illustrated by S. Maidens)

CHAPTER 7 ACTIVITY

Targeting Effective Strategies

Using the "target" format, choose one of the topics listed below and write the topic name in the centre of the target. Working individually or in a group, fill in the spaces on the outer ring of the target with detailed information, identifying key concepts about the chosen topic. Be prepared to share this information with the whole class.

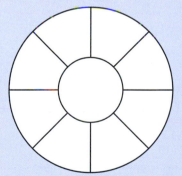

Topics:
Questioning	Bloom's Taxonomy
Groupings	Wait time
Transmission	Cooperative learning
Transaction	Transformation
Classroom management	Integrated Day

Some guiding questions:

• What are some ramifications of using simplistic modes of questioning?
• How might Miller's "3 Ts" be implemented within the classroom?
• How can cooperative learning strategies enhance student learning?
• How does teacher attitude affect classroom management?

CHAPTER 8

THE CURRICULUM:
Organizing Pieces
of the Puzzle

"*Fellow educators—are we not lost? Do we know where we are, remember where we have been, or foresee where we are going?*"

~ Huebner, 1999, p. 231

STUDY OBJECTIVES

The purpose of this chapter is to
- examine the differing views (orientations) of curriculum
- review curriculum research
- study the curriculum review, development, and implementation cycle
- learn how to map the curriculum
- explore problem-based learning
- differentiate between technical rational approaches to curriculum and those that are more transformative

INTRODUCTION

This chapter raises questions about the shape of the curriculum in a democratic society. If, as has been noted throughout this book, people are naturally curious learners, then education can either develop or stifle the inclination to question and learn. A curriculum that avoids asking questions is not neutral, but reflects a determination to have students accept received knowledge and passively accept the status quo. Friere (1985) noted that education that tries to be neutral supports a dominant ideology. If a curriculum encourages questions, students are initiated into further developing their intellectual, social, and emotional powers to examine the conditions of their lives.

In the view of education presented in this chapter, teachers are mediators who work with the multiple relationships between the externally imposed curricula, the formal knowledge required, and the individual students who come to school with various kinds of knowledge. In this latter view, teachers are decision makers whose choices reflect the ways in which they construct the world. Yet novice teachers need to understand how the curriculum works and is shaped in schools. As a result, although the long-term goal is for teachers to be able to negotiate multiple relationships in the classroom and school community, the immediate focus is to begin to understand and work within the structures that enclose the curriculum and the institution of the school.

VIEWS OF CURRICULUM

There have been various definitions of curriculum over the years, ranging from Foshay's (1980) comment that the curriculum is all the experiences that a child has under the guidance of the schools, through to Tanner and Tanner's (1975, p. 38) casting of the curriculum as:

> The planned and guided learning experiences and intended outcomes, formulated through the systematic reconstruction of knowledge and experience, under the auspices of the school, for the learner's continuous and wilful growth in person-social competence.

Influenced heavily by Ralph Tyler's (1969) early conceptions, curriculum was seen as a question of scientific inputs, outputs, and consensus of what should be taught. Tyler's focus saw the curriculum as something that could become efficient and measured. Many suggest that the curriculum processes developed and argued for under these conditions could be labelled as technical rational; in other words, if only the sequence of knowledge, information, and activities was adjusted properly and delivered in the appropriate manner, students would learn. In contrast, other curriculum theorists such as Michael Apple (2000) argued that the Tylerian curriculum did little more than take students in, put them through a curriculum, and process them out the other end. The difference between Apple and Tylerian notions was that Apple was sensitive to the hidden curriculum in which more than official knowledge was taught. Apple suggested that as the curriculum was taught, other aspects of societal imbalance were also systematically introduced. Thus schools themselves continued to reproduce the imbalances that were evident in society.

By the mid 1980s, some curriculum theorists began to reflect more broadly on education and its meaning. Researchers like Connelly and Clandinin (1988, p. 1) noted that:

> Curriculum is often taken to mean a course of study. When we set our imaginations free from the narrow notion that a course of study is a series of textbooks or specific outline of topics to be covered and objectives to be attained, broader more meaningful notions emerge. A curriculum can become one's life course of action. It can mean the paths we have followed and the paths we intend to follow. In this broad sense, curriculum can be viewed as a person's life experience.

Or in Madeline Grumet's words: "Curriculum is what the older generation chooses to tell the younger generations" (Grumet, 1988). These notions of curriculum continue to inform the ways in which provinces and school districts decide what students are to learn.

At the same time as those in curriculum were beginning to think differently about their field, many other theorists and researchers influenced by the changing face of society and of schools began to question what schools did and how schools have been implicated in replicating some of the inequities in education. Gaile Cannella goes so far as to suggest that the conceptualization and practice of curriculum development—combined with methods of teaching and management and evaluation as an educational practice—act to control teachers and children (1999).

Certainly if the curriculum is conceptualized as in Figure 8.1, as the interaction between and among the teacher, the child, and the subject matter within a context that reflects the school and the society in which the school is embedded, there may well be some legitimacy to Cannella's claim that there is an intimate relationship between teacher, student, and curriculum. In this view, teachers and students operate within a context that is fraught with political issues.

Figure 8.1 Conceptualization of Curriculum

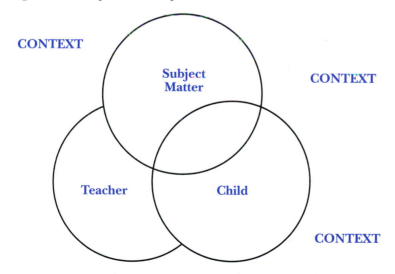

If teachers recognize the political nature of their endeavour, they actively work toward creating a community in which teachers and students become co-learners. Schools, the curricula for which teachers are responsible, the children who come from diverse backgrounds, and the cultures within which all are located reflect a complexity that is all too often disregarded in a drive to keep it simple. If the complexity of a learning community is recognized, then there is an acknowledgement that the community works toward a collaborative common good in which all community members have access to all programs of the school. It is not easy to move into the role of co-learner if the teacher does not recognize the political and contested nature of the curriculum and the ways in which the teacher is involved in social and cultural reproduction, for example as government employees, teachers in their classrooms have a role in reproducing society as it exists. The failure to recognize that role means that teachers may not question the curriculum that they are asked to deliver since they assume that it is value neutral. For example, if one examines curriculum documents or textbooks from the 1950s, one sees that the norm represented is the white single-parent family. As times change there have been different representations of the family. Now because Canada has an increasingly diverse population with diverse values, these values find a place in the curriculum and in the classroom.

It is important to remain aware that educational policies and the curriculum are controlled through the implementation of provincial curriculum standards. These standards, geared toward increasing student knowledge through a common curriculum, fail to recognize that students and their locations in culture are different. However, the standards are hailed by many as part of a modern curriculum that attempts to ensure that all students ultimately become productive wage earners who can compete in the global economy.

For the politically aware teacher, the common curriculum with it standards and focus can be balanced by the notion of a caring curriculum. This means that educators who work within the context understand that educational caring means activism and taking a stand against racism and injustices. Teachers with this orientation are currently caught in a system that, although it may articulate democratic goals, fosters high stakes curriculum in a drive to ensure higher test scores. The recent emphasis on assessment and accountability in the form of high stakes testing often requires curriculum materials or programs that are mandated by governments and school boards, which are then closely monitored to insure implementation and resultant student achievement. Many school boards implement specific forms of assessment designed to evaluate whether students have indeed learned from the curriculum.

If high stakes curriculum is invoked, there seems little room for questioning the knowledge that is transmitted. Yet there is a need to recognize that although high stakes curriculum is in place in many areas, there are other purposes for the curriculum in schools. For example, curriculum can be oriented toward academic rationalism, personal relevance, developing cognitive processes, technology, and social adaptation/social reconstruction.

As noted above, some researchers talk about the difference between the hidden and the explicit curricula, while others concentrate on the influences on curricula, which include the following:

- parents
- subject disciplines
- local school communities
- assessments
- teachers

- politics
- boards of education
- principals
- students

Table 8.1 summarizes some of the varying viewpoints on curriculum. It is important that teachers think about where each viewpoint is located, and how changes in perspective happen during the school year.

Table 8.1 *Summary of curriculum viewpoints*

Curriculum Focus	What It Means
Academic Rationalism	• the school is responsible for sharing the ideas of the past, including concepts, generalizations, methods of the academic disciplines, and works of art • becoming educated means being initiated into these disciplines and becoming informed about the content of these disciplines (Hirst and Peters, 1974) • subject matter or content knowledge is critical
Personal Relevance	• emphasis on personal growth, integrity, and autonomy • the goal is for learners to become self-actualized, autonomous, and authentic human beings • body and intellect are equally important • education involves holistic growth toward personal and humane goals as cognitive, creative, aesthetic, moral, and vocational dimensions are integrated • Eisner (1979) and Klein (1986) are proponents of this model
Cognitive Process	• the foundation of the spiral curriculum that is discussed later • reflects the notion that environmental and experiential factors have an impact on development (Bruner, 1956) • students do not grow out of stages—different stages assume importance along the life path • the motives for learning are internal • students should want to learn out of interest in the material • students who pursue concepts independently gain a better understanding. Teachers provide guidance to students and engage them in dialogue to encourage learning" (Bruner, 1956)
Social Reconstruction	• the curriculum is designed to empower teachers and students to get involved with global issues and concerns • encourages students to use collaborative methods to solve problems locally
Transformative	• may involve critiques from feminist, critical, multicultural, popular, and democratic human rights perspectives • the goal is to encourage students and teachers to advocate for social change and influence social policy (Henderson & Hawthorne, 2000)

Curriculum, then, can be seen as a cultural construction (lived curriculum) and not simply a collection of ideas, concepts, and policies that have to be implemented in the classroom (curriculum as plan). When the curriculum is viewed as a cultural construction, teachers recognize that subject matter, pedagogy, students, and the school community at large interact to shape it. Curriculum and curricular activities then move toward praxis as all aspects are in relation and being shaped and changed by multiple interactions.

The following questions are central to any consideration of curriculum. The answers to these questions begin to hint at a particular curriculum perspective.

1. What counts as knowledge? What should students know and do when they leave school? Should the curriculum be oriented toward discrete sets of skills or be more integrated?
2. Who controls the selection of knowledge? In what ways are governments at various levels involved? How do lobbying groups get their perspective into the curriculum?
3. In what ways is the knowledge that finds a place in school linked to the distribution of power in society?
4. What knowledge is valued? Whose knowledge is it? Whose voices are not present? Why?
5. How is knowledge made available to students? What is the relationship between knowledge and pedagogy?
6. In what ways can curriculum knowledge be linked to life history and the personal experiences of students' lives?
7. How does the curriculum signal ways to behave responsibly and justly?

CURRICULUM: A CONTESTED ARENA

Researchers have specific interests in curricula. The work of curriculum researchers includes examining:

- teacher thinking during decision making
- schools as professional communities (Hargreaves, 2003, Hibbert & Rich, 2005, Wenger, 1998)
- curriculum as the focus of discourse (Kincheloe, 1999)
- history of the disciplines in schools (Taba, 1999)
- conceptual change and cognitive processes (Bruner, 1956)
- social constructivism (Searle, 1995)
- multiple sources of knowledge (Gardner, 2004)
- problem solving and curriculum as lived experience (Connelly & Clandinin, 1988)

Curriculum, what it is and how it is played out in schools, is a contested area. For example, in the case of social studies education in Canada, most boards focus on citizenship education. More recently, a citizenship curriculum or a module within a social studies curriculum has been developed in many provinces including Ontario, New Brunswick, and British Columbia in the hope that changing the curriculum to put a focus on a particular social issue will have an impact on future citizens and the way in which they operate in the world. Sears and Hughes (1996) note that the concept of citizenship is contested, and when trying to implement citizenship education, there has to be a recognition that what passes as citizenship education will depend on the conception of citizenship that informs the curriculum.

In their analysis of social studies curriculum, Sears and Hughes quote Resnick (1990) who suggests that in Canada, there was an institutionalization of authority, attributing order, and a certain pessimism that dominated social studies curriculum in the past. This perception of citizenship and what it was to be Canadian had an impact on generations of students, since the social studies curriculum tended to be a consensus version of history with little room for controversy. The citizens who left school after exposure to this curriculum took what was presented as authoritative and raised few questions about their position in the world (Conley, 1989). Today, an analysis of curriculum and policy documents from across the country reveal a more activist conception of citizenship, but this does not necessarily mean that the interest is taken up in classroom practice. As has been pointed out by many (Sears & Parsons, 1991; Fullan & Connelly, 1985), there is often a discrepancy between what is articulated in curriculum and policy documents and what happens in the classroom. Indeed, Iannacci (2005) and Cummins and Danesi (1990) found that the rhetoric of Canadian multiculturalism is at odds with a dominant culture that favours white, middle class families. In these studies, the researchers found that although the curriculum discussed the multicultural practices of Canada, the reality in many classrooms was food, festivals, and fun. In the Iannacci study, it was noted that even though an early years (Kindergarten) classroom had predominantly Muslim children, the school participated in a "multicultural Santa Claus" day in which all children were introduced to Santa and asked what they expected Santa to bring. Thus, the experience of the school did not reflect the culture of the children, but the culture of the mainstream.

Although the politics of curriculum is perhaps most evident in the case of social studies, it is also present in other subject areas. The questions posed in the previous section could be applied to social studies, language arts, mathematics, or science, and examination of any curriculum policy document from a particular era will provide a picture of what was valued by society at that time. For example, today's classrooms emphasizing literacy education of a particular type is the result of an on-going fear of adult illiteracy and the notion that without a literate population, society will be unable to compete in a global economy. Indeed, when examining patterns from country to country, the curricular processes put into place within education systems to ensure literacy bear a remarkable resemblance to each other. Yet classroom teachers, who are at the forefront of the curricular debates and act daily as employees of a school board, have a responsibility to implement the curriculum. The challenge for the reflective teacher is to keep abreast of the critiques of curriculum and the research in the field, while understanding personal conceptions of curriculum and working with a curriculum policy document that will inevitably change as society evolves. Classroom teachers recognize that although the curriculum is a contested area, they must make sense of it and be able to use it in the classroom as a basis for planning and organizing student learning.

CURRICULUM CONTROL IN CANADA

In Canada, each province has control over education and the curriculum for the province. This means that because governments are elected bodies, the shape of the curriculum produced in each province reflects the influence and desires of various groups within the province. Provinces have to balance the demands of various groups in creating the curriculum. Like classroom teachers who must be aware of the various influences in the local community as they make choices about what aspects of the curriculum to enhance and deliver in what ways within the classroom, the policy document that forms the provincial curriculum is the result of deliberation, discussion, and decision making. In planning and organizing the curriculum, the classroom teacher must balance knowledge gleaned from curriculum research and theory, knowledge of subject matter, the demands of the provincial government, and knowledge of the local community.

REFLECTIVE PRACTICE

In Ontario, the elementary program of studies (the Little Grey Book) was put into place in 1937 and was used for several decades after that. By the mid-seventies after *Living and Learning* was presented, curriculum became less rigid and provided more flexibility for the teacher. By the end of the twentieth century however, curricula became more prescriptive with expectations and learning outcomes clearly delineated.

Think about the following questions:

- What is the curriculum process in your jurisdiction?
- What curriculum documents are you responsible for?
- What is the orientation of these documents?
- In what ways do the official documents differ from what you have seen and experienced in a classroom?

A quick examination of any of the provincial documents reveals that they are organized as a spiral in that concepts are introduced and reinforced over time. In a spiral curriculum, ideas are introduced early and reinforced until the learner has the conceptual maturity to fully comprehend them. Gardner speaks about this spiral as a pathway in which members of a community have agreed on the goals of the system and the steps that should be taken to achieve the goals. He suggests:

> *...in elementary school, that's basically not a time for disciplined learning. It's a time for getting excited about learning, to be curious about things, to be motivated, to want to find out more...*
>
> ~ *Howard Gardner, 1999, p. 215*

MORE INFORMATION
See the companion website for more information on the curriculum documents for the various provinces.

The classroom teacher then has a document from which to work, but also has a series of decisions to make about how the document is to be taken up in the classroom within the particular context in which the school is located. Other influences on the decisions made include the nature of assessment, the cultural context of the class, and the demands of the subject matter

Classroom teachers' decisions

The following scenario demonstrates some of the conflicts that emerge when orientations to curriculum clash. Read through the scenario and respond to the questions either in a small group or in your journal.

 **REFLECTIVE PRACTICE**

Conflicting Conceptions

Sarah Huxtable has taught at Penfield Elementary school for the past five years. She has worked successfully with the students in her grade 5 class and especially enjoys teaching language arts to the children who come from the surrounding farms. The students who leave her classroom generally perform well on the external standardized assessments in literacy. She has been asked by the principal to serve on a provincial curriculum committee to provide advice in developing a new provincial document for language arts. She has also been told that one of her former instructors from her Faculty of Education, Dr. Ida Kno, will be on the committee that is to develop the curricu-

lum. Somewhat excited and thrilled to be asked to serve on what she perceives as a significant committee, Sarah looks forward to the first meeting.

The Meeting

At the first committee meeting, the committee members are presented with a draft document that contains a number of curriculum expectations for language arts. The committee members, seven of whom come from urban areas with a large numbers of ESL students, read through the expectations and the conversation begins:

Dr. Kno: Well this was certainly not what I had expected to see. There seems to me to be very little subject content in this document. It is all about skills that require a context for delivery. How can one teach critical thinking without having to think about something?

Sally H. (a Teacher from an urban core area school): Well don't you see that is just the issue. With these open-ended skills I can select content to meet the needs of my students. I like the way the expectations are open-ended. I can use whatever material I want to help students acquire the skills.

Sarah: I'm worried about the list of expectations. How can I guarantee that all of my grade fives will achieve these? I am creative and like to have some freedom to plan creative activities in my class. This list of expectations means that I will have to teach one skill at a time and then test to see if the skill has been acquired. There will be no joy in my teaching.

Dr. Kno: Well I certainly agree with you. If you knew for example that you had to teach a set number of novels you could ensure that everybody had the right content and then you could make sure that you taught the skills with these novels.

Sarah: I don't think you understand what I mean. Teaching from a set of novels will also limit my teaching. I have classes in which the boys won't read novels.

Sally: Yes, at least we agree. There is more to the curriculum than content or skills. We have to pay attention to the students as people. There are so many issues that students have to face. There is the environment, their different cultures, and in my class the fact that some can't speak English. I don't think that learning about subject matter and skills alone is the way to approach the language curriculum. In language classes we have to help students learn to care for each other and the planet.

Brad (an inner city teacher with 10 years experience): Well we all know that we don't really have to decide anything here. We will just be given another document and we will do the best we can with it. The thing to do is pay attention to the assessments at the end. My question is how is the curriculum going to be assessed?

Fartook (a teacher new to the district but with experience in Iran): Yes I agree with Brad. We have to know what is to be tested. Only then can we determine what the curriculum should be. These students have to learn to compete.

Sally: They are only eleven years old. They have lots of time to think about competition later.

Sarah: Do we know what the grade 4 documents say? Maybe that will help with our deliberations. Dr. Kno, have you seen the previous grade's curriculum?

Think about the following questions:

- What curriculum orientations are reflected in the positions taken at the meeting?
- In what ways might these orientations be resolved?
- What influences might be reflected in the orientations?
- What can a teacher do when his/her philosophy and practices are in the minority and don't fit with those proposed by the school system, other teachers, and parents?

CURRICULUM DEVELOPMENT AND IMPLEMENTATION

Curriculum goes through a process of systematic review in which those responsible assess the content to determine how well it matches with the current state of society, the knowledge in the subject area, and the developmental stages of the students for whom it is designed. In short, periodically in every system, the curriculum is reviewed to determine how well it is serving the needs of society at large. All teachers therefore have to be prepared to learn about and use different curriculum documents over the course of their career. That is why it is important for teachers to learn how to critique curricula and recognize the orientations reflected in the documents.

At every level, once the existing curriculum has been reviewed, there may be major or minor changes made in the content. In most provinces in Canada, major revisions were undertaken in the 1990s in response to a move toward high stakes curricular outcomes. This period of development was followed by a period of implementation in which teachers were introduced to new documents and provided with ways in which the documents could be used in the classrooms. In many cases, during the implementation period teams of teachers were in-serviced on the documents and then told to in-service peers in local school boards. This process of "train-the-trainer" was designed to ensure that all teachers were familiar with the basic content of the curriculum policy document.

Once teachers knew the challenges of the documents, they were to design a classroom curriculum that began with the expected outcomes and work backwards to develop activities that would ensure student success. This process is called backward design and was discussed in some detail in chapter 5. However, as a reminder, here are Wiggins & McTighe's (2001) five steps in designing backwards:

1. Decide on the essential understanding to emerge from the unit of study.
2. Decide on a summative assessment for the unit of study.
3. Align the unit with the local curriculum outcomes.
4. Select the resources to help teach the outcomes.
5. Move back and forth across the curriculum map as revisions and refinements are made.

CURRICULUM MAPPING FOR THE CLASSROOM TEACHER

Teachers also follow a process of curriculum review, development, and implementation in the classroom to develop a program that works for the students. Teachers who plan curricula for their classrooms likely follow steps similar to those outlined below:

1. Gather the relevant subject matter documents (language arts, science, mathematics, etc.)
2. Read through the documents to identify those skills, expectations, outcomes, and objectives that are deemed as essential for students at a particular grade level
3. Gather material to use to teach specific outcomes or expectations; content, process, and skills
4. Decide what activities would allow students to demonstrate specific outcomes
5. Decide how to teach specific subject content
6. Determine the type of assessment that will evaluate student achievement
7. Decide how to organize material for presentation to students

[handwritten margin note: How to Plan Classroom Curricula?]

Once the curricular content has been decided, teachers develop unit and lesson plans that allow them to map the curriculum in each subject area so that the students and parents can easily see the ways in which the curriculum has been shaped for the year. Curriculum maps allow teachers to organize the year by month or semester and provide an overview of the essential learning goals, skills, and concepts (drawn from the curriculum documents), along with the materials and methods of assessment that may be used throughout the year. Curriculum maps provide a framework for decision-making and allow teachers and others to see the basis on which educational decisions have been made. Table 8.2 is an example of a curriculum map.

Table 8.2 *Curriculum Map*

Month	Essential expectations	Content Materials	Activities	Assessment	Planning for diverse groups	Across the Curriculum
Sept.	Identify three or four which you will concentrate on for the month	Note materials that will enable students to practise skills/ gain content knowledge	List key activities	Suggest how learning will be assessed (observation, teacher-made test, student demonstration of skill)	What activities will meet the needs of different groups of learners (high/ low achievers, ESL)	Suggest how expectations can be met in other subject areas

REFLECTIVE PRACTICE

Use the curriculum map above as a framework for mapping the curriculum in one subject area. Draw from the provincial curriculum document to determine essential expectations or outcomes.

Think about the following questions:

- What do you need to find in addition to the curriculum documents?
- Once you have completed your map think about what had to be left out. Why?
- On what basis did you make your curriculum decisions?

Look at the samples available on the various curriculum mapping websites. Each site offers a slightly different approach to curriculum mapping. The type of mapping used reflects the teacher's orientation to curriculum, as well as the documents the teacher is required to use. There are multiple ways to map the year's program; but teachers should be able to explain the choices they make with respect to the ways in which they plan and organize the program.

MORE INFORMATION
For more information on curriculum mapping, see 'Sample maps' on the companion website

REFLECTIVE PRACTICE

Outcomes, Objectives or Expectations?

Curriculum documents use a number of different terms to describe what students are to learn; some documents use the term objectives, others expectations, and still others outcomes. In each case, the outcome relates to something that students will be able to know or do.

Note the following sample of outcomes and expectations from curriculum documents from across the country.

1. It is expected that students will demonstrate an understanding that print conveys meaning. (English Language Arts K–7, British Columbia Department of Education, 1996)
2. By the end of Grade 1, students will read a variety of simple written materials (e.g., signs, pattern books, rhymes, children's reference books) for

different purposes including for practice, information, vocabulary building, and enjoyment. (Language Arts 1–8 Curriculum, Ontario Ministry of Education, 1995)
3. Students will be expected to select, read, and view with understanding a range of literature, information, media, and visual texts. (Atlantic Canada English Language Arts Curriculum K–3, New Brunswick, 1998)

Think about the following questions:

- What are the similarities and differences between and among the statements?
- What does each statement mean for the teacher? For the students?
- What are the implications of these statements for assessment?

SUBJECT MATTER: DOES IT MATTER?
(OR SHOULD THERE BE CONTENT-FREE CURRICULUM?)

Some people think it does not matter whether teachers know a great deal about the subjects they teach. Good teaching is determined by the how (teaching method or style) rather than the what (content), or so the thinking goes.... However, there is a deep truth in the statement "you are what you teach." A math teacher is not (or should not be) just somebody who teaches math. A real math teacher is a person who embodies math, who lives math, who in a strong sense is math. We can often tell whether a teacher is real or fake by the way that person stylizes what he or she teaches

~ Max Van Manen, 1986, p. 45

As noted earlier, there is on-going debate about what should be taught in schools. If the task of the curriculum is to ensure that students have the basic necessities for education and later life, then there is a need for students to acquire specific knowledge that all adults need to have to function in society. Generally speaking, most jurisdictions mandate curriculum in English or French in which listening, speaking, reading, and writing are required skills. As students progress through the grades, the language arts curriculum focuses more on literature. In many instances, selecting literature for the classroom can become controversial as different groups argue for maintaining a cultural heritage (Hirst & Peters, 1974), while others argue for notions of multi-literacies and multi-literatures (Toohey, 2000).

Another area that is seen as essential in all jurisdictions is mathematics education. Students are expected to be able to understand mathematical relationships and be able to demonstrate a working ability in basic branches of the discipline of mathematics (arithmetic, basic algebra, geometry). Science and technology are seen as increasingly important, consisting of essential information that all future citizens should possess. Basic science at the elementary level becomes physics, chemistry, and biology at the secondary school level. Without an understanding of basic science, future citizens cannot be expected to be able to participate in a democracy and understand the nature of the decisions they will be expected to make.

In all jurisdictions, social studies—the combination of history, geography, and citizenship—are seen as essential. Although at the elementary level the curriculum may be called social studies, by the middle years social studies is often broken out into component disciplines. The one discipline that requires a further level of complexity is that of geography, which can be translated into either social geography (the study of people and place) or physical and scientific geography (the study of the physical outline of the planet and the ways in which it can have an impact on the economic and scientific understanding of the world).

The arts (music, visual art, drama) provide a set of aesthetic understandings and, although in recent years they have not been valued as much as those subjects directly related to the economics of work in many jurisdictions, they have been deemed to deserve a place in the curriculum. Finally, especially in some jurisdictions, there has been an increased emphasis on physical education. In part this may be a response to the higher cost of health care and the notion that if citizens possess a sound mind in a sound body, there will likely be a decreased cost to the health care system. It seems apparent that although there are many orientations to curriculum, academic rationalism still plays a dominant role in the way in which curriculum is constructed. Table 8.3 suggests ways in which academic rationalism is played out in both elementary and secondary schools. Consider the ways in which certain groups of students may feel systematically excluded from school because of the academic focus. What seem to be the assumptions about what is valued when this approach is taken?

Table 8.3 *Relationships Between Elementary and Secondary School Curricula*

ELEMENTARY CURRICULA	SECONDARY SCHOOL SUBJECT DISCIPLINES	
Language Arts – in English or French (reading, writing, speaking, listening, viewing, responding)	English Communication Studies	
Mathematics	Algebra Geometry Calculus	
Social Studies	History Geography-social or physical Citizenship Education	
Science and Technology	Chemistry Physics General Science	Biology Computer Science Broad-based technology
The Arts	Music Drama	Dance Visual Art
Physical and Health Education	Physical Education	
Second Language Education	French Spanish Mandarin	

A CURRENT CURRICULUM ISSUE: DOES ONE SIZE FIT ALL?

The notion of high stakes curriculum was raised earlier in this chapter, where it was noted that high stakes curriculum is the result of an increased emphasis on standardized assessment. In many areas, curriculum documents have been made prescriptive in an attempt to ensure that teachers are all teaching the same material to various groups of students. Linda Darling Hammond (1997, pp. 52–53) notes that:

> The use of highly prescribed curricula has been most prominent in large urban school systems and in a number of Southern states with traditions of strong centralized controls. These are often places where lagging investments in education make it difficult to recruit and retain an adequate supply of well-prepared teachers.

She goes on to note that even in systems where curriculum is highly prescriptive, many students can master the skills in isolation but still not read or write. Darling Hammond suggests that in these situations, the students' learning is inert and is not transferred from one context to another. Thus, although they may perform well when tested, their understanding is limited to the specific assessment context. Required coverage of massive amounts of material can lead to students who move from one topic to another without any deep understanding of subject matter. If teachers apply what is known about learning theory to the curriculum, then alternative approaches to curriculum organization and implementation become apparent. The section below presents approaches to the curriculum that move away from worksheets and drills, and demands that students apply concepts in practice from the outset.

STUDENT ENGAGEMENT AND ALTERNATIVE CURRICULUM APPROACHES

Brian Cambourne, a linguist and learning theorist, identified several conditions to enhance student learning. These conditions—immersion, demonstration, expectations, responsibility, approximation, employment, response, and engagement—occur in no special order and are recursive. Cambourne (1995, p. 188) also noted that "if students didn't engage with language no learning would occur". He then suggested four principles of engagement that contribute to the student's involvement with the curriculum. These principles are:

Principles of Engagement?

1. Learners engage with the subject when they believe they have the capability to learn.
2. Learners engage with demonstrations of learning if the activity is meaningful to their lives.
3. Learners are more likely to be engaged if they are free from anxiety.
4. Learners are more likely to engage if they have a positive model.

The notion of engagement has recently been taken up by many others and reflected in approaches to curriculum development. Engagement theory suggests that for students to be involved with their learning, they must be meaningfully engaged in interacting with others as they complete authentic learning tasks. Consistent with constructivist approaches to learning, engagement theory focuses on experiential, self-directed learning in which students have control over what is learned and how it is learned. In engaged learning, all cognitive processes are involved and students are intrinsically motivated because the tasks in which they are working are of importance to everyday life. When applied to the curriculum context, engagement theory has three aspects that are important to consider:

• Create—which considers the ways in which learning is a creative activity that demands application of skills
• Relate—a summary of the relationship aspects of communication and skills involved in group work
• Donate—which suggests that the outcome of the curriculum experience will be shared with the community outside of the classroom

Interestingly, many believe there is much to be gained from considering the ways in which subject areas are integrated. According to some, integrating subjects for particular purposes can allow students to address particular problems that cannot be addressed in a single subject area. For example, students may learn to read in the language arts class but need to be able to apply those skills in other subject areas. Some curriculum specialists argue that an integrated approach to school subjects provides for better student learning that is then more easily transferred from one subject area to another. Just as critical thinking needs to be applied within a discipline, so too do other types of skills that are identified in other curriculum documents.

Those who favour a traditional disciplinary approach—developing specialization in one area only—may see integrated studies or interdisciplinary work as "soft" and without rigor. The next section explores three approaches to integrated learning: problem-based learning, project-based learning, and integrated studies. Note that each one provides an alternative to academic rationalism, and alleviates some of the issues that Darling Hammond raised about the impact of high stakes curriculum on student learning.

PROBLEM- OR PROJECT-BASED LEARNING

Problem-based learning (PBL) begins with the assumption that students have some basic information that is not always translated into new contexts. It is a both a curriculum and a process that challenges students to engage in cooperative group learning. Finkle and Torp (1995) suggest that problem-based learning is a curriculum development and instructional system that develops problem solving strategies and disciplinary knowledge. Figure 8.2 places problem-based learning on a continuum with traditional curriculum.

Figure 8.2 *Traditional and Problem-Based Curriculum*

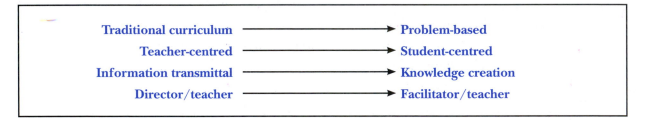

Initially, problem-based learning (PBL) may not seem to be as efficient in assisting student learning since traditional measures of assessment may not capture the skills and knowledge acquired. However, over several years, PBL may foster knowledge retention and transfer because the problems created cause students to use critical skills across several disciplines. As a result, PBL seems to be a good way to encourage skill development across the curriculum, especially in social studies and science classrooms. It should be noted that problem- or project-based learning is not peripheral to the curriculum, but central to it. The problems or projects form the curriculum since the problem is the central teaching strategy encountered by students. Through the project, students learn central concepts. Of course, designing a problem- or project-based curriculum implies that the teacher has a solid grasp of the skills, processes, and concepts are required in a subject area. According to Bereiter and Scardemelia (1993), problem- or project-based learning always involves the construction of new knowledge as students interact, draw from prior learning, and apply knowledge in new contexts.

One of the keys to developing effective problem-based learning is ensuring that students have the opportunity to reflect on why they are involved in an activity. For example, in science many teachers will have students engage in a rocket design and launching activity. However, without the extension of a scaffold of carefully constructed questions to guide student thinking as they work through a process, the activity does not meet the final goal of student learning. In a problem-based environment, one of the key issues is the nature of the interaction surrounding searching for the solution to the problem. Thus the teacher's and students' ability to ask critical questions is a significant part of the teaching/learning process in PBL.

Finkle and Torp (1995) suggest that students involved in PBL go through a seven-stage process that includes the following:

1. identifying a problem
2. creating a problem statement
3. identifying the information needed to solve the problem
4. identifying resources to help solve the problem
5. generating potential solutions
6. analyzing the solutions
7. presenting the best solution orally or in a written report

If students have to go through the process identified above, then what do teachers do to create a problem-based learning environment? To construct a problem-based curriculum, the teacher examines the relevant curriculum and then considers the following:

• What ideas are central to the course?
• What are the required outcomes/expectations for the course?
• What problems will help students demonstrate the required outcomes? In identifying the problems, the teacher needs to know the interdisciplinary parameters of the problem, as well as ensuring that

the problems as stated contain all of the dimensions that the students will need to explore. What questions will extend student thinking?
• Divide the problem into parts.

Teachers then begin with a problem that is not well defined and that lends itself to many possible solutions. For example, in social studies it is often helpful to begin with an anchor story that appeared in the local paper so that the problem is relevant to students' daily lives, for example:

Red Hill Creek is an environmentally sensitive area located in the city of Hamilton on the Niagara escarpment. The creek and its ravine are home to several species of frogs and other wildlife that have co-existed with the few large houses in the area. Recently, the city has determined that there is a need for an expressway to enable people from the west end of the city to quickly get to jobs in the east. The expressway is scheduled to cut through the Red Hill Creek ravine.

This social and environmental problem could engage students in a variety of activities, from interviewing local politicians to researching the history of the area and finding out about the geological underpinnings of the creek. Science, social studies, and of course language arts are all involved in the problem.

Before presenting the problem to students, teachers should be aware of the specific scientific, geographic, and historical information they would like learners to gain from the problem. In addition, because language is central to all learning, teachers need to decide what language skills are going to be the focus of any assessment of the problem.

After being presented with the problem, students engage in the following steps:

- How do I understand the problem? What do I know about it? What are potential solutions?
- What do I need to know to solve the problem? How can I get the information I need? Who can help me? How can I work with others in my group?
- How do I apply my new knowledge?
- In what ways can the group present potential solutions to the problem?

 **REFLECTIVE PRACTICE**

Consider the ways in which engagement theory is reflected in problem-based curriculum planning. Think about the following questions:

- What are the strengths of problem-based learning?
- What are its limitations?

INTEGRATION ACROSS THE CURRICULUM

Unlike problem- or project-based learning, integration across the curriculum provides opportunities for teachers and students to see the ways in which skills and processes are carried forward or reinforced from one subject area to another. In some ways, an integrated approach to the curriculum provides teachers with the perception of more control over what students might be learning. Many teachers choose to carry out integrated curricular activities by using thematic units. Others look for skills or processes that are involved in all subject areas. As noted above, language is central to the development of curriculum and to the development of student thought and expertise in various subjects. Integration is a way of teaching and experiencing information that enables students to make new connections and develop new knowledge.

Generally, "big ideas" work best in developing an integrated approach to curriculum. Look at Figure 8.3 and think about the ways in which skills and process can be integrated across the curriculum.

Figure 8.3 Organizing integrated units using webs

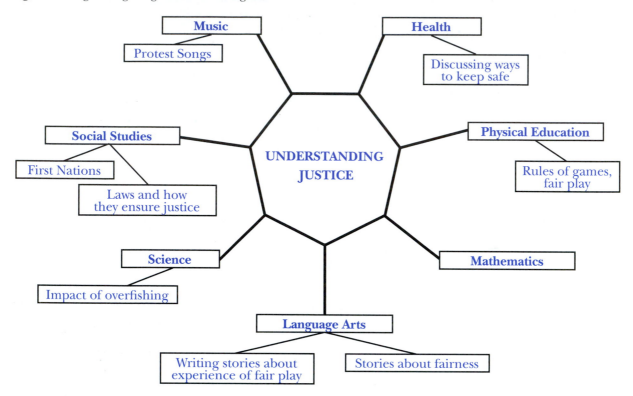

Think about what subject areas lend themselves to integration around the notion of "Understanding Justice." Note that it is more likely with this topic that social studies and language arts can be mutually reinforcing and that other subjects may need to be taught in isolation. Another unit may have a better relationship between and among other subjects.

An alternative way to think about integration is around specific skills. For example, if students are to learn to read to follow directions, the skill may be best introduced in a science class or physical education class rather than a language arts class.

Figure 8.4 Integration using specific skills

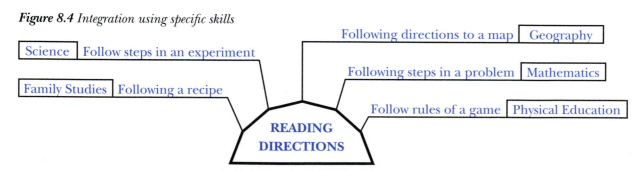

Integrated studies can also be developed as a result of reading a particular book. For example, the following integrated studies plan emerged after a class read the book *Children of the Earth Remember* by Schim Schimmel.

Figure 8.5 Integration using a book

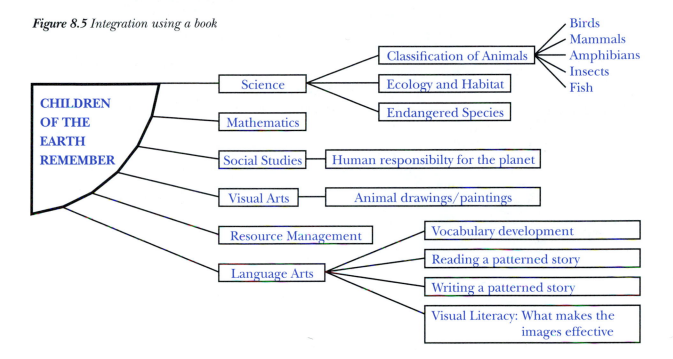

Note that using literature can be a good starting point for integrated studies, but again the teacher has to be aware of the sequence of skills that are to be developed at each level. In many ways, the only limitation to integration is the imagination of the teacher and the understanding of the subject matter.

CURRICULUM ORIENTATION

The following stories have been developed from diaries and interviews conducted with pre-service teachers in a faculty of education. They seem to represent different ends of the spectrum of early experiences with teaching.

Read through the stories and think about your own experiences. What is your story of teaching and in what ways does it differ from Lisa and Eileen's stories?

# PERSONAL STORIES

Lisa's Story

Lisa was confused from the very first day in the Faculty of Education because she had believed she had something to offer students, but she couldn't quite name what that was. And then when she found out how much she was expected to learn in order to become a teacher, she was left feeling empty and anxious. She wondered what she thought she had to give. She remembered the voices that they told her to "be a teacher." She was good with kids, they said. She loved to play and be dramatic with them.

If she thought about it, she realized that she had little idea of how to be a teacher, and most of her thoughts around teaching focused on how not to teach. She began to fear that she was learning how to teach in a way that reflected her notions of how not to. So much to learn and so little that she could recognize as worthy. Resentment was her constant companion as she struggled with her need to succeed and her failing faith in the system that demanded objectives, outcomes, and expectations.

She moved through her days feeling small and insignificant, unrecognized and unappreciated. Judgment and assessments followed her, paralyzing her with fear, reducing her even further. She was back in grade two again, locked in her struggle with Ms. Doright to do it her way. But back then she had a mother who loved her no matter what. Mother showed her how to write and draw anyway she wanted. She had taken delight in her markings and so had she.

But now she was expected to be the teacher and could not do it her way. Her heart ached as she imposed order and watched small hands

Eileen's Story

The first three weeks at the Faculty of Education were a test of the compromise that Eileen had made. She had apprehensions about teaching, many of which had grown out of her own school experiences. She certainly didn't have many positive early school memories. For her, school was a means to an end. She had to get through it and she knew it was valued by those around her, particularly her parents. She could certainly read and was good at math, but she was bored and indifferent about content. Being poor at sports just added to her hate for school. By university, however, Eileen had a new insight about education. It wasn't what you learned but how. For the first time she found herself trying to solve problems. Content still did not appeal, but the process of learning was fascinating. By teacher's college, she decided she would manage the dullness of content while mastering the how of teaching.

Then to her surprise, somewhere during the first three weeks, the content, the technical side of teaching, grabbed her imagination. Language arts, the structure and beauty of math, the issues surrounding spelling: all captured her attention. For the first time, content intrigued her. Without yet making connections between the how and what, she was open to challenges of the education she had known and about which she was learning. As she began to sort out notions of traditional and child-centred education and other seemingly dichotomous issues, she relished discovering new ideas.

Confidence grew as she engaged in self assessment. As she entered her first practicum, Eileen was consciously aware of and articulated the tensions inherent as she entered the classroom. Her own

Personal stories continues...

labour to make perfect B's and A's and C's. Her voice sounded muffled as she gave directions for things she in which she did not believe. And sometimes it was almost a relief when the children seemed not to hear her, as if complicity existed between them.

But order was demanded of her and them. She sensed that she must strike a balance, for to become lost in chaos was not the freedom she sought. At times anger would well up in her when she thought they were keeping the answers from her, and she frantically searched the knowledge for the key to her dilemma. Occasionally an illusive fragment confirmed what her heart refused to give up, but it did not take the shape of something she could actually use. She had little to show her assessors for it seemed to her a lie to write a meaningless version of reality. She wondered what it might mean to submit a daybook that would read: Lesson #1: Crushing the Spirit; Lesson # 2 Stifling the creative, but didn't think that she would be understood.

Think about the following questions:

1. What is Lisa's theory of curriculum? In what ways might her theory have an impact on the ways in which she approaches teaching and learning?
2. In what ways are you like Lisa? In what ways are you different? Lisa's Story

(Rich, Langford, Kronick & Scinderson, 1990)

educational history informed her decisions about content and process. She weighed theory as interpreted by the faculty against her own knowledge of practice, and she modelled after her associate teacher. She learned to disagree with some practices that didn't fit her emerging belief system, but she was able to successfully negotiate her way through the landmine that was practicum.

She began to visualize the kind of teacher who could make a difference. Eileen drew from her teacher-parents and used constructs they had represented in developing her own. For Eileen, the excitement of the concrete teaching experience, the definite nature of the lesson plans, the tidy objectives made her course work finally seem practical. She wanted teaching techniques presented faster and she wanted explicit connections drawn between theory and practice. Caught up in her own goal-directedness, Eileen had little patience for own theory. She wanted the pedagogic content of teaching and she wanted it now. Eileen had waited years to be excited by content, and now it was being held from her. She knew her goals and she knew herself. Her quiet determination led her from agonizing over what to teach. She simply decided what to do then went about it. For Eileen, the only real problem was discovering the appropriate content to teach, and she found it by reading the curriculum material. That was all she needed. Her task as teacher was to simply organize what others gave her.

Think about the following questions:

1. What is Eileen's theory of curriculum? In what ways might her theory have an impact on the ways in which she approaches teaching and learning?
2. In what ways are you like Eileen? In what ways are you different?

SUMMARY

This chapter presented various approaches to curriculum planning and suggested that the curriculum and the way it is developed and implemented reflect political choices on the part of school jurisdictions. Curriculum is a contested area in which the classroom teacher plays a frontline role that may not always reflect the teacher's orientation toward teaching and learning. For some teachers the contradictions between what they are required to do by the curriculum documents for which they are responsible and by their own orientation can become problematic. Others recognize that their job involves a reconciliation of their own orientation with the curriculum. For most teachers, the ultimate test of how the curriculum is to be modified and changed depends on the students that they are teaching. The key issue for all teachers is to develop an understanding of the relevant research in a subject area, to know the developmental levels of their students, and to understand the nature of their community context. When the teacher has a grasp of these three factors he or she can best make the appropriate accommodations in the teaching and learning context of the classroom. It was noted that teachers who display professional knowledge that is grounded in a combination of disciplinary awareness along with the nature of human development are better able to make curricular decisions that support student learning. It was also noted that professional teachers will make use of curriculum mapping as well as the alternative approaches to curriculum planning and delivery suggested in the chapter. Finally, the notion of high stakes curriculum was introduced as a reflection of high stakes testing discussed in chapter nine.

CHAPTER 8 ACTIVITY

Now that you have a sense of the issues that are involved in the planning and development of curriculum you can better examine the curriculum documents that you are expected to use in your province.

Examine the introduction of one curriculum document and answer the following questions:

- What orientation seems to be reflected in the document?
- What groups or stakeholders does the document represent? Is it parents, teachers, researchers, or another group altogether?
- In what ways do the expectations outlined in the document fit with the students that you have encountered?

Now consider the classroom environment. Invite a teacher to comment on the curriculum that is in use today. Ask the teacher in what way the curriculum is similar to or different from a previous document in the same subject area. What do you notice about the response?

Finally observe one lesson taught from the curriculum document. Now answer the following questions:

- How does the lesson "fit" within the curriculum?
- What is the lived experience of the curriculum, and how does it differ from the curriculum policy document?
- Why might this difference occur?

CHAPTER 9

ASSESSMENT AND EVALUATION:
The Glass is Half Full

> *"The report card. Cradle of Truth. The child's burden ever since school began. The dynamic flesh-and-blood life of the classroom reduced to cold, sterile facts and statistics. Undeniable. Unsinkable. Unshakeable."*
>
> ~ Gary Jones, 1991, p. 52

STUDY OBJECTIVES

The purpose of this chapter is to
- examine the nature of high stakes testing
- understand the need for accountability
- differentiate between assessment and evaluation
- define authentic assessment
- learn how to use rubrics
- understand the role of observation in the classroom
- develop a plan for evaluation

INTRODUCTION

Assessment and **evaluation** are critical aspects of every teacher's and every child's life in school. It is important for teachers to understand the strengths and limitations of various forms of assessment so they can make appropriate educational decisions. This chapter begins by framing assessment and evaluation within the current context of global education, and then considers the specifics of the classroom teacher's role with respect to both. Teachers need to understand the pressures that have created the demand for standardized assessments in the global economy. However, at the same time, teachers need to be accountable to parents and children and ensure that not only can students respond to test questions, but they can apply knowledge in everyday contexts.

GLOSSARY

Assessment—the process of gathering information about the student over a period of time. Diagnostic assessment gathers information about what students already know and can do. Formative assessment is the process of monitoring student's learning development. Summative assessment or EVALUATION is the final assessment during which time a value is placed on the student's work and a judgment is made about progress.

Evaluation—the process of judging what has been gathered during the process of assessment to provide a clear indication of how well a student performs. The results of evaluation are usually communicated to others, including parents and other teachers, through the reporting process.

ASSESSMENT: THE CONTEXT OF PUBLIC ACCOUNTABILITY

Accountability can be examined from many different perspectives. One way in which provincial governments have tried to ensure accountability to the public is through the prescription of curriculum and outcomes. For example, Charles Ungerleider (2003, p. 241) notes that in many jurisdictions, politicians "have flocked to testing, standards, accountability contracts, and school councils." Yet he also suggests that such simplistic measures fail to reflect what we know about students and learning, especially in an overcrowded curriculum. According to Ungerleider, the following minimal conditions must be in place to ensure student success:

- ensuring there is broad agreement about essential outcomes for all students
- ensuring these outcomes are clearly articulated and supported with time and instructional material
- articulating high but reasonable expectations for student success
- holding students, parents, and teachers responsible for those outcomes
- assessing progress in those areas at different times over school careers
- using practices and policies that increase learning outcomes for all students
- examining rates of student progress, as well as gradients in student progress, associated with such factors as socio-economic standing, gender, and ethnicity

Yet as Ungerleider noted, those in the public sphere want concrete evidence that schools are producing students who can compete. For example, in Canada, the **School Achievement Indicators Program (SAIP)**, introduced by the Council of Ministers of Education in 1993, is designed to assess the performance of 13- and 16-year-old students in mathematics content, mathematics problems solving, reading, writing, and science. This three million dollar program was designed not to replace testing programs already in place in the various provinces, but to provide a better mechanism for inter-provincial comparisons.

The push for accountability was intensified in the year 2000 with the advent of the Organization for Economic Cooperation and Development (OECD) Programme for International Student Assessment

(PISA) tests that were administered to 15-year-old students. These tests attempted to determine how far students had come in acquiring the skills and knowledge necessary for participation in the global economy. Forty-three countries participated in 2000 and by 2006, 57 countries will participate in testing mathematical literacy, scientific literacy, reading literacy, and problem solving. The tests are a mixture of multiple-choice items and those requiring students to produce their own responses. Technical reports are produced for each participating country, and students and provinces are ranked within the country list. Available online or for purchase, each report asks whether students are ready for the challenges of the future. What is not asked in the reports, nor is it within the scope of the reports to raise the issue, is whether or not the best questions are being posed, or whether the tests as they are constructed really measure the skills and knowledge needed for an uncertain future.

For educators, tests like PISA will be a fact in the foreseeable future. Yet what teachers need to know is that standardized tests are designed to compare children with one another, and now not only children but also schools and school districts are being compared.

With a standardized assessment, some children will inevitably not meet the standard. A potential hazard is that schools and school boards will no longer conduct the thoughtful, authentic assessments that have long been part of their programs.

> Note that there are differences between a **Norm Referenced** and a **Criterion Referenced Assessment**. A Norm Referenced Assessment measures student achievement against a sample of other students of the same age or grade level. A Criterion Referenced test measures student achievement against a specific learning objective or performance standard.

Increasingly, educational researchers and practitioners are raising the types of questions suggested by Ungerleider's conditions for student success. In the United States, the *No Child Left Behind* Act promised that schools would be made better by yearly testing and would result in every child being proficient in reading by 2014 (Meier, Kohn, Darling-Hammond, Sizer, & Wood, 2004). One consequence of that program of testing was that if children failed to meet the standard, then school districts had to purchase approved "scientifically proven" programs to teach students. The scientific experts on the panel often had their own reading programs to sell, and even with the new materials, many students did not meet the requisite standard.

Teaching to the test through materials designed to help students demonstrate achievement, combined with the notion that testing itself improves student achievement, are both flawed assumptions. Berliner and Biddle (1995) hypothesize that high stakes assessment causes teachers to narrow their focus to teaching to the content of standardized tests, thus ultimately limiting student achievement in other areas such as the arts. Others, including Ungerleider (2003), argue that rather than dismissing standardized assessment out of hand, teachers need to be more intelligent about using the tests and placing them alongside all of the other forms of assessment in place in schools.

Large-scale assessments in and of themselves are but one part of a giant assessment and accountability puzzle. With thoughtful analysis and interpretation, test scores can point to areas that do need some remediation. Further, teachers who are politically aware and able to argue sensibly for students can begin to educate policy makers as to what is appropriate assessment and what counts as accountability in the classroom. However, teachers also need to be aware of what counts as evidence for policy makers, and should be willing and able to provide such evidence.

> *Now, it is the view of the Ministry that a theoretical knowledge will be more than sufficient to get you through your examination, which after all, is what school is all about*
>
> ~ *J.K. Rowling from Harry Potter and the Order of the Phoenix*

PRINCIPLES OF AUTHENTIC ACCOUNTABILITY

Neill (2004) identifies the following principles for authentic accountability. Teachers should think about how aware they are of the principles in their own classrooms. To what extent does realizing these principles require that teachers become politically astute?

- Shared vision and goals—schools and their local communities should be the primary authorities in the accountability process; from the shared community vision, decisions about the focus of the school programs are developed.

- Resources—adequate resources should be provided and used, while children who need more should be provided with more; if schools are to be equitable, children should receive what they need to develop
- Participation and democracy—individual voices of teachers, administrators, parents, and students should be heard; they should share in making decisions, which also means respecting diverse experiences and cultural backgrounds
- Prioritized goals—assessment information should be focused on goals rather than on those items most easily measured
- Multiple forms of evidence—both qualitative and quantitative data have a place in accountability; standardized assessment is one measure
- Inclusion—all students must be assessed with appropriate tools; demographics should be taken into account
- Improvement—the goal of accountability should be school improvement; to accomplish this goal, teachers need time to collaborate
- Equity—the goal should be to close the achievement gap between and among race, culture, and gender
- Balance—accountability should mean the teacher is accountable for student performance, and the system is accountable for providing adequate resources

Wiggins & McTighe (2001) suggest that backward design, in which the teachers decide on the form of assessment early in the planning process, is one way to ensure accountability. In short, as teachers plan units, they should think about what students will be able to know and do once the unit has been completed, and the ways by which students will be able to demonstrate their knowledge and skills.

!! PLO !!

> **MORE INFORMATION**
>
> For more information on principles of backward design, see the "Principles of backward design" on the companion website

 ## REFLECTIVE PRACTICE

The strengths and limitations of backward design were discussed in previous chapters. Now, consider what you have read in the preceding section and think about the following questions:

- How does backward design assist or inhibit planning for authentic assessment?
- Why is this so?

TESTING, TESTING, AND MORE TESTING: CHILDREN, TESTS, AND TEACHER EXPECTATIONS

Most students undergo a variety of tests, ranging from the standardized ones outlined above to informal screening that begins at birth (e.g., physicians use observation scales to determine whether children are reaching the appropriate developmental milestones). By the time the child is of school age, he or she will likely experience other forms of screening, such as physical development (can you jump on one foot) and simple cognitive tasks (a story retell). Such readiness screens are almost taken for granted at schools, and are at times the first indicator that the child may not have a background that closely matches that of the school setting. For example children may be asked to complete a simple task such as placing an item above a table or distinguishing between numbers and letters. Other such tests will examine children's book handling knowledge—do they know top from bottom, left from right. Once the child is in school, there are likely to be paper-and-pencil tests, such as a sign-in book in kindergarten, or more formal teacher-made tests designed to assess whether or not the child has learned what the teacher thinks has been taught. Some children may be offered individual intelligence tests like the Wechsler Intelligence Scales for Children, while others will only ever be subjected to group-administered tests.

As noted above, standardized assessments, particularly in language and mathematics, have been a part of most school boards for years. However, they have become increasingly more pervasive and are often part of decisions made about a child's performance and placement. And, given what we know about the performance of some groups on tests, these decisions can have a profound impact on what happens to students at school. It is important to be cautious about using tests, particularly when they are administered to young children. As noted in early chapters, children's developmental levels vary, and what is deemed as lack of readiness or of limited performance may simply be a reflection of a child not having reached a specific level of development.

Another area that should be considered when looking at test performance is the issue of expectation. Riley (2005), in her research examining teacher expectations, relates the following anecdote:

The one piece of advice seniors would always give to juniors at my high school was to ace your first exam. The rumour was that if you nailed that first assignment, teachers would place you on a pedestal and you could spend the remainder of your high school years riding on the coattails of first term paper success. However, the pitiful souls who failed their first term assignments would be sentenced with the task of desperately trying to regain credibility with unforgiving teachers for the duration of their high school lives. As teenagers we were prone to hyperbole.

Riley's study indicated that teachers' expectations of students and their tacit ascription of certain characteristics to groups of students influenced their decision-making about students and their subsequent placement in academic programs. She found that some teachers made differential placement decisions concerning English as second language learners and Aboriginal students, even though the objective data on students (academic achievement data, test scores, and so forth) were the same. Riley's research provides a reason for all teachers to reflect on expectations about students, and serves as a reminder that objective data is interpreted by human beings with their own personal histories.

REFLECTIVE PRACTICE

Check Your Assumptions

Think about students you have known or groups with which you have come into contact. Think about the following questions:

• What were your expectations of the individuals or of the group?

• In what ways were you surprised by their performance? Why?

• How did the teacher's (or your own) expectations influence your performance in particular tasks?

Of course the classroom teacher, in spite of all of the cautions and caveats, is still responsible for being accountable to students, parents, and the public. The question then becomes, what does classroom assessment look like and what do teachers need to know to fulfill their obligations?

EVALUATION AND ASSESSMENT: THE SAME OR DIFFERENT?

Many members of the public equate the notions of evaluation and assessment. Yet to the educator, these terms have distinct and important differences, both in terms of what they do and how they look in practice. Assessment is the process of gathering information about the student. In gathering information, the teacher draws on many aspects of classroom life, such as:

• using the forms of standardized assessment referred to above
• gathering samples of students work
• incorporating information gained from parent interviews

The purpose of assessment is to enable students to demonstrate what they are able to do and what they know. It is on-going and happens over time. Further, assessment can, and at times should, result in decisions to make significant programming changes.

On the other hand, evaluation places a judgment on what has been gathered in the process of assessment. Evaluation provides a clear indication of how well a student performs. Results of evaluation are usually communicated to others, including parents and other teachers, through the reporting process.

Figure 9.1 shows the process of assessment, evaluation, and reporting schematically.

Figure 9.1 The assessment, evaluation, and reporting process

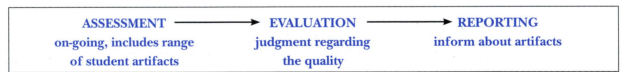

ASSESSMENT →	EVALUATION →	REPORTING
on-going, includes range of student artifacts	judgment regarding the quality	inform about artifacts

Types of Assessment

Diagnostic assessment gathers information about what students already know and can do. Gathering a sample of student writing at the beginning of the year can be the basis of a diagnostic assessment.

Formative assessment is the process of monitoring student's learning development. It may include samples of types of writing completed over a period of time, a checklist of observed written language skills, and so forth.

Summative assessment is the final assessment during which time a value is placed on the student's work and a judgment is made about progress.

McTighe (1999) distinguishes between and among the dimensions of students' achievement, progress, and work habits during the assessment process. Confusion about how these areas are reported and the ways in which information is gathered in each area can be problematic for teachers and parents. McTighe identifies student achievement as performance relative to identified learning outcomes. In most instances, this includes how well the student has performed vis-à-vis the curriculum document in a specific subject area. Progress considers the degree of growth toward the outcomes, while work habits include whether the student demonstrates characteristics of effort, assignment completion, etc.

The primary purpose of assessment and evaluation in any classroom is to inform teaching and learning. To achieve this purpose, any assessment must be on-going and part of the teaching/learning cycle. In addition, any assessment should reflect what has been taught. For example, assessing students to determine whether they grasp the concept of measurement after a unit on addition of whole numbers does not make sense. Neither does using only paper-and-pencil tasks to assess whether or not students have acquired speaking skills. Ultimately, in real life we assess our own performance in our jobs and in our daily activities. The long-term goal then, of any assessment practice, is to encourage all learners to engage in self-assessment and evaluation.

REFLECTIVE PRACTICE

Self-Assessment

Donald Schon (1986) talks about reflection in action and reflective practice. He suggests that all professionals engage in this—especially when they are involved in complex and messy situations.

Think about the following questions:

- To what extent does your own performance evaluation reflect what you know about teaching and learning?
- When and how do you assess your performance?

In any assessment process, a series of decisions must be made, as shown in Figure 9.2.

Figure 9.2 *Decision-making in the assessment process*

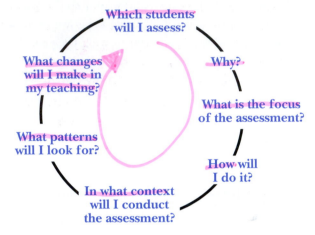

AUTHENTIC ASSESSMENT: WHAT IS IT?

Much educational literature discusses the need for authentic assessments that focus student performance on tasks that relate to activities in the world outside of the classroom. Authentic writing assessment demands that students write for a purpose; if a letter is written, it is for a specific audience and requires a response. Wiggins (1990) suggests that authentic assessment

- presents students with a range of tasks that represent all aspects of student learning; it may involve report writing, discussion, research, interviewing, etc.
- focuses on whether students can craft polished answers or performances
- involves "ill-structured" challenges and roles that help students rehearse for adult life

Wiggins goes on to note that emphasizing and standardizing the criteria for scoring such varied products achieves validity and reliability, and that validity depends in part on whether the target test simulates "real-world activities." Authentic assessment then requires a knowledgeable teacher who is aware of the demands of the curriculum and can use it as a guide for determining tasks in which students can engage to demonstrate their learning.

Before setting an assessment, the teacher needs to be clear about what is to be assessed. This requires setting clear goals and objectives for instruction that indicate exactly what learning outcomes are expected. If a goal is a general statement, then an objective is the framework on which that goal is based. For example, a goal in the writing curriculum might be that students will write to persuade. An objective related to that goal might be that students will view three advertisements and identify four techniques used to persuade the viewer to purchase the product. Students will then use one technique to draft an advertisement for a book they have recently read. Table 9.1 provides an example of this process.

Table 9.1 *Setting goals, objectives, and performance tasks*

GOAL	OBJECTIVE	PERFORMANCE TASK
Students will write to persuade	1. View three advertisements 2. Identify four persuasive techniques	Write an advertisement to "sell" a book they have read

 # REFLECTIVE PRACTICE

Consider one goal from a curriculum document with which you are familiar. From the goal, identify two learning objectives and then design a performance task that will enable students to demonstrate they have achieved the goal.

Think about the following questions:

- What are the challenges in the activity?
- What kinds of questions must you ask yourself to design the performance task?

STRATEGIES FOR ASSESSMENT

Performance Tasks

Performance tasks should represent something that may be required in a venue outside of the school context and that has value. A performance assessment allows students to demonstrate their skills in relation to real situations. In designing performance tasks, Airasian (1991) suggests the following steps:

1. Identify the task to be performed and either perform it yourself or imagine your performance.
2. List the important aspects of the performance.
3. Limit the number of performance criteria to be observed.
4. Request a colleague review the task.
5. Use clear language to describe the performance criteria.
6. Express the performance criteria in terms of student observable behaviour.
7. Arrange the criteria in the order that they are likely to emerge.

Since there is no right or wrong answer to a performance task, many teachers use **rubrics** to assess them. In addition, many school boards have developed rubrics to help teachers determine whether students are developing their skills. When developing a rubric for performance tasks in the classroom:

- decide on a scale (level of performance)
- provide descriptors for each level on the scale
- use an outline similar to the one below to help design a task observation sheet

A rubric

- is a set of criteria students see prior to engaging in a task
- can be established for a single task
- can be developed by viewing and/or preparing established criteria prior to the activity; students clearly know what is expected

The worksheet in Table 9.2 may help organize the development of rubrics.

GLOSSARY

Rubric—a set of criteria students see prior to engaging in a task.

MORE INFORMATION

For more information on a variety of rubrics check the companion website.

Table 9.2 *Rubric worksheet*

Performance Task	Level 4 Exemplary	Level 3 Accomplished	Level 2 Developing	Level 1 Beginning
	Is able to perform well above the standard expected	Has mastered the standard	Has some of the aspects of the tasks completed but not yet at the mastery level	Shows a beginning level of performance

There are two main types of rubrics: analytic and holistic. An holistic rubric measures the overall quality of a task, while an analytic rubric measures specific aspects of a task. When developing rubrics, teachers need to review the content of the curriculum document and identify what performance tasks are to be assessed. Many curriculum documents contain rubrics that have been developed for specific subject areas. Teachers should first review the relevant documents to determine what standards have been identified as appropriate rubrics for the subject area, then using these as a basis, they can make modifications to suit their specific group of students.

Observation

Considerable research supports the reliability of informed teacher judgment about student achievement based on observations of students as they engage in various learning activities. The notion of "kidwatching" is not new and is particularly significant when students are engaged in performance tasks. In the primary grades, observation is a good way to conduct an assessment of a child without being overly intrusive.

To observe well, teachers need to understand child development, the curriculum, and the influences of context and culture on children's behaviour. If these are not in place, a teacher may make faulty assumptions about children's behaviour and performance in specific settings. It is therefore imperative that teachers are aware of their own histories and the assumptions they hold about the performance of specific groups. For teacher observations to be valid, they need to have the following characteristics:

- **Systematic**: The teacher needs to have specific tasks that are being observed and needs to know how to look at the child during the period.
- **Timely:** The teacher needs to be aware of when it is appropriate to look at performance.
- **Repeated:** The judgment should not be made based on one observation.
- **Continuous:** Observation should be extended over time if the teacher is to gain a picture of the student's development in complex tasks.
- **Recorded:** Simply making a mental note of the observation is not sufficient; the observation needs to be recorded and dated.

MORE INFORMATION

For more information on performance assessments, check "The definition of performance assessment and performance assessment for science teachers" on the companion website.

• **Interpreted:** The information needs to be weighed against what is known about the student and the context; in making interpretations, the teacher needs to guard against bias and stereotyping.

Observation is not simply standing back and looking at the classroom and the students. Observation methods include but are not limited to:

• watching students engage in performance tasks
• listening to students interact
• conferring with individuals and groups
• marking products created by students
• making anecdotal records
• collecting work samples and recording why the samples were collected
• interacting with students and determining how their language might be extended

The teachers who are the most effective at observation have a plan for conducting observation in the classroom. For example, they may use a class list as an organizational device and decide on a rotation schedule for observing students. This plan may be for the complete program, or may be more focused for individual subject areas. See Table 9.3 for an example.

Table 9.3 *Sample rotation schedule for observing students*

Name	Dates to be observed in Language Arts	Dates to be observed in Social Studies	Dates to be observed in PE	Dates to be observed in Arts
Marissa	Sept 24, Oct 24, Nov 24	Sept 5, Oct 5, Nov 5	Sept 10, Oct 10, Nov 10	
Farhan	Sept 5, Oct 5, Nov 5	Sept 24, Oct 24, Nov 24		
Sahar				

Note that the teacher will have observed each student at least three times in each subject area over the course of a semester. Organizing a schedule like the one in Table 9.3 reminds the teacher that each student should receive particular attention in a specific area. The teacher might also decide that these observation periods could include writing or reading conferences and/or gathering specific artifacts from the subject. This does not mean that there will not be informal observations throughout the semester. For example, if Farhan (in the schedule above) demonstrated a particularly strong performance on a task, the teacher would make note of that performance and include an observation about the performance in the student record. The anecdote below highlights the types of spontaneous observation a teacher might record.

 REFLECTIVE PRACTICE

Galan, a grade one student, demonstrates little interest in reading or writing. He prefers to be active and will do anything to avoid looking at books. His journal writing is a rapid scribble so that he can get on to activities in the block corner.

Mrs. H., his teacher, notes his skill in running games and the way he tries to organize the other children to play soccer. After one reading lesson, she sees that Galan has returned to his desk; and she thinks that once again it will be a struggle to have him attempt any writing. Much

to her surprise, when she passes his desk, she notes that he has turned his worksheet over and on the back has written SOCA SKR. When she asks him about his writing, he says it wasn't writing, but is a plan for playing soccer. The "words" translate as "Soccer Score."

Think about the observation note Mrs. H. might write. Think about the following questions:

• What was Galan demonstrating by his action?
• What skills is he demonstrating?

When conducting observations, teachers look for information from a variety of areas, including:

• attitude toward the learning task
• learning strategies the student uses
• attention to the learning task
• interaction and communication of learning
• acquisition of concepts

As teachers work in classrooms with students, they are aware of all of these dimensions and make a systematic attempt to note student performance in each area.

Observation and Questioning

Many teachers find it useful to have a series of questions to guide observations, while others use checklists as a way to monitor what is expected of various groups of students. Table 9.4 outlines a series of questions to guide observations about problem solving.

Table 9.4 *Questions to guide observations about problem solving*

Area being considered	Questions to guide teacher observation	Description of expected behaviours
Problem Solving	• Does the student risk finding solutions to problems? • Does the student seek assistance in problem solving? • Does the student find problem solutions independently? • Does the student use relevant information to solve problems? • Does the student classify, compare, or match concrete materials to solve problems? • Does the student recognize similar solutions to problems?	• Searches for solutions to simple problems • Tries to solve problems independently • Requires assistance to solve problems • Is able to distinguish relevant from irrelevant information in seeking solutions • Uses relevant information to find solutions • Is able to relate present problems to those solved in the past

REFLECTIVE PRACTICE

With a group of peers, develop a list of questions to guide observation of a student's development in a subject area. Consider why certain questions are seen as more important than others.

Think about the following questions:

• What types of questions demand that inferences be made?
• What assumptions are embedded in the questions?

By having a set of questions to guide observation in specific areas of development, the teacher's observations in the classroom can be more focused.

Knowing what to observe and thinking about the kinds of questions to ask as teachers interact with students will help their observations become more aligned with the curriculum and with the tasks students are expected to perform.

 **REFLECTIVE PRACTICE**

In the interaction sequence below, which set of comments will elicit more focused observations? Why?

COMMENT 1	COMMENT 2
I like your painting.	What did you do to produce this picture?
You used colour well.	Tell me why you decided to put colour into your landscape.
Your painting is great.	Your painting helped me understand the story you told. How did you decide what to include in the illustration? Why did you decide to include the chipmunk in your drawing?

Observation Checklists

Although many teachers find that checklists help focus their observations, others find that checklists limit what they want to record. A checklist can provide a good outline of what might be expected in a subject at a particular time. When a checklist is combined with an observational record, the teacher has a powerful vehicle for evaluating student work. Checklists can also be developed with students as a way to help them understand what is valued in the subject and in the classroom (e.g., a behavioural checklist). The key to the value of any checklist is ensuring that it is not too detailed, since a detailed list will become unwieldy and will not be used. Many teachers use curriculum documents as a basis for developing checklists. Table 9.5 provides an example of a checklist for beginning writing behaviours.

Table 9.5 *A checklist for beginning writing*

	Consistently	Sometimes	Not yet observed
Understands that words convey the meaning of the story			
Uses words from classroom environment in stories			
Writes one sentence stories			
Leaves spaces between words			

Uses consonants' sound to represent words:
    Initial
    Final
    Medial			

Uses vowels as placeholders			

Anecdotal Records

A key to all observational record-keeping is the **anecdotal record**. These are most often found in the primary classroom, but middle school and senior teachers also find that anecdotal records are an excellent way to record student progress in areas related to problem solving, group work, and collaboration. Anecdotal records are short narratives about events in the classroom. Teachers who keep anecdotal records often use a binder with notes for each student and add pages to the binder as the year progresses. Over time, anecdotal records lead to the development and interpretation of patterns of learning and help teachers make judgments about student progress.

Some teachers use a two-step method for anecdotal recording. The first step is a file folder ruled with space for each child in the class. The space for each child is large enough for a sticky note. The child's name is printed at the top of each space and sticky notes are added. Any observations made during the day are jotted on the sticky note and then at the end of the day are transferred to a binder in which the child has a page or pages. At the end of each month (or a period determined as appropriate), the teacher reads through all of the notes that have been transferred to the child's page(s) in the binder and looks for themes or patterns in the child's learning. The teacher then writes a summary comment on the binder page. In this way the teacher maintains an accurate record of what has happed in the classroom and, because the original notes are still available, can refer to them when writing report card comments. Many teachers also use the binder as a way to reference specific pieces of student work that have been noted.

Conferences and Interviews

Many teachers conduct conferences and interviews of various types with students. Conferences are likely to happen in language arts, but teachers who use problem-based learning often find that conferences provide a way to keep up with what students are doing in their learning. Conferences are also a great way for teachers to provide feedback to students. Indeed, Shulman (1986) notes that during conferences, the teacher has perhaps the best opportunity to demonstrate his or her pedagogic content knowledge base and form of professional understanding. During the conference, the teacher's knowledge of the subject combines with the student's acquisition of content and results in the greatest potential for an extension of learning. The teacher's ability to ask good questions in the conference not only assists with assessment, but can also forward student learning. Conferences provide a good way to gather information about

- learning processes and strategies
- student goals for future learning
- attitudes
- understanding of concepts
- interests

At the end of each conference, the teacher again keeps an anecdotal record that goes into the student file and can be revisited over the course of the year.

Work Samples

One source of data for student assessment that should not be overlooked is student work samples. Student artifacts such as worksheets, writing selections, artwork, block constructions, reports, and role playing activities all provide insight into student learning. Student work samples should all be dated and notes made about why a particular sample is kept (see Figure 9.3). Many teachers use portfolios to store student work, and when combined with the teacher's anecdotal records, they provide the basis for assessment. Once dated work samples have been placed in the portfolio, teachers can look across the year to determine much about the students' development.

Teachers may use a set of criteria to examine the portfolio, some of which may be drawn from the curriculum documents. Students themselves can use the portfolios to compare work from the beginning of the year with work completed at a later stage during the year. This can be useful when a student seems to have reached a plateau in learning and is concerned about lack of progress. Examining early work provides a framework for considering the whole year and can help parents and their children see the progress that has been made over the year.

Figure 9.3 Student work sample and teacher notes

Teacher-Made Tests

In most classrooms, at some point in the year, teachers will likely want to administer a test to determine whether or not students have acquired the content. In an outcomes-based classroom, teacher-made tests should be linked directly to the outcomes articulated in the curriculum. Tests are not designed to replace all of the forms of observational assessment noted earlier, but are one more item in the repertoire of assessment tools available to the teacher. Any artifact could be considered a test of some type, but this section focuses on designing a test that considers specific content. Over time, teacher-made tests will ideally reflect a balance between and among a variety of types, as indicated in Table 9.6.

Table 9.6 *Types of tests and sample questions*

Type of Test	Sample Question
Short answer/long answer questions	Short answer: Why did the poet use a metaphor in the first stanza?
	Long answer: In a short essay, discuss the relationship between Harry Potter and Dumbledore.
Easy/difficult questions	Easy: What colour was Clifford the big red dog?
	Difficult: Why was Clifford the big red dog an important character in the book?
Factual knowledge/knowledge application	Factual: List three effects of global warming.
	Knowledge application: In what ways does global warming have an impact on human activity?
Word based questions and diagram/image based questions	Word based: Provide a definition of the water cycle.
	Diagram: Illustrate the water cycle with a sketch.
Game tests	You have just completed a unit on Canadian society during the sixties. Design a game that highlights key events of the time. Be prepared to teach your peers how to play.
Matching tests	Match the mother with its offspring.
	cow piglet pig lamb doe calf ewe fawn
Multiple choice tests	Which of the following sentences contains a spelling error?
	a) The dog chased the cat. b) Where were you? c) Peeple played tag. d) The balloon burst.

No matter what type of test is chosen, it is important to make sure there is adequate time to develop the test and for students to take the test. It is equally important to pay attention to the evaluation criteria for each test item and for the test as a whole. The value placed on each item should reflect the value placed on the purpose of the test. If the teacher wants to know what information (facts) students have acquired during a period of study, the test and its items may be factually oriented and may simply ask students for names of objects. If, on the other hand, the interest is in application, the teacher may decide on a performance assessment that requires a demonstration of the activity, or a pencil-and-paper test that requires students to use words to indicate how they would produce a certain artifact.

Tests that simply assess recall of information do not serve teachers or students well. To develop tests of higher order thinking and of students' ability to apply knowledge, think about using an adaptation of the types of questions noted in Table 9.7.

Table 9.7 *Types of test questions*

Type of Test	Suggested terminology
To assess knowledge of information	Use terms like label, name, match, reproduce
To measure comprehension	Use terms like defend, estimate, explain
To measure application	Use terms like prepare, operate, produce
To measure analysis	Invite students to diagram, compare and contrast, subdivide
To measure synthesis	Use terms like combine, categorize, revise
To measure judgment or evaluation	Ask students to justify, interpret, describe

Note the similarity between this chart and Bloom's taxonomy that was introduced in Chapter 7. Teachers' questioning skills in the context of classroom instruction also have a place in classroom assessment.

Finally, the nature of the subject matter will also have an impact on the type of test that is used. Ideally, all test questions should be placed in a meaningful context so that rather than simply asking true or false questions, students might identify statements as true or false but then rewrite false statements as true. In this way, the test is a challenge for students and pushes their thinking further.

REFLECTIVE PRACTICE

Find a test that has been designed for a specific grade level. Analyze the test to determine how well it works in terms of student evaluation.

Think about the following questions:

- In what ways could the test have been improved?
- Did it test what it was designed to test?

Portfolios and Assessment

Portfolios are used to store samples of student work over time, and many teachers recognize them as a way toward authentic assessment. Portfolios and **portfolio assessment** assume the following:

- The collection has been meaningfully gathered—it is not just a collection of stuff, and each artifact has a purpose.
- Students are involved in the development of criteria for inclusion of specific artifacts in the portfolio (e.g., using a "yours, mine, and ours" approach in which the student and the teacher select artifacts individually, and together decide on artifacts to be included); this approach ensures that teachers include a piece of work that indicates a specific growth step.
- They may have input from parents and administration.
- The artifacts represent everyday activities of students.
- There may be subsections within a portfolio.
- There will be a range of artifacts from multimedia to print.

To build toward a self-evaluation at the end of each semester and each year, teachers should encourage students to write a reflective note on the contents of their portfolio and document what they think they have learned. The purpose of this activity is to develop reflection as students consider why they have chosen the various artifacts and suggest how the artifacts demonstrate their learning. The process of reflection and setting goals for future learning gives power to students as they recognize that they have responsibility for their own learning outcomes.

GLOSSARY

Portfolio Assessment—A collection of artifacts related to a specific subject area. Periodically teacher and student review the portfolio to determine what has been learned.

MORE INFORMATION

For more information on classroom assessment techniques, see "Classroom assessment techniques and practical assessment, research and evaluation" on the companion website.

DATA, DATA, AND MORE DATA: ANSWERING THE "SO WHAT?" QUESTION

From the strategies above, it is apparent that there are indeed multiple data sources for gaining information about student progress. The types of assessment discussed can be placed on a scale like the one in Figure 9.5.

Figure 9.5 *Types of assessment*

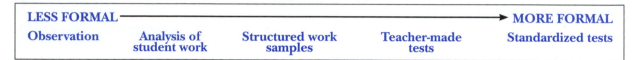

Teachers have to make decisions about the balance in the assessment practices in their classroom. The following factors help bring a balanced perspective to assessment practices.

• Diversity in student needs and learning strengths and weaknesses need to be considered when choosing instructional and assessment strategies.
• Each criteria category within the achievement level needs to be observable, i.e., knowledge/understanding, thinking/inquiry, communication, and application.
• Assessment methods need to include pencil-and-paper tests and applications, performance tasks, and personal communication.
• Different types of assessment—diagnostic, formative, and summative evaluation—need to be incorporated throughout the teaching/learning cycle.
• Forms of assessment include tests that address standards, teacher-directed assessment tools, student-directed self and peer assessment, and student–teacher interaction.

It is useful for teachers to map strategies for assessment as they plan the curriculum over the year. If the curriculum and assessment practices are considered simultaneously, there is little likelihood that a critical skill or process will not be addressed. A worksheet like the one in Table 9.8 helps organize each curriculum unit and determine the appropriate assessment.

Table 9.8 *Curriculum planning worksheet*

SUBJECT	INSTRUCTIONAL FOCUS	METHODS/ACTIVITIES	ASSESSMENT STRATEGIES
Language Arts	Writing to persuade	• Use video ads • Sustained writing time • Group conferences • Writing an ad	• Peer conferences • Performance assessment (develop ad for book)
Science	Hydrologic cycle	• Experiment with steam for condensation • Water table • Weather observations (establish weather station) • Library research	• Student report on steps in experiment • Test to label water cycle • Student logs

Wiggins and McTighe (2001) suggest prioritizing assessment and planning according to the following categories:

1. What is worth knowing but not vital to development.
2. What is important to know and vital to development.
3. What is necessary for enduring understanding and develops key skills and knowledge.

Once the types of assessment have been decided and periods for evaluation determined, the teacher needs to periodically review all of the gathered data. The teacher may be somewhat less evaluative during the assessment process, however at the end of an assessment period, the teacher places a value on the data that has been gathered. During the review process, the teacher draws on the curriculum documents, what is known about the student, and what has been completed during the instructional cycle.

Once all of the data on a student is gathered, the teacher begins the process of content analysis. This process likely includes examining work samples, documents, and records to look for trends, attitudes, and performance. Teachers note instances of concept development or acquisition, as well as areas in which there has been little or no progress. From the analysis of the evidence of student achievement, the teacher can make decisions about the direction of instruction for the next period of work and decide what needs to be reported to parents and documented in the student's official record. When preparing to evaluate and write a report on a student, think about the following questions:

- Who wants/needs this information? (Is it parents, other teachers, or the student?)
- What are the key things they need to know?
- What evidence documents these key things?
- What evidence is most credible to each audience? Why?

Most teachers do not wait until the end of a semester to evaluate the material they have gathered on students, but have a plan for reviewing and evaluating achievement and progress at the end of each instructional unit. Compiling all of these separate evaluations makes up the final report to parents and to the teacher in subsequent years.

Any reporting should reflect the use of multiple sources of data gathered from a range of contexts and should use language that is accessible to the intended audience. Specifically, parents are often interested in what the student has done since the last reporting period and future goals for instruction for the student.

TEACHER PERFORMANCE APPRAISALS

performance assessment
outcome-based assessement
multiple choice tests
formative summative
observation scales
standardized tests
accountability
essay tests
reporting
reliability
validity
rubrics

It should be apparent from reading through this chapter that just as teachers are expected to be able to assess students, teachers themselves are subject to assessment. Teacher performance appraisals have recently become an integral part of most school boards, with the principles of assessment discussed above as part of the process. Many boards have developed their own appraisal process, but the pattern set out here should enable teachers to begin to develop their own portfolio that in turn can become a part of their performance appraisal.

To develop a portfolio for performance appraisal, teachers first should establish a set of professional goals for the year. This draft annual learning plan should include specific areas on which the teacher plans to focus (see Table 9.9). Aspects of the goals can relate to personal professional development, while others may relate to the school curriculum.

Table 9.9 *Performance appraisal guidelines*

PROFESSIONAL LEARNING GOALS	WHY THIS GOAL NOW	HOW I PLAN TO ACHIEVE IT
Personal professional development (take a graduate course in action research)	• Would like to examine my classroom practice in some detail • My teacher mentor has agreed to be a critical friend during the process	Register for a masters program and take one course in the fall semester
Curriculum-related (learn more about literacy development strategies)	This is my first year in a grade one classroom and I have never worked with young children before	Find out who the literacy contact is for the board Sign up for summer literacy institute

It is better to have a limited number of goals each year, but teachers might want to consider developing a three-year plan so that, as with students, they can plot where they would like to be and what they will be able to know and do after three years.

The annual learning plan can become part of a professional portfolio. This portfolio, like those kept by students, provides an opportunity to make decisions about what showcases a teacher's work. Professional portfolios are useful during a performance review and when applying for positions. They are underpinned by several assumptions, especially the notion that professional development is most effective when teachers have the opportunity to set their own goals and determine their own ways to learn.

In deciding to construct a portfolio, teachers should identify specific purposes and goals for the portfolio; these goals will help them decide what to include. The artifacts selected may be samples of student work, credentials, letters from parents, etc. Just as students are expected to have a rationale for the items in their portfolio, teachers should have a rationale for including documents in the professional portfolio. The portfolio should have a table of contents and the goal for the portfolio. Here are some ways of getting started with a portfolio:

• Select an item that best indicates the purpose of the portfolio and demonstrates development toward achieving goals.
• Choose another item and decide what will be added to the portfolio if it is included—then decide if it should be included or not. Continue this process until the portfolio reflects the goals.
• Decide how to organize the items. Think about the various categories of experience to showcase.

- Create a table of contents to indicate how each item reflects progress toward a goal.
- Think about the goal statement and rationale. Is this the way you want to present yourself as a teacher?
- Share the portfolio with a friend to see what they learn about you from reading it.
- Make the necessary changes.

SUMMARY

In this chapter the various types of assessment available to teachers in classrooms have been highlighted. It was suggested that results from these various tools could be examined in order to evaluate the learner's progress. The problematic nature of standardized global assessments has been raised as it was suggested that these assessments are but one tool in the range of evaluation instruments available to teachers. Considerable time was spent in discussing classroom observation as a way of gathering on-going information about the students. Finally teachers were encouraged to develop a plan for classroom assessment as well as to begin to gather information for their own self assessment in their professional portfolios.

CHAPTER 9 ACTIVITY

Create an Assessment Plan

Select a grade or division; decide what types of assessment would be needed to determine a student's development over the year. Determine the assessment appropriate for each subject area, and give reasons why the assessment would be appropriate for that area. Consider your options if the assessment does not reveal progress in a particular area. A chart similar to the one below might help you organize your assessment plan. (One type of assessment has been completed for you.)

Type of assessment	Time used	Subject area in which it is appropriate	When to summarize the assessment results and evaluate them	What can be done if progress is not made
Observation	Throughout the year	All	At the end of each month	Try specific intervention to see if student can complete task in alternative contexts

PART III

ENHANCING CHILDREN'S THINKING

CHAPTER 10

ADJUSTING THE PROGRAM:
One Size Does Not Fit All

"Why anyhow, this unrelieved emphasis on sameness when the most obvious facts are the manifold differences among people—differences of all sorts, in native ability, in interests and inclinations, in temperament, in every taste and aptitude for learning, in home upbringing, in economic status and opportunity, in ethnic and racial heritage …. Any program of basic schooling that does not take them into account flies in the face of facts that will defeat it."

~ Adler, 1982, p. 42

STUDY OBJECTIVES

The purpose of this chapter is to
- understand the range of diversity in a classroom
- recognize cultural and linguistic diversity
- program for special needs students
- identify the role of the school team
- understand multiliteracy
- develop educational plans for students

INTRODUCTION

This chapter looks at the diversity and differences in the classroom. Diversity is a factor in all schools and teachers need to critically assess how they can provide for diverse populations. Having diverse learners in the regular classroom is a challenge for teachers; understanding the nature of diversity is the first step in planning to meet individual needs. We know that students benefit socially from being integrated with peers, and we know that integration or inclusion can promote tolerance for diversity. Yet for the classroom teacher, the need to foster academic achievement is of paramount concern. Indeed, when dealing with the student who is different from the norm, some of the major contradictions in education may find their way into the classroom.

One of these tensions is between child- and teacher-centered approaches to programs—a tension that has been around since Plato (cited in Cooper, 1998) and Rousseau (cited in Cranston, 1991) and which is further reflected in the work of Thorndike (1903) and Dewey (1992). Thorndike suggested that all skills can be programmed, packaged, taught, and then tested. In contrast, Dewey (1992) suggested that each student has a unique learning pattern and can be apprenticed into more mature learning. In this, Dewey was more like Vygotsgy (1962), whose work was discussed earlier in this book. Attending to the tension is particularly important when considering diversity and difference, since the teacher needs to be aware of assumptions about diversity and how these are taken up in the classroom. This chapter begins with an overview of the types of diversity found in the classroom, then goes on to provide strategies for working toward inclusion.

GLOSSARY

Diversity—Refers to the nature of students in the classroom. Diversity includes both culturally and linguistically diverse populations as well as special needs students

WHAT IS DIVERSITY?

The notion of **diversity** in schools is complex and is based on the tacit assumption that there is a norm that all learners strive toward. Yet in reality, all students are different from one another and from the teacher. ==Diversity encompasses both special needs learners as well as those who are culturally and linguistically different.== Fewer students fit the norm, and teachers who are teacher-centered rather than focused on individuals are not likely to be able to meet individual needs. It is therefore important for teachers to be aware of the ways in which they think about and make assumptions regarding what these students bring to the classroom. Dei & James, (2002, p. 62) suggest that

> Concepts of inclusion and exclusion in societal institutions like schools, charged with promoting collective norms and personal growth, are inextricably linked to definitions of equity and success.

Success for all students depends on the ability of the school to respond to the needs of diverse learners. Teachers are responsible for being aware of who they are as people in the classrooms in which they work. All too often, if teachers do not think about the experiences that have shaped their attitudes and perceptions about others, they can assume that all others share the same experiences. Read the excerpt below from Tasha Riley (2005). Think about how being confronted by difference might have an impact on interactions.

PERSONAL STORIES

Confronting Differences

Not that I minded or anything. I was used to it by now. I recalled the first time I really noticed I was the minority in a place. It was three years earlier and I was teaching English in Korea. Once again I was on the bus. This time I was standing. It was another hot day but the bus was so packed you not only had to peel yourself off of the seat, you also had to peel yourself away from whoever had been unfortunate enough to stand beside you.

Sudden movements became risky as you never knew exactly whose gut you might elbow or foot you could step on. The hot sun poured through the open windows and played against the golden hairs of my arms. Not something I would usually pay attention to except for the fact that the children in the seat beside me were pointing at my arms and giggling uncontrollably. I looked in their direction and they promptly covered their laughing mouths with their hands in a failed

Personal Stories continues…

attempt to smother another burst of giggles that flew from their mouths in a torrent breaking through the cracks between their fingers. One brave girl reached out to touch my arm. I felt her fingers press lightly upon my skin, pause for a moment, and then dart away like the flick of a snake's tongue. She glanced up at me to gauge my reaction and seeing as I hadn't turned into a ferocious monster in the short time it had taken to pull her hand away, she ventured out again to make a second attempt. Placing her tiny hand upon my arm, she strokes the golden hairs that jet upward and out of my skin. Soon all the other children began to touch. I remember feeling a little strange, rather like a caged dog in a pet store. A young Korean woman closer to my age notices my predicament and then snaps sharply at the children. The children stop abruptly putting their hands between their knees, casting their eyes down still desperately trying to stifle in giggles. The woman turns to me. "They are fascinated by the hair on your arms." she explains. "They have never seen a white person before."

Think about the following questions:

- In what ways might this situation reflect the context of some of the children you may teach?
- How might one begin to confront difference?

CULTURAL AND LINGUISTIC DIVERSITY

A little over 50,000 of the 229,091 immigrants who arrived in Canada in 2002 were children under the age of 14. Many of these children do not have English or French as their first language. When the language factor is combined with cultural differences, it is clear that students in today's classrooms come from diverse backgrounds; social class, ethnicity, and language distinguish them. A good teacher pays attention to differences and acknowledges that fair treatment of students does not necessarily mean equal treatment. It is important to recognize that some students may participate in two distinct cultures: the mainstream and the ethnic. When there are discontinuities between the two cultures, students may have difficulty in school, especially if the teacher assumes that the majority culture is the one that has the greatest value. **Culturally responsive instruction** pays attention to issues of diversity, while at the same time recognizes that culturally diverse students need the same curriculum and academic skills as those in the mainstream.

Teachers who are aware of their attitudes and assumptions about others are more likely to be able to work effectively with students. If teachers do not have this awareness, they may discriminate because they are unaware of their own bodily presence, their place within society, and its impact upon others. In Canada, where fair-skinned, able-bodied people are the norm, people whose skin colour is different

GLOSSARY

Culturally responsive instruction—Instruction that recognizes the differences present in the classroom between and among students of different cultures and language backgrounds. In short it does not assume that all students have the same histories.

or whose physical presence does not match the norm have visible markers of difference. Because such people are considered to be the norm, they may be perceived as "natural." Students who are different may be subject to various forms of discrimination. Indeed, when examining social studies texts presented in schools, the texts present others in ways that are all too often taken for granted. Willinsky (1998) writes about an activity in which he has students examine photographs from social studies texts to see how others are portrayed. He encourages students to think about their position vis-à-vis the people in the photo, and asks that they begin to read the text and the photos separately to first see how they interpret the photo, then to see any disparity between the photo and the text. Through discussion students are led to think about the ways in which their assumptions about the people in the photos are affected by their own world experience. The text then can provide another way of thinking about the world.

REFLECTIVE PRACTICE

Recall, from your own experience in school, a time when you were confronted by your difference from others.

Think about the following questions:

- How did you feel?
- What would have helped you in that situation?
- How will you bring this understanding into the classroom?

MAINTAINING AND FOSTERING SOCIO-CULTURAL AWARENESS

It is important for all educators to know about culture and understand what it is and how it operates in schools. One simple way of thinking about culture in schools is to recognize that culture is not static but rather is dynamic, and it provides a set of norms by which groups of people live and work. These conventions are arbitrary, but our awareness of our own norms and those of others can help create a classroom context in which all students have a better opportunity to learn. To help people think about their culture and place in society, Piper and Piper (1996) developed a set of questions and activities that can be used to help make a distinction between individual and group values. The questions and activities are listed below. As you read through and complete them, think about how your values shape who you are. How will these have an impact on your work with diverse learners ?

REFLECTIVE PRACTICE

How to Separate Individual and Group Values

Think about the following questions:

1. If someone handed you a blank piece of paper and asked you to describe your cultural status, what would you write? What would you leave out? Why?
2. If you were asked the question by the president of a club to which you belong, what would you say?
3. To how many cultural groups do you belong? List two other people who share your cultural profile.

4. Have you ever felt excluded from a group? How did you feel? Why?
5. Have you ever excluded anyone from your group? Why?
6. When travelling to another country, have you ever experienced concern about not knowing how to satisfy basic needs such as nutrition and hygiene, or not knowing how to ask for something in a foreign language? How did you feel?
7. Have you ever felt like a stranger in a strange land? Why? What helped you overcome your concerns?

(Adapted from Piper & Piper, 1996)

United Nations Educational, Scientific and Cultural Organization (UNESCO) documents the notion of cultural diversity and suggests that cultural rights are a part of human rights. The United Nations' convention on the Rights of the Child (1989), to which Canada became a signatory in 1991, suggests that children have rights and require special care and protection. The treaty contains four principles which deal with the following:

1. the best interests of the child
2. protection from discrimination
3. the right to life, to survival, and to optimum development
4. the opportunity for children to participate in matters that concern them

MORE INFORMATION

The Canadian Coalition for the Rights of Children has developed several guides pertaining to the treaty. To find out more, see the following on the companion website:

- Education and the United Nations Convention on the Rights of Children

- Child Care and the United Nations Convention on the Rights of Children

Knowing about the rights of the child as documented by UNESCO can help teachers marshal arguments for creating curricula that are culturally responsive and respect the rights of all learners. Indeed, when teachers respect a basic tenet of the convention—that all children have the right to be treated with dignity and respect—then many of the issues related to diversity in education have a sound rationale and a foundation in **equity** and social justice. In education, this means that although it may seem simpler to strive for uniform solutions—a one-size-fits-all for all learners—there is a need for schools to build on students' cultural and linguistic diversity. The students' culture influences the ways in which they view the world and has an impact on the types of experiences in which the students engage.

Attending to diverse cultures value can assist teachers in planning activities for students. In literacy learning, it is important to recognize that particular experiences related to literacy acquisition are embedded in cultural practices. The assumptions made by some teachers about what constitutes effective literacy practice may have to be modified as they learn more about the different ways literacy is constructed in the home. For example, children whose culture is founded on an oral tradition may not place the same value on traditional storybook reading as other cultures.

To accommodate diverse cultural and linguistic backgrounds, teachers need to be aware of those aspects of culture that shape the learners' approach to school. In a study of culturally and linguistically different early years' students, Iannacci (2005) found that all too often what children brought to school from their home experiences was not a part of the everyday classroom experience. Indeed, rather than building on what the children brought to school, in many instances the school actively worked toward a cultural and linguistic replacement so that a child's first language, and in some cases literacy, was not the foundation on which English language acquisition was built. The school instead worked toward eliminating the first language and too often demanded that it not be spoken at school.

Yet increasingly, researchers and practitioners are arguing for an approach to diversity that has been labelled multiliteracies. A **multiliteracy** approach calls for a recognition of diversity and the fact that students increasingly have to negotiate multiple cultural and linguistic differences to function effectively in the world. Those in the New London Group (1996) call for a broader approach to literacy that accepts that the student will have to be capable of pragmatically interacting across cultural and linguistic boundaries in order to have access to the evolving language of work and the community. Multiliteracies accept that there are multiple sign systems in the world (semiotics) that include multi-media such as DVDs, CDs, computers, art, music, as well as multiple languages and cultures. Going beyond the simple recognition that literacy includes oral and visual, a multiliteracy approach recognizes that in a diverse world, increasingly various sign and symbol systems are important and all have an impact on our ability to communicate. The New London Group suggests that when a multiliteracy approach is taken, there is a greater likelihood that those from diverse populations will be able to interact successfully within the mainstream. Although it may seem complex, a multiliteracy approach has a few simple stages embedded within it that are outlined in the next section.

MULTILITERACY PEDAGOGY: AN OVERVIEW

A multiliteracy pedagogy means that teachers and students work together to use various sign and symbol systems to make sense of the environments in which they are located. Classroom practices begin with the students' own knowledge and move out from there. Ideally, the curriculum is co-created by the students as they interact with each other, the texts from the environment, and the world around them. Central to the notion of multiliteracies is that students learn together about things that matter to them in their own world. The five steps below outline some of what can happen in a multiliteracy pedagogy. It is important to remember that the stages are recursive and move backwards and forwards as students and teacher negotiate meaning.

1. Start with the students themselves. Provide an imprecise outline of the type of projects in which students might be involved. For example, if middle school students are asked to design books for primary children, review some of the basics of book making with them and provide many contextual clues to help them get started. Make sure there are expert and novice students in each group to facilitate scaffolding.

2. Provide a language to discuss the process. The language reflects the terminology students will need to use to communicate their processes to others. This overt instruction encourages students to

talk and share using their own language first, then gradually supplement this language with the technical language that focuses on the project at hand.

3. Recognize that the final product may involve more than print literacy; students may produce visual texts to share or may conduct a performance art piece. At this stage, talk again about the ways in which the project reflects both old and new learning.

4. Frame the project within the broader context of making meaning. How do the student-produced texts reflect others that are available? In what ways are they the same/different? Questions about the purpose of the project might emerge: Who is this for? Why was it constructed in this way? Encourage students to think about the affects of the project on others. How does this project fit with others that have been completed before?

5. Specify what was learned and apply it to another context. How might things change if this were a different place/time?

In short, in a multiliteracy approach, students are simultaneously

- functional users of language and text (broadly constructed as print, visual, hardware, software)
- meaning makers—they understand the purpose and use of text
- analyzers of discourse—they recognize the ways in which language reflects positions of power
- transformative practitioners—they use developing skills and knowledge in new ways to create new texts

MORE INFORMATION

For more information about multiliteracies see "The multiliteracy project" and "About the New London Group and the international multiliterarcies project" on the companion website.

VALUING CULTURAL AND LINGUISTIC DIVERSITY

Although it may seem to be an impossible task, structuring the classroom environment to enhance and support cultural and linguistic diversity is not totally unlike structuring the classroom environment to support a student. Table 10.1 organizes some of the ways in which student goals reflect values and impact instruction. Think about other instructional activities that can be added to column three in Table 10.1 based on other sections of this text.

Table 10.1 *The impact of student goals and values on instruction*

Goal	Value	What it means in the classroom
To develop confidence and self reliance	independent learning and the ability to self evaluate	• need for independent projects rather than teacher directed ones • projects that are constructed to involve learning in many subject areas
To be able to work in groups and appreciate what others have to offer	collaborative learning and accepting the various roles of novice/expert learner	• group work with students assigned to various roles (recorder, chair, etc.) • opportunities to reflect on group processes
To appreciate others	the need to respect individual contributions to any activity	• share stories of who students are as people • provide opportunities for peer assessment
To develop independent thought and joy in learning	the need to foster originality and thinking outside of the norm	• opportunities for students to engage in problem-based and case-based learning
To actively pursue learning opportunities	the need to complete a task and develop a work ethic	• Provide opportunities for peer- and self-evaluation

ANOTHER FORM OF DIVERSITY: THE SPECIAL NEEDS STUDENT

There has been some confusion in recent years over the definitions of terms surrounding special education and diversity in schools. Recently, the Crucial Terms Project (Bunch et al., 2005) attempted to gather definitions that could be used to ensure that those interested in diversity across the country have a consistent vocabulary. They suggest that inclusion refers to educational practices based on the philosophical belief that all students (those with and without disabilities), have the right to be educated together in age appropriate classrooms, and to benefit from education in regular classrooms within community schools

One of the issues that rapidly becomes apparent in any classroom is that the teacher-centered approaches of the past do not fit well in an environment shaped by a diverse population. For years there has been debate about how to best meet the needs of diverse students. With respect to the special needs learner, the debate has focused on where students with special needs should be taught, along with how they should be taught. In the past, classrooms for students with behaviour problems, learning disabilities, or gifted needs were segregated from the norm. This model was based on a system of standardized assessment and labelling of students who were deemed to require specialized assistance in segregated environments.

Today, in part because of the recognition that society itself is increasingly diverse, the trend is away from segregation and toward integrating students with special needs into the mainstream classroom. This inclusive approach is based on a more holistic paradigm that recognizes that special educators and regular classroom teachers can work together to meet the needs of special students. This paradigm is shaped by the socio-cultural perspective of teaching and learning which views the classroom context as an ecological one that evolves over time. As noted in the section on culturally and linguistically diverse students, this has implications for the teacher. In order to work in this environment, teachers, like students, need to work together as teams and design multifaceted approaches to curriculum and teaching methodology. **Inclusive education** means that all students are welcomed into the school and have their individual needs met within the classroom. As a result, classrooms may include non-English speaking students, physically handicapped students, and students with learning disabilities. Inclusion means that teachers are constantly seeking different ways to organize and plan for learning in the classroom, and should also be able to communicate effectively with members of the school team involved with an individual student's program.

In thinking about working with students with special needs, it is important to recognize the need for a team approach and to understand what various members of the school team do to help the classroom teacher work with an individual learner. A school team may be organized in a manner similar to the one outlined in Table 10.2. Think about the roles and the expertise that each member brings to the team.

Table 10.2 *The organization of a school team*

Who	Role
Classroom teacher	• Knows the student in the classroom and has the most contact with the student in school • Documents what has been tried in terms of the curriculum and how the student responds • Presents the learner to others in the team • Often brings the team together (since the student is in class with him/her)
Administration (Principal)	• Provides necessary support for teachers and team to assist the student • Assists in facilitating the meetings and may arrange for specialists to visit • May have a series of meetings planned for the academic year
Parents	• Know the child better than anyone else • Can provide history of schooling and of family culture
Psychologist, social worker, attendance counselor, speech and language pathologist	• May have expertise to deal with a particular case • Not all schools have these partners available
Special education teacher, learning resource specialist	• A teacher with knowledge of special education who may be able to suggest resources or plan activities
Teacher's aid	• Assists with a learner who has a specific disability

REFLECTIVE PRACTICE

It is often a little intimidating to enter the first school team meeting, since there are many people on the team with different skills and expertise from that of the classroom teacher. There may be a social worker or school psychologist and perhaps a special education specialist. In addition, the school principal is on the team; he or she has overall responsibility for the school and for conducting teacher evaluations. All of these people have knowledge of cases in general. The classroom teacher, however, has specialized knowledge of the learning context.

Think about the following questions:

- As a classroom teacher, how might you want to negotiate entry?
- What kinds of questions might you have when you first participate in a school team?
- What questions might you have for each member?

All members of the school team must be able to practise active listening and collaborate with others to design an appropriate program for students. The knowledge base of each team member must be respected, and it is important that the facts are presented in as clear a manner as possible in any discussion of an individual learner. The team itself will likely make judgments about the best program possible after gathering data from multiple sources. School teams generally follow a process similar to the one identified below:

1. The problem is defined in concrete terms.
2. The items that have an impact on the problem are identified. For example, it may be that a student has difficulty concentrating when there is noise in the classroom.
3. Strategies for dealing with the problem are identified and evaluated for potential success.
4. Individuals responsible for implementing the strategies are targeted.
5. Strategies are implemented and given a timeline for evaluation of effectiveness.
6. Changes are made once an evaluation of the strategy has been completed.

Use this process as you think about 'The Case of Steven' in the Personal Stories Section.

Another approach to preparing for a school team meeting is to organize the case in the following manner:

1. What is the current situation with this student? Be specific about the reason for the referral.
2. Consider what the school knows about the family and the parents. In what ways might they like the case to be considered?
3. Decide whether the concerns are cognitive, emotional, social, or behavioural. Have some strategies in mind.
4. Meet with the parents and ask them about the child to determine whether the behaviour occurs at home.
5. Describe the current context of the student at school and note any behavioural patterns.
6. Suggest whether the student is benefiting from current instruction—is the student frustrated, unmotivated?
7. Does the student find the curriculum challenging? Is it too easy? What is the student like affectively (i.e., attitude)?

PERSONAL STORIES

The case of Steven

Steven, a seven-year-old boy in a grade 1/2 classroom, seems to have little or no interest in reading. Today, like every day, the teacher has all of the twenty-five students in the classroom on the floor for a shared reading activity that is to be followed by a phonemic awareness activity and then a journal writing activity. Many children sit quietly, but Steven, as is also usual, consistently plays with the Velcro on his runners and when he tires of that, begins to poke Christopher who sits beside him on the carpet. When asked to move, Steven does so reluctantly, and sits in front of the teacher who is directing the children's attention to the words on a large sheet of chart paper. Steven begins to make animal sounds then starts to crawl away from the teacher and the chart. Suddenly the teacher asks him to come and circle the word "the" from a series of fifteen words on the chart and he does so. When he is asked how he knows that is the correct word, he says "I dunno. I just know and there's another one there." This time he points to the word "the" on the calendar. The teacher makes note of this activity then sends the children to their tables with a journal activity in which they are to write about the favourite part of the story she has just read. Steven shouts "this is boring," tears up the paper, and throws it at the teacher. He then moves to the classroom library and takes out a chapter book on hockey and seems to be paging through it. When the teacher settles the other children to their tasks, she goes to Steven and asks what he is doing. Calmer now, he picks up the book and says "I'm reading, stupid." Taken aback, the teacher asks him to read a page to her. He does so effortlessly.

The teacher decides to take Steven's case to the school team. Why?

Individual Education Plan (IEP)

Once a student has been taken to the school team, he or she may be assessed by a teacher who is trained to work with special needs children or by another specialist such as the school psychologist. The teacher may be asked to complete a detailed observational profile of the student. After the information gathering, which likely includes interviews with parents or guardians, the school team may meet again and decide that an **Individual Education Plan (IEP)** has to be developed and implemented for the student. It is likely that the team will take into account different sets of strategies for the student that may include a modification of the curriculum, a modification of the setting, and/or a modification of the teaching approaches. The IEP becomes a part of the student's file and is reviewed systematically over the course of the year, with necessary changes being made as the learner develops skills. Generally the classroom teacher, often with the support of a special education specialist, implements the IEP. Because of the current practice of inclusion, many teachers will have several students with IEPs in their classroom, and they must be skilled at modifying and tracking student learning. IEPs have specific learning goals for each student, and in Steven's case the specialist might suggest that he be placed on an individual reading program with a focus on developing skills in written language. However, before an IEP is developed, more information than what was provided in the case above would have to be gathered.

When developing IEPs and working with special needs students, it is important to remember that flexible planning is essential. However, the degree to which teachers are comfortable with such flexibility is a combination of their professional knowledge and skills. The experienced teacher recognizes that lesson plans for the whole class can often be modified to meet the needs of the students on IEPs. The strategies outlined in the subsequent sections provide ways to begin to think about such planning.

Most school boards have developed their own individual education plan forms, but generally they contain the type of information noted in Table 10.3.

Table 10.3 *Example of an Individual Education Plan (IEP)*

Student Name:
Date of Referral:
Assessments: (A list with results)
Goals:
  1.
  2.
  3.

Objectives: How to Achieve Evaluation (date)
  1.
  2.
  3.

Follow-up

Organization for Inclusion

It is not within the scope of this chapter to provide details on the various types of special needs that may be present in any inclusive classroom. Difficulties may include physical issues, behavioural problems, learning disabilities, and psychological difficulties. Classroom teachers have control over the ways in which they organize the physical setting, classroom routines, students, and the use of support personnel. The type of structure imposed on the classroom will vary depending on the needs of the students. Those who have issues with attention may benefit from well-established and consistent routines with little extra stimulation, while those who have had limited stimulation will need more. For example, a three-sided study carrel may work well to keep a distractible child focused, and a hearing impaired child may benefit from being close to the teacher. In any case, it is important that teachers have clear sight lines throughout the classroom for issues of safety and classroom management.

In thinking about strategies for helping students from diverse backgrounds and with diverse needs, a three-pronged approach is sometimes useful: this is a set of strategies that can be constructed around, with, and on behalf of students. Strategies that are built around learners include program or classroom placement and structuring the learning environment. Items that involve working with the student include tutoring activities or activities that help the student take control of his/her own learning. Classroom organization is a factor that teachers can control in the classroom, and that has a definite impact on helping to meet the needs of diverse learners. A single correct room arrangement does not exist; every arrangement depends on the size and nature of the classroom. The key thing for any teacher to remember is that to meet the needs of all students, the classroom arrangement should meet the needs of the tasks that are planned. Ideally, to maintain classroom control, the teacher will want to have ready access to groups in the classroom. In addition, given what has been suggested about the role of problem-based learning, there will need to be places for groups to meet.

Traditional classrooms, organized in rows of desks facing the teacher, reflect a particular orientation to teaching and learning that does not necessarily meet the needs of all students.

Jones & Edmunds (2005) suggests that the ideal classroom arrangement should provide teacher mobility and allow opportunities for teachers to interact with individual students and groups of students.

Look at the following four diagrams of classroom arrangements in Figure 10.1. What style of teaching/learning is reflected? How would the needs of diverse learners be reflected in each? Why?

Figure 10.1 *Sample classroom arrangements*

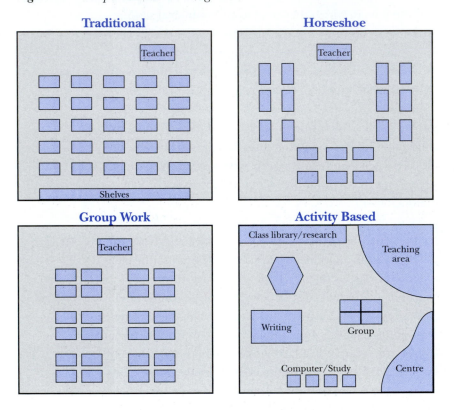

In Figure 10.2, a somewhat different approach is taken. This approach includes places for students to learn in large groups, small groups, and independently. Note that the type of furniture available in the school may influence the ways in which teachers can structure the classroom. Remember too that when teachers have diverse students, they may also need to be able to accommodate spaces for quiet times in the classroom. The following three basic areas need to be accounted for in the classroom:

1. Whole class meeting spaces
2. Independent workstations
3. Small group work areas with or without teacher direction

Figure 10.2 A different approach to classroom organization

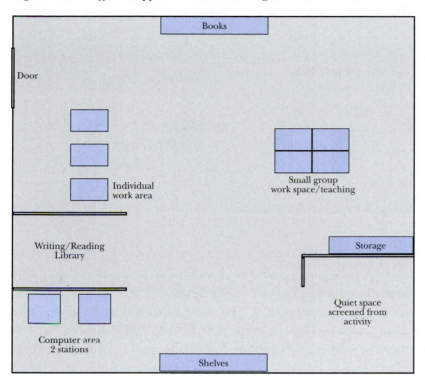

For all classroom arrangements, it is important that all learners understand the conventions of the classroom and the ways in which materials
are to be used. It is also important, especially when incorporating technology into the classroom to help meet the needs of diverse learners,
to pay attention to the location of electrical outlets and placement of
computers so they are not in the flow of traffic and are not exposed
to glare. Safety issues in the classroom are of particular consideration
when children with physical disabilities are in the room.

What is in the classroom will vary depending on the age and needs
of the learners. Younger children may need more areas for activities
such as sand or water or manipulatives that can facilitate working with
concrete materials before moving to abstract conceptual work; older
children will benefit from writing and reading centres. The way in
which the classroom is structured ultimately depends on the physical
space, the furniture available, and the teacher's approach to teaching
and understanding learning.

REFLECTIVE PRACTICE

Think about the different classrooms that you have experienced. Some were likely visually stimulating while others may have had little on the walls. Some had desks while others had tables. If you have ever visited a school museum you will note that some have desks attached to each other. All of these classrooms were organized by teachers who had reasons for organizing the learning space in particular ways.

The next time you go to a school, map a classroom and if possible ask the teacher why the space has been organized in that way. Share your observations with your peers.

• What differences, if any, do you notice between regular and inclusive classrooms?

INCLUSIVE PEDAGOGY

It is important that the teacher model for all students, but especially those who have special needs, what is expected of a learner and a citizen in a democratic society. This means that the language teachers use to refer to groups or to speak to boys and girls matters, because language itself conveys attitudes and expectations. Teachers need to be aware of issues such as wait time; that is, students need time to respond to questions, especially if they are cognitively demanding. The issue of cultural sensitivity becomes important here because in some cultures it is not appropriate to ask questions of the teacher. William Purkey (1999) speaks of invitational approaches to learning in which the teacher establishes a classroom context where students feel they are part of a learning community. Like Max Van Manen (1985), Purkey notes that referring to students by name and greeting them as they come into the classroom are part of creating a space in which all students are welcomed. Research indicates that human learning takes place in a social context. The teacher who creates a community in the classroom is more likely to establish a positive learning environment than one who does not attend to the physical and social space.

All classrooms also need routines and structures, particularly classrooms with special needs students. In addition, these routines can be thought of as being somewhat like the laws that govern our daily lives in society. Like these laws, routines should be developed with the community itself. Establishing clear expectations for behaviour and work completion at the beginning of the year can make the classroom a better place for all students. Many teachers develop a list of classroom rules in cooperation with their students. Figure 10.3 shows a primary classroom list developed by Mr. Hussain's grade one classroom. Figure 10.4 shows a list of classroom rules from a grade eight classroom.

Figure 10.3 *Primary classroom rules*

> **Mr Hussain's Grade One Rules**
>
> **To get along in our class we:**
>
> - **Use indoor voices.**
> - **Walk in the classroom.**
> - **Smile at each other.**
> - **Wait our turn.**
> - **Put our things away neatly.**

Figure 10.4 *Middle school classroom rules*

> **Survival in Grade 8**
>
> - **Respect each other.**
> - **Complete our work promptly.**
> - **Return items to the right storage area.**
> - **Plan our day.**
> - **Accept responsibility for our actions.**

GLOSSARY

Task Board—A bulletin board on which teachers place an outline of the tasks that students have to complete each day.

Bell work—Independent work that is assigned for students to complete immediately after the entrance bell rings. This work enables teachers to complete organizational tasks.

Some teachers also designate specific rules for homework completion or have a **task board** or **bell work** that students complete at the beginning of each class. These are all strategies that reinforce routines and help establish independent learning. It is also important that all students are aware of the expectations for tasks and projects as they are assigned. Telling students that a project will be assessed using a specific rubric helps them to organize their own learning, and also enables the teacher to speak with parents about these specific expectations.

It was mentioned earlier in this book that students have different learning styles and modalities. It is critical to attend to these differences in the inclusive classroom. Visual learners will benefit from lessons and a classroom that contains many visual supports, while auditory learners will benefit from the addition of audiotapes and read alouds in the classroom. In terms of visual supports, graphic organizers often help students (see Figure 10.5).

Figure 10.5 Sample graphic organizer

When considering how to organize the classroom, note that all visuals should be related to lessons and units that are developed in the classroom (i.e, they should serve more than a decorative purpose). A visually appealing classroom should also relate to the students' learning so that bulletin boards contain story charts or student projects, and primary classrooms feature word walls with words students need to use in daily writing activities (see Figure 10.6).

Figure 10.6 Classroom organization

Kinesthetic learners benefit from opportunities to use their bodies and tactile senses in lessons. Using manipulatives in math or concrete models in science helps many students understand difficult concepts. In addition, there is research which indicates that giving students the opportunity to dramatize or dance to stories stimulates creativity in writing. The multiliteracy approach noted earlier in this chapter uses technologies in the classroom to simultaneously provide auditory, visual, and kinesthetic supports to students.

In addition to providing support for different types of learning styles, teachers with special needs students in the classroom modify the curriculum and their teaching approaches to accommodate students' needs. These modifications may include making decisions about the ways in which lesson content is to be presented. For example, one way of delivering content is through a lecture type lesson in which information is given using Power Point presentations or overheads that have a logical and clear organization. It may be useful to use verbal cues or visual highlighting to draw students' attention to specific points. For example, in a lesson on the water cycle, students might be asked to provide an illustration in which key terms are labelled. Teachers might encourage students to use art to express ideas, then reinforce the art with scientific terminology as shown in Figure 10.7. The teacher might give students a cue to emphasize key concepts by saying "Remember these words...." All students, not simply those with learning problems, benefit from having attention called to the key points of the lesson.

Figure 10.7 *The water cycle*

At other times, a demonstration may be useful to vary presentation and stimulate student interest. When using manipulative materials in mathematics, it is helpful to model for students one way of grouping a set of materials, then challenge them to group the materials in a different way. In this way, students have a model to which they can refer. This is another way to structure learning and ensures that all students have the opportunity to participate.

Finally, activity-based learning provides students with the opportunity to physically engage in an activity. Such learning can follow teacher demonstrations or be structured so that students have a particular set of steps to follow to complete activities. Activity-based learning works well when there are mixed abilities in the classroom; it allows the more expert learner to assist the less expert student in completing tasks.

Teachers in inclusive classrooms also think about different ways in which the curriculum can be presented and organized. Teachers need to explore ways of modifying the curriculum while keeping in mind that for some students, going beyond the curriculum content is necessary and desirable, while for others it may be a struggle to master the important content. In planning for special needs students and thinking about the ways in which the curriculum can be modified, teachers need to make decisions about what aspects of the curriculum are critical and what can be left for later development. A chart like the one below might help teachers organize curriculum content.

Table 10.4 Organizing curriculum content

BASIC CONTENT	CONTENT	DESIRABLE BUT NOT ESSENTIAL CONTENT
Essential for the next unit of learning	Establishes the basis for the next unit and hints at what is to come	Introduces more sophisticated language and concepts related to but not essential for the content

With each level of curriculum content, teachers might think about the ways in which content could be introduced to students in ways that engage them and motivate them to learn. The following list provides different approaches to curriculum that might be used in various units and lessons. Think about when you might use them and in what subject areas they would be most appropriate.

- model making
- audio-taped stories
- variations on games like Jeopardy
- cooperative groups
- board games
- card games
- charades
- puzzles
- enlarge print
- strategy games
- drama
- simulation

The illustration features projects that indicate different ways in which students can demonstrate their knowledge. What skills would these students have demonstrated in completing the project?

Different ways of demonstrating knowledge

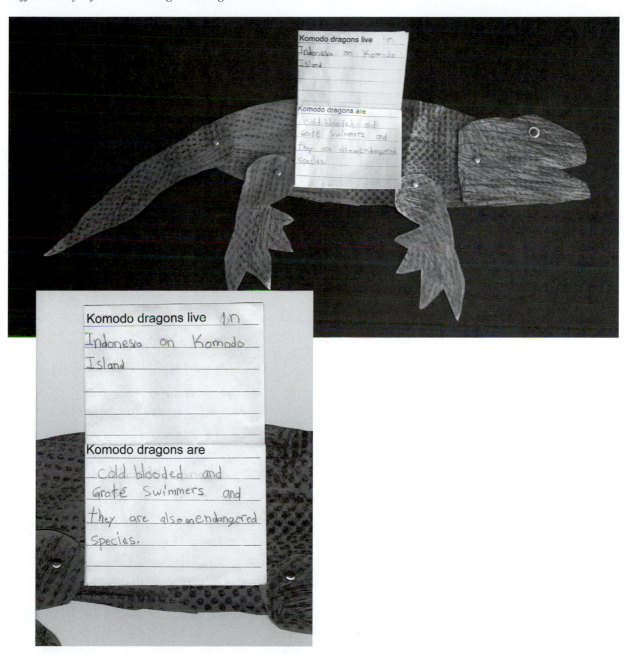

REFLECTIVE PRACTICE

For your professional portfolio, develop a curriculum project that can be used in an inclusive classroom. Suggest how the project can be modified for different types of students.

A key factor in accommodating diverse learners in the classroom is facilitating student engagement. In the case discussed earlier in this chapter, Steven was not engaged because he clearly was not being challenged by a one-size-fits-all approach to reading instruction. Research is increasingly indicating that students who are not engaged with school lack motivation and fall behind in terms of achievement.

DIVERSITY, ENGAGEMENT, AND STUDENT ACHIEVEMENT

One of the key elements in issues of diversity is whether or not students maintain a sense of engagement with schools. The Organization for Economic Cooperation and Development (OECD) conducted a study in 2003 that questioned whether the education system could meet the needs of students who have become disengaged from school. All children need to have genuine access to community, and this is perhaps especially true of students who have special needs. One of the factors that has an impact on student engagement is whether or not they are involved in learning that attends to more than simple retention of facts. The OECD study found that students who were asked to identify and become involved in solving problems that involved multiple data sources were more engaged, and that activities involving real-world learning and problem solving also contributed to engagement. This finding reflects the notion of multiliteracies discussed earlier.

In general, students are engaged when they

• are able to develop connections between school activities and those outside of school
• feel competent about their accomplishments
• have opportunities to share their learning with others

The challenge then is to create a learning environment that capitalizes on all or most of these attributes.

The Northwest Regional Education Laboratory (2000) suggests that to make an environment engaging, the following must be considered:

- Relate in-school activities with those that happen outside of the school. This type of activity allows students to build on prior learning and to bring what they already know into the classroom. Students are then valued for their background and histories.
- Students need to have some degree of control over what they learn or about the topic being covered. This does not mean that the school does not have the right and the responsibility to deliver a curriculum, but it does mean that there should be places for students to pursue topics in which they have an interest within the larger boundaries of the curriculum. There will be times when the students become the experts in the classroom who share their knowledge with others.
- Tasks should be challenging but achievable. In the case of Steven mentioned earlier, he was not engaged in a challenging task. He didn't seem to be interested in reading, as the teacher defined it, because he was already a reader. It is important to note that just as rote tasks can be defeating for students, tasks that are too challenging can be equally defeating. Don Holdaway (1979) spoke of a tension line in terms of school activities (see Figure 10.8). He noted that all learning tasks have a degree of tension as the student attempts to attain mastery. However, if the task is within the student's grasp, that tension is gradually eased. If the task is repeatedly too difficult, then the tension becomes so great that the student wants to get out of the context.

Figure 10.8 *Tension line*

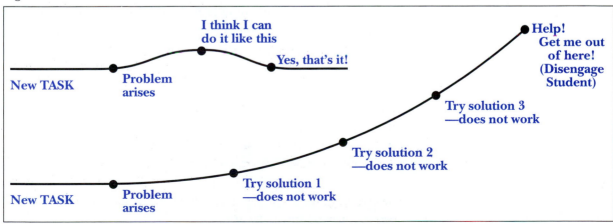

- Pique students' curiosity about topics. In journalism and advertising, a technique called a teaser is used to gain interest about a new product. In a classroom, a similar technique can be used to highlight student interest in various topics. For example, present a bit of information about a topic then ask the students to form their own hypothesis, or provide contradictory information and challenge them to decide which information is correct.
- Design culminating activates that allow students to share what they have learned. Culminating activities or celebrations allow students the opportunity to demonstrate their understanding and confirm knowledge by talking about it.

A key factor in facilitating engagement and enhancing student achievement is the creation of a classroom context in which all students become part of a community. In this way students learn that they have a responsibility to themselves and to the community as a whole. Those who are engaged because the classroom climate is welcoming and enables them to experience trust and security will be better able to learn. In such an environment, the curricular modifications that must be made to meet individual needs will support all learners.

REFLECTIVE PRACTICE

All teachers need to think about evaluating student learning. In inclusive classrooms, students and teachers should always be asking themselves, "What have we learned?"

Think about the following questions:

- What did the students learn?
- What did I learn about them?
- What did I learn about my teaching?
- How would I change this lesson if I taught it again?

SUMMARY

This chapter introduced various aspects of diversity in the classroom. It considered linguistic and cultural diversity, as well as diversity issues created by students with special needs. The focus was on direct aspects of instruction over which the teacher has some control and that can be used to help scaffold students' learning. The chapter also emphasized the design of the classroom climate and the creation of a learning community in which all students have a role. As the chapter developed, strategies for working with diverse learners and for engaging with school teams were provided. Finally, teachers were encouraged to develop an activity-based project for special needs students.

 **CHAPTER 10 ACTIVITY**

Developing Strategies for Diversity

Think about the information that you have gathered from this chapter. What questions remain for you about the issues related to diversity? To help you identify areas in which you may wish to gain further information complete the chart below:

What I learned about diversity		What questions still remain?	How will I find answers to my remaining questions?	What resources do I need to gather?
Cultural/ Linguistic	Special Needs			

Now think about what you have learned with respect to teaching strategies for diverse populations. Begin a list of strategies that can be used with those who are culturally and linguistically different and another list for those who have special needs. Do your lists consist of similar strategies? What are the implications of these strategies for inclusive classrooms?

CHAPTER 11

ENRICHMENT: Letting the Genie Out of the Bottle

"

The mind is not a vessel to be filled but a fire to be ignited.

~ Plutarch, AD *46–120*

STUDY OBJECTIVES

The purpose of this chapter is to
- explore the development of creative and critical thinking
- understand the importance of reflection and make connections between and among different ideas
- apply these understandings in the context of the classroom

INTRODUCTION

This chapter builds on information from previous chapters and explores the underlying factors that enhance learning and teaching by fostering deeper levels of thinking. The chapter examines the development of creative and critical thinking, along with the logical extensions of thinking into problem solving and metacognition. The contributions of reflection and making connections between and among ideas are explored as essential components for promoting life skills. Practical applications for the development of thinking skills within the classroom setting are also examined.

THE PROCESS OF THINKING

Due to the complexity of the topic, few people would agree on just how many different kinds of thinking are associated with the myriad of human interactions and reflections engaged in daily. Over the last 25 years, many different ideas about this topic have been postulated, and the trend has been to categorize different kinds of thinking.

Terms such as **creative thinking** versus **critical thinking**, divergent versus convergent thinking, and higher-level versus lower-level thinking are just a few of the terms associated with the development of thinking skills. The problem with these terms is that they produce a dichotomy that separates one from the other and results in an impression that one is exclusive of the other, both in function as well as in worth. Instead, it is important to consider how two different kinds of thinking can work in tandem with one another for the benefit of both. For example, memorizing (considered to be a lower-level thinking skill) can be just as important as synthesizing (considered to be a higher-level thinking skill) when establishing a common base of knowledge or needing automatic recall of certain items. In order to understand this dichotomy, it is important to examine these two dimensions of thinking: creative and critical thinking.

There are two major categories of thinking processes, namely creative thinking and critical thinking. Each kind of thinking is important and each is mutually supportive of the other. The following overview examines how cognitive instruction has evolved over the years with respect to the evolution of thinking skills.

> **1980 Critical Thinking Skills**
> focus on examining the specifics of thinking and dealing with problem solving in a systematic manner.
>
> **1985 Critical/Creative Thinking**
> realization that critical thinking alone does not account for all types of thinking; creative thinking focus added.
>
> **1990 Thoughtful Classroom/Mindful School Approach**
> focus on teaching *about*, *of*, and *for* thinking; actively promoting reflection as the key to metacognition.
>
> (Fogarty, 1997; Costa, 2001)

Most educators would agree that if we want children to optimize the power of their thinking, then we must challenge them to go beyond basic forms of reasoning and make both creative and critical thinking a priority in their schooling. These types of thinking are essential because once they have been established, they form the base from which problem solving and metacognition ultimately arise.

Decision making must be an underlying factor throughout this process so that children are actively involved in the construction and reconstruction of their own thinking, and gain confidence in their own abilities to make good decisions. The concept of autonomy is intertwined with this process and provides an overriding structure for the development of good decision making. If we want children to become responsible in their actions, independent in their thinking, and clear about their values, then we must provide them with ongoing opportunities to develop these vital life skills (Coloroso, 1995).

The following chart illustrates the hierarchical nature of thinking, moving from the bottom level to the top in terms of development.

Figure 11.1 *Development of a framework of thinking processes*

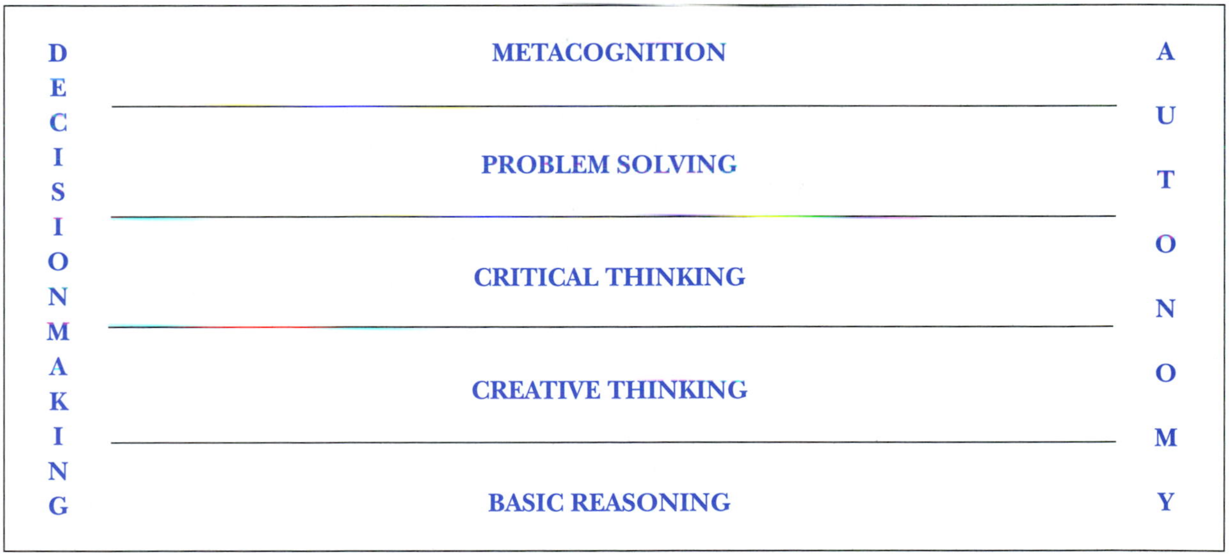

D E C I S I O N M A K I N G	METACOGNITION	A U T O N O M Y
	PROBLEM SOLVING	
	CRITICAL THINKING	
	CREATIVE THINKING	
	BASIC REASONING	

In this framework, basic reasoning becomes the foundation for all subsequent thinking skills. Once basic reasoning is established, creative thinking becomes evident and builds upon this base. There is a definite developmental component in operation; the manifestations of creative thought can be observed in very young children, before they have the neurological capability of engaging in the kind of analytical thought that characterizes critical thinking. Around 7 years of age, children tend to become more systematic, begin to analyze, and start to make a gradual transition into more critical thinking (Jensen, 1998). Problem solving capabilities are added as they are experienced and actively incorporated into the children's learning by the teacher. Lastly, metacognition develops as children engage in more reflective thought and self-evaluation. All of these capabilities are set within a framework of experiences that is supported by decision-making and the development of autonomy.

CREATIVE THINKING

In order to teach creatively, teachers must be aware of what creativity is and be able to think in creative terms. Creative teachers tend to be independent in their thinking and have a vision for teaching and learning. They tend to be risk-takers, since they appreciate the value of what risk-taking can ultimately produce for them. When creative teachers are supported by their administrators and by parents, they are "able to move mountains" and to do amazing things for the children who are entrusted to their care. Creative teachers tend to be strongly self-motivated, seeking out new materials, techniques, approaches, and challenges. Creative teachers tend to be committed to their students and work as long and as hard as it takes to achieve what is best for them. They are passionate about appropriate teaching and learning and go to inordinate lengths to ensure what they do with their students is of high quality (Sternberg, 1996; Gardner, 1999; Eisner, 2005).

> *Teachers can awaken the creative impulse in their students and in themselves.*
>
> ~ *Robert J. Sternberg, 1996, p.152*

Creative teachers tend to become very involved with their students and derive great satisfaction from each individual student's growth and achievement. They work best when given guidelines rather than directions, as well as the time and space to accomplish what is expected of them. Creative teachers need to be given this leeway to pursue

MORE INFORMATION

For more information on teaching for thinking, see "Teaching gifted children (and all others) to think better" by Kathy Checkley (2003) on the companion website.

these goals in their own unique ways and in accordance with their own individual teaching styles. Since creative teachers will naturally value creativity, they are more likely to support creativity in others. Creativity involves being a productive thinker. Some aspect of productive thinking include:

- Fluency—generating many different ideas/alternatives
- Elaboration—adding new ideas to make something more interesting
- Originality—coming up with unusual or unique ideas
- Flexibility—being open to different thoughts and approaches

(J. Juntune, personal communication, 1987)

When the list above is examined, commonalities emerge. Most importantly, all of these approaches are *generative* in nature—they involve creating something rather than dissecting or analyzing it. The unusual or novel is at the heart of creative thinking.

Creativity means different things to different people, since establishing personal connections and contexts are at the heart of creativity. Because of this, a definitive definition for creativity is difficult to ascertain—it may perhaps even be impossible. Many theorists have attempted to determine a definition, but it remains elusive. However, Bob Samples persisted in this endeavour and created the following list which captures the essence of the importance of creativity, the interesting juxtaposition of its various dimensions, and the impact that creativity can have on people's lives (Samples, 1987).

> *Creativity is more than mere change.*
> *Creativity includes accuracy and precision.*
> *Creativity is possible in all modalities, intelligences and styles.*
> *Creativity is both public and private.*
> *Creativity results in useful and aesthetic expression.*
> *Creativity begins in diversity and ends in specificity.*
> *Creativity requires both openness and closeness.*
> *Creativity is evolutionary.*
> *Creativity is attitudinal.*
> *Creativity is manifested in lifestyle.*
>
> *~ Bob Samples, 1987, p. 163*

CREATIVITY AND THE ARTS

The points outlined above highlight the importance of integrating ideas from various sources/subject areas and providing the freedom to express understanding in individualistic ways, as a basis for appropriate learning and teaching. Children have a natural capacity for using the Arts as an enriching form of communication and expression for all aspects of their learning. By using this capacity, they open up a wealth of opportunities for decision making and problem solving, which can ultimately translate into enhanced life skills. The Arts can also have a profound influence on personal development as children gain self-esteem and confidence through their own efforts. In terms of interpersonal relationships, the Arts help students learn to respect the contributions of others. Ultimately, the Arts impact on students' capacity to enjoy fulfilling and satisfying lives (Eisner, 2005; Gardner, 2005). The Arts are not a "frill" to be treated lightly, but instead are an essential part of every child's educational experience —they are every child's right!

HOW TEACHERS CAN FOSTER CREATIVITY

Robert Sternberg (1996) identifies 12 strategies for fostering creativity.

1. Serve as a role model for creativity.
2. Encourage questioning of assumptions.
3. Allow mistakes.
4. Encourage sensible risk-taking.
5. Design creative assignments and assessments.
6. Let students define problems for themselves.
7. Reward creative ideas and products.
8. Allow time to think creatively.
9. Encourage tolerance of ambiguity.
10. Point out that creative thinkers invariably face obstacles.
11. Be willing to grow.
12. Recognize that creative thinkers need to have nurturing environments.

(Sternberg, 1996)

Educators are lucky to be welcomed into the world of children and, in doing so, gain many insights into their own lives. When looking at young children who are still relatively new to the school system, consider how they are among the most creative creatures on earth. They can make magic out of nothing, and create art out of junk and beauty out of chaos. They can brighten their teacher's day with their naïve but sweet perceptions of the world. They can make everything seem better with their often straightforward acceptance of what life has to offer.

Even very young children have tremendous capacity to represent very complex images, but this is dependent upon the richness and quality of the experiences that they have had in their lives. The following picture of a Canada goose was drawn by a child who was only 2½ years old. The degree of detail in the representation of the body form and the proportion of the bird are really quite astounding! Every evening after supper, Emma (the artist) would go down to the local pond to feed the Canada geese with her father. This example highlights the need for children to have rich experiences to draw from for representing their own personalized understanding of their world. How limiting it would have been to give this child a prepared black outline drawing of a Canada goose to colour, especially since she might not have had the physical dexterity to colour within the lines!

EMMA, aged 2½ yrs.

In contrast, an all too common complaint heard from adults is that, "I am just not creative." Indeed, for some people, developing their own creativity becomes a personal goal as they get older, as indicated perhaps by the current preoccupation with crafts. What happens to all of the openness and acceptance that is so prevalent in children? Some earlier research by Howard Gardner provides some insights into this perplexing puzzle.

Gardner's Stages of Creativity

Howard Gardner identified three stages in the development of creativity (Gardner, 1982). The characteristics at each of these stages are as follows:

1. **Spontaneous Creativity** (1–7 years)
• instinctively creative
• delight in original art, music, drama, and language
• combine ideas in unusual ways
• use art as a means of gaining mastery over concerns or worries
• generally uncritical of their own creations and those of others

2. **Literalism** (8–12 years)
• become less imaginative
• concentrate more on rules and practical ideas than on creativity
• become more self-critical
• often feel frustrated by their own efforts
• search for literal rather than metaphorical meanings
• prefer to copy or collect pictures rather than create their own
• valuable as a necessary "latency period" to enable consolidation and mastery, and ultimately to promote risk-taking
• beneficial for practising specific artistic skills

3. **Mature Creative Expression and Appreciation** (adolescent years)
• able to create original artistic forms or ideas
• continue to practise artistic skills
• appreciate the artistic works of others
• intense evaluation of their own work

It is interesting to note that the characteristics and stages of brain growth and development, reveal similar patterns to those described by Gardner in his stages of creativity (Gallagher & Reid, 1981; Healy, 1987; Jensen, 1998).

When children come to school, they have already used their natural curiosity to formulate some personal understanding about how the world works. Young children tend to have more holistic and visually oriented views of the world (Healy, 1987; Pearce, 1977; Jensen, 1998; Yardley, 1991). Therefore, they are more concerned with overall configurations and are less focused on details at this particular time. As a consequence, the visual art they produce reflects this more global approach to representation (Yardley, 1991).

As they gain experience and mature, they gradually show more awareness of patterns and relationships, begin to analyze, and, consequently, begin to show more detail in their representations. This awareness and analysis becomes more evident around 7 years of age, and parallels the mylenation which occurs in the corpus collosum. This development facilitates the communication between the two hemispheres and enables children to coordinate their thoughts both in holistic as well as specific terms (Healy, 1987; Shore, 1997; Jensen, 1998). In particular, the switch to more literal, critical views of their artwork parallels the development and accessing of more analytical processing within the brian.

Toward the end of the Junior division, at about 11 or 12 years of age, many children enter a stage of being able to better deal with abstract notions, although they remain dependent upon concrete referents for verification of their ideas for some time (Gallagher & Reid, 1981; Huitt, 2003). At this age, they become better able to synthesize, hypothesize, evaluate, and apply or transfer their understanding to a variety of new situations (Hewitt, 1995). All of these capabilities lend support to the coordination of creative and realistic evaluative skills described by Gardner for this age group.

Serious Implications for the Development of Creativity

The Arts in general, and Drama in particular, can play a critical role in helping children express their growing understanding in non-threatening ways (Wilkinson, 1993). The importance of trying something new and risking being wrong cannot be overemphasized. In this way, the connections to constructivist theory and the development of autonomy become more obvious. The intellect moves forward when individuals feel able to take risks, make the necessary modifications to their existing notions of the world, and learn from these approximations or "mistakes" in all aspects of the curriculum—constructivism in action!

Children cannot make any mistakes in water, or any lasting mistakes in sand. But once they put pencil to paper, they are open to be judged and therefore may be less willing to take risks.

~ A. Yardley, personal communication, July 1991

Children today are under a great deal of pressure to compete and be perfect. However, there is an inherent danger in expecting children to deal with learning in the same ways that adults would. With more and more parents appearing to impose an adult model of perfection on their children's performance, even in the very early years of their schooling, it becomes a serious issue that needs to be addressed. Indeed, value must be attached to the reality that children learn more from the mistakes they make than from always being correct, since errors demand reorganization of their thinking. So if children are afraid to make mistakes, they will "play it safe" and only produce that which they are sure will be acceptable and correct from an adult perspective. In doing so, they will produce less and will not open themselves to as many new possibilities in their learning. While this whole notion of risk-taking might make some adults feel decidedly uncomfortable, especially in these times of accountability, it is time that risk-taking—and the attendant mistakes that result—be valued for the contribution it makes to children's growth and development, as well as to the evolution of their thinking.

Key Points on Creativity

The issue for teachers is how to help children, in very practical ways, to develop their creativity so that their life experiences are enhanced. The following points summarize some key suggestions for facilitating creative development in children:

• Make learning enjoyable. Children will be most creative when they enjoy what they are doing.
• Encourage children to take pride in their own work rather than relying on extrinsic rewards.

- Minimize competition between the children.
- Encourage cooperation and collaboration among children.
- Help children to recognize their own strengths and weaknesses in their work through realistic self-evaluation.
- Offer children choices in what they do and how they do it.
- Help children to build self-esteem and confidence in their abilities.
- Encourage children to be active and independent learners.
- Give children ample opportunities for free play with materials before they do something specific with them or a "finished" product is expected.
- Encourage children to fantasize and express their thoughts and feelings freely.
- Show children that their teachers value creativity.
- Model creativity as a teacher by actively engaging in it yourself and discussing your thoughts and feelings with the students.

(Cohen, 1988; Sternberg, 1996; Noddings, 2005; Eisner, 1972, 2005)

The challenge, then, is for teachers to create an appropriate environment that will ensure quality learning experiences and the enhancement of creativity. In order to accomplish this, they need to establish a setting that is rich in possibilities for individual expression and focus on children's interests as the starting point. Creativity will be enhanced if imagination is encouraged and if imagery/visualization techniques are incorporated into class interactions. A spirit of connectedness will also enhance children's learning as they begin to see how artistic responses can be used across different subject areas (Cohen, 1988; Samples, 1987).

There is another benefit to be gained when teachers model creative behaviours and foster a creative sense in children: they become more aware of the creative processes within themselves (Wassermann, 1992).

> *The freedom to create and invent appears to be closely connected with the development of creative, innovative adults.*
>
> *~ Selma Wassermann, 1992, p. 134*

It is difficult to find a definition for creativity as it applies specifically to children. It may be that the very developmental nature of children precludes such a definition being written in specific terms. Perhaps creativity in children is the process of exploring possibilities which can result in enhanced awareness and understanding to be applied at some point in the future. Sometimes the process of creativity can be limited by developmental parameters as well as by the quality of the learning environments provided, both in a concrete as well as a social sense. Teachers need to be alert to experiences that enable children to explore and represent their creative thoughts without undue pressure to produce similar creations.

> *We are meant to, designed to, engineered to evolve in creativity and intelligence throughout life.*
>
> *~ Arntz et al 2005, p. 153*

The importance of creativity for individuals, as well as for society as a whole, is undeniable. In this ever-changing world with future problems that cannot even be imagined, it is no longer enough to be capable of giving back bits of information as they were presented in their original form. With societal problems, environmental problems, and the technological capability to obliterate every living creature on this planet, the need for creative people is even more critical than at any other time in history.

Perhaps no one sums up this need for creativity better than Jean Piaget. His ideas could be thought of as a talisman for a better world!

> *The principal goal of education should be creating people who are capable of doing new things, not simply repeating what generations have done before."*
>
> *~ Jean Piaget, 1969*

Creative thinking enables people to look at things differently and make unusual or unique connections. It helps them retain a sense of wonder in the world around them and develop a deep and abiding respect for the contributions of others. It is an important part of the human condition.

REFLECTIVE PRACTICE

A Visual Activity

The following illustration shows how creativity can be represented in visual terms. This image looks quite different when viewed from two different perspectives.

Look at the image displayed below. It shows a cityscape as seen at night.

Next, turn the book upside down and look again. Now it is a cityscape as seen during the day! Such is the capricious nature of creativity!

Think about the following questions:

- How is creativity represented in this image?
- How can we encourage students to represent their ideas creatively?

What does creativity look, sound, and feel like?

Figure 11.2 Dimensions of creativity

MORE INFORMATION

For more information on creativity, see "Creativity—its place in education" by Wayne Morris (March 2006) on the companion website.

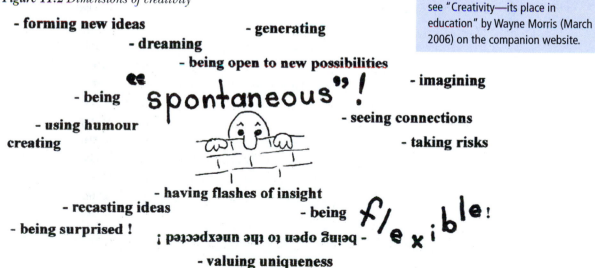

These descriptors highlight important aspects of creative thinking, the kind of thinking with the potential to enrich us in all aspects of our lives: visually, physically, socially, emotionally, cognitively, morally, and spiritually. However, it does not and cannot stand alone. Critical thinking is also an important part of the human condition and it plays a complimentary role to creative thought.

CRITICAL THINKING

The growth of critical thinking is strongly linked to the developmental level of children. Primary children appear to be naturally creative thinkers, since they tend to process information more holistically in their early years (Gardner, 1982; Jensen, 1998). However, critical thinking skills appear to develop over a long period of time, as children are exposed to different ideas and as neurological development proceeds (Shore, 1997; Jensen, 1998). This development parallels one of the major shifts in thinking which becomes evident around 7 years of age. As more reliable communication begins to occur between the brain's two hemispheres, the earlier holistic thinking begins to shift toward more analytical processing.

Teachers need to recognize the characteristics of both kinds of thinking so that, as they begin to appear, teachers can foster facility in both kinds. It is interesting to note how the changes occurring in thinking relate back to similar cognitive changes in terms of Piagetian stages, and also the stages in creative development outlined previously by Gardner. There are major shifts in thinking around age 7 and again at 11 years of age in all of these areas.

Teachers can facilitate children's creative thinking by encouraging multiple responses to different learning experiences. Teachers can also facilitate children's critical thinking by presenting them with experiences in thinking things through in more systematic ways. Taking things apart to show component parts, making lists, creating categories, and labelling are all examples of how critical thinking can be represented in concrete forms. Thinking skills for primary children must respect the developmental parameters of young learners and will, of necessity, be more elemental in form.

What does critical thinking look, sound, and feel like?

Critical thinking is:

- Purposeful
- Linear
- Systematic
- Analytical
- Specific
- Dealing with component parts
- Comparing
- Contrasting
- Categorizing
- Labelling
- Goal-oriented
- Predictable

When comparing the way in which the items are outlined above with the descriptors for creative thinking from Figure 11.2, the contrast in the format alone speaks for itself. Unlike creative processing, critical thinking functions much more deliberately and is more focused on achieving a specific goal. Critical thinking involves solving a problem in ways that are systematic, predictable, and obvious. Just as creative thinking parallels the processing of the right hemisphere, critical thinking mirrors the kind of processing going on in the left hemisphere (Jensen, 1998; Renzulli et al, 2004).

MORE INFORMATION

For more information on critical thinking, see "Maximizing learning for all students" by Kathy Checkley (2003) on the companion website.

REFLECTIVE PRACTICE

Creative and Critical Thinking

Draw a T-chart and label the two columns as follows: Creative Thinking, Critical Thinking.

Examine the list below and categorize each item under the appropriate column:

- make a timeline for the early explorers of North America
- design a home for the future
- make a postcard to send to a friend about a tropical location
- make a list of endangered species found in the Brazilian rainforest
- contribute a square to a book quilt written by a specific author
- outline the steps you would take to solve a problem involving long division
- draw a geometric shape and make a list of all of its physical characteristics (faces, edges, corners, etc.)

PROBLEM SOLVING

Learning is always more meaningful and relevant when it is set within a problem-solving context. It encourages children to become more involved and explore different possibilities. Pattern recognition is an essential skill that children need for problem solving (Renzulli et al, 2004).

The human brain is very good at recognizing patterns. Indeed, it tends to seek patterns wherever they might be, and to create patterns even when they don't exist in obvious terms. Patterns enable us to bring order to our impressions of the world around us and, in doing so, see interrelationships and gain better understanding about the unknown.

Sometimes people have to make a concerted effort to break away from old habits and outdated patterns of thinking. When they are able to do this, they become more aware of different viewpoints, more open to various possibilities, and more receptive to the change process itself. Unfortunately, in response to the recent emphasis on accountability, the educational community has become more conditioned to the notion that there is one definitive "right answer" for many problems. A much more beneficial approach is to look at the errors that children make and help children use them as stepping stones to greater understanding. One of the major obstacles in the path of children's learning is that the teaching community tends to focus more on the answers to be remembered than the problems to be solved.

All too often, teachers subconsciously train children that right answers are good and wrong answers are bad. This value has become deeply embedded in the rewards systems used prominently in many schools. As a result, children strive to be right as often as possible, and try to keep their mistakes to a minimum. The problem with this attitude is that it can result in conservative patterns of thinking that preclude the use of unique thought patterns, and it can short-circuit the creative problem-solving process.

Such limited thinking can have serious ramifications because no one can fully or accurately anticipate what kinds of problems or solutions will be needed in the years ahead. In order to address this, creative problem solving needs to be considered a survival skill for the future, and it should be a basic right for all children in their schooling.

The very nature of creative thinking demands that it be viewed as not only constructive but also, in a sense, destructive—old notions often have to be broken down, completely revamped and totally new ones created. Flexibility in thinking is a key component of this process.

Think of activities that encourage creative problem solving, for instance ask students to reflect on the similarities between a group of words, e.g., the words 'car', 'spoon', and 'paper bag'. At first glance, the relationship between and among these items may be not be all that obvious. However, on further examination, the conclusion could be that they all carry something. Children need to engage in many of these associative kinds of activities to become aware of less obvious connections and to think beyond the usual. Roger Von Oech provides some interesting and somewhat whimsical perspectives on this in both of his books (Von Oech, 1983, 1985).

ENCOURAGING THINKING & PROMOTING METACOGNITION

Teachers play a major role in developing thinking skills. As a teacher questions his or her students, the quality of the students' thought processes follows the teacher's lead. If questions have depth and breadth and encourage making connections, they enhance thinking. If the focus of the questions is narrow and not challenging, then students' thinking will not be optimized. A simple question that Piaget frequently used was his "justification" question: "*Why do you think so?*" The value of this kind of question is that it requires children to explain their thinking, and in doing so clarify their thoughts.

When creative and critical thinking combine, the results can powerfully enhance deeper levels of understanding and encourage more connections between and among ideas/concepts. Taken to the ultimate conclusion, it promotes **metacognition**, which is a deeper understanding that transcends our knowledge of what we know to include not only how but also why we know something. Metacognition has several dimensions and functions, such as

> **GLOSSARY**
> Metacognition—the ability to reflect and think about one's own thinking.

- a **planning** function when we consider what we already know about something as we begin to prepare for a new situation
- a **monitoring** function when we consider how something is proceeding as we engage in an activity
- an **evaluating** function when we reflect on the effectiveness of something we have completed

(Costa, 2001)

How Teachers Can Facilitate Metacognition

Teachers can encourage depth and breadth in children's thinking by

- creating learning situations that have *personal relevance* and meaning to children
- providing children with many opportunities to *make decisions* about their learning and their impressions about what they are learning
- providing many opportunities for children to *discuss and exchange points of view* with their peers
- using *visualizing activities* which encourage an emotional response to learning
- attending to *metaphorical thinking* since it enhances interconnections between and among ideas

(Costa, 2001; Fogarty, 1997)

Teachers need to consider how they can incorporate as many activities as possible that encourage metacognitive thinking. For many teachers, the following questions or self-evaluative prompts can be a valuable aid in reminding them to attend to this important focus throughout the school day.

1. What opportunities did I provide today for children to *reflect* on their own thinking and the thinking of others?
2. What opportunities did I provide today for children to *use and practise* their problem solving skills?
3. What opportunities did I provide today for children to *plan, organize, and present* their learning?

(Fogarty, 1996)

" *Facts are just bits and pieces of knowledge. They acquire meaning only when combined into significant patterns.* "

~ Howard Gardner, 2000, p. 5

One of the most powerful things that teachers can do is have their students engage in reflection. Opportunities to reflect can easily be accommodated and incorporated into regular classroom routines. Reflective journals can become a part of responding to different subject areas so that reflective practice becomes integrated across the curriculum.

As children engage in reflective practice, they will be:

RE- thinking

    RE- visiting

        RE- searching

            RE- focusing

                RE- fining

                    RE- considering

                        RE- directing

                            RE- examining

In the early 1980s, Schon created the term "*reflective practitioner*" to describe people who routinely engage in reflective thought (Schon, 1983). He believed that reflective thinking was a necessary and powerful tool when used by teachers to promote and augment their own professional growth. Reflective practitioners use their propensity for inquiry to enhance their own self-knowledge and guide themselves toward deeper levels of understanding. The benefit is that teachers, who are committed to using an inquiry approach for themselves, can also stimulate similar processes in their students.

It is important to note that children in the early years of school have not yet reached a stage where they can reason clearly (Jensen, 1998). In addition, they are strongly influenced by physical impressions/experiences gained from the environment. For this reason, they are often referred to as "concrete learners." This term highlights their ongoing need to seek affirmation of their perceptions from physical objects in the environment and can limit their ability to think critically. As a result, some levels of thinking may be beyond the developmental parameters of young children.

> **MORE INFORMATION**
>
> For more information on metacognition, see "Educational principles of learning: metacognition" by PaperToolsPro on the companion website.

THE IMPORTANCE OF THINKING SKILLS

If we want children to become more independent and responsible for their own thinking, they must become more aware of how they think and how others think as well. To do this, they must be taught to talk about their own thinking and communicate with others about their thinking. In doing so, they become more mindful of how they think and what they know, and take control of their own thinking processes. This process ultimately helps them gain personal insights into their own thinking (Fogarty, 1996).

Teachers play a major role in this process by establishing a learning environment where risk-taking is facilitated, truth is valued, and openness is rewarded. In such supportive environments, children learn to believe in their own capabilities for identifying and solving problems. They begin to learn that being able to think for themselves is something to embrace.

Teachers play an essential role in helping children discover how they perceive thinking. Some of the strategies that teachers can use include the following:

- engaging in active listening
- asking questions that probe for meaning (going beyond the obvious)
- requesting reasons and evidence to explain or support their thinking (justification)
- facilitating elaboration on a topic (extending ideas into new areas)
- encouraging children to listen to the ideas of others (active listening)
- guiding students to make comparisons and see contrasts (similarities and differences)
- making children aware of contradictions and inconsistencies (judging relevancy)
- having children discuss implications and consequences (predict outcomes)
- perceiving learning as a shared endeavour within the classroom
- listening to the students and ensuring they feel free to express their ideas
- appreciating individuality and valuing the ideas of others
- encouraging open discussion and challenging the ideas of others
- promoting active learning and full involvement
- allowing children time to think and change their ideas
- celebrating errors as ways to enhance and refine thinking
- providing positive feedback and encouraging elaboration of ideas

(Fogarty, 1996; Costa, 2001; Eisner, 2005;
Checkley, 2003; Sternberg, 1996)

THINKING SKILLS REVISITS QUESTIONING

Questioning accounts for about 80 percent of the learning time in the classroom, with the average teacher asking about 400 questions a day (Bloom, 1956) Given the sheer volume of questions asked of children on a daily basis, and the fact that about 70 percent of these will be lower-level questions (at the Knowledge or Comprehension levels), this becomes an issue too important to ignore. Bloom's research indicated there is a strong relationship between the kinds of questions that children are asked and the kinds of thinking that these questions encourage. When questioning initiated by teachers offers little challenge to children, this becomes an area of serious concern.

As mentioned previously, no one can deny the significant contribution the research of Benjamin Bloom made to questioning. For many decades, teachers have used Bloom's Taxonomy to guide their questioning and discussions with children (Bloom, 1956). There are, however, many educators who feel that his ideas were not particularly "user friendly" considering the number of different examples of questions that teachers have to remember at each level of the taxonomy. Another problem is that his taxonomy is perceived as far too abstract for regular use in a practical sense. As a result, consistent application of Bloom's Taxonomy has varied over the years, from teacher to teacher.

One method designed to address the problems associated with using Bloom's Taxonomy is the Q-Matrix approach, which was developed by Chuck Wiederhold (1995). The Q-Matrix is a 6 × 6 cell matrix containing word pairs that serve as prompts to use when formulating questions at particular levels.

An important benefit of using the Q-Matrix is that it can be used for any subject area. By moving across the matrix, the subject matter can remain the same but the level of complexity in processing can be adjusted to fit the circumstances. For example, the teacher might begin by asking simple recall questions to establish a common base of knowledge or to review some factual information at the start of a lesson, for example, "**What did** King John do that upset his subjects?" (Knowledge)

Once this base of knowledge is determined, the teacher can proceed to ask more complex questions that elicit deeper levels of understanding and involve more "process" types of questions, for example, "**How did** this affect what the barons decided?" (Comprehension), or "**Why might** this become a problem for the king?" (Synthesis).

GRAPHIC ORGANIZERS

Many teachers realize the value of using graphic organizers with their students to help them see connections between and among ideas. Some of the uses for graphic organizers include:

- showing how information is related
- helping students organize their thinking for speaking and writing
- depicting key concepts
- promoting a clear understanding of content
- serving as a visual record of complex relationships
- involving students in active learning

The following list provides some specific examples of how to use graphic organizers in the classroom:

- Use Venn diagrams help to emphasize how things can be categorized and where areas of overlap exist.
- Use T-charts to help students compare and contrast various ideas.
- Use target formats to help focus specific attention on a topic and surround it with related ideas or components.
- Use mind maps help students see the interconnections between and among concepts.

These are but a few of the many types of graphic organizers that are used in classrooms. Most are simplified recording formats, but some, like the mind map, can be rather complex and require specific teaching and guidance before independent use.

MIND MAPPING

A mind map is a visual form of note-taking or recording of information. It allows students to record a lot of ideas within a relatively small space, and at the same time, show key relationships. Since it also provides an opportunity to represent information processed by both sides of the brain, it is a way for students to access and use their preferred style of learning. Some key points about mind mapping include the following:

- Pick a central focus (word or image).
- Let ideas flow without judgments in initial brainstorming.
- Use key words to establish topics and subtopics for the mind map.
- Print one key word per line.
- Use arrows to show relationships and connections.

- Use images and symbols to illustrate ideas (drawings/pictures).
- Augment ideas with "clouds."
- Enhance ideas with different print styles.
- Use colour for emphasis.
- Use connected or branching lines to organize associations (with words, phrases)
- Draw words in ways that convey meaning (e.g, disappear)

(Nancy Margulies, 1991)

The teacher will want to have several sessions working with the whole class to demonstrate exactly how a mind map is developed. Children should be given ample opportunities to practise each one of the skills outlined above before attempting to do a mind map on their own. If this skill is developed carefully, mind mapping can greatly enrich not only the recording that students do on a daily basis, but also the value of creating a mind map for study purposes.

MAKING CONNECTIONS

One of the greatest gifts that teachers can give to their students is to help them see their learning as being interconnected. When learning is perceived to be isolated bits of information, it is difficult for students to organize and interpret what the learning means (Jensen, 1998). The importance of having a relevant context cannot be over-emphasized. Human beings are constantly searching for patterns and organizing structures so that what they are exposed to can begin to make sense. Teachers who set learning in a context that has meaning and personal relevance are already ensuring that the students will learn what is intended.

There are many diverse strategies that can assist teachers in this endeavour. Using a variety of graphic organizers, providing visual clues for extending thinking and questioning skills, promoting metacognition, incorporating both creative and critical thinking into classroom activities, setting learning within a problem solving venue, and promoting autonomy are essential for today's learners.

Children need to develop their thinking skills in order to "learn how to learn." No one person can teach all that needs to be taught or learn all that is possible to learn, especially in these times of rapid change and technological advancement. Indeed, the sheer volume of what is possible to learn grows exponentially every day! Thinking skills, then, become a way of managing not only how to learn, but also what is most essential to learn or to apply in a specific circumstance. By having many opportunities to discuss problems and try out various ideas, children begin to understand and internalize which actions are the most appropriate to use, in a particular scenario, to achieve their goals.

PERSONAL STORIES

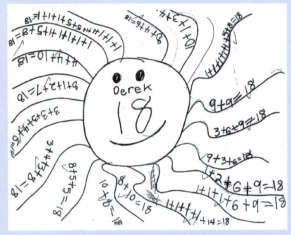

Being Open-ended: What Children's Creations Can Teach Us

A simple but effective strategy that many teachers use is to provide an open-ended learning application. The following is a magnificent example of this strategy.

Child-created graphic organizer

Derek, aged 8 years, was reviewing number facts for "18" at the start of the school year and was told to write as many number facts as he could where the answers added up to 18—an open ended task. The results can be seen in the graphic organizer that Derek created for himself. If examined carefully, some amazing insights are revealed about how Derek was thinking.

Start on the right hand side at the "double," 9 + 9 = 18, and then proceed clockwise around Derek's organizer. It is evident that Derek has started to take some of the previous numbers apart to make new combination, e.g. 3 + 6 (formerly a "9"); he then uses the *commutative property* of numbers to reverse the order of these same numbers, as 3 + 6 + 9 = 18 becomes 9 + 3 + 6 = 18. He continues to deconstruct some numbers

even further as "3" becomes "1 + 2" and then "1 + 1 + 1." Continuing around the shape, a wealth of information is revealed about when and how Derek changed his thinking patterns.

If Derek had not been given such an open-ended task, these insights would never have been revealed to his teacher. The teacher learned so much more from this creative product than ever could have been gained from merely providing answers to some questions laid down in standard rows on a page of number facts. It demonstrated not only a creative finished product, but also the process that produced it!

When the teacher commented at the end that she really liked his drawing of the "sun," she was told, rather indignantly, that it was a spider!

SUMMARY

Education is not just for today, but must go beyond traditional views of reasoning so that children will be better prepared to deal with whatever problems they encounter in the future. In a world where rapid retrieval of information is a technological reality, there must be a shift in emphasis to more holistic approaches so that *how* children learn is valued as much as *what* children learn. If the products that children produce are seen in the broader context of the process that produced them, they are made more meaningful and will thus result in learning that has deeper worth for the individual as well as greater assessment value for the teacher.

School programs need to encourage a questioning attitude on the part of both teachers and students so that critical and creative thinking can flourish. Reflective practice, which promotes deeper levels of personal understanding and, ultimately, the development of metacognition, needs to be a priority for incorporation into the curriculum. To foster this, children need sensitive adults with whom to interact so they can clarify and extend their own ideas, as well as incorporate the ideas of others into their learning.

Educators must recognize that valuable learning occurs not only within the school environment, but is also drawn from those experiences in the outside world of the child, both in a physical and a social sense. Such experiences enrich learning experiences and enable children to connect, on deeper levels, to the world around them.

> *...how powerful it can be if the teacher comes in and says, "Did any of you see the sunrise this morning?" Sharing those experiences briefly gives kids a glimpse of everyday spirituality. Students realize that they're not the only people in the world who are moved by these things. You know how kids like to lie flat on the grass and feel the earth spin? Did you do that when you were a little kid? I know I did. To acknowledge such things is a part of everyday spirituality.*
>
> *~ Nel Noddings, in Montgomery Halford, 1998–99, pp.30–31*

By incorporating real-life experiences and problems into the curriculum, there is the potential to powerfully motivate learning, since issues of personal relevancy are automatically addressed through such approaches. This, in turn, fosters collective responsibility while encouraging children to become ultimately true, autonomous citizens of the world in a global sense. By incorporating broader contexts, enriched and interactive learning environments, a focus on ongoing problem solving, and more holistic global approaches, cognitive growth can be enhanced and enriched.

 **CHAPTER 11 ACTIVITY**

This is an opportunity for you to "think outside the box"!

The following list contains five different *answers*. Write a question for each answer.

• a purple apple
• it was my dog!
• a hamburger
• a gold medal
• 649–8891

Added challenge:
Now devise a scenario in which all of the above can be combined!

PART IV

LOOKING AT THE BIG PICTURE

CHAPTER 12

ESTABLISHING BALANCE:
Putting It Together

> *When a day passes it is no longer there. What remains of it? Nothing more than a story.*
>
> ~ Singer, 1976

> *The truth about stories is that's all we are.*
>
> ~ King, 2003

STUDY OBJECTIVES

The purpose of this chapter is to
- understand the role of story in helping teachers and students make sense of the classroom
- recognize the concept of co-learning and be able to participate in a co-learning context
- understand the role of parents in the co-learning context
- recognize the role of critically reflective practice in growing into the profession
- understand the need to develop professional relationships
- understand the role of balance in developing a classroom that focuses on both work and play

INTRODUCTION

Teaching is a complex activity and although there has been much research it is still a profession that is not fully understood. Many studies have focused on the technical aspects of teaching, and indeed much of this book provides insights into what those aspects are, as well as summarizing what good teachers need to know and do to begin to teach. Yet recently a number of studies have focused on the teacher as a person. In these studies, there is a recognition that the teacher's own story or autobiography influences the way in which the teacher structures the classroom. For example, Connelly and Clandinin (1994) consider the role of story in the curriculum; James Britton (1982) suggests that memories of past experiences are in story form; and Jerome Bruner (1990) argues for recognition of narrative as a primary form of knowing. Brookfield (1995) argues that to become critically reflective, teachers must move away from innocent practice that assumes that just because intentions in teaching are sincere, the practice that results may not reflect the power dimension inherent in any human relationship. Brookfield goes on to suggest that teachers who want to be critically reflective need to understand who they are as persons, and in so doing begin to unpack their assumptions about the ways in which they operate in the world.

This chapter explores critical reflection and narrative as a way to understand who teachers might become. In so doing, concepts of co-learning are introduced, as well as notions of standing beside parents as partners and learners to support student development.

BEGIN AT THE BEGINNING: WHAT MAKES A GOOD TEACHER

Unfortunately, what inhibits development as teachers is all too often their own histories. For example, what do teachers see when their students sit before them in class? What assumptions do they make about who the students are? What assumptions do the students make about who the teachers are? Teachers are often too quick to label, too quick to assume that they know who the students are, and the students equally assume they know who the teachers are.

Brookfield (1995) suggests that teachers need to consider the taken for granted assumptions about the world and their place within it. Yet he also notes that as people, we tend to resist this examination, in part because of our fear about what we might discover. He goes on to outline three broad categories of assumptions.

1. **Paradigmatic**—assumptions about the fundamental ways in which the world is categorized. For example, we may assume that all adults are self-directed learners and it would take a great deal of evidence to the contrary to change the basic assumption.
2. **Prescriptive**—assumptions that describe the "oughts" in our lives. Good teachers ought to behave so that learning is self-directed. These assumptions also outline the ways in which we come to expect both teachers and students to behave.
3. **Causal**—assumptions that influence the ways in which we organize the classroom and the teaching–learning situations. For example, Chapter 6 explores the causal assumption that if teachers are well organized there will be fewer management issues in the classroom. Brookfield suggests that causal assumptions are the easiest to expose, but are only the beginning of reflective practice.

All too often, voices in classrooms are silenced by assumptions about who teachers and students are and about what teaching and learning look like. Teachers may not listen to students' stories because no one listens to them. Yet in telling their own stories, teachers take control of who they are as professionals and who they might become in the students' lives. As authors or authorities, teachers have the power to tell or not tell. The plot is shaped and the characters in the story assume the assigned roles. At times, the structure of the story imposes causality on random events. The structuring provides elegance to the tales and makes them seem more real and more polished. Yet often, when the elegantly constructed story is revisited and assumptions challenged, it is discovered that the lens through which the experience was viewed was flawed or opaque. Growth as a person and as a professional depends on the ability to revisit the original story to determine how it can be retold.

Take the example of a teacher who considered her classroom to have a rather democratic environment, where students had the freedom to choose activities and actions. The teacher was shocked by the result of an **action research** project in which a "critical friend" observed her teaching over a period of several days. The critical friend noted that rather than behaving in a democratic manner, the teacher's actions were those of a benevolent dictator who seldom relinquished control and created forced choices for the students' own good. In this case the teacher was able to reflect on those aspects of her behaviour that were causing her actions to differ from the story she had created about her classroom world. Once confronted with the difference between her story and the way in which she behaved in the classroom, she could begin to change her behaviour and create a new story.

> **GLOSSARY**
>
> **Action research**—A form of research that pursues action as it tries to understand what is happening in a specific context like the classroom. It uses a spiral process which uses both action and critical reflection on the results of the action. For teachers, action research involves problems of teaching practice.

Proponents of democratic schools also realize, sometimes painfully, that exercising democracy involves tensions and contradictions.

~ M. Apple, 1995, p. 8

Just as great authors are embedded in their culture and time, the stories teachers tell are culturally embedded. The language used by Dickens, for example, is representative of Victorian England; the sensibilities and the social structure that he wrote about and implicitly criticized are specific to a time and place. When teachers make sense of the world, meaning is made from a social location. Teachers who tell stories from their classrooms are confined by their experiences of the classroom. All too often, re-inscription of cultural stories occurs, rather than casting for new meaning. If teachers do not recognize that they are often privileged by their status and their culture, they may assume that all children share the same **cultural capital**. They may believe that all children should have experiences similar to their own and should eagerly accept opportunities to gain that cultural capital. The failure to recognize that different cultures have differing world views and need to be respected can create issues in the classroom. Thus understanding their own positions and histories is significant for teachers. The challenge is discovering how their stories have been shaped and in what ways they might be re-cast.

 # REFLECTIVE PRACTICE

Think about your story. Jot down a few sentences about a time when you first thought about being a teacher. If you were a teacher's assistant at the time, recall what you thought about the classroom. Think about the following questions:

- In what ways did you see yourself working with students?
- How old were your students?
- What were you teaching?
- Share your story with a partner. Were there similarities and differences between your story and that of your partner?
- What metaphor begins to shape your understanding of what it is to be a teacher?
- In what ways does that metaphor arise from your history?

The media recognizes the influence of story in shaping the understanding of various professions. Think about the films *Stand and Deliver, Lean on Me, Dead Poet's Society,* or *The Prime of Miss Jean Brodie.* How was the teacher portrayed in each of these films? Biklen (1987) notes that "teaching has suffered because of its reputation as a haven for the ordinary and unambitious," and goes on to suggest that the heroic metaphor portrayed in the films noted here suggests that teachers act as heroes when they are significant figures in the lives of students. Yet for all of its positive notions, the hero figure tends to be a loner who does not act in relation to others, but who instead sacrifices personal relationships for the good of the students.

Researchers who write about teacher autobiography attempt to encourage teachers to label their experiences, to name them so that in the process of naming they can begin to understand who they are and why they teach as they do. Richert (1992, p.142) notes:

> As teachers talk about their work and name their experiences, they learn about what they know and what they believe. They also learn what they do not know. Such knowledge empowers the individual by providing a course for action that is generated from within rather than being imposed from without… Agency, as it is described in this model, casts voice as the connection between reflection and action. Power is thus linked with agency or intentionality. People who are empowered—teachers in this case—are those who are able to act in accordance with what they know and believe.

Only when teachers understand who they are as people and as teachers can they begin to assume the stance of co-learner.

BECOMING A CO-LEARNER: ASSUMING A CRITICALLY REFLECTIVE STANCE

To become co-learners, teachers assume critically reflective stances in everyday teaching practices. Teachers who adopt this stance are willing to take risks with teaching and begin to think differently about professional lives. They reconsider past, taken-for-granted patterns of interaction with students and with colleagues, and assume responsibility both for shaping the curriculum and for determining what type of personal professional development is needed. Such teachers know what works in the classroom because they know and understand their students. At the same time, they may challenge the system in which they work because it seems unresponsive to the individual hopes and dreams of learners. Thus they practise a balancing act in which they simultaneously maintain their roles as teachers who are responsible for educating students, and at the same time critique their profession and its practices so that it can become stronger and more responsive.

> *Teachers learn just as their students do: by studying, doing, and reflecting; by collecting their work; and by sharing what they see.*
>
> ~ *Linda Darling-Hammond, 1997, p. 319*

In **co-learning** classrooms, teachers act in conjunction with rather than in opposition to learners. In this new position, qualitatively different relationships with students, colleagues, and knowledge evolve as nothing in the classroom is static or taken for granted. When teachers take a critically reflective stance, the micro-knowledge of practices and procedures, and the relationship of knowledge to the broader social and political contexts, are called into question. Teachers, together with students, are responsible for displaying the complexities of knowledge. In these classrooms, the relational nature of knowledge is articulated so that inconsistencies can be examined and action taken. In the context of the classroom this means that when presenting the story of Native land claims for instance, teachers will examine various perspectives and not present only one dimension of the situation. Students will have opportunities to discuss and debate varying perspectives in order to see that knowledge and what counts as valuable depends on the standpoint. **Critical reflection** is essential in any co-learning context. The interactions between classroom participants are in flux as each participant assumes alternative teacher and student roles depending on the specific context of the discussion and content. Interaction in the co-learning context opens rather than limits the possibility of considering alternative forms of knowledge.

In traditional classrooms, teachers and students enter a unique and specialized relationship in which teachers have power because they have knowledge. However, in co-learning classrooms, the power relationship changes because at different times both teachers and students hold the position of expert. The expert role contains similar assumptions about knowledge and power in that the expert has specialized knowledge that can be shared with others. When the expert role shifts from teachers to students, the teacher assumes the role of learner and the location of power and authority changes. Since both teachers and students at different times can assume the expert mantle, the context becomes reflexive as the teacher enters a relationship in which teaching and learning are activities engaged in by all classroom participants. It is not simply a question of the teacher creating the context in which the student can share particular expertise, but the student must also consider the implications of holding particular expertise. All of these actions are conducted within the complex social setting of the classroom.

Since co-learning involves close human interactions, the context in which it occurs acknowledges a process of persons-in-relation in which, through critical reflection, the participants consider the meaning of alternative voices and roles. Unlike collaborative learning contexts, the co-learning classroom provides opportunities for a critique of the structures of power that form the context. Teachers and students are together in a democratically shaped classroom; although there are places and times for authority, there are also times when all members of the community have their voices heard. In a co-learning context, the teacher and the students make a deliberate attempt to be transformative and systematically raise issues of power and control for discussion.

As a co-learner, the teacher moves between the roles of expert disseminating knowledge and a more fluid, dynamic relationship within the class. Teachers create a context for learning, involve students in discussion, begin to raise questions, and then gradually answer questions posed by students. As the teacher discusses with students, the traditional lesson format—where the teacher questions, the student answers, and the teacher evaluates the student's response—becomes more like normal conversation. By engaging in real conversation, there is the possibility for dialogue that relates to the expertise of the learners. In the classroom, the teacher's role shifts from that of leader to that of member and partner. At different times, teachers and students negotiate knowledge on equal terms. Thus the traditional expert-novice relationship is reconstructed as co-learning and a learning community is formed.

A LEARNING COMMUNITY: WHAT IS IT?

A classroom learning community consists of a group of people linked by a common set of problems and a common search for solutions. As noted above, the teacher creates the learning community by recognizing that all students have something of value to contribute. The members of the community share and develop ideas and expertise as they engage with skilled practice. A learning community includes both the individual student and the class itself, which becomes an entity that learns and develops its own identity.

Driven by a passion for learning, the members of the class are committed to collective goals that all members of the community are aware of. Characterized by talk and story-telling, the students in these communities know that they can trust each other and find support when needed. As the trust in the classroom grows, and indeed to foster that trust, the teacher may take the lead in establishing communication with the community at large and the parent group in particular. Teachers who understand what it is to be a student and be excited by new ideas foster the most effective communities of practice.

The following set of questions will help teachers determine whether a learning community is growing in a particular classroom:

• Do class members take responsibility for their own learning?
• Do class members share their learning with each other?
• Do class members believe that they can improve their skills and knowledge?
• Do class discussions show development of ideas?
• Do class members see themselves as constructivist knowers?

Table 12.1 The stages of development in a learning community

Stage	Period	Development Characteristics	Typical Activities
Potential	The beginning of the school year	Students face similar situations but do not have shared history	Discovering commonalities
Coalescing	The first months as students begin to trust each other	Students come together and recognize their potential	Negotiating community
Active	The period between November and March	Students develop common practices or routines for accomplishing goals	Engaging in joint activities, creating artifacts, adapting to change, renewing interest, commitment, and relationships
Dispersed	End of June	Students no longer engage intensely but the community is active and a force as a centre of knowledge	Staying in touch, calling for advice and reunions
Memorable	Re-visiting the experiences over the summer and later	The classroom community is no longer central but it remains a significant part of people's identities	Telling stories about the experience

(Adapted from Wenger, 1998)

Wenger suggests that to foster a learning community, leaders (i.e., teachers) have to demonstrate some of the following characteristics:

• Inspire as well as have skills and expertise
• Be able to organize daily activities and know when to delegate to students

- Track learning of the community (assessment)
- Display interpersonal leadership by fostering mutual respect and understanding of the social fabric of the classroom
- Foster connections between and among classrooms in the school and connect the school community to the larger world outside the school
- Think outside the box

MORE INFORMATION

The notion of learning communities has been recently expanded to include professional learning communities. To learn more about professional learning communities and what is necessary to foster learning communities, see 'Professional learning communities" by Rick DuFour on the companion website.

REFLECTIVE PRACTICE

Identify someone in your school board or school who displays one or more of the characteristics of a learning community leader. Think about the following questions:

- Do you agree that learning community leaders often have informal power that is significant in the functioning of the institution?
- What role do they play in developing a learning community?
- To what extent is their leadership acknowledged?

Think about a school in which you have worked.

- To what extent were there learning communities in that school?

See the companion website for the article, "Professional Learning Communities" by Rick DuFour. Think about the following questions:

- How do Rick DuFour's notions from this website fit or fail to fit those suggested here?
- What role does a professional learning community play in your development as a teacher?

Learning Journals

Brookfield (1995) suggests that keeping a **learning journal** can help teachers begin to view the classroom through the eyes of their students. Keeping a learning journal can also help teachers understand what it means to assume the role of co-learner because in assuming the responsibility of a learning journal, teachers can understand their expectations of students. A learning journal provides some insights into the emotional and cognitive aspects of being a learner. Just as with students in a classroom, a learning journal maintained by the teacher has a specific purpose and should contain specific directions for input. Sometimes it is helpful to designate a specific time to record thoughts and feelings in the learning journal so that time for reflection is valued.

GLOSSARY

Learning Journal—A way in which learners can track what they are learning during the course of a lesson or unit.

Brookfield suggests that a learning journal can be guided by the following questions:

- What have you learned about yourself as a learner this week?
- What have you learned about your emotional responses to learning?
- What were the most exciting things you learned this week?
- What caused you the most distress?
- What learning tasks were the easiest? What were the most difficult? Why?
- What was the most significant thing that happened to you as a learner?
- What learning activity or emotional response surprises you the most?
- What do you feel proudest of this week?
- What is the area in which you are most dissatisfied? Why?

(Brookfield, 1995)

REFLECTIVE PRACTICE

Keep a learning journal for a week.

Think about the following questions:

- What part of your program created the most distress for you?
- What was the most rewarding?
- What have you learned about yourself as a learner?

- In what ways will that learning influence your teaching?

After completing a learning log, think about using a **critical incident** questionnaire such as the one below to help understand yourself as a learner.

Critical Incident Questionnaire for the Classroom

- When did you feel most engaged in your classes this week? What was happening?
- When did you feel most out of it during classes this week? What was happening?
- What action did someone take (teacher or fellow student) in class that was most helpful?
- What action did someone take (teacher or student) that was puzzling or confusing?
- What surprised you the most in classes this week?

(Brookfield, 1995)

Teachers can use these **critical incident** questions with their students to help them gain an insight into how well their students are relating to incidents in the classroom. Reviewing student responses to the lessons over the course of the week can help to build trust between teacher and students. The experience of having their opinions regularly solicited makes students feel they have ownership of the classroom. Not all actions will be changed because of student responses; however, knowing how and why students react to situations in particular ways can help the teacher become a co-learner. Teachers will likely also note that different students respond to different activities in different ways. Some may find an experience engaging, while others will find it boring. This again makes the case for ensuring that teachers use a range of strategies and methods to meet the needs of all students.

Community is ultimately about the ways in which people—parents, students, teachers, and administrators—experience their daily lives in schools. The practice of community means that all individuals, in the context of the school, care for and about others. In a postmodern world, a school or classroom that evolves into a community of co-learners is based on an ethic of accepting others regardless of social class, race, language, or culture. In such contexts, there may be a conscious examination of the ways in which difference is constructed in schools and in society at large. In other words, once the teacher understands who she or he is as a person, the teacher may be able to assist students to understand the ways in which "differences between and among social groups are constructed and sustained within and outside of the school…" (Giroux, 1992). Teachers can begin to highlight some of the ways in which these differences are constructed both for themselves and for their students by using action research in the classroom.

ACTION RESEARCH AS A MEANS TO UNDERSTAND TEACHING

Teachers interested in the notion of developing a community of learners are also interested in maintaining their own professional growth. Many teachers elect to engage in action research as a way to challenge their assumptions about their own teaching and to begin to articulate their own theories of practice. Action research can help teachers

- evaluate their own teaching styles
- see different ways of teaching
- understand how to better interact with children as they move into the position of co-learners

However, some teachers may be concerned about the notion of research, assuming that research is only done by those outside the classroom not involved in day-to-day practice. Yet teachers are always asking questions about the process of learning. Teachers involved in action research may explore a range of questions, such as:

• How do I enable students with learning difficulties in my classroom to succeed?
• What can I do to create a co-learning context?

To get started on an action research project or to begin thinking like a researcher, the teacher simply asks questions. At times the seemingly easiest yet often most difficult question is, "What's going on in my classroom?" Asking this question signals the intent to begin a process of information-gathering and reflection that can change the classroom context dramatically. The big question of "what's going on here" is refined over days and weeks as teachers look at the class in different ways or begin to reflect on issues and articles in the media about education. In the classroom context, once teachers can think about what stands out they can then ask themselves, "What do I wish I knew more about?" Ideally, at this point the teacher may want to share these initial questions with colleagues, which could mean the beginning of a professional support group or a professional learning community. Some teachers find it useful to brainstorm ideas about their teaching, then begin to categorize them in order to focus. Others find that involving students in this process engages students as co-learners (see Figure 12.1). Here is a list of questions that could be investigated further:

• How might I organize the classroom to facilitate better traffic patterns?
• Are my centres used effectively?
• How might I raise student achievement scores?
• Are my reading conferences producing higher order thinking?
• Will contracts help establish improved behaviour?
• Are manipulatives an effective tool for teaching multiplication?
• To what extent are my homework books improving communication with parents?
• How might I help students check their own spelling?

• Will peer conferencing improve students ability to revise their work?
• How might I integrate the use of the classroom library into the program?

These questions are then categorized according to whether they are curriculum related or management related:

Figure 12.1a Brainstorming and categorizing—issues related to classroom management

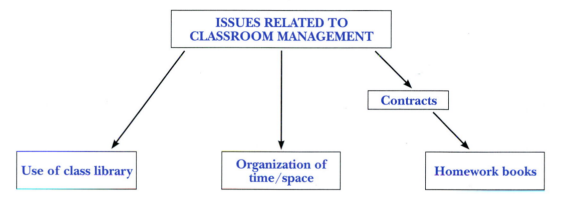

Figure 12.1b Brainstorming and Categorizing—issues related to curriculum management

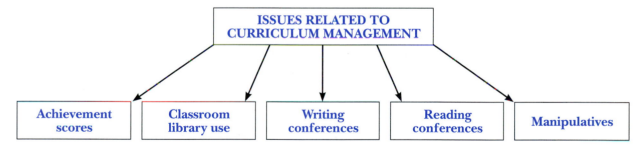

Once the questions are generated, they can then be focused through conversation with peers or by reading professional literature. Teachers should think about what they want to accomplish with the questions, answering for both themselves and their students. Teachers then need to think about how they will know when they have found some answers. Teachers who use action research may find that the chart below helps organize information and plan the project. Note that this chart is equally helpful for students organizing their own research.

Table 12.2 Information gathering process (a sample)

What I know about the question/topic	What I think I know or believe about the question/topic	What I must do to find information (be specific)	Where will I find information
• Professional literature suggests that directed reading can help improve reading comprehension	• I could model effective questions	• Read *Constructing Meaning in the Elementary Schools* for ideas	• Library
• My students seem to only skim read and not attend to text	• Students are interested in working independently	• Re-visit Bloom's taxonomy of questions	• In this text
• Students do not ask each other effective question during reading			• Ask students about their reading habits

Once a question has been determined the teacher may find that there are many sources of information, some of which will come from the literature while other information may be available from direct sources such as interviews. Here is a list of sources that teachers can tap to gather information:

• Observation (direct observation of students)
• Research (look up student records)
• Field notes
• Consult colleagues
• Survey other teachers
• Talk with parents
• Professional books

Teachers who engage in action research often begin by deciding whether to gather quantitative or qualitative data. One way of organizing this data is presented in Figure 12.1. It is important to think about the nature of the question since the question will determine what type of data is needed. Qualitative data is gathered through strategies such as interviews, diaries, and observation. Often the teacher's own files are a great source for qualitative material. On the other hand, quantitative data uses scores on tests, numbers, and frequencies to present information. For example, a teacher might want to conduct a behavioural analysis and use a checklist to observe and code specific behaviours. This information can then be used to help make decisions about program modifications.

Once the question has been designed and the decision made about the type of data needed, teachers can begin to gather data. At this stage they are observing, collecting samples of student work, making field notes, talking with students, and/or developing checklists and surveys for students and/or their parents to complete. Teachers interested in the development of student writing skills, for example, already have a head start if they have been asking students to sign and date all writing samples. This particular type of action research then uses the basic process of assessment that occurs in any classroom as a source of data. Once the data has been analyzed and themes discovered, the teacher–researcher can make the curricular changes that will further support student learning.

Like any researcher, the teacher–researcher has to analyze and interpret the gathered data. Once again, it is important that teachers be aware of their assumptions about students and learning as they make these interpretations. To discover what is important about the gathered data, teachers need to reflect on it, read it, and place it within the context of similar work that has been completed. This is a great opportunity for professional sharing and for learning from colleagues. Finally, teachers think about the audience for the research findings; is it for their classroom only (to assist in making professional decisions), or is there a need to share the findings more broadly? Engaging in action research in the classroom is certainly an important way for teacher to learn more about their practices and to further discover who they are as teachers and as learners.

> **MORE INFORMATION**
>
> For further information on classroom action research, see the following articles on the companion website: "Using action research and provincial test results to improve student learning" by Ron Wideman, and "The history of action research" by Janet Masters.

REFLECTIVE PRACTICE

Fostering reflective practice is one way to develop a healthy workplace atmosphere, since reflective practice treats teachers as professionals who have control of their own learning. To help you think reflectively about practice

Think about the following questions:

• Why did you decide to become a teacher? What or who influenced you?

• As a student teacher, what did you think teaching would be like? Why? What influenced your ideas?

• As a practising teacher, have your ideas changed over the years? What events contributed to the changes?

• When do you feel most valued/fulfilled in your work? Why?

• When have you felt least valued, connected to your work? Why?

Action Research and Teacher Knowledge

Teachers are in authoritative positions imbued with expertise and power by virtue of the acceptance of their knowledge by those outside the classroom who license them to teach. If teacher expertise is recognized because of external judgments about what knowledge is important and who owns knowledge, then a teacher's decision to share responsibility for both ownership and determination of the value of knowledge is fairly radical. Critiquing the very system that gives teachers status may place them at risk with colleagues, employers, and credentialing agencies. Yet critically reflective teachers who engage in classroom research take this risk, and in so doing enter into new relationships with knowledge and students.

When knowledge is viewed as fluid, as something that can be created and recreated, there is a recognition that expertise can change depending on both the particular definition of knowledge and on the context in which it is created. There are tensions between public and private knowledge that affect everyday life, particularly when private knowledge is not respected or valued by the school context. Thus in a language education class, rap may not be valued by the teacher whose education suggests that only Shakespearean sonnets are worthy of study. Yet critically reflective teachers may use rap as a way to examine the disjuncture between the curriculum and personal knowledge. They can then work with students to provide a commentary on the different ways in which languages and cultures value different forms of knowledge.

To teach reflectively, teachers have to learn to teach within the culture even as they question the fabric of the culture. Their actions are not such that they tear the fabric apart, but instead they highlight aspects of the culture and of knowledge that need to be questioned. They are moving in two directions at once: suggesting to students the possibility of opting into the present structure of power, but also highlighting the features of the system that may have negative consequences for everyday life. Through their actions, they maintain a dialectic role that demonstrates for students both possibility and limitations. In the classroom, this dialectic balance enables informed decisions and a constant critique that is shaped by the role of teacher as researcher.

PARENTS, TEACHERS, AND SCHOOLS: PARTNERS?

Mrs. Jones, a language arts consultant, walks through the front door of her neighbourhood school early one Friday morning. Mr. Keifer, the new kindergarten teacher, accosts her and tells her that parents of the kindergarten classroom helpers are to enter by the back door only; the front door is reserved for officials. When Mrs. Jones explains who she is, Mr. Keifer apologizes and offers to take her to the staff room for coffee.

All too often, parents have a formal relationship with schools that does not welcome them into the school's everyday life. Yet research increasingly indicates that parent involvement in schools is a positive attribute and has an impact on student achievement. The involvement of parents and teachers in the school is a relationship that has been ambivalent at best. Recently, however, in recognition of parents' growing concern for greater involvement in education, most school boards in Canada have created some formalized role for parents in school councils. In these councils, parents have an official voice in decisions and activities in the local school. However, as Fine (1991) notes, at times the involvement is more window dressing than real. In addition, Fine states that often only middle class parents tend to get involved, those who have the time or the opportunity to systematically participate in issues related to school governance. It is not within the scope of this chapter to discuss the full range of opportunities with relation to formal parental involvement within school councils and other forms of governance, however this section does raise some issues about, and provides some suggestions for, ways in which parents might be involved with their child's education on the classroom and school level.

MORE INFORMATION

For more information on school councils in Ontario, see "School Council: A guide for members" on the companion website.

Figure 12.2 *Types of families*

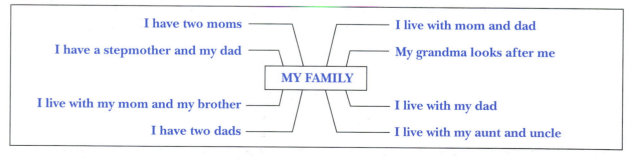

I have two moms — I live with mom and dad

I have a stepmother and my dad — My grandma looks after me

MY FAMILY

I live with my mom and my brother — I live with my dad

I have two dads — I live with my aunt and uncle

REFLECTIVE PRACTICE

To what extent is the scenario described in the school council guide for Ontario the same as or different from your province or board? What could be some of the issues that may be faced by school councils?

Think about the following questions:

- Who becomes a school council member? What is their ethnicity, gender and age?
- Who is heard on the council? Teachers? Parents? You?
- Does the school council have real decision-making power? Fine (1991) says they do not.
- Why are some voices under-represented in school councils?
- To what extent are school councils really about democracy?

Think about your own family and your school experiences.

- In what ways did your parents or guardians relate to your teachers?
- In what ways did the relationship between the school and your parents or guardians change as you moved from grade to grade?

Now look at Figure 12.2. Think about your family in relation to the types of families indicated.

- How might your experience influence the way in which you interact with different families?

There is likely one teacher and 25–30 students in any given classroom. Each of these students has parents or guardians (Figure 12.2) who are very concerned about the well-being and academic achievement of their child, regardless of the nature of the guardianship relation. The classroom teacher has to be able to interact with each set of parents and their child in a respectful and caring manner. In all cases, it is likely that the parent(s) and guardian(s) have one child's welfare at heart more than all others, while the teacher has to be mindful of accepting and treating all children equitably. Parents or guardians may not be as likely to see faults in their own child as they might in others. Consider the following scenarios and think about what you would do and say to the parents involved.

REFLECTIVE PRACTICE

Scenario One

Cassie is a lively 6-year old who tends to wander about the classroom and borrow items from other children's work stations. She raids other children's cubbies for their snack which she hides in her own cubby. She also pokes other children to get their attention. When they cry out, Cassie is not to blame. Cassie's parents are sure that Cassie would never take items that didn't belong to her and are certain that the teacher is picking on her. They say that she never had problems in kindergarten and perhaps it is just that Cassie is bored by the grade 1 program. After all, she has been reading for a year.

Scenario Two

Nabila is a 12-year-old girl who recently arrived in Canada from Saudi Arabia. Her family is Muslim and they are quite aware of some of the liberal attitudes of Canadian families. They do not want Nabila to walk home from school alone, so her older brother meets her every day. She has become a problem since her arrival in Canada since she no longer keeps her room tidy and has on more than one occasion spoken back to her parents. Mr. Arsam was quite concerned when Nabila came home with a Harry Potter book. He was concerned that the children in the book seemed to lack the supervision of adults and that was not a good model for his daughter. When Nabila failed to meet her brother at 3:45 pm one day, Mr. Arsam arrived at the school to berate the teacher for keeping Nabila behind to receive assistance in mathematics.

Scenario Three

Kevin was not making progress in his grade 3 class. At 8 he had not yet learned to read, but was very good with numbers and mathematics. When asked about applying for an assessment, his mother suggested that Kevin was "not a dummy, he just needs to be smacked to get to his work."

Think about the following questions:

- As a teacher, how would you handle each scenario?
- What issues do you identify?
- Which issues are within the scope of the school?

Think too about the assumptions that are made about each case. It is important to remember that all schools and families are different and your perspective as a teacher is also framed by your own experiences as a human being.

Today there are many issues that have an impact on children and their families. Consider the issues below and think about the impact on the family and on classrooms.

- Geographic mobility—families move from place to place
- Erosion of neighbourhoods—most people are away from home during the day; the front porch has given way to the back deck
- Segregation of neighbourhoods—different groups in different areas
- Increased poverty levels—gaps between the wealthy and the poor
- Increase in single parent families
- Both parents working outside the home
- Funding for cooperative programs to support families

GETTING TO KNOW PARENTS: WHAT TO DO?

Ideally the first contact with a child's parent or guardian is not after an incident in which there has been a behavioural problem or an academic disaster. The basic reason for contacting parents is to establish communication so that the parents understand who the teacher is and the nature of the program. Once a basis of understanding is established, it is easier to make contact if a more challenging situation arises. Many schools organize a meet-the-teacher evening (sometimes known as "meet the creature") early in the school year so that parents and teachers can meet in an informal setting. However, the teacher who really wants to establish a positive relationship with parents will have already engaged with them before this event.

Strategies

The following are a series of strategies that teachers can use to introduce themselves to the parents. As you read through Table 12.3, think about which one suits your personality. How might you modify these strategies to your own situation?

Table 12.3 Introduction Strategies

Strategy	When used
Letter of introduction • Include information about the class • Introduce yourself • Suggest what items will be needed for the year (pencils, special notebooks etc.)	• At the beginning of the school year • Usually sent home on the first day
Monthly calendar • Contains information about special dates and events during the month • May include suggestions for homework	• At the beginning of each month
Sunshine calls • Let parents know something positive about their child	• As early as possible in the school year and whenever a child does something special
Home visits • An opportunity to meet the child in the context of the home	• Usually done in early years contexts since it lets the child meet the teacher on familiar territory
Monthly newsletter • Summarizes special events of the month • An opportunity to tell parents what student has accomplished • Highlights learning outcomes	• Monthly or at the end of key units
Interviews • More formal opportunity to discuss child's progress	• Formal interviews may be required by the local school board and formally scheduled twice a year • Less formal interviews may be requested by the parent or teacher
Class yearbook • Good opportunity to get parents involved in creating a memory book of the child's school year • Includes photos and work samples • Highlights key school events	• End of year
Email notes • An opportunity for parents to get quick notes on their child's progress *Caution: not all parents may have access to email and others may expect instant responses*	• At any time
Homework books/contracts • Inform parents about daily or weekly expectations for their child	• Daily or weekly (decided by teacher, parent, and child)
Other ideas	

Figures 12.3 and 12.4 provide a sample calendar and letter of introduction.

Figure 12.3 Sample calendar

SUNDAY	MONDAY	TUESDAY	WEDNESDAY	THURSDAY	FRIDAY	SATURDAY
Healthy Snack 26 Challenge: Breads & Cereals Dog Bite Idea: Dry, unsweetened cereal (with or without milk)	DAY 4 February 27 *Library*	DAY 5 February 28 BBQ Day *Gym*	DAY 6 1 ASH WEDNESDAY *Music*	DAY 1 PIZZA 2 KINDERGARTEN PARENTS 12:45 P.M. – "How is my child smart?" NEWSLETTER GOES HOME BAHA'I FAST BEGINS	DAY 2 3 *Gym*	4
5 Healthy Snack Challenge: Milk & Dairy Dog Bite Idea: yogurt tube, yogurt drink, yogurt cup	DAY 3 6 SPRING FLING MONEY TO BE RETURNED TO THE SCHOOL *Music*	DAY 4 BBQ 7 *Library*	DAY 5 8 TOP DOG ASSEMBLY 1:30 *Gym*	DAY 6 PIZZA 9 SCHOOL COUNCIL MEETING 6:30 p.m. *Music*	DAY 1 10 SCHOOL COUNCIL DANCE-A-THON FUNDRAISER 9:00 A.M. TO 2:00 P.M. *Computers* REPORT CARDS GO HOME	11
12 Healthy Snack Challenge: Milk & Dairy Dog Bite Idea: Cheddar Cheese (bite size chunks)	13 MARCH BREAK	14 MARCH BREAK PURIM JUDAISM NEW YEAR SIKHISM	15 MARCH BREAK	16 MARCH BREAK	17 MARCH BREAK	18
19 Healthy Snack Challenge: Fruits & Vegetables Dog Bite Idea: Vegetable sticks, any fruit... grapes, bananas, cantaloupe	DAY 2 20 BOOK FAIR MARCH 20-23 LADYDAY-WICCAN BAHA'I FAST ENDS *Gym*	DAY 3 BBQ 21 FEAST OF NAW RUZ ZOROASTRIAN *Music*	DAY 4 22 *Library*	DAY 5 PIZZA 23 BOOK FAIR EVENING 4:00 – 8:30 P.M. EVENING PARENT REPORT CARD CONFERENCES *Gym*	24 MORNING PARENT REPORT CARD CONFERENCES *No Sched*	25
Healthy Snack 26 Challenge: Fruits & Vegetables Dog Bite Idea: Applesauce, fruit cups KHORDAD SAL (BIRTH ANNIVERSARY OF ZARATHUSHTRA FASLI CALENDAR)	DAY 6 27 *Music*	DAY 1 BBQ 28 *Computers*	DAY 2 29 NEW YEAR/VASANT NAVARATRI HINDUISM *Gym*	DAY 3 PIZZA 30 APRIL CALENDAR GOES HOME *Music*	DAY 4 31 *Library*	

Figure 12.4 Sample letter of introduction

Dear………………..

I am excited to be starting the year with your children. Grade two is a busy year in terms of the curriculum and there are so many stories to share. I have many interesting and challenging learning activities planned. I will be calling each one of you to talk about your child sometime during the next two weeks.

This year I plan to work with a number of themes beginning with *Getting to Know You*. To help with the unit I would like you to send a picture of your child as a youngster. Label the picture with your child's name and age at the time of the photo. I plan to use these in an "All About Us" bulletin board. In addition, talk with your child about a favourite memory. We will use these memories as the beginning of our writing in this unit.

If you are interested in helping your child you might engage him or her with some of the following activities: making grocery lists, reading a bedtime story, talking with them about their reading or their favourite television show, cooking together, playing a game outdoors or indoors, going to the library, having fun.

In the meantime, do not hesitate to contact me at the school should you have any concerns. Remember that during the day I am busy with your children but I am available during the noon hour most days or after school, usually until 4:30 pm.

When any material is sent home, it is important that it is grammatically correct and free from spelling errors. The material demonstrates to parents that the teacher is an appropriate role model for their child.

PREPARING TO MEET PARENTS: FIRST IMPRESSIONS MATTER

The Informal Meeting (Meet-the-Teacher)

There are pitfalls in every social occasion, and meet-the-teacher night, afternoon, or morning is no different. Teachers can prepare by learning and remembering the names of the children in their class and trying to have one positive comment to make about each child. Some schools make the situation a little easier for teachers by arranging a short time in the classroom before a less formal event, such as a family food night. If this is the case, having nametags for parents will help the teacher associate them with their child. In this, as in all instances of meeting parents, the key is to maintain a sense of humility and patience, and remember that each parent unconditionally loves the child that arrives at the classroom door each morning. The teacher's knowledge of that child is tempered by what Van Manen calls pedagogic tact (Van Manen, 2005), in that the teacher's knowledge of the child is informed by his or her understanding of child development, pedagogy, and history.

Formal Meetings: Parents' Evening

Many schools have a more formal parents' evening sometime after the first encounter. During this evening, teachers may be expected to discuss the curriculum and certainly to have their classroom ready to show. Sometimes parents bring their children to these events to share with their parents some aspect of their daily lives. Organizing the classroom for parents' night is important because parents will want to see where their child sits and where his or her work is displayed. On these occasions, parents expect that the teacher will be dressed professionally and be able to greet each parent and child with enthusiasm, even though the day before may have been long and hectic. It is also useful to have curriculum documents available so that parents can see what their child is expected to accomplish during the year. These documents, combined with samples of their children's work (notebooks, displays, reading material), will help parents understand the teacher and the program a little better.

The Interview (dictated by the board or required by parents and teacher)

The key is to be prepared and to have samples of the student's work available to provide evidence to the parents of the child's progress. If a behavioural issue is involved, it might also be useful to have documented examples of the behaviours over the course of a week or more so that parents can see that the behaviours are not isolated instances. Always make sure there is something positive to communicate, and be prepared to suggest some possible actions to take as a result of the meeting. For those starting their teaching careers, it can sometimes come as a surprise when parents look to teachers for assistance with parenting. However, it is important to remember that teachers do have specialized knowledge that may be useful to parents.

In any meeting, make sure the agenda is clear. Just as teachers have a full day, most parents or guardians also have other activities in which they could be engaged. When the interview is arranged, let the parents know why the meeting is being held and be as specific as possible. The following guidelines for meetings will help develop a relationship with parents and provide some assistance for the child.

- Listen to what the parents say. All too often, teachers want to express the situation from their perspective. Listening to the other in the interview, just as in the classroom, can provide a more rounded picture of the child. In addition, active listening will help to establish a relationship with the parents that will benefit the child in the long run. Remember that parents know their child well, although they may not want to hear criticism.
- Decide and agree with the parents on the outcomes of the interview. For example, if the outcome is to be a focus on a set of specific skills over the coming term, indicate that; if it is to be an attempt to introduce some form of behaviour modification, indicate that. Keep track of what has been suggested and plan to follow up.
- Teachers should think about how they feel when they go into an unfamiliar situation or a situation in which they have had difficulty in the past. Remember that some parents have not had success in

schools. The interview may bring forth some unhappy memories for them.

What can teachers do to alleviate their concerns?

• Tell parents good news as well as negative news.
• Teachers need to be honest in what they tell parents about their child. Parents and children need to know what progress is being made and how it can be improved or what the consequences are.

UNDERSTANDING PERFORMANCE APPRAISAL: TEACHER EVALUATION

In any school board, in addition to teachers' involvement in their own reflective practice, they are also systematically involved in some form of performance appraisal or evaluation. In some provinces like New Brunswick, new teachers are involved in a Beginning Teacher Induction Program (BTIP), while other jurisdictions are also developing initiatives in this area. In Ontario, the performance appraisal process involves:

1. A minimum of two classroom visits once every three years for experienced teachers.
2. A minimum of two classroom visits every year for two years for teachers new to the board or to the profession. Figure 12.5 outlines the evaluation process in Ontario. Discover what the evaluation process is like in your province by visiting the appropriate website.

Figure 12.5 *Teacher evaluation process in Ontario*

Notification of evaluation to teacher **(within 20 days of the beginning of the evaluation year)**
Pre-observation meeting
Classroom observation
Post-observation meeting
Summative report *Completed within 20 days of the classroom observation and submitted* *with the Annual Learning Plan to the district school board*
Unsatisfactory *Principal must prepare an improvement plan within 15 days*
Review Status
Unsatisfactory* *Principal produces another improvement plan after 2 consecutive unsatisfactory ratings*
Satisfactory *Principal to visit classroom within 60 days*
Review Status
Satisfactory* *2 consecutive satisfactory ratings*
Third appraisal within 120 days
Process ends
Unsatisfactory *Notice to terminate, suspension/reassignment*
Termination *Complaint sent to OCT (Ontario College of Teachers)*
Reinstatement *Only possible if the board of trustees does not agree to the termination* *within 60 days of receiving the recommendation to terminate.*

SELF EVALUATION

Although any accountability scheme may seem onerous, the intent behind the process is to ensure that children have the most competent teachers in front of them. Consider Table 12.4 below and think about where you fit in terms of your approach to self evaluation.

Table 12.4 *Approaches to self evaluation*

Strength Theory	Fault Theory
I achieve excellence through a focus on developing strengths.	I need to find my weaknesses and fix them.
I achieve excellence by managing weaknesses. I overpower my weaknesses with strengths.	I ignore my strengths since they are obvious.
I am aware of what makes people successful teachers.	I believe that success is the opposite of failure so I study failures to achieve success.
I believe that focusing on weaknesses wastes time and energy.	I believe that success comes from working on weaknesses long enough and hard enough.

THE CREATION OF THE CONTEXT FOR SHARING: NO MORE BOUNDARIES

Human beings have the capacity to stand outside the self and objectively view the self in relation to others. As participants in a socially and historically constructed world, both teachers and students need to develop the capacity to see the roles in which they have been cast if they are to become critically reflective. The task is to challenge prior assumptions and begin to reconstruct a different way of thinking about the world. One of the difficulties is that it is very hard for people within a context to overcome the socialization processes that have been part of the everyday experience. Much research suggests that in daily interactions with students, many teachers systematically reinforce traditional stereotypes and cultural patterns. Until teachers are aware of the ways in which they are implicated in cultural reproduction and of the assumptions they hold about teaching and learning, it is difficult to initiate any change in practice.

Further complicating attempts to create contexts for sharing is the teacher's role as representing a profession that is accountable to the public. Little wonder that for those new to teaching, the first concern is maintaining control and discipline, and then finding the right material to teach to implement the curriculum appropriately. Survival concerns often override any concern for the individual student, and indeed may inhibit teachers from becoming reflective. Further, since so much of the teacher's life is constrained by the day-to-day realities of the bureaucracy in which they work, yielding any power, however minor, may seem to be somewhat threatening because of a worry about loss of disciplinary control or fear of reprimand for not teaching appropriate content. In addition, from the vantage of the new teacher, critical reflection may seem time-consuming and problematic when juxtaposed with the reality of day-to-day tasks.

SUMMARY: FINDING BALANCE— TAKING CARE OF THE SELF

There is no denying that teaching is a demanding profession that embodies stresses and strains that are unlike those in any other profession. Responsibility for the education of the next generation is, in and of itself, a challenging task. Accepting responsibility for the day-to-day well being of numbers of children and their families adds another dimension of stress. In all of this, it is important to remember that teachers need to take time for themselves. New teachers in particular often have to be reminded that in order to be present for students, they need to be physically and mentally fit.

As teachers move into their new career, they need to take time to exercise regularly to maintain the required physical stamina. They should not work every day of the week. They too need a passion outside of the school—walking, scrap booking, photography, reading, etc.—to ensure they have a life beyond the walls of the school. That passion for living and for life can inform their work with students. Remember too there is a need for spaces for quiet contemplation and for simply enjoying being in the world. There are times when "a bear needs to be by himself to think his own thoughts and dream his own dreams." (Hayes, 1976) Like their students, teachers also occasionally need a time out to be in the world and marvel at what it has to offer. Only then can they bring that world back into the classroom to share with their students.

CHAPTER 12 ACTIVITY

Write a letter to yourself in which you highlight your hopes and dreams as a teacher. Outline where you want to be at this time next year. Will you be teaching? Where? What new knowledge do you hope to have gained? What life experiences will matter to you? Once you have written the letter, put it into an envelope and mail it to yourself. Write on the back of the envelope: To be opened "same time next year." When you receive the letter, file it until next year at which point open it and evaluate whether your hopes/dreams are the same. What have you learned? What was unexpected? What made you happy? In what ways has your story changed?

CHAPTER 13

CLOSING THOUGHTS:
"This Way to the Egress!"

"This Way to the Egress.

Famous showman P.T. Barnum used the above sign as a device to expedite the move-ment of his customers through the last part of his circus sideshow. On seeing the sign, they thought that they would be treated to the sight of yet another exotic creature. Instead, this led them to the exit. And so, the final chapter...

STUDY OBJECTIVES

The purpose of this chapter is to
- make connections between theory and practice
- understand the expanded role of professional development within the context of professional learning communities
- examine the impact of mentoring, moral development, and character education on the role of the teacher
- recognize the various dimensions of the process of change

INTRODUCTION

Many ideas about teaching and learning have been presented throughout this book, and, perhaps, many previously held beliefs have been challenged. This chapter presents a dichotomy of endings and beginnings—endings because this is the final chapter in the book, and beginnings because it is hoped that the ideas in this text will stimulate new thoughts as well as openness to new ideas. It will attempt to bring about a sense of closure by using some of the concepts and ideas developed within this text and, at the same time, providing some practical ideas and reminders for future reference. Finally, the chapter will challenge teachers to consider where they will go from here by engaging in some personal reflection that will, hopefully, promote further professional growth and change.

ALPHABET SOUP... THE 3 RS

Many teachers have heard, or may even relate on a personal level, to the sentiment that the "3 Rs" should be the prime focus and responsibility of teachers. This perception arose during the middle of the nineteenth century when the focus was on creating a public school system that would educate, as expeditiously as possible, a potential work force for the factories that were being built during the Industrial Revolution. Darling-Hammond even goes so far as to argue that the bureaucratic structures set up during this period continue in part to this day, and such approaches sustain "engendered passive and predictable patterns of teaching and learning" (Darling-Hammond, 1997, p. 67). And so, for many generations, teachers taught "reading, 'riting, and 'rithmetic," and assumed that children would learn in the way they were taught. This was also a time when society subscribed to such notions as "spare the rod and spoil the child," and "children should be seen and not heard." Fortunately, both for children and for the teaching profession as a whole, times change, societies evolve, and children's needs again come to prominence.

These earlier, more inflexible views of the teaching and learning process have been tempered by several factors, such as

- the passage of time
- researchers who based their beliefs on observations of and working with children
- teachers who have worked with children in a variety of authentic settings
- an overall increase in the knowledge base of the professional teacher

In response to these factors, there has been a gradual shift away from the notion of conformity and standardization as the prime goals of education, toward a focus on developing the teamwork and collaborative skills that will be more useful in the future.

The amount of research that has accumulated on how children learn is impressive. It guides today's educators toward truly meeting the varied needs of children through developmentally appropriate practice. The work of major theorists outlined earlier in this text, along with information on brain research, social constructivism, multiple intelligences, and the role of emotional well-being are but a few of the important sources that guide teachers in their work with children.

Teachers acknowledge that to ignore this body of information and continue using methods not consistent with current research would be an abdication of their professional responsibilities.

It is a truism that teachers are expected to teach and children are expected to learn. Indeed, many traditional subjects are still the basis of much of today's curriculum: children are still taught spelling and grammar, use phonics to help them decode words, and work toward automatic recall of basic facts in arithmetic. The biggest differences in schools today are not so much in *what* children are taught, but rather in *how* they are taught. Currently, the emphasis is on helping students to develop personal connections to knowledge. Attention to how these connections are being made helps promote deeper levels of understanding about what children are learning. The benefit for children is that when they truly understand something, they don't have to memorize it!

"From this ……… to this"

While dealing with issues and problems has always been a part of teachers' professional responsibilities, teachers are currently facing additional and unique challenges, which include the following:

- greater diversity in the student population (linguistically, experientially, culturally, and socio-economically)
- an ever-increasing curriculum load (conflict management, character development, etc.)
- a higher degree of accountability to a wider range of stakeholders
- a broader definition of teacher responsibilities (responsibility for the physical, social, emotional, as well as cognitive well-being of students)

When all of these are taken into consideration, a teacher's task of dealing effectively with the needs of the individual child, of continuing to refine their professional knowledge base of child development, and of handling an ever-expanding curriculum can appear at times to be not only an awesome responsibility, but also an almost insurmountable task. Most importantly, teachers must keep in mind that the prime reason for their being in the classroom is the children.

> *The habits we form from childhood make no small difference, but rather they make all the difference.*
>
> ~ *Aristotle, 384–322* BC

WHAT IS EFFECTIVE TEACHING?

Before considering how to improve education, it is important to determine what is effective teaching. The research of Stronge, Tucker, and Hindman identifies certain key features associated with the qualities of effective teaching (Stronge et al, 2004). Their findings indicate that some of the basic prerequisites for effective teaching include verbal ability, content knowledge, educational coursework, teacher certification, and teaching experience.

Once the researchers established this base of prerequisites for what comprised effective teaching, they went on to identify the qualities of effective teachers, including:

MORE INFORMATION

For more information on effective teaching, see "Embracing teacher quality & excellence: Perception, reality and casualty" by Mary D. Monsour (2006) on the companion website.

- the presence of the prerequisites (as outlined above)
- the teacher as a person (what they bring personally to the classroom)
- organization and classroom management (natural inclination and learned skills)
- organizing for instruction (natural inclination and learned skills)
- implementing instruction (learned skills)
- monitoring student progress and potential (learned skills)

(Stronge, Tucker, and Hindman, 2004)

REFLECTIVE PRACTICE

Think of the following questions:

• What skills do you bring to your teaching that would make you an effective teacher?

• What does effective teaching look, sound, and feel like?

Make a mind map to summarize your ideas.

Fulfilling all of these responsibilities can be a daunting task for teachers, especially for those new to the profession or new to a division or grade. The following diagram highlights some of the classroom teacher's obvious responsibilities on a daily basis (see Figure 13.1).

Figure 13.1 Balancing the many responsibilities of the teacher

The Arts

Health & Physical Education

Language

Mathematics

Science & Technology

Social Studies
Geography & History

The Kindergarten Program

Physical Development
– Health

– Safety

Affective Development
– Emotional/Social

– Spiritual

Cognitive Development
– Knowledge

– Thinking Skills

– Problem Solving

(WFA, 2006)

A major issue facing teachers is the ongoing task of learning how to balance all of these responsibilities, while still maintaining a sense of humour as well as enthusiasm and joy for their teaching. It is not an easy task, and it cannot be accomplished alone. Just as students require appropriate assistance as they progress through school, teachers also need ongoing support in meeting the daily challenges they encounter on their professional journey. Otherwise, the profession will run the risk of not only losing many new teachers from classrooms, but also of losing the potential contributions which they could have made to the profession overall. Berliner indicates that it takes between three to eight years for a teacher to master the skills of teaching (Scherer, 2001). Retention and support of new teachers in these beginning years then becomes of paramount concern. In order for this to happen effectively, the responsibility for the education of children must not rest with teachers alone, but must be shared by the entire educational community and even by society as a whole.

If teachers are to continue to be effective and to be viewed as exemplars of appropriate practice, it is essential that they become active participants with their peers in developing **professional learning communities** that will enable them to take responsibility for their own professional growth.

PROFESSIONAL LEARNING COMMUNITIES

It is important at this point to digress and briefly revisit Lev Vygotsky's concept of the Zone of Proximal Development. Vygotsky believed that children could be guided to master some tasks or skills that would ordinarily be considered too difficult for them to do on their own if they had the assistance of an adult or more highly skilled peer. When they were challenged to work beyond their level of independent functioning, they were operating within their Zone of Proximal Development (Vygotsky, 1978). For many years, educators have applied this principle to their work with students, but it is also appropriate to consider how the same principle could be applied to foster growth in the professional learning of teachers.

When new teachers are coached by more experienced colleagues who mentor, challenge, and support them, then they too are working in *their* Zone of Proximal Development and, therefore, there is the potential for everyone to benefit.

- Students will benefit from their teachers' enhanced level of skills.
- New teachers will benefit from the expertise of their peers.
- Experienced teachers will benefit from clarifying their own views on teaching and learning, and from making a contribution to the next generation of teachers and students.

GLOSSARY

Professional Learning Community—a group of professionals working together to provide mutual support for devising solutions to a set of issues they hold in common. This collaboration should facilitate their collective professional growth and is characterized by a commitment to student learning, a culture of collaboration, and a focus on achieving results.

MORE INFORMATION

For more information on Lev Vygotsky, see "Vygotsky" on the companion website.

LEARNING WITH COLLEAGUES

In order to enhance their teaching skills and sense of professionalism, teachers must be prepared to be more reflective, to become more autonomous learners, and to demonstrate leadership in achieving these goals. Such a process naturally involves working with colleagues and requires teachers to look at professional development in new ways. Two essential components include the concept of schools as learning communities and collaborative learning.

In the previous chapter, specific information was shared about the value of developing a learning community within the classroom. It is now appropriate to expand upon this idea to include looking at how teachers individually, and the teaching profession as a whole, could benefit from such parallel approaches. Wenger (1998) suggests the following stages of development toward building a learning community. Although the focus of this research was on learning communities within the classroom, the ideas are easily adapted to parallel the work of building a professional learning community for teachers.

1. **Potential**

   At the beginning of the process, there is a recognition of a lack of history and time is spent getting to know one another so that shared commonalities among teachers can be identified.

2. **Coalescing**

   As the process continues, potential strengths and limitations within the group, are recognized and the teachers negotiate what their professional learning community will be like. Professional goals are then set cooperatively.

3. **Active**

   At this stage in the process, the focus is on developing ways of accomplishing goals through changing practices. There is renewed interest in the profession and in strengthening relationships within their support group.

4. **Dispersed**

   The group dissolves and individuals works on achieving the goals set by the group; ongoing professional support for one another continues.

5. **Memorable**

   Lastly, the experiences of the group are revisited individually and are, in turn, related to others.

(Adapted from Wenger, 1998)

Now that the process has been ascertained, the following strategies outline what teachers can do to foster growth in the professional learning community with their colleagues:

- sharing leadership, expertise, and skill
- ongoing leadership by organizing regular meetings of colleagues
- documenting the learning of the professional learning community (journals, records, etc.)
- interpersonal leadership through fostering mutual respect and understanding the social fabric of the professional group
- boundary leadership by fostering connections to other professionals/groups
- creative thinking to develop new and unique approaches ("thinking outside of the box")

(Adapted from Wenger, 1998)

Darling-Hammond's research provides further insights into school reform and the value of learning within a professional community. She strongly advocates establishing systems that will support both students' and teachers' learning. Her ideas focus on teachers working in concerted ways to create an ideal of a learning community. She believes that certain principles and practices must be in place if this is to happen effectively.

- Shared governance must be a part of the process.
- Teacher knowledge must be a prime consideration and must be valued.
- All parties must develop and articulate a shared vision of what good teaching is, and then agree upon and set goals, commitments, and practices.
- Small, ongoing learning groups must be set up for both students and teachers.
- Time must be provided for teachers to plan and work collaboratively with others.
- Strategic mentoring must be provided, especially for new teachers.
- A rich array of learning opportunities must be made available (e.g., explore the idea of professional learning schools)

(Darling-Hammond, 1997)

Darling-Hammond (1997) has issued a further challenge to the teaching profession as a whole, and policy makers in particular, to release some of the more rigid controls imposed on teachers and to encourage more teacher flexibility, adaptability, and creativity. She stresses that "what matters most is the commitment of teachers and their capacities" (Darling-Hammond, 1997, p. 293).

DuFour and Eaker have added a further distinction to the discussion of school reform and improvement of student achievement by emphasizing that schools need to shift their focus from "ensuring that students are *taught*, to ensuring that students *learn*" (DuFour & Eaker, 2005, p. 32). Their research suggests that when this shift in thinking occurs, teachers work more collaboratively to find appropriate practices that will ensure student success. For DuFour, student achievement is influenced in positive ways by the following factors:

• shared vision
• collective responsibility and commitment to high levels of learning for every student
• collaboration and commitment between home and school
• monitoring and intervention to ensure a systematic response to individual student needs
• stipulating a requirement that students receive additional assistance and spend extra time on working through their problems
• active monitoring of the process by school leaders

(DuFour, 2004)

> *The collective commitment to high levels of learning for every student led these schools to assess the impact of their efforts and decisions based on tangible results. When teachers in schools are truly focused on student learning as their primary mission, they inevitably seek valid methods to assess the extent and depth of that learning.*
>
> *~ DuFour, 2004, p. 2*

REFLECTIVE PRACTICE

Consider some of the schools you have visited. Think about the following questions:

• What evidence is there that teachers are engaged in developing a professional learning community?

• How might you initiate the development of a professional learning group in your school next year?

Support for school reform continues to gain momentum, and many researchers are adding significantly to the knowledge base. Discussions abound about the changes occurring within the educational community. Most recently, Andy Hargreaves has added a new perspective to the issue by outlining seven characteristics necessary for sustaining educational reform in schools (Hargreaves & Fink, 2006).

Seven Characteristics of Educational Reform

1. **Depth**: Dealing with learning that matters with a focus on understanding and connecting to all students.
2. **Endurance**: Distributing leadership to many so that change lasts over time with a legacy in people, in principles, and in practices.
3. **Breadth**: Developing a community of learners so that real input is injected into conversations about reform.
4. **Justice**: Considering the effect of one aspect on every other part; competition does not improve matters.
5. **Diversity**: Many are now moving away from the idea of standardization since a given reform is not a solution for everyone or every circumstance.
6. **Resourcefulness**: The profession needs to release the energy of the young and support them in developing and implementing new ideas.
7. **Conservation**: The profession should not demean the past but should retain what has been learned and, from this base, embrace change for the future.

(Hargreaves & Fink, 2006)

Without these characteristics, lasting and meaningful reform will be very difficult to achieve. For many researchers, the keys to reform are:

Involvement—ensures that the talents and perspectives of all parties can be accessed to make a more comprehensive and balanced process.

Openness—ensures receptiveness to the ideas of others as well as transparency so that critical examination and accountability will be vital components.

Authenticity—ensures that the process and, ultimately, the goals will have real-life meaning and applications for all parties.

Further support for these ideas is also evident in earlier research by Elliot Eisner.

> *Much of what we attempt to do in education is predicated on standardization and uniformity... a shift needs to be made from a conception of schooling as a horse-race or educational Olympics to a conception of schools as places that foster student's distinctive talents.*
>
> ~ *Elliot Eisner, 1999, pp.56–57*

> **MORE INFORMATION**
>
> For more information on professional learning communities, see "Leading edge: Culture shift doesn't occur overnight —or without conflict" by Rick DuFour on the companion website.

BENEFITS OF PARTICIPATION IN A PROFESSIONAL LEARNING COMMUNITY

When teachers agree to be part of a professional learning community, many benefits become evident for students, for teachers, and for the profession as a whole. As part of the process, teachers assume responsibility for their own personal professional growth and in doing so, also become more autonomous learners. By experiencing the power of autonomy firsthand, there is the potential for making teachers more sensitive to the value of autonomy in the learning process of their students as well as for themselves.

As teachers have input into shaping the curriculum, it becomes more relevant and meaningful for their students and learning is enhanced. A necessary skill for improving professional practice involves engaging in critical thinking about their professional practice.

When teachers act in conjunction with other professionals to set collective goals, examine inconsistencies, and take appropriate actions, they develop specialized and more dynamic relationships with their colleagues. In response to this, support groups develop to facilitate professional growth within the profession. Relationship roles become more flexible and interchangeable, with complexity of social relationships resulting.

As issues of relevance are raised and alternate viewpoints are taken into consideration, a context is created for critiquing and discussing professional issues. Professionalism is enhanced as research is examined as a resource and support for the ideas being considered. This provides opportunities for professionals to transform the structure, content, and system from within the educational community. The end result is that the professional autonomy of teachers is enhanced (Darling-Hammond, 1997; DuFour & Eaker, 2005).

Just as it is essential for students to learn within a caring classroom community, the same is also true for their teachers. They must see their colleagues as a positive force for enabling change, both in their individual practice as well as in the profession as a whole. One way in which the change process can be facilitated is if teachers are assisted in their growth by a strong mentorship program.

The Role of Mentoring

One of the dimensions of participating in a professional learning community is the role of **mentoring**. Without strong role models and supportive colleagues, little advancement could be sustained within the teaching profession. Depending on where a teacher happens to be in his or her professional career, the role of mentoring can be considered in different ways—benefits for new teachers and value for experienced teachers. If new teachers are expected to grow naturally into their professional roles, then mentoring programs must be established to support them, especially in their beginning years in the profession. Similarly, experienced teachers also require mentoring to enable them to continue in their professional growth and to become lifelong learners.

Good mentoring involves many different skills and capabilities. It thrives in an atmosphere where mentors are able to adjust their interactions to suit the needs of the person being mentored, to use their own self-knowledge as a starting point in communicating with a person new to the profession, and to adopt a positive attitude toward the mentoring process (Rowley, 1999).

GLOSSARY

Mentoring—occurs when a role model offers support to another person and shares their knowledge, expertise, and experiences with that person.

According to Rowley (1999), there are several qualities that characterize a good mentor which include:

- a strong commitment to the role of mentoring
- an accepting attitude toward the beginning teacher
- skill in providing instructional support
- effective interpersonal skills in different contexts
- model of being a continuous learner
- communication of an attitude of hope and optimism

> *If we want to grow in our practice, we have two primary places to go: to the inner ground from which good teaching comes and to the community of fellow teachers from whom we can learn about ourselves and our craft... The resources we need in order to grow as teachers are abundant within the community of colleagues. Good talk about teaching is what we need—to enhance both our professional practice and the selfhood from which it comes.*
>
> *~ Parker Palmer, as cited in Scherer, 1998, p. 5*

REFLECTIVE PRACTICE

Think about the following questions

- How might you set up a mentoring system with your students within the classroom setting?
- How might this be extended to include mentoring with colleagues?

When considering the valuable contributions made by mentors to their peers within the teaching profession, some other dimensions of sharing knowledge and expertise within the professional learning community must be examined. Two important underpinnings of success in teaching and learning are moral and character development.

MORAL DEVELOPMENT

A person's ability to be reflective about his or her thinking and to have empathy in the face of another's trouble are key factors that have a serious impact on student learning and on their receptiveness to new ideas. The teacher plays a crucial role and provides a powerful influence in this

MORE INFORMATION

For more information about mentoring, see " The good mentor" by James Rowley (1999) on the companion website.

aspect of the teaching/learning process. When teachers have a strong ethical sense and model this in their daily work with students, it has a powerful impact on students' learning and on their overall development.

Weissbourd (2003) recognizes the impact that strong role models can have on student behaviour and providess some guidance for teachers in this important area. He identifies the following characteristics within teachers that facilitate moral development in their students.

• Teachers influence students by being good role models and also by what they bring to their relationships with their students.
• Teachers need to appreciate and respect students' perspectives.
• Teachers should face issues squarely and not shy away from them.
• The strength of the relationship with individual teachers is paramount.
• Teachers must realize that moral qualities are shaped in these relationships.
• Teachers must be aware that trust promotes fierce loyalty in students.
• Teachers need to be fair, generous, caring, and empathetic educators.
• Teachers must value the teacher–student relationship since this is what shapes students' moral development.
• Teachers must recognize the influence of emotional development on students' learning.
• Teachers who make a difference reach out to struggling students.
• Teachers must respect and nurture their students' sense of idealism.

(Weissbourd, 2003)

" *Schools can best support students' moral development by helping manage the stresses of their profession and by increasing teachers' capacity for reflection and empathy.* "

~ Rick Weissbourd, 2003, p.6

Barriers to Effective Moral Development

The road to developing a strong moral sense in students will not always be smooth. No matter how good the teacher's intentions are or how thoroughly the teacher plans, there can always be impediments. For example, two potential barriers to the development of moral development can be students who have a history of behaviour problems and those who experience a sense of isolation. It is a definite challenge for some students to overcome being labelled as a "problem" and, for those who do not feel connected with either the learning process or other learners, it can be especially difficult. In both of these instances, teachers must make a concerted effort to break down these barriers by providing the necessary assistance and support to help these students start again, with a "clean slate", on a more positive footing.

The student–teacher relationship is of extreme importance here since communication to support moral development will not be as effective unless personal connections have been made between both parties and a level of trust has been established. This needs to be the starting point to facilitate the development of a strong moral sense.

 **REFLECTIVE PRACTICE**

What teachers bring to their relationships with their students has a strong influence on moral development.

Think about the following questions:

- How would you go about sharing your own personal beliefs with your students?
- How could this be systematized within the classroom setting?

CHARACTER EDUCATION

It is difficult to contemplate the whole issue of mentoring and moral development without taking **character education** into consideration. Since people generally relate more strongly to those for whom they have respect, character education would seem to be an essential component if participants are to be receptive to the messages given to them by their mentors.

For Rushmore Kidder (2000), the issue of character education cannot be left to chance. He proposed seven qualities of successful character education to guide educators in developing effective character education programs.

> **GLOSSARY**
>
> **Character Education**—involves teaching children about basic human values including honesty, kindness, generosity, courage, freedom, equality, and respect.

The Seven "Es" of Character Education

1. **Empowered**: Teachers have a role to play in this because society is concerned about this issue and expects some kind of response on the part of the schools.
2. **Effective**: There is a bank of evidence supporting the value of character education and its impact on student attitude; students begin to understand a lot of things not understood before and improve their moral reasoning abilities.

3. **Extended into the community**: When important values are identified, they can be supported; community involvement is essential to avoid differences of opinion on this potentially volatile issue.

4. **Embedded**: Ensure that character education is an integral part of the curriculum; it can be a part of every subject area.

5. **Engaged**: Solicit community support for this initiative so that all stakeholders are involved and committed to the process; ensure it is made relevant to the students.

6. **Epistemological**: Make a concerted effort to deal with character education by developing a conceptual framework for how this can be accomplished in a formalized sense; don't leave its development to chance in informal discussions.

7. **Evaluative**: Devise some ways of assessing the effectiveness of what has been developed by the school community.

(Kidder, 2000)

On a practical level, Gloria Rambow Singh (2001) provides some suggestions for encourageing character education within the regular classroom setting. She outlines the following sequence of strategies for facilitating the development of character education:

• Build a sense of community right from the start of the school year.
• Involve students in all aspects of the life of the classroom.
• Incorporate language that emphasizes the development of character for example, honesty, kindness, generosity, courage, freedom, equality, respect.
• Incorporate cooperative learning techniques into the teaching/learning process, so that students can practice and become comfortable with these concepts.

MORE INFORMATION

For more information on character education, see "Talking about ethics and character education" on the campanion website.

REFLECTIVE PRACTICE

Brainstorm as many ideas as possible about what "character language" might sound like. Once these have been recorded, see if you can categorize the language into specific types of character language for example, personal, group, societal, etc.

THE ONLY CONSTANT IS CHANGE

… the call to change is a call to learn …

~Marge Scherer, 2006, p. 7

When considering the whole concept of change, it is possible to use "learning" and "change" interchangeably; when a person learns something new, he or she is not the same as before. This is true physically, emotionally, as well as cognitively, because when something new has been experienced and learned, restructuring and rewiring occur within the brain. Change occurs as a result of new neural pathways being created during the learning process, and these become available to transmit new information in the future.

While change can be exciting, it can also be uncomfortable. Whenever something new is experienced, there can be, at the very least a sense of minimal discomfort, a feeling of something not being quite the same. For example, fold your hands together in front of you and note which thumb is on top. Now, refold your hands, ensuring that the opposite thumb is on top this time. How does it feel? Change is often accompanied by a feeling of unease.

Such feelings arise when old views have to be discarded or when prior understandings have to be completely revamped. There seems to be a human tendency to want to hold on to the familiar, and this can be a serious challenge to the change process as a whole.

While personal change can be acted upon privately, change that goes on within the educational community occurs, by its very nature, within a public forum, and this can be problematic. The fact that such a forum may not always be one in which total support for change is forthcoming can make it even more difficult for educators. Due to the threat of potential criticism, teachers may even shy away from change simply because it is easier to maintain the status quo.

Teachers need to be aware of the benefits that change can offer them on a personal as well as on a professional level. By embracing change, teachers open themselves to new ways of thinking, responding, and being. When teachers demonstrate an openness to change, this can provide a powerful role model for students so that they gain confidence in their abilities to become active participants in the change process. In essence, change is the ultimate form of risk-taking!

> *Kaleidoscope*
> *Infinite patterns of constant change*
> *A turn of the wrist*
> *A twist of Fate*
> *And nothing is the same again.*
>
> ~ *WFA, 1996*

By modelling a positive attitude toward change, encouraging openness to new ideas and approaches, and welcoming uniqueness into their lives, teachers can make a positive contribution to how students respond to change. This exposure will be invaluable since students' receptiveness toward change can have a strong effect on their personal sense of well-being in the future. Indeed, many people believe that today's youth will live in a world characterized by a constant state of change.

EDUCATIONAL REFORM AND LEADERSHIP

For several decades, Michael Fullan has explored various dimensions of curriculum development and school reform, particularly as it relates to the role of leadership in the educational system (Fullan, 2000). It is important for teachers to be aware of these issues since they ultimately have an impact on what happens in the classroom.

Fullan has identified some interesting points concerning the change process across the different panels within the education system.

- Successful change in student performance takes about *three years* to accomplish at the elementary school level.
- Successful change in student performance takes about *six years* to accomplish at the secondary school level.

The world of teaching has undergone some intense changes over the past ten years and ever-increasing influences, on both teachers and the teaching profession, have become the norm. Fullan identifies five powerful external forces that schools must deal with in implementing school reform:

- parents and community
- technology
- corporate connections
- government policy
- the wider teaching profession

In response to these forces, Fullan (1998) has outlined four key strategies to deal with these influences:

1. **Respect those you want to silence.**
   It is important to try and learn from those who are not in agreement with you. Unique alternatives may arise from different perspectives.
2. **Move toward the danger in forming new alliances.**
   School reform and community reform must occur in tandem, and strong, supportive school–community relationships are essential. If such relationships are not strong, then they must be a priority and open communication is crucial.
3. **Manage emotionally as well as rationally.**
   The change process and resistance to change can be very stressful for all parties. A concerted effort must be made to manage the stress that will inevitably result from change (e.g., exercise, meditation, peer support groups, etc.).
4. **Fight for lost causes.**
   Be hopeful when it counts. Teachers need reminders that they are connected to others and to the "greater good." Being hopeful serves to energize people, reduce stress, and point the way to new ventures.

MORE INFORMATION
For more information on educational reform, see "The three stories of educational reform" by Michael Fullan (2000) on the companion website.

INITIATIVES IN TEACHER EDUCATION

Only through experiencing the complexity of the classroom does a teacher learn. A degree in education… prepares you to be a beginner in a complex world.

~ David C. Berliner, in Scherer, 2001, p.6

In response to changes within the teaching profession and in anticipation of how new teachers will be required to deal with these changes in the future, the Association of Canadian Deans of Education recently approved an accord on teacher education. This accord outlines 12

MORE INFORMATION
See the companion website for the ACDE's Accord on Intial Teacher Education.

principles of initial teacher education to provide direction to the educational community.

 # REFLECTIVE PRACTICE

Make a list of personal changes that have occurred over the last year.

How did you cope with these changes?

Examine the list of 12 principles outlined in the ACDE's Accord on Initial Teacher Education and identify any that have affected you personally

The message from all of the sources in this chapter is consistent throughout the educational community: When entering the teaching profession, be prepared to deal with change on an ongoing basis.

Where do I begin?

Teaching is an interesting mixture of trial and error, problem solving, prediction, inquiry, estimation, and, most of all, hard work. When faced with setting up one's own classroom for the first time, it can appear to be a rather daunting task. Thankfully it is not something that has to be done alone. Over the years, an incredible bank of wisdom has accumulated and the following ideas are but a summary gleaned from many collective years in education. These ideas are offered as a starting point with the hope that they will assist and inspire you as you start your work with elementary children. They are presented in a format that is easy to access, and they provide some practical reminders for getting the school year off to a positive and productive start. It is hoped that these ideas will be an on-going reference for teachers and that they will add their own ideas to these pages in the years to come. Teachers might wish to copy these two pages and file them in the front of their daybook. An expanded version of these ideas can be found in Appendix 13C on the companion website.

THE ABC'S OF BEGINNING TEACHING

A
- authentic
- accepting attitude/ approachable
- accessible/available
- accountability/assessment

B
- blocks of time
- books! books! books!
- bulletin boards
- bus schedule

C
- celebrate
- collect/categorize
- consistent/calm/curious
- cooperative learning

D
- developmental factors
- daybook
- displays
- dismissal routines

E
- engagement
- expectations (clear)
- empowerment
- evaluation (holistic)

F
- firm/fair/friendly
- familiarize (OSRs, colleagues)
- formulate plans/lists
- feedback

G
- greatness (foster)
- guidance
- generate ideas
- groupings (whole to individual)

H
- hand out materials
- have fun activity ready (day one)
- helpful tone
- humour

I
- interesting
- involvement
- invitational learning
- inquiry

J
- justify rules/routines
- journals (set up)
- jobs (schedule)
- join in (extracurricular)

K
- keen interest
- keep (good files, binders, plans)
- kind approach
- knowledgeable

L
- lessons (plan first week)
- learning styles
- listening
- lists (make and check off)

M
- make room attractive
- management
- meet them at the door
- mentoring (students, colleagues)
- metacognition
- memorable learning

N
- natural approach
- negotiate (themes/rules/ routines)
- name games
- newsletter (begin to collect info now)

O
- optimize learning
- observations
- organize (labels)
- obligation (a "calling")

P
- plan ahead
- predict/prioritize
- participation (optimize)
- plan for change (flexibility)
- portfolios
- professional practice

Q
- quality (strive for)
- quiet, productive learning
- questions (variety)
- queries (welcome)

R
- respect/reflect/risk-taking
- resources (many, varied)
- rules/routines/rights
- rubrics

S
- smile!
- seating plan
- specific instructions/ directions
- supplies

T
- think creatively
- time (don't waste it)
- teach something new
- timetable

U
- understanding (teach for …)
- useful tasks
- use all talents
- up-to-date/upgrade

V
- vibrant
- viable learning
- visual/visualization
- volunteers from community

W
- welcome warmly
- well-ordered
- "withitness"
- work (first day)

X
- Xerox (in advance, copyright)
- extra challenges (open ended)
- x-ray eyes (see all)
- extra-curricular

Y
- year plan (flexible)
- "yes" (positive focus)
- "you" (catalyst)
- young and incomplete (they are …)

Z
- zest for teaching
- zero tolerance (for some things)
- zoom in (be energetic)
- zeal (advocate for students)

FINAL INSPIRATIONAL THOUGHTS: A CREDO FOR CHILDREN

1. What a person is, is more important than what a person knows.
2. Education should fit the individual rather than aim to make the individual fit the system.
3. It is the right of every individual to attain a sense of self-fulfillment.
4. Individuals should be encouraged to use their gifts in the service of others.
5. Education should be a living experience, not just a preparation for living.
6. Since children are born learners, the many years which they take to mature provides them with unique opportunities to add breadth and depth to their learning. Rushing this serves no valuable purpose.
7. Learning through the involvement of all the senses precedes learning through communication.
8. The system should be based on respect for the individual rather than on accountability.
9. The mind of the teacher is of supreme importance since it influences the quality of what is encouraged in the mind of the child.

A. Yardley, personal communication, April 1993

SUMMARY

The focus of this chapter—and of this book—has been change in all of its dimensions. For members of the teaching profession, change is a constant companion; as they teach, their students change, and as they interact the students change their teachers. While change is not always a comfortable process, it is necessary to keep growing and learning as life- long learners. The challenge of change and its attendant growth engages teachers in a continuous pattern that will keep them renewed and vital in their own professional growth, as well as for the children in their care. This last chapter presented many ideas, some practical and some philosophical, to assist teachers in this endeavour. Teachers have always been challenged to be open to new ideas, to examine their belief system, and to be flexible in their thinking.

> *A paradigm is a set of assumptions that are not meant to be tested; in fact, they are essentially unconscious. They are part of our modus operandi as individuals, as scientists, or as a society.*
>
> ~ *Arntz et al, 2005, p. 24*

CHAPTER 13 ACTIVITY

Changing One's Beliefs

Reflect on the many ideas you encountered in this text. Answer the following questions concerning how you feel about children and learning, as well as your own role in the teaching/ learning process.

Think about the following questions:

• What is a PARADIGM SHIFT?
• Why would you want to shift one?
• How would you shift your own paradigm?
• Will it be painful?

See Appendix 13A for some potential answers.

APPENDIX 13A

DISCUSSION POINTS FOR CHAPTER 13 ACTIVITY

(Note: Since responses will be of a personal nature, a range of possible answers is provided.)

1. A paradigm shift is basically the changing of one's belief system or philosophy.

2. You might want to shift your paradigm because
   - of personal dissatisfaction with how you are working
   - you don't feel challenged
   - of pressure from peers or administration, etc.

3. You might shift your paradigm by
   - professional reading
   - taking a course
   - challenging the beliefs of colleagues
   - discussions with colleagues
   - teaching a course
   - teaching in a new grade/division/subject, etc.

4. Change is usually accompanied by at least a bit of discomfort, but the rewards in terms of personal satisfaction are more than worth it!
   - challenging another's beliefs can be a delicate issue that must be approached with great sensitivity
   - an atmosphere of trust must be established first
   - there needs to be some form of "exit strategy" in place so that if problems arise and tempers flare, all concerned parties have a "soft place to land" and a way of defusing a volatile situation

The book *What the "Bleep" Do We Know?* by Arntz (2005), will challenge your beliefs about a lot of things, and maybe even precipitate a paradigm shift!

GLOSSARY

Action research—A form of research that pursues action as it tries to understand what is happening in a specific context like the classroom. It uses a spiral process which uses both action and critical reflection on the results of the action. For teachers, action research involves problems of teaching practice. (p. 355)

Anecdotal records—a series of comments that are based on a teacher's systematic observation of student learning. (p. 284)

Assessment—the process of gathering information about the student over a period of time. Diagnostic assessment gathers information about what students already know and can do. Formative assessment is the process of monitoring student's learning development. Summative assessment or EVALUATION is the final assessment during which time a value is placed on the student's work and a judgment is made about progress. (p. 267)

Autonomy—being governed by oneself. (p. 76)

Backwards design—Planning with the assessment measures decided before the unit/lesson begins. (p. 146)

Bell work—independent work that is assigned for students to complete immediately after the entrance bell rings. This work enables teachers to complete organizational tasks. (p. 315)

Character education—involves teaching children about basic human values including honesty, kindness, generosity, courage, freedom, equality, and respect. (p. 397)

Classroom management—a multifaceted process which depends upon an engaging curriculum, student responsibility, appropriate teacher modelling, effective instruction, and management skills to work toward conflict resolution with individuals and the whole class. (p. 196)

Co-learning—the concept that teachers and learners alternate between the expert and novice roles so that both are at times teacher and learner. (p. 358)

Cognitive development—learning which occurs over a period of time and which involves changes in one's thinking. (p. 5)

Community—a group of people with a common focus or vision. In classroom learning, communities consist of people who are learning together. Learning is the common purpose. (p. 144)

Constructivism—an approach to learning and teaching that is based on research about how people learn. In this approach, individuals play an active role in constructing their understandings directly from their experiences and in concert with others. (p. 42)

Constructivist theory—a general framework of instruction based on the study of cognition. (p. 42)

Cooperative small group learning—an approach which focuses on small groups of students working together to solve or resolve a common problem. Individual group members are responsible for their own learning and for facilitating the learning of other group members. This approach is characterized by positive interactions, individual accountability, equal participation, and shared social skills. (p. 66)

Creative thinking—generating ideas or materials that are unique, unusual, or that did not exist before. (p. 326)

Critical incident (in the classroom)—An occurrence in a classroom or within a learning context that stimulates further thought about future action. (p. 363)

Critical reflection—a term introduced by Donald Schon as he studied professionals in action. Schon suggested that professionals, when confronted with the everyday problems of their profession, could begin to engage in critical reflection that would place their everyday action within the context of both their world of practice and the readings and theory that they had completed. (p. 358)

Critical thinking—making decisions, analyzing, and breaking down something systematically into its component parts. (p. 326)

Cultural capital—knowledge, skill, and education which may endow a person with a higher social status. (p. 356)

Culturally responsive instruction—instruction that recognizes the differences present in the classroom between and among students of different cultures and language backgrounds. In short it does not assume that all students have the same histories. (p. 299)

Curriculum expectations—these are listed within curriculum documents and outline what students are expected to be able to know, do, or understand at the end of each year. (p. 141)

Daybook—the teacher's record of what is to happen each day of the school year. It will contain daily lessons and schedules. (p. 180)

Daylighting—the concept that classrooms should have natural light that falls over a student's left shoulder. (p. 166)

Decentering—a transformational process by which individuals gradually let go of a strong adherence to their own ideas, make comparisons with the thinking of peers, become more self-critical, and look for the potential reasons behind their own thinking. (p. 92)

Diversity—refers to the nature of students in the classroom. Diversity includes both culturally and linguistically diverse populations as well as special needs students. (p. 298)

Emotional intelligence—the capacity for recognizing our own feelings and those of others, for motivating ourselves, and for managing emotions well in ourselves and in our relationships. (p. 30)

Equilibration—the on-going process of self-correction or self-regulation, keeping just the right balance between assimilation and accommodation, by which the individual strives to keep a feeling of balance or equilibrium as he or she makes sense of the world and changes his/her way(s) of thinking. (p. 15)

Equity—the treatment of others characterized by fairness and justice. (p. 302)

Evaluation——the process of judging what has been gathered during the process of assessment to provide a clear indication of how well a student performs. The results of evaluation are usually communicated to others, including parents and other teachers, through the reporting process. (p. 267)

Five-day cycle—this is an organizaton in which the traditional week is Monday–Friday. The problem in the school context is that professional development days and holidays can interfere with the schedule so that some subjects consistently have reduced time. (p. 178)

High stakes assessment or testing—any programme of testing that compares students across jurisdictions and has consequences for the type of curriculum that is in place in schools. (p. 270)

High stakes curriculum and testing—testing that is standardized and administered to groups of students on a systematic basis. Results are used to compare groups of students across the country. This term also encompasses the influence of test results on the curriculum whereby the curriculum is designed to produce good test results rather than good learning outcomes. The assumption here is that only knowledge and skills that can be measured are worthwhile. (p. 145)

Inclusive education—providing education for students with diverse needs within the regular, mainstream classroom. Inclusive education means that the classroom teacher has to be able to plan for diverse needs. (p. 306)

Individual Education Plan (IEP)—a plan developed by the school team that outlines the provision of an individual program for a student with special needs. (p. 309)

Intellectual development—the process of deriving meaning from experience through acquiring, structuring, and restructuring knowledge. (p. 14)

Invitational learning—a phrase coined by William Purkey, invitational learning suggests planning the teaching and learning activities and space so that students are welcomed into the environment. Inviting schools are places where students are welcomed and respected. (p. 173)

Learning journal—a way by which learners can track what they are learning during the course of a lesson or unit. (p. 361)

Mentoring—occurs when a role model offers support to another person and shares knowledge, expertise, and experiences with that person. (p. 394)

Metacognition—the ability to reflect and think about one's own thinking. (p. 341)

Multiliteracy—there are many forms of literacy all of which use a number of sign and symbol systems to help individuals make sense of the world. Generally a multiliteracies approach crosses cultural and linguistic boundaries. (p. 302)

Neuroplasticity—the brain's ability to change and make new connections. (p. 114)

PISA—developed by the Organization for Economic Cooperation and Development (OECD), the Programme for International Student Assessment (PISA) tests are administered to 15-year-olds in an attempt to determine whether students have acquired the skills and knowledge necessary for participation in the global economy. (p. 269)

Proactive—to anticipate potential problems in advance and have a plan for addressing these issues. (p. 200)

Problem-based learning—experiential learning which is organized around investigations of real-world problems. (p. 66)

Professional learning community—a group of professionals working together to provide mutual support for devising solutions to a set of issues they hold in common. This collaboration should facilitate their collective professional growth and is characterized by a commitment to student learning, a culture of collaboration, and a focus on achieving results. (p. 338)

Progressivism—is an educational philosophy that assumes that humans are interactive, social beings. Relying on the notions of John Dewey, **progressivists** believe that students learn by doing and involve students in activities that require that they make decisions and evaluate their learning. (p. 172)

Portfolio assessment—a collection of artifacts related to a specific subject area. Periodically teacher and student review the portfolio to determine what has been learned. (p. 289)

Reactive—to give a primary response to a situation or stimulus when it occurs. (p. 200)

Rubric—a set of criteria students see prior to engaging in a task. (p. 278)

SAIP—School Achievement Indicators Program (SAIP), introduced by the Council of Ministers of Education in 1993, is designed to assess the performance of 13- and 16-year-old students in mathematics content, mathematics problems solving, reading, writing, and science. (p. 268)

Scaffolding—the skilful use of questions used by the teacher to enable children to understand and use concepts that would be beyond their level of thinking if they were doing this independently. (p. 24)

Schema (Schemata – Plural)—the mental frameworks that are created as children interact with their physical and social environments. (p. 16)

Self-concept—a person's self-image or how one feels about oneself and the belief that one has in one's own capabilities. (p. 89)

Six-day cycle—a cycle in which days are numbered 1–6 and repeat over time. Monday in week 1 becomes day 1 and the following Monday becomes day 6. Tuesday is day 2 in week 1 but day 1 in week 2. With this cycle certain subjects are not neglected due to holidays. (p. 178)

Social Constructivism—the process by which knowledge is actively created through social relationships and interactions. (p. 22)

Spiral of knowing (The)—a model of learning which expresses the openness and dynamic nature of the concept of stages in learning. As children encounter different experiences, they are prompted to reorganize their earlier views of the world and create new categories by building upon previously held beliefs. (p. 68)

Task board—a bulletin board on which teachers place an outline of the tasks that students have to complete each day. (p. 315)

Zone of Proximal Development (ZPD)—the range of tasks too difficult for children to master alone, but that could be mastered with guidance and assistance from adults or more highly skilled children. (p. 23)

REFERENCES

CHAPTER 1

Arlin, P.K. (1975). Cognitive development in adulthood: A fifth stage. *Developmental Psychology*, 11, 602–606.

British Columbia Ministry of Education. (2000). *The Primary Program: A Framework for Teaching*. Province of British Columbia.

Berk, L.E. (1996). *Infants, children, and adolescents*. Toronto: Allyn and Bacon.

Bredekamp, S., & Copple, C. (1997). *Developmentally appropriate practice in early childhood programs*. Washington, DC: National Association for the Education of Young Children.

Caine, G., & Caine, R.N. (1997). *Education on the edge of possibility*. Alexandria, VA: Association for Supervision and Curriculum Development(ASCD).

Dewey, J. (1969). *Experience and education*. New York: Macmillan/Collier Books. (Originally published in 1938; reprinted in 1969.)

Elkind, D. (1976). *Child development and education: A Piagetian perspective*. New York: Oxford University Press.

Gallagher, J. McCarthy, & Reid, D.K. (1981). *The learning theory of Piaget and Inhelder*. Austin, TX: Pro-Ed.

Gardner, H. (1983). *Frames of mind: The theory of multiple intelligences*. New York: Basic Books.

Gardner, H. (1991). *The unschooled mind: How children think and how schools should teach*. New York: Basic Books.

Gardner, H. (1999). *Intelligence reframed: Multiple intelligences for the 21st century*. New York: Basic Books.

Gardner, H. cited in preface to Armstrong, T. (2000). *Multiple intelligences in the classrooms*, (2nd ed.). Alexandria, VA: ASCD

Gardner, H. (2005). *Multiple lenses on the mind*. Paper presented at the ExpoGestion Conference, Bogota, Columbia, May 25, 2005.

Goleman, D. (1998). *Working with emotional intelligence*. New York: Bantam Books.

Harter, S. (1990). Causes, correlates and the function of self-worth: A life span perspective. In J. Kolligian, & R. Sternberg (Eds.), *Competence considered*. New Haven, CT: Yale University Press.

Healy, J.M. (1987). *Your child's growing mind*. Toronto: Doubleday

Hewitt, J.D. (1995). *Teaching teenagers: Making connections in the transition years*. Vancouver: EduServ.

Inhelder, B. cited in J. McCarthy Gallagher, & D.K. Reid (1981). *The learning theory of Piaget and Inhelder*. Austin, TX: Pro-Ed.

Jensen, E. (1998). *Teaching with the brain in mind*. Alexandria, VA: ASCD.

Kamii, C. (1984). Autonomy: The aim of education envisioned by Piaget. *Phi Delta Kappan*. February.

Norris, D., & Boucher, J. (1980) *Observing children through their formative years*. Toronto: Toronto Board of Education.

Peterson, R., & Felton-Collins, V. (1986). *The Piaget handbook for teachers and parents*. New York: Teachers College Press.

Piaget, J. (1950). *The psychology of intelligence*. London: Routledge.

Piaget, J. & Inhelder, B. (1969). *The psychology of the child*. New York: Basic Books.

Roehler, L., & Cantlon, D. (1996). Scaffolding a powerful tool in social constructivist classrooms. Retrieved July 2, 2006 from http://ed-web3.educ.msu.edu/literacy/papers/paperlr2.htm

Santrock, J.W., & Yussen, S.R. (1992). *Child development: An introduction*. Dubuque, IA: Wm. C. Brown.

Shore, R. (1997). *Rethinking the brain: New insights into early development*. New York: Families and Work Institute.

Sylwester, R. (1995). *A celebration of neurons: An educator's guide to the human brain*. Alexandria, VA: ASCD.

Vygotsky, L. S. (1978). *Mind in society: The development of higher psychological processes*. Cambridge, MA: Harvard University Press.

Wright, O. (1984). *Observing adolescents in their developing years*. Toronto: Toronto Board of Education.

CHAPTER 2

Alderson, S. (1985). Play: The natural basic. *FWTAO Newsletter*, April/May, 6–9.

Allen, R. (2001). The project approach to learning. *Curriculum update: Early childhood learning*. Spring.

Berk, L.E. (2000), *Child Development.* (5th ed.). Toronto: Allyn & Bacon.

Bodrova, E., & Leong, D. (2003). The importance of being playful. *Educational Leadership*, April, 50–53.

Bredekamp, S., & Copple, C. (1997). *Developmentally appropriate practice in early childhood programs.* Washington, DC: National Association for the Education of Young Children.

Brooks, M.G., & Grennon Brooks, J. (1999). The courage to be constructivist. *Educational Leadership*, November, 18–24.

Bruner, J. (1966). *Toward a theory of instruction.* Cambridge, MA: Harvard University Press.

Bruner, J. (1996). *The culture of education.* Cambridge, MA: Harvard University Press.

Cambourne, B. (1988). *The whole story: Natural learning and the acquisition of literacy in the classroom.* Auckland, NZ: Ashton Scholastic.

Cunningham, P., & Allington, R. (2003). *Classrooms that work.* Boston, MA: Pearson Educational.

Eisner, E. (2005). Back to whole. *Educational Leadership*, September, 14–18.

Fine, J. (1987). The importance of play in the young child's cognitive development. *Research Bulletin*, February 51, 1–2.

FWTAO (1986). *Active learning in the early school years.* Toronto: Author.

Gallagher, J., McCarthy & Reid, D. K. (1981). *The learning theory of Piaget and Inhelder.* Austin, TX: Pro-Ed.

Gardner, H. (1999). *Intelligence reframed: Multiple intelligences for the 21st century.* New York: Basic Books.

Ginsburg, S., & Opper, H. (1969). *Piaget's theory of intellectual development: An introduction.* New Jersey: Prentice-Hall.

Gredler, M. (1997). *Learning and instruction: Theory into practice.* (3rd ed.). Upper Saddle River, NJ: Prentice-Hall.

Hewitt, J.D. (1995). *Teaching teenagers: Making connections in the transition years.* Vancouver: EduServ.

Huitt, W., & Hummel, J. (2003). Piaget's theory of cognitive development. *Educational Psychology Interactive.* Valdosta, GA: Valdosta State University. Retrieved July 2006, from http://chiron.valdosta.edu/whuitt/col/cogsys/piaget.html

Johnson, D.W., & Johnson, R.T.(1991). *Learning together and alone: Cooperative, competitive, and individualistic learning.* Alexandria, VA: ASCD.

McBrien, J.L., & Brandt, R. S. (1997). *The language of learning: A guide to education terms.* Alexandria, VA: ASCD.

Miller, J.P. (1993). *The holistic curriculum.* Toronto: OISE Press.

Noddings, N. (2005). What does it mean to educate the whole child? *Educational leadership*, September, 8–13.

Ontario Ministry of Education. (1995). *The principles of education for grades 1 to 9.* Toronto: Queen's Printer for Ontario.

Perkins, D. (1999). The Constructivist classroom: The many faces of Constructivism. *Educational Leadership*, November, 57, (3), 6–11

Santrock, J.W., & Yussen, S.R. (1992). *Child development: An introduction.* Dubuque, IA: Wm. C. Brown.

Smilanski, S., & Shefatya, L. (1990). *Facilitating play: A medium for promoting cognitive, social, emotional, and academic development in young children.* Gaitherburg, MD: Psycho–Social & Educational Publication.

Torp, L., & Sage, S. (2002). *Problems as possibilities: Problem-based learning for K–16 education*, (2nd ed.). Alexandria, VA: ASCD.

Turner, T., & Krechevsky, M. (2003). Who are the teachers? Who are the learners? in the first years of school. *Educational Leadership.* 60 (7).

Weininger, O. (1979). *Play and education.* Illinois: Chas. C. Thomas.

CHAPTER 3

Alderson, S. (1985). Play: the natural basic. *FWTAO Newsletter*, April/May, 6–9.

Bennett, N., Wood, L., & Rogers, S. (1997). *Teaching through play.* Buckingham, UK: Open University Press.

Berk, L.E. (1996). *Infants, children, and adolescents*. Toronto: Allyn and Bacon.

Branden, N. (1994). *The six pillars of self-esteem*. New York: Bantam.

Bredekamp, S., & Copple, C. (1997). *Developmentally appropriate practice in early childhood programs*. Washington, DC: National Association for the Education of Young Children.

Canfield, J., & Wells, H.C. (1976). *100 ways to enhance self-concept in the classroom*. NJ: Prentice Hall.

Chilton Pearce, J. (1992). *Evolution's end: Claiming the potential of our intelligence*. New York: Harper Collins.

Coloroso, B. (1994). *Kids are worth it*. Toronto: Somerville House.

Eisner, E. (2005). Back to whole. *Educational Leadership*, September, 14–18.

Fine, J. (1987). The importance of play in the young child's cognitive development. *Research Bulletin*, February, 51, 1–2.

Hewitt, J. D., (1995). *Teaching teenagers: Making connections in the transition years*. Vancouver: EduServ.

Johnson, R.T., & Johnson, D.W. (1987). *Structuring cooperative learning*. Edina, MN: Interaction Book.

Kamii, C. (1984). Autonomy: The aim of education envisioned by Piaget. *Phi Delta Kappan*, February, 410–415.

Kamii, C. (1991). Toward autonomy: The importance of critical thinking and choice making. *School Psychology Review*, 20, 382–388.

Kamii, C., Clark, F.B., & Dominick, A. (1994). The six national goals: A road to disappointment. *Phi Delta Kappan*, May, 672–677.

Kohn, A. (1996). *Beyond discipline: From compliance to community*. Alexandria,VA: ASCD

Lewis, C., Schaps, E., & Watson, M. (1996). The caring classroom's academic edge. *Educational Leadership*, September, 16–21.

Miller, J.P. (1993). *The Holistic Curriculum*. Toronto: OISE Press.

Piaget, J., & Inhelder, B. (1969). *The Psychology of the Child*. New York: Basic Books.

Postman, N. & Weingarten, C. (1969). *Teaching as a subversive activity*. Harmondsworth, England: Penguin Books.

Purkey, W.W., & Novak, J.M. (1984). *Inviting school success: A self-concept approach to teaching and learning*. Belmont, CA: Wadsworth.

Samples, B (1987). *Open mind, whole mind: Parenting and teaching tomorrow's children today*. Rolling Hills Estates, CA: Jalmar Press.

Santrock, J.W., & Yussen, S.R. (1992). *Child Development: An introduction*. Dubuque, IA: Wm. C. Brown.

CHAPTER 4

Arntz, W., Chasse, B., & Vicente, M. (2005). *What the "bleep" do we know?* Deerfield Beach, FL: Health Communications.

Bredekamp, S. & Copple, C. (1997). *Developmentally appropriate practice in early childhood programs*. Washington, DC: National Association for the Education of Young Children.

Caine, G., & Caine, R.N. (1997). *Education on the edge of possibility*. Alexandria, VA: ASCD.

Diamond, M., & Hopson, J. (1998). *Magic trees of the mind*. New York: Dutton.

Dispenza, J. as cited in Arntz et al (2005). *What the "bleep" do we know?* Deerfield Beach, FL: Health Communications.

Erlauer, L. (2003). *The Brain-compatible classroom: Using what we know about learning to improve teaching*. Alexandria, VA: ASCD.

Fogarty, Robin (1997). *The mindful school: How to integrate the curriculum*. Palantine, IL: Skylight

Gallagher, J.McCarthy, & Reid, D.K. (1981). *The learning theory of Piaget and Inhelder*. Austin, TX: Pro-Ed.

Gardner, H. (1991). *The unschooled mind: How children think and how schools should teach*. New York: Basic Books.

Gardner, H. (2005). *Multiple lenses on the mind*. Paper presented at the ExpoGestion Conference, Bogota, Columbia, May 25, 2005.

Given, B.K. (2002). *Teaching to the brain's natural learning systems*. Alexandria, VA: ASCD.

Goleman, D. (1998). *Working with emotional intelligence*. New York: Bantam Books.

Healy, J.M. (1987). *Your child's growing mind*. Toronto: Doubleday.

Hebb, D. (1970) cited in R. Restak (1979) *The brain: The last frontier*. New York: Doubleday.

Jensen, E. (1998). *Teaching with the brain in mind*. Alexandria, VA: ASCD.

Jensen, E. (2005). *Teaching with the brain in mind* (2nd ed.). Alexandria, VA: ASCD.

Kohn, A. (1993). *Punished by rewards: The trouble with gold stars, incentive plans, A's, praise, and other bribes*. Boston: Houghton Mifflin.

Kohn, A. (1996). *Beyond discipline: From compliance to community*. Alexandria, VA: ASCD.

Meister Vitale, B. (1982). *Unicorns are real: A right-brained approach to learning*. Rolling Hills Estates, CA: Jalmar Press.

Piaget, J., & Inhelder, B. (1969). *The psychology of the child*. New York: Basic Books.

Restak, R. (1979). *The brain: The last frontier*. Garden City, NY: Doubleday.

Restak, R. (1993). *Receptors*. New York: Bantam Books.

Russell, P. (1979). *The brain book*. New York: Hawthorne Books.

Santrock, J.W., & Yussen, S.R. (1992). *Child development : An introduction*. Dubuque, IA: Wm. C. Brown.

Shore, R. (1997). *Rethinking the brain: New insights into early development*. New York: Families and Work Institute.

Sylwester, R. (1995). *A celebration of neurons: An educator's guide to the brain*. Alexandria, VA: ASCD.

Wittrock, M.C. (1997). *The human brain*. Toronto: Prentice-Hall.

Wolfe, P. (2001). *Brain matters: Translating research into classroom practice*. Alexandria, VA: ASCD.

Chapter 5

Blythe, T., & Associates. (1998). *The teaching for understanding guide*. San Francisco: Jossey-Bass.

Bruner, J. (1969). *The process of education*. Cambridge, MA: Harvard University Press.

Murdoch, K. (1998). *Classroom connections: Strategies for integrated learning*. Melbourne, Australia: Eleanor Curtain Publishing.

National Research Council (2000). *How people learn: Brain, mind experience, and school*. (Expanded Ed.) Washington, DC: National Academies Press.

Schwartz, D. L., Bransford, J. D., & Sears, D. (2006). *Maps of inquiry*. Retrieved May 2006 from www.instruction.greenriver.edu/kclay/highschoolscience/mapsofinquiry.doc

Shulman, L., & Sparks, D. (1992). Merging content knowledge and pedagogy: An interview with Lee Shulman. *Journal of Staff Development*, 13(1), 14–16.

Van Manen, M. (1986). *The tone of teaching*. Toronto: Scholastic

Vygotsky, L. (1978). *Mind and society: The development of higher mental processes*. Cambridge, MA: Harvard University Press.

Wiggins, G,. & McTighe, J. (2001). *Understanding by design*. New York: Prentice Hall.

Chapter 6

Lackney, J. A. (2003). Trends in school design and construction. *Business and professional people for the public interest, architecture for education: New school design* (pp.3.23–3.27) From the Chicago Competition.

Lackney, J., & Jacobs, J. (2005). *Creating spaces for teaching and learning*. Thousand Oaks, CA: Corwin Press.

Lortie, D. (1979). *School teacher: A sociological study,* (2nd ed.). Chicago, IL: University of Chicago Press

McGuffey, C. (1982). Facilities. In H.J. Walbert, (Ed.), (1987) *Improving educational standards and productivity*. (pp 237–288). Berkley, CA: McCutchan.

Novak, J., & Purkey, W. (2003). *Inviting educational leadership: Fulfilling potential and applying an ethical perspective to the educational process*. London: Pearson.

Purkey, W. (1999). *What students say to themselves: Internal dialogue and school success*. Thousand Oaks, CA: Sage.

Rafferty, M. (1969). *Forty years of school planning*. California: California State Department of Education.

Schikendanz, J. A. (2003). Engaging preschoolers in code learning: Some thoughts about preschool teacher's concerns. In D. M. Barrone, & L. M. Morrow, (Eds.) *Literacy and Young Children, Research-Based Practice*. New York: Guilford Press.

CHAPTER 7

Bennett, B., Bennett, C., & Stevahn, L. (1991). *Cooperative learning: Where heart meets mind.* Toronto: Educational Connections.

Bennett, B., & Smilanich, P. (1991). *Classroom management: A thinking and caring approach.* Toronto: Bookation.

Bloom, B., Englehart, M., Furst, E., Hill, W., & Krathwohl, D. (1956). *Taxonomy of educational objectives: Cognitive domain.* New York: Longman.

Curwin, R., & Mendler, A. (1999). *Discipline with dignity.* Alexandria, VA: ASCD.

Dreikurs, R., Bronta, G., & Pepper, F. (1971). *Maintaining sanity in the classroom: Illustrated teaching techniques.* New York: Harper & Row.

Eisner, E.W. (2005). Back to whole. *Educational leadership,* September, 14–18.

Faber, A., & Mazlish, E. (1995). *How to talk so kids can learn: At home and in school.* New York: Scribner.

Hewitt, J.D. (1995). *Teaching teenagers: Making connections in the transition years.* Vancouver: EduServ.

Jensen, E. (1998). *Teaching with the brain in mind.* Alexandria, VA: ASCD.

Johnson, D.W., & Johnson, R.T. (1991). *Learning together and alone: Cooperative, competitive, and individualistic learning.* Alexandria, VA: ASCD.

Kagan, S. (1992) *Cooperative learning.* San Juan Capistrano, CA: Kagan Cooperative Learning.

Kamii, C. (1991). Toward autonomy: The importance of critical thinking and choice making. *School psychology review,* 20, 382–388.

Kounin, J. (1970). *Discipline and group management in classrooms.* New York: Holt, Rinehart, and Winston.

Lewis, C., Schaps, E., & Watson, M. (1996). The caring classroom's academic edge. *Educational leadership,* 54 (*1*),16–21.

Lyman, F. (1992). Think-Pair-Share, Thinktrix, Thinklinks, and Weird Facts: An interactive system for cooperative thinking. In N. Davidson, & T. Worsham (Eds.), *Enhancing thinking through cooperative learning,* (pp.169–181). New York: Teachers College Press.

Miller, J.P. (1993). *The holistic curriculum.* Toronto: OISE Press.

Noddings, N. (2005). What does it mean to educate the whole child? *Educational leadership,* 63(*1*): 8–13.

Rowe, M.B. (1974). Wait-time and reward as instructional variables, their influence on language, logic and fate control: Part 1. Wait time. *Journal of research on science teaching,* 11, 81–94.

Samples, B. (1987). *Open mind/Whole mind: Parenting and teaching tomorrow's children today.* Rolling Hills Estates, CA: Jalmar Press.

CHAPTER 8

Apple, M. (2000). Between neoliberalism and neoconservatism: Education and conservatism in the global context. In N.C. Burbules & C.A. Torres (Eds.), *Globalization and education: Critical perspectives.* (pp. 57–77). New York: Routledge.

Bereiter, C., & Scardamalia, M. (1993). *Surpassing ourselves: An inquiry into the nature and implications of expertise.* La Salle, IL: Open Court.

Bruner, J. (1956). *Towards a theory of instruction.* Cambridge, MA: Harvard University Press.

Cambourne, B. (1995). Toward an educationally relevant theory of literacy learning: Twenty years of inquiry. *The reading teacher,* 49(*3*),182–192.

Cannella, G. (1999). The scientific discourse of education: Predetermining in the lives of others—Foucault, education and children. *Contemporary issues in early childhood education,* 1: 1.

Conley, M. (1989). Theories and attitudes towards political education. In K.A. McLeod (Ed). *Canada and citizenship education.* (pp. 137–156). Toronto: Canadian Education Association.

Connelly, M., & Clandinin, J. (1988). *Teachers as curriculum planners: Narratives of experience.* Toronto: OISE Press.

Cummins, J. & Danesi, M. (1990). *Heritage languages: The development and denial of Canada's linguistic resources.* Our Schools/Our Selves Education Foundation.

Darling-Hammond, L. (1997). *The right to learn: A blueprint for creating schools that work.* San Francisco: Jossey Bass.

Eisner, E.W. (1979). *The educational imagination.* New York: Macmillan Publishing.

Finkle, S.L., & Torp, L.L. (1995). *Introductory documents.* (Available from the Center for Problem-Based Learning, Illinois Math and Science Academy, 1500 West Sullivan Road, Aurora, IL 60506-1000.)

Foshay, A. (1980). *Considered action for curriculum improvement.* Alexandria, VA: ASCD.

Gardner, H. (1999). *Intelligence reframed.* New York: Basic Books.

Gardner, H. (2004). *Changing minds: The art and science of changing our own and other people's minds.* Cambridge, MA: Harvard University Press.

Grumet, M. (1988). *Bittermilk: Women and teaching.* Amherst: University of Massachusetts Press.

Hargreaves, A. (2003). *Teaching in the knowledge society: Education in an age of insecurity.* New York: Teachers College Press.

Hibbert, K., & Rich, S.J. (2005). Virtual communities of practice. In J. Nolan & J. Weiss, J. Hunsinger, & P. Trifonas (Eds.). *International Handbook of Virtual Learning Environments.* Berlin: Springer Academic Publications.

Hirst, P.H., & Peters, R.S. (1974). The curriculum. In E.W. Eisner & E. Vallancy (Eds.), *Conflicting conceptions of curriculum.* Berkeley, CA: McCutchan Publishing.

Henderson, J., & Hawthorne R. (2000). Transformative curriculum leadership. Hirsch, E.D. (1987). *Cultural literacy: What every American needs to know.* Boston: Houghton Mifflin.

Huebner, D. (1999). *The lure of the transcendent.* Mahweh, NJ: Lawrence Erlbaum Associates.

Iannacci, L. (2005). *Othered among others: A critical narrative of culturally and linguistically diverse (CLD) children's literacy and identity in early childhood education (ECE).* Unpublished doctoral dissertation: The University of Western Ontario, London, ON.

Kincheloe, J. (1999) School where Ronnie and Brandon would have excelled. In W. Pinar (Ed.), *Contemporary curriculum discourses.* (pp. 346–363). New York: Peter Lang.

Klein, M.F. (1986). Alternative curriculum conceptions and designs. *Theory into Practice.* 25(1), 31–55.

Pinar , W. (2004). *What is curriculum theory?* Mahweh, NJ: Lawrence Erlbaum Associates.

Rich, S.J., Langford, H., Kronick, C. & Scinderson, S. (1990). *Learning to teach in the early years.* Unpublished report of the Teacher Development Project. University of Western Ontario.

Scrivens, M. (1999). *Groundless belief: An essay on the possibility of epistemology.* Boston: Princeton University Press.

Searle, J.R. (1995). The construction of social reality. New York: Free Press.

Sears, A.M., & Hughes, A.S. (1996). Citizenship education and current educational reform. *Canadian journal of education.* 21, (2), 123–142.

Sears, A.M., & Parsons, J. (1991). Towards critical thinking as an ethic. *Theory and research in social education.* 19, 45–68.

Taba, H. (1999). *The dynamic of education: A methodology of progressive educational thought.* London: Routledge (Reprinted from 1932).

Tanner, D., & Tanner, L. (1975). *Curriculum development: Theory into practice.* New York: Merrill.

Toohey, K. (2000). *Learning English at school: Identity, social relations and classroom practice.* Buffalo, NY: Multilingual Matters.

Tyler, R. (1969). *Basic principles of curriculum and instruction.* Chicago, IL: University of Chicago Press.

Van Manen, M. (1986). *The tone of teaching.* Toronto: Scholastic.

Wenger, E. (1998). *Communities of practice: Learning, meaning and identity.* Cambridge, UK: Cambridge University Press.

Wiggins, G., & McTighe, J. (2001). *Understanding by design.* New York: Prentice Hall.

CHAPTER 9

Airasian, P.W. (1991). *Classroom assessment.* New York: McGraw-Hill.

Berliner, D.C., & Biddle, B.J. (1995). *The manufactured crisis: Myths, fraud, and the attack on America's public schools.* Redding, MA: Addison-Wesley.

De Fina, A. A. (1992). *Portfolio assessment: Getting started.* Toronto: Scholastic.

Neill, M. (2004). *Leaving no child behind: Overhauling NCBL.* In D.Meier, A. Kohn, Darling-Hammond, L., Sizer, T.R., & Wood, G. (2004) (Eds.). *Many children left behind.* Boston, MA: Beacon Press.

Jones, G. (1991). *Crocus Hill notebook.* London, ON: The Althouse Press.

Meier, D., Kohn, A., Darling-Hammond, L., Sizer, T.R., & Wood, G. (2004). *Many children left behind.* Boston, MA: Beacon Press.

Riley, T.A. (2005). *The face of achievement: Influences on teacher decision making about Aboriginal students.* Unpublished Master's thesis. Vancouver: The University of British Columbia.

Schon, D. (1986). *The reflective practitioner.* New York: Teachers College Press.

Shulman, L.S. (1986). Those who understand: Knowledge growth in teaching. *Educational Researcher*, 15, 4–14.

Ungerleider, C. (2003). *Failing our kids: How are we ruining our public school system?* Toronto: McClelland & Stewart.

Wiggins, G., & McTighe, J. (2001). *Understanding by design.* New York: Prentice Hall.

Wiggins, G. (1990). The case for authentic assessment. *Practical assessment, research & evaluation*, 2(2). Retrieved March 10, 2006 from http://PAREonline.net/getvn. asp?v=2&n=2.

Richert, A. E. (1992). Voice and power in teaching and learning to teach. In L.Valli (Ed.) *Reflective teacher education: Cases and critiques.* Albany, NY: State University of New York Press.

Singer, I. B. (1976). *Naftali the storyteller and his horse.* Sus, NY: Farrar, Strauss and Giroux.

Van Manen, M. (2005). *The tone of teaching.* London, ON: The Althouse Press.

Wenger, E. (1998). *Communities of practice: Learning, meaning and identity.* Cambridge, UK: Cambridge University Press.

CHAPTER 10

Bunch, G., Finnegan, K., Humpheries, C., Dore, R. & Dore, L. (2005) *Finding a way through the maze: Crucial terms used in education provision for Canadians with disabilities.* Toronto: The Marsha Forest Centre.

Cooper, J.M. (1998). *Reason and emotion.* Boston: Princeton University Press.

Cranston, Maurice. (1991) *The noble savage: Jean-Jacques Rousseau, 1754–1762.* Chicago, IL: University of Chicago Press.

Dewey, J. (1992). *How we think.* Amherst, NY: Prometheus Books.

Dei, G. J. & James, I. M. (2002). Beyond the rhetoric: Moving from exclusion, reaching for inclusion in Canadian schools. *Alberta Journal of Educational Research.* 48(1), 61–87.

Holdaway, D. (1979). *Foundations of literacy.* Toronto: Scholastic.

Iannacci, L. (2005). *Othered among others: The CLD student in the early years classroom.* Unpublished doctoral dissertation. The University of Western Ontario, London, ON.

Jones, F. & Edmunds, A. (2005). *From chaos to control: Understanding and responding to behaviours of students with exceptionalities.* London, ON: The Althouse Press.

New London Group (1996). International multiliteracies project. Retrieved July 02, 2006 from http://edoz.com. au/educationaaustralia/archive/features/mult3.html

Northwest Regional Education Laboratory (2000). *Increasing student engagement and motivation: From time-on-task to homework.* Retrieved July 02, 2006 from http://www.nwrel. org/request/oct00/textonly.html

Organization for Economic Cooperation and Development OECD (2003). *Student engagement at school: A sense of belonging and participation.* Toronto: OECD Publishing.

Piper, D. & Piper, T. (1996). Maintaining and fostering socio-cultural awareness in a community of secondary school learners. In J. Andrews (Ed.), *Teaching students with diverse needs.* Toronto: Thomson Nelson.

Purkey, W. (1999). *What students say to themselves: Internal dialogue and school success.* Thousand Oaks, CA: Sage.

Riley, T. (2005). *Teachers' attribution of characteristics to students.* Unpublished master's thesis. The University of British Columbia, Vancouver.

Thorndike, E. L. (1903). *Educational psychology.* Chicago, IL: University of Chicago Press.

Van Manen, M. (1985). *The tone of teaching.* Toronto: Scholastic.

Willinsky, J. (1998). After 1492–1992: A post colonial supplement for the Canadian curriculum. In Satu Repo (Ed.) *Making schools matter: Good teachers at work.* Toronto: James Lorimer.

CHAPTER 11

Arntz, W., Chasse, B., & Vicente, M. (2005). *What the "bleep" do we know?* Deerfield Beach, FL: Health Communications.

Bloom, B. S. (Ed.) (1956). *Taxonomy of educational objectives: Classification of educational goals.* New York: Longman, Green.

Checkley, Kathy (2003). Teaching gifted (and all others) to think better. *Classroom Leadership,* 7(*3*).

Cohen, L.M. (1988). Developing children's creativity, thinking, and interests. *Oregon School Study Council,* 31,(*7*).

Coloroso, B. (1995). *Kids are worth it: Giving your child the gift of inner discipline.* Toronto: Somerville House.

Costa, A.L. (2001). *Developing minds: A resource book for teaching.* Alexandria, VA: ASCD.

Eisner, E.W. (1972). *The development of creative thinkers.* New York: Macmillan.

Eisner, E. (2005). Back to whole. *Educational Leadership,* September.

Fogarty, R. (1997). *The mindful school: How to integrate the curriculum.* Palatine, IL: Skylight.

Fogarty, R. (1996). Workshop notes—Conference for Program Dept.(Scarborough Board of Education).

Gallagher, J. McCarthy & Reid, D. (1981). *The learning theory of Piaget and Inhelder.* Austin, TX: Pro-Ed.

Gardner, H. (1982). *Art, mind, and brain: A cognitive approach to creativity.* New York: Basic Books.

Gardner, H. (1999). *Intelligence reframed. Multiple intelligences for the 21ˢᵗ century.* New York: Basic Books.

Gardner, H. (2000). Make the most of young minds. *Educational Digest,* February, 5–6.

Gardner, H. (2005). *Multiple lenses on the mind.* Paper presented at the ExpoGestion Conference, Bogota, Columbia, May 25, 2005.

Healy, J.M. (1987). *Your child's growing mind.* Toronto: Doubleday.

Hewitt, J.D. (1995). *Teaching teenagers: Making connections in the transition years.* Vancouver: EduServ.

Jensen, E. (1998). *Teaching with the brain in mind.* Alexandria, VA: ASCD.

Margulies, N. (1991). *Mapping inner space: Learning and teaching mind mapping.* Tucson, AZ: Zephyr.

Montgomery Halford, J. (1998–99). Longing for the sacred in schools: A conversation with Nel Noddings. *Educational Leadership,* December–January, 28–32.

Noddings, N. (2005). What does it mean to educate the whole child? *Educational Leadership,* September, 8–13.

Pearce, J. (1977). *Magical child: Rediscovering nature's plan for our children.* New York: E. P. Dutton.

Piaget, J. & Inhelder, B. (1969). *The psychology of the child.* New York: Basic Books.

Renzulli, J.S., Gentry, M., & Reis, S.M. (2004). A time and a place for authentic learning. *Educational Leadership,* 62(*1*), 73–77.

Samples, B. (1987). *Open mind. Whole mind: Parenting and teaching tomorrow's children today.* Rolling Hills Estates, CA: Jalmar.

Schon, D. (1983). *The reflective practitioner.* New York: Basic Books.

Shore, R. (1997). *Rethinking the brain: New insights into early development.* New York: Families and Work Institute.

Sternberg, R.J. (1996). Investing in creativity: Many happy returns. *Educational Leadership.* January, Article 30: 152–155.

Von Oech, R. (1983). *A whack on the side of the head: How to unlock your mind for innovation.* New York: Warner Books.

Von Oech, R. (1985). *A whack on the other side of the head.* New York: Warner Books.

Wassermann, S. (1992). Serious play in the primary classroom. *Childhood Education,* 68(*3*): 133–139.

Wiederhold, C. (1995). *Cooperative learning and higher level thinking: The Q-Matrix.* San Juan Capistrano, CA: Resources for Teachers.

Wilkinson, J.A. (1993). *The symbolic dramatic play-literacy connection: Whole brain, whole body, whole learning.* Toronto: Ginn.

CHAPTER 12

Apple, M. & Beane, J. (Eds.)(1995) *Democratic schools.* Alexandria, VA: ASCD.

Britton, J. (1982). "Spectator role and the beginning of writing." In G.M. Pradl (Ed.). *Prospect and retrospect: Selected essays of James Britton,* (pp. 46–67). Montclair, NJ: Boynton/Cook.

Brookfield, S. (1995). *Becoming a critically reflective teacher.* Toronto: John Wiley & Sons.

Bruner, J. (1990). *Acts of meaning.* Cambridge, MA: Harvard University Press.

Clandinin, J., & Connelly, M. (1995). *Teachers' professional landscapes.* New York: Teachers College Press.

DuFour, R. and Eaker, R. (2005). *On common ground: The power of professional learning communities.* Blomington, IN: National Educational Service.

Darling-Hammond, L. (1997). *The right to learn: A blueprint for creating schools that work.* San Francisco: Jossey Bass.

DuFour, R. (2004). What is a professional learning community. *Educational Leadership.* 61(8) 6–11.

Fine, M. (1991). Ap[parent] involvement: Parent participation in schools. *Language Arts.* 43(12): 24–43.

Giroux, H. (1992). *Border crossings: Cultural workers and the politics of education.* New York: Routledge.

Hayes, G. (1976): *Bear by himself.* New York: Harper Collins.

King, T. (2003). *The truth about stories.* Toronto: CBC Canada, The Massey Lectures.

Richert, A. E. (1992). Voice and power in teaching and learning to teach. In L.Valli (Ed.) *Reflective teacher education: Cases and critiques.* Albany, NY: State University of New York Press.

Singer, I. B. (1976). *Naftali the storyteller and his horse. Sus.* NY: Farrar, Strauss and Giroux.

Van Manen, M. (2005) *The tone of teaching.* London, ON: The Althouse Press.

Wenger, E. (1998). *Communities of practice: Learning, meaning and identity.* Cambridge, UK: Cambridge University Press.

Chapter 13

Arntz, W., Chasse, B., & Vicente, M. (2005). *What the "bleep" do we know?* Deerfield Beach, FL: Health Communications.

Darling-Hammond, L. (1997). *The right to learn: A blueprint for school reform.* San Francisco: Jossey-Bass.

Dufour, R. (2004) *Leading Edge: Culture shift doesn't occur overnight —or without conflict.* Retrieved 1 July, 2006 from www.nsdc.org/library/publications/jsd/dufour254.cfm

DuFour, R., Eaker. R., & DuFour, R. (2005). Recurring themes of professional learning communities and the assumptions they challenge. In R. DuFour & R. Eaker (Ed.), *On common ground: The power of professional learning communities* (pp. 7–29). Bloomington, IN: National Educational Service.

Eisner, E. (1999). Performance assessment and competition. *Phi Delta Kappan,* September, 54–58.

Fullan, M. G. (1998). Leadership in the 21st century: Breaking the bonds of dependency. *Educational Leadership,* 55(7): 6–10.

Fullan, M. (2000) *The Three Stories of Educational Reform.* Retrieved 1 July, 2006 from http://www.pdkintl.org/kappan/kful0004.htm

Hargreaves, A. & Fink, D. (2006). Challenging the status quo. *Educational Leadership,* Volume 63(8). 16–21.

Palmer, P. J. (1998). *The courage to teach.* San Francisco: Jossey-Bass.

Rambow Singh, G. (2001). How character education helps students to grow. *Educational Leadership,* Volume 59(2), 46–49.

Scherer, M. (2001). Improving the quality of the teaching force: A conversation with David C. Berliner. *Educational Leadership,* 58 (8), 6–10 .

Scherer, M. (1998). Perspectives/ The importance of being a colleague. *Educational Leadership,* 55(5):5.

Scherer, M. (2006). Perspectives/ The challenge to change. *Educational Leadership,* 63 (8), 7.

Stronge, J. H., Tucker, P. D., & Hindman, J. L. (2004). *Handbook for qualities of effective teachers.* Alexandria, VA: ASCD.

Vygotsky, L. S. (1978). *Mind in society: The development of higher psychological processes.* Cambridge, MA: Harvard University Press.

Wenger, E. (1998). *Communities of practice: Learning, meaning, and identity.* Cambridge, UK: Cambridge University Press.

Weissbourd, R. (2003). Moral teachers, moral students. *Educational Leadership,* 60 (6), 6–11.

WEBSITE RESOURCES

These websites were active at the time of printing. Please refer to the companion website for updates to this list.

CHAPTER 1

(p.5) For more information on comparing different theories of learning, see "Psychological Theories: A brief survey of the changing views of learning" at
http://www.uib.no/People/sinia/CSCL/web_struktur-4.htm

(p. 7) For more information on how parents and teachers can become more aware of the value of play and the potential problems associated with too early an emphasis on formal learning, see "Too much learning damaging children's play" at
http://education.guardian.co.uk/print/0,3858,5280243-115179,00.html

(p. 13) For more background on Piaget, see

"Genetic Epistemology (J.Piaget)" at
http://tip.psychology.org/piaget.html

"Piaget's Stages: Inventions by Children" at
http://www.artifacts.com/11children.html

"Papert on Piaget" by Simon Papert at
http://www.papert.org/articles/Papertonpiaget.html

(p. 22) For more information on Vygotsky, see

"Lev Vygotsky" by Solrun B. Kristinsdottir at
http://starfsfolk.khi.is/solrunb/vygotsky.htm

'Social Constructivism' at
http://gsi.berkeley.edu/resources/learning/social.html.

(p. 25) For more information on scaffolding, see "Scaffolding: A powerful tool in social constructivist classrooms" by Roehler & Cantlon at
http://ed-web3.educ.msu.edu/literacy/papers/paperlr2.htm

(p. 27) For more information on multiple intelligences, see "Howard Gardner and Multiple Intelligences" by M. K. Smith at http://www.infed.org/thinkers/gardner.htm

CHAPTER 2

(p. 42) For more information on constructivism, see "Social Constructivism and the World Wide Web—A Paradigm for Learning" by Mark McMahon at
http://www.ascilite.org.au/conferences/perth97/papers/Mcmahon/Mcmahon.html

(p. 43) For more information on Bruner see "Constructivist Theory (J. Bruner)" at
http://www.infed.org/thinkers/bruner.htm

(p. 45) For more information on social constructivism in learning, see "Social Constructivism" by Beaumie Kim at
http://www.coe.uga.edu/epltt/SocialConstructivism.htm

(p. 66) To learn more about play, see

"Too Much Learning Damaging to Play" by Sue Rogers (2005) at
http://education.guardian.co.uk/print/0,3858,5280243-115179,00.html

"Active Learning Through Play" by the Iowa Department of Education at
http://www.state.ia.us/educate/ecese/is/ecn/active_learning.html

(p. 67) For more information on Piagetian stages of development, see "Piaget's Theory of Cognitive Development" by Huitt & Hummel (2003) at
http://chiron.valdosta.edu/whuitt/col/cogsys/piaget.html

(p. 71) For more information on Constructivist classrooms, see "Design of constructivist learning environments" by D. Jonassen (2001) at
http://www.tiger.coe.missouri.edu?~jonassen/courses/CLE/

CHAPTER 3

(p. 79) For more information on the importance of autonomy in learning, see "What does research on Constructivist Education tell us about effective schooling?" by Rheta DeVries at www.finefoundation.org/IAE/iae-z-op-devries-1.pdf

(p. 83) For more information on Kamii's views on autonomy, see "Teachers need more knowledge of how children learn mathematics" by Constance Kamii at
www.nctm.org/dialogues/2000-10/needmore.htm

(p. 84) For more information on the role of choice and how this facilitates the development of critical thinking, see "Choices for children: Why and how to let children decide," by Alfie Kohn at www.alfiekohn.org/teaching/cfc.htm

(p. 85) For more information on self-esteem, See "Review of Self-Esteem Research" by Robert Reasoner at www.self-esteem-nase.org/whatisselfesteem.shtml

CHAPTER 4

(p. 110) For more information on brain structures and functions, see "Brain facts and figures" by Eric Chudler at http://faculty.washington.edu/chudler/facts.html

(p. 112) For more information on the role of active learning, see " Why hands-on tasks are good" by Kathie Nunley at http://help4teachers.com/hottopics.htm#scc

(p. 113) For more information on the pruning of unused/underused pathways within the brain, see "Brain Biology: it's basic gardening" by Kathie Nunley at
http://help4teachers.com/gardening.htm

Chapter 5

(p. 146) For more information on Teaching for Understanding, see "Introducing TFU: What is the teaching for understanding framework?" at
http://learnweb.harvard.edu/alps/tfu/about3.cfm

(p. 155) To view a student developed lesson plan see "A sample lesson plan: Preservation of Westminister Ponds" on the companion website.

(p. 161) Many provinces have developed electronic curriculum planners to assist teachers with planning units. For more information on curriculum materials and resources for teachers across Canada, see 'The curriculum foundation' at
http://www.curriculum.org/tcf/index.shtml

Chapter 6

(p. 166) For more information on classroom design see Blackstock school smart classroom designs at **http://blackstock.huensd.k12.ca.us/html/rm_desi.htm**

(p. 167) For more information about these design principles and to discover the research base from which they have been developed, see "33 principles of classroom design" by Jeffery A. Lackney at **http://schoolstudio.engr.wisc.edu/33principles.html**

(p. 173) To read more about invitational learning, see Invitational education at
http://www.caringeducation.net/html/want.html#item3

Chapter 7

(p. 192) For more information on the effect of teacher attitude on learning, see "Student behaviours and teacher approval versus disapproval" by Dan Laitsch (2006) at
http://www.ascd.org/portal/site/ascd/template

(p. 203) For more information on classroom management, see "Rewarding democracy/ class management" by Constance Kamii at
http://portfolio.washington.edu/jeraldg/tep/96027.html

(p. 206) For more information on useful questioning techniques, see "Maximizing learning for all students" by Kathy Checkley at
http://www.ascd.org/affiliates/articles/cl200302_checkley.html

(p. 219) For more information on cooperative learning, see "Cooperation works!" by Dianne Augustine at
http://www.ascd.org/ASCD/pdf/journals/ed_lead/el_198912_augustine.pdf

CHAPTER 8

(p. 246) Visit the following websites for curriculum documents for the various provinces:

British Columbia   http://www.bced.gov.bc.ca/pubsadmin.htm
Alberta   http://www.education.gov.ab.ca/K_12/
Saskatchewan   http://www.sasked.gov.sk.ca/
Manitoba   http://www.edu.gov.mb.ca/
Ontario   http://www.edu.gov.on.ca/eng/relsites/elemen.html
Quebec   http://www.mels.gouv.qc.ca/
New Brunswick   http://www.gnb.ca/0000/anglophone-e.asp#cd
Nova Scotia   http://www.ednet.ns.ca/
Prince Edward Island   http://www.gov.pe.ca/educ/
Newfoundland   http://www.ed.gov.nl.ca/edu/
Nunavut   http://www.gov.nu.ca/education/eng/index.htm
Yukon   http://www.education.gov.yk.ca/
North West Territories http://www.ece.gov.nt.ca/

(p. 251) For more information on curriculum mapping, see 'Sample maps' at
http://www.curriculumdesigners.com/resourcesmapsamples.htm

CHAPTER 9

(p. 269) For more information on OECD and PISA testing, visit
http://www.pisa.oecd.org/

(p. 271) For more information on principles of backward design, see the "Principles of backward design" at
http://www.ltag.education.tas.gov.au/Planning/models/princbackdesign.htm

(p. 278) For more information on a variety of rubrics visit the following websites:
http://canadaonline.about.com/od/rubrics/
http://school.discovery.com/schrockguide/assess.html

(p. 279) For more information on performance assessments, see

"The definition of performance assessment" at
http://www.ascd.org/portal/site/ascd/
menuitem.4427471c9d076deddeb3ffdb62108a0c/

"Performance assessment for science teachers" at
http://www.usoe.k12.ut.us/curr/science/Perform/PAST5.htm

(p. 289) For more information on classroom assessment techniques, see

"Classroom assessment techniques" at
http://www.siue.edu/~deder/assess/catmain.html

"Practical assessment, research and evaluation" at
http://pareonline.net/Home.htm

CHAPTER 10

(p. 301) The Canadian Coalition for the Rights of Children has developed several guides pertaining to the UN's convention on the Rights of the Child. Visit the following websites to find out more:

Education and the United Nations Convention on the Rights of Children
http://www.rightsofchildren.ca/pdf/ed.pdf

Child Care and the United Nations Convention on the Rights of Children
http://www.rightsofchildren.ca/pdf/care.pdf

(p. 304) For more information about multiliteracies see

"The multiliteracy project" at http://www.multiliteracies.ca/

"About the New London Group and the international multiliterarcies project" at http://edoz.com.au/educationaustralia/archive/features/mult3.html

CHAPTER 11

(p. 328) For more information on teaching for thinking, see "Teaching gifted children (and all others) to think better" by Kathy Checkley (2003) at http://www.ascd.org/affiliates/articles/cl200311_checkley.html

(p. 337) For more information on creativity, see "Creativity—its place in education" by Wayne Morris (March 2006) at http://www.leading-learning.co.nz/newsletters/2006-no27.html

(p. 339) For more information on critical thinking, see "Maximizing learning for all students" by Kathy Checkley (2003) at http://ascd.org/affiliates/articles/cl200302_checkley.html

(p. 343) For more information on metacognition, see "Educational principles of learning: metacognition" by PaperToolsPro at http://www.papertoolspro.com/Research.htm

CHAPTER 12

(p. 361) To learn more about professional learning communities and what is necessary to foster learning communities, see 'Professional learning communities" by Rick DuFour at http://info.csd.org/staffdev/rpdc/darticle.html

(p. 367) For further information on classroom action research, see

"Using action research and provincial test results to improve student learning" by Ron Wideman at http://www.ucalgary.ca/~iejll/volume6/wideman.html

"The history of action research" by Janet Masters at http://www.scu.edu.au/schools/gcm/ar/arr/arow/rmasters.html

(p. 369) For more information on school councils in Ontario, see "School Council: A guide for members" at
http://www.edu.gov.on.ca/eng/general/elemsec/council/guide.html

CHAPTER 13

(p. 386) For more information on effective teaching, see "Embracing teacher quality and excellence: Perception, reality and casualty" by Mary D. Monsour at
http://etd.library.pitt.edu/ETD/available/etd-03222006-074841/unrestricted/monsourmd_etd2006.pdf

(p. 288) For more information on Lev Vygotsky, see "Vygotsky" at
http://gsi.berkeley.edu/resources/learning/social.html

(p. 393) For more information on professional learning communities, see "Leading edge: Culture shift doesn't occur overnight —or without conflict" by Rick DuFour at
www.nsdc.org/library/publications/jsd/dufour254.cfm

(p. 395) For more information about mentoring, see " The good mentor" by James Rowley at http://www.ascd.org/ed_topics/el199905_rowley.html

(p. 398) For more information on character education, see "Talking about ethics and character education" by Rushworth Kidder at
http://www.ascd.org/ed_topics/eu200006_19.html

(p. 401) For more information on educational reform, see "The three stories of educational reform" by Michael Fullan at
http://www.pdkintl.org/kappan/kful0004.htm

(p. 401) See the companion website for the ACDE's Accord on Intial Teacher Education.

PHOTO CREDITS

INDEX